NOT SO BLACK AND WHITE

KENAN MALIK

Not So Black and White

*A History of Race from
White Supremacy to Identity Politics*

HURST & COMPANY, LONDON

First published in the United Kingdom in 2023 by
C. Hurst & Co. (Publishers) Ltd.,
New Wing, Somerset House, Strand, London, WC2R 1LA
© Kenan Malik, 2023
All rights reserved.

Distributed in the United States, Canada and Latin America by
Oxford University Press, 198 Madison Avenue, New York, NY 10016,
United States of America.

A Cataloguing-in-Publication data record for this book
is available from the British Library.

ISBN: 9781787387768

This book is printed using paper from registered sustainable
and managed sources.

www.hurstpublishers.com

Printed in Great Britain by Bell and Bain Ltd, Glasgow

CONTENTS

For Osman Kavala
May you soon be free

ACKNOWLEDGMENTS

A book is always both an intensely personal project and a collective endeavour, the product of hundreds of conversations, disagreements and debates. *Not So Black and White* is no different. Not only have many contributed through years of discussing the issues in this book, but many have pored over the manuscript, dissecting it and correcting it. I would particularly like to thank Ahlam al-Samman, Toby Andrew, Kwame Anthony Appiah, Philipp Blom, Veronica Buckley, Vivek Chibber, Barbara J. Fields, Mike Fitzpatrick, John Gillott, Paul Gilroy, Jo Glanville, Alex Gourevitch, Alex Hochuli, Cheryl Hudson, Nasreen Khan, Keri Leigh Merritt, David Olusoga, Adam Rothman, Adam Shatz, Selina Todd, Thomas Chatterton Williams and Robert Yates. I have not always taken their advice (probably to my detriment) but they have all helped shape the book. My thanks also to my editor Lara Weisweiller-Wu for the care with which she read the draft, to Ross Jamieson for saving me from my errors in subbing the book, and to Michael Dwyer who has been unfailingly supportive of the project.

INTRODUCTION

RETELLING THE STORY OF RACE

I cannot remember the first time I was beaten up because of my skin colour. It was certainly before I reached my teens, but so normal was the experience of having to defend myself against racists that I have kept no mental tally. By the time I was a teenager, it was difficult to think of many days when I wasn't in a fight with racists. By the end of my teens I was organizing street patrols to protect Asian families from racist attacks.

The Britain in which I grew up in the 1970s was very different to the Britain of today. Racism was vicious and visceral and woven into the fabric of society in a way difficult to imagine now. "Paki bashing" was a national sport. Stabbings were common, firebombings almost routine events; and if you went to the police for aid you were more likely to be arrested than the racists. It was that experience that drew me into political campaigns against street violence, police brutality and racist deportations. But if it was racism that drew me to politics, it was politics that made me see beyond the narrow confines of racism. I came to learn that there was more to social justice than challenging the injustices done to me; and that a person's skin colour, ethnicity or culture provides no guide to the validity of his or her political beliefs.

Through politics, I was introduced to the ideas of the Enlightenment, and to the concepts of a common humanity and universal rights. Through politics, too, I discovered the writings of Karl Marx and John Stuart Mill, of Thomas Paine and Mary Wollstonecraft, of James Baldwin and Rosa Luxemburg, of CLR James and Frantz Fanon, of Hannah Arendt and Sivanandan. Most of all, I discovered that I could often find more solidarity and commonality with those whose ethnicity or culture was different to mine, but who shared my

1

values, than with many with whom I shared a common ethnicity or culture but not the same political vision. My politics, in other words, was not shackled to my identity, but helped me to reach beyond it. It allowed me to see that my personal experiences and background were insufficient to help me formulate my values and ideals. It allowed me also to distinguish between *identity* and the *politics of identity*. Identities are of great significance to all of us. They give each of us a sense of ourselves, of our grounding in the world and of our relationships to others. Politics, though, is a means, or *should* be a means, of taking us beyond the constricted sense of identity given to each of us by the specific circumstances of our lives and the particularities of personal experiences.

I was able to unshackle my politics from my identity in large part because the struggles of British Asian communities at that time, organized through groups such as the Indian Workers' Association and the Asian Youth Movements, were intimately bound up with wider struggles. Migrant workers were at the forefront of industrial action, from the first significant postwar "immigrant strike" at Red Scar Mill, near Preston, Lancashire, when Asian workers took action against the practice of forcing non-white employees to work more machines for less pay, to Grunwick, a photo processing plant in north-west London, where in 1976, 137 mainly Asian women went on strike in protest at appalling conditions, racist intimidation and the banning of unions. Within weeks of the Grunwick walk-out, the women received support from other workers. Miners and electricians, builders and bus drivers, joined mass pickets—20,000-strong on one day—while postal workers refused to move the company's orders. Eventually, the trade union leadership withdrew its support, an act of betrayal that led to the women being defeated, ending their action after nearly two years. Devastating though the defeat was, the support from rank-and-file workers marked a significant moment in the struggle against racism and sexism and in developing cross-racial working-class unity.[1]

This history provided the grounding for the struggles of my generation. We recognized, almost without thinking about it, the commonality of values, hopes and aspirations that bound together Asians, blacks and whites. If I was growing up in today's Britain, though, I am not sure I would feel the same. Many of the organizations that allowed us to make those wider connections—such as the Asian Youth Movements—have disappeared. Countless groups in wider society that helped foster solidarity, whether within the anti-racist or the labour movements, have disintegrated, too. Making those broader connections, seeing the bigger picture, breaking the shackles of identity, is more difficult today. Far from taking us beyond our narrow identities, contemporary politics is frequently circumscribed by them. In the past, the identities that defined us politically were often distinct from our personal identities. Today, they are regularly intertwined. Many imagine that to be Muslim or white or gay or European is to accept a particular package of values and beliefs and ideals. What we are defines what we should cherish or value or believe.

* * *

Not So Black and White is a book about the history of the concept of race. It is also a book about the politics of identity. The two, as we shall see, are inextricably linked. To tell the story of one, we also have to tell the story of the other. Many imagine that identity politics is a new phenomenon, and one that is associated with the left. A long view reveals something different: that the origins of the politics of identity lie not on the left but on the reactionary right. It developed in the late eighteenth century and its primary expression was in the concept of race. Of course, it was not called "identity politics" then. But that is what it was.

The concept of a "racial type" as it developed through the nineteenth century was of a group of people linked by a set of fundamental characteristics and differing from other types by virtue of those attributes. These included not just mental and physical traits, but also social needs, aspirations and value. One's being—one's identity—determined one's moral and social place in the world. Here was the original politics of identity. Today, the idea that one's beliefs, values and social location is defined by one's identity is frequently found within antiracist circles. Many antiracists suggest that black or Asian people who are conservative, or do not follow the set script of what minorities should believe or how they should behave, are not really black or Asian but straining to be white. Many

3

demand that white artists or writers should not engage with "black pain" and insist that there are certain aspects of the histories and cultures of non-white groups that should be off-limits to white intellectuals. I look more closely at these "stay in your lane!" arguments in Chapter 9. To understand why racists and identitarians often end up in the same place, we need to understand the complex relationship, both historical and contemporaneous, between racial beliefs and the politics of identity. That is what *Not So Black and White* sets out to do.

There are four interwoven narratives in this book. The first is a retelling of the story of race. Most people assume that racism emerges when members of one race begin discriminating against members of another; that racism is what develops when races collide. I will show that historically the opposite is the case: intellectuals and elites began dividing the world into distinct races to explain and justify the differential treatment of certain peoples. The ancestors of today's African Americans were not enslaved because they were black. They were eventually deemed to be racially distinct, as black people, to justify their enslavement.

What made such justification necessary was that from the eighteenth century onwards, America, France, Britain and other European nations began to define themselves by their attachment to equality and liberty. In practice, though, their policies denied both to much of the population. "Race" became the means to bridge the contradiction between the assertion that "We hold these truths to be self-evident, that all men are created equal", the claim of the American Declaration of Independence, and the reality of a slave-owning nation. The contradiction was waved away by insisting that certain people were by nature unequal and not deserving of liberty and equality.

I retell the story of race in a different way, too. Today, we think about race primarily in terms of skin colour or of continent of origin ("black", "white", "Asian", and so on). But that was not how nineteenth-century thinkers imagined race which, for them, was a description of social inequality, not just of skin colour. Certainly, they saw blacks and whites and Asians as distinct races. But they also often saw labourers and farmhands in the same way. It may be difficult to comprehend now, but nineteenth-century thinkers looked upon the working class as a racial group, physically and anthropo-logically distinct from the rest of society, in much the same way as many now view black people as racially dissimilar to whites. Even in America, where slavery ensured that the black/white divide was paramount, other groups—European migrants, especially from southern and eastern Europe, Jews, sections of the working class and the poor—were racialized, too. Understanding the real history of race is important not just as an intellectual exercise but also because it challenges many of the ways in which we think about race and race relations today.

Interlaced with the history of race is my second story—that of the resistance to racism and colonialism, and of how that resistance expanded the meaning of equality and universality. Through the twentieth century, and especially in the last decades, there devel-oped an impassioned debate about the Enlightenment, and espe-cially about the concept of universalism, which many came to see as Eurocentric, even racist. Both supporters and critics of the Enlightenment present it as a peculiarly European phenomenon. Both miss the importance of the non-European world in shaping many of the ideas we associate with the Enlightenment. It was, as we shall see, through the struggles of those denied equality and liberty by the elites in Europe and America that ideas of universal-ism were invested with meaning. And it is the demise of that radical universalist tradition that has shaped much of what we now call identity politics.

The third story is that of the relationship between race and class. In the age of Trump and Brexit, many on the left have come to despise the working class as racist, xenophobic and ignorant. David Rothkopf, professor of international relations, CEO of *Foreign Policy* magazine, and a member of Bill Clinton's administration, described Trump supporters as people who "are threatened by what they don't understand, and what they don't understand is almost every-thing". Many within the working class feel betrayed and abandoned by the liberal elites, rail against globalization and view migrants and minorities as threats to their livelihoods and social position. These are themes that have haunted the fractured relationships between different sections of workers from the seventeenth century onwards. I track some of the collisions between race and class, explore attempts to forge class unity across the fissures of race, and look at why the construction of cross-racial solidarity has proved so challenging. I also look at why the disproportionately working-class character of many black and minority communities makes for a more complex story than much of the discussion allows. Issues that on the surface seem straightforwardly as the product of racism—even ones as apparently black and white as the shocking police killings of African Americans that gave rise to the Black Lives Matter movement—are, as I show in chapters 8 and 9, often better seen through the prism of class than of race. Our preoccupation with race frequently hides the realities of injustice.[2]

The final thread in my story is that of the emergence of modern identity politics. I look at the complex set of developments that has allowed it to occupy centre stage, examine the relationship between modern identity politics and that of the past, and explore, too, the connections between the identitarianism of the left and that of the right. Woven into this history is also a critique of many of the concepts of contemporary leftwing identity politics, especially the understanding of "whiteness" and of "white privilege", and of trends such as the calling out of cultural appropriation.

* * *

This book is both narrow and expansive. It is narrow because the history it tells is largely a Western history, the story of race primarily in Western Europe and America. This is not because this is the only story I could tell. The history of the concept of race in China or Japan or Russia or India is important and fascinating, and some scholars have begun to sketch out such histories. Japan, as we shall see in Chapter 3, challenged ideas of white supremacy by introducing the ideal of equality into the debate in 1919 over the founding charter of the League of Nations. The Japan that talked of equality was also the Japan that imposed its own forms of national and racial superiority on subject peoples in East Asia. To have included these histories, however, would have made this book too unwieldy and so they have been left out.

In Western debates, I focus much on developments in America, especially in Chapters 7, 8 and 9. This is not because I think that these are particularly insightful or significant in themselves. On the contrary, debates and policies in other parts of the world are too often unreflectingly shaped by ideas and movements that originated in America, whether Sixties Black Power or the contemporary culture wars. That influence, underpinned by America's economic, political and cultural weight, demands that we look even more carefully at those ideas and developments, unpack the myths and unpick the arguments. And in understanding the American debates we understand more also about the debates beyond the USA.

The focus on American debates, and on the black/white divide, means that many Asian and Middle Eastern thinkers, from Sadiq al-Azm to Pankaj Mishra, and the specific questions with which they have been involved, are missing from the narrative. I recognize that this leaves a hole, but, again, to have included those thinkers and those debates would have made the book too unmanageable. What I have tried to do is focus on those debates that most illuminate broader concerns.

Not So Black and White is narrow, too, because it retells the history of race against the background of contemporary concerns—in particular, the debates over identity politics and the relationship between race and class. The themes I have picked out, and the questions I have asked, bear the stamp of those concerns.

It is expansive, though, because in retelling that story, *Not So Black and White* both questions the way we think about race and identity, and argues that to understand both issues we have to take in a much broader social and political canvas. It shows how race is not simply a description of particular groups of people, but also a lens through which many themes of modernity have been brought into focus—equality and inequality, progress and decay, the nature of class and of class politics, the social function of science, the meaning of radicalism, the character of capitalism and the possibilities of social transformation. It is expansive, too, because while it is a history of Western thought, it challenges the idea that Western thought can be understood simply by looking at Europe and America. To understand the Enlightenment, for instance, we have to understand the degree to which Enlightenment ideas, and in particular notions of equality and universalism, were subsequently shaped by intellectuals and movements from well beyond Europe and America, through their engagement with Euro-American ideas and their struggles against racial thinking and colonial rule.

Part One of the book—"The Barbarism of Race"—tells the story of the rise of the concept of race, and of white supremacy; Part Two—"The Struggle to Transcend Race"—of the development of movements against racism and their decay into contemporary identity politics. The chapters are both historical and conceptual. They often cover the same historical period but tell a different narrative or look at it from a different perspective.

Chapters 1–4 tell the story of the modern invention of, respectively, equality, race, whiteness and antisemitism. They show how the coming of modernity transformed the ways in which people thought about human relationships and how the Enlightenment embrace of equality as an ideal posed new questions about how to understand inequality and difference. It is in wrestling with the new conundrums thrown up by modernity—especially the tension between an abstract belief in equality and social practices that ensured not just inequality but enslavement, too—that concepts of race and of whiteness emerged.

Chapter 5, the last chapter in Part One, looks at Nazism and the Holocaust against the background of racism and colonialism. Hitler brought to Europe practices that Europeans had long pursued in their colonies. The result was both to unleash barbarism on a hitherto unimaginable scale in Europe and to help undermine those practices, and the ideas from which they developed, as their true consequences became clear. The post-Holocaust world looked upon race in a very different way.

Part Two explores the debates over universalism, the belief in the equal moral worth of all human beings, and in there being certain norms and forms of governance under which all humans best flourish. It shows the necessity of a universalist perspective in both building movements against racism and in transcending the very concept of race. It also shows the difficulties in constructing universalist movements, the divisions that have continually rent antiracist and anticolonial struggles, the obstacles to creating solidarity across racial lines and the constant temptation for antiracists to mimic racial thinking by themselves adopting ideals and organizations rooted in racial categories.

Chapter 6 begins with a discussion of the Haitian Revolution, one of the three major revolutions of the eighteenth century, but which, when compared to the place that the American and French Revolutions occupy in our culture, is barely remembered. Yet, it was through the Haitian Revolution, in which the slaves of the French colony of Saint-Domingue dismantled their chains and declared an independent nation, that the emancipatory logic of the Declaration of the Rights of Man was for the first time seen through to its revolutionary conclusion. I look at the reverberations of the Haitian Revolution over the next two centuries, at how radical forms of universalism, inspired by Haiti, developed in contrast to a liberal universalism that tolerated slavery and welcomed colonialism, and at how the practices of racism and of imperialism posed great dilemmas for those combating them, creating new doubts about the Enlightenment that would flourish in the twentieth century.

Chapters 7, 8 and 9, all of which focus on developments in America, look at how the promise of universalism became degraded. Chapter 7 tracks the fraught relationship between the battles for black emancipation and working-class struggles and of the attempts to sustain a universalist vision in the face of opposition from both without and within. Chapter 8 tells of the long arc of the struggle for black rights in twentieth-century America, and at how early attempts to forge unity between black and working-class struggles foundered, how the battles for economic and for political equality became separated and how, in the process, black identity was remade. It is a story that takes us from the case of the Scottsboro Boys, nine black teenagers fitted up for rape, who would probably have gone to the electric chair but for the extraordinary intervention of the Communist Party, through the Black Power Movement of the 1960s to Black Lives Matter.

Chapter 9 looks at how the endpoint of these developments was the emergence of identity politics. It examines the complex set of changes in the postwar world that nurtured the politics of identity. And it casts a sceptical eye on issues such as Critical Race Theory, cultural appropriation and white privilege.

Finally, Chapter 10 shows how the identity politics of the left allowed racist ideas to be rebranded as "white identity". It brings us almost full circle as the reactionary right, marginalized in the postwar world because of its rootedness in prewar racial thinking, has been able to reclaim its original heritage. Chapter 10 examines how the far right has exploited the language of pluralism and diversity to remake racial ideas. It looks, too, at how mainstream conservatives have helped rehabilitate some of the most vicious messages of reactionary identitarians. The chapter, and the book, ends with a reflection on how to escape the identitarian trap and uncage ourselves from our obsession with race.

We live in an age in which in most societies there is a moral abhorrence of racism, albeit that in most, bigotry and discrimination still disfigure the lives of many. We also live in an age in which our thinking is saturated with racial ideology and the embrace of difference. The more we despise racial thinking, the more we cling to it. It is like an ideological version of Stockholm syndrome. *Not So Black and White* does not provide a readymade cure for the syndrome. I hope, though, I can show how we have ended up where we are, and in understanding that, we can understand also how to release ourselves from our fetters of both race and identity.

1

THE INVENTION OF EQUALITY

I

"We hold these truths to be self-evident, that all men are created equal." It's a line that every American knows as intimately as their phone number, and one that millions across the globe recognize. A line from the American Declaration of Independence that declares the founding of a nation on an eternal, inviolable principle.

Except that there is nothing either eternal or inviolable about that principle. The idea that "all men are created equal" may seem unexceptional today. Belief in equality and in a common humanity oxygenates the bloodstream of the modern world. And yet, at the time it was written, in 1776, the sentiment was anything but self-evident. So extraordinary was it that even those who wrote that line, and signed the Declaration, did not accept it. They held it self-evident that all men were equal but also held slaves. Not till almost a century after the Declaration was slavery formally abolished with the passing of the Thirteenth Amendment in 1865. Not till three years later, with the Fourteenth Amendment, were African Americans deemed constitutionally to be American citizens. And not till 1870 were they afforded the constitutional (though not necessarily the actual) right to vote when the Fifteenth Amendment guaranteed citizens suffrage irrespective of "race, color, or previous condition of servitude".

For the men who signed the Declaration of Independence, and for those who subsequently framed the American Constitution, "all men" clearly meant "all white men" or, more precisely, "all propertied white men". We can read this as revealing the gross hypocrisy

11

of America's Founding Fathers, and the degree to which notions of "liberty" were racially stained. "How is it", as Samuel Johnson asked, "that we hear the loudest yelps for liberty among the drivers of negroes?". We can also read it, however, as showing how remarkable is the claim that "all men are created equal" and how difficult it has proved historically to turn that sentiment into social practice. Today, equality may be the "default setting", as Dutch historian Siep Stuurman puts it, and inequality acceptable only "to the extent that it is justified by good reasons". For virtually the whole of human history, however, the reverse held: "Inequality was the habitual and reasonable standard, while equality stood in need of justification, if it was considered at all. Inequality was omnipresent, palpable, and realistic, while equality had to be imagined, argued for, conjured up from nowhere." Equality had "to be *invented*".[1]

Concepts of equality and of a common humanity run deep into human history. We find whispers in Ancient China and Ancient Greece, in Buddhism and Stoicism, and stronger echoes within the monotheistic faiths. In the premodern world, such ideas were relatively marginal, and cut against the grain of social reality. Even those few individuals who dared to dream about equality mostly accepted the reality of societies steeped in hierarchy and difference.

It was not till the Enlightenment in the eighteenth century that the modern concept of equality was nurtured. The Enlightenment was also the period in which modern racial theories began to surface. In the decades between the American Revolution of 1776 and the European revolutions of 1848, the concept of race moved into mainstream thinking and became the principal lens through which Western societies viewed social differences. This paradox—of modernity as the age that invented the concepts both of equality and of race—still shapes our consciousness today. It is the paradox at the heart of this book.

The common-sense view of racial inequality is that certain people are treated unequally because they belong to, or are seen as belonging to, distinct races. African Americans or British Asians face discrimination because they are viewed as racially distinct. Our tendency to categorize people by race, and to infer different qualities in different races, has led to racial inequality.

The trouble with this argument is that race, like equality, is a social not a natural concept. It, too, had to be "invented". If there is nothing natural about races, why do some societies feel compelled to categorize people by race? To answer that, we need to turn the common-sense argument on its head. It is not racial differences that have led to unequal treatment but the persistence of social inequalities in societies with a commitment to equality that has led many to view such inequalities as ineradicable, and hence natural, and to place people into different racial categories. Race did not give birth to racism. Racism gave birth to race.[2]

II

The "axis of world history", the "most deepcut dividing line in history", lay, the twentieth-century German philosopher and theologian Karl Jaspers claimed, in the centuries between 800 and 200 BCE, the period in which "Man as we know him today came into being". What Jaspers called the "Axial Age" was indeed a transformative moment in the great civilizational centres across the globe. In China and India, in Greece and Palestine and Persia, the old heroic age, in which human lives and moral conduct were shaped largely by myth and legend, whether the *Iliad* and the *Odyssey* in Greece or the *Mahabharata* and *Ramayana* in India, gave way to a more philosophical, self-reflective time. New philosophies, faiths and moral ideas were seeded, from Judaism in Israel, to the teachings of Zoroaster in Persia, the rise of Confucianism and Mohism in China, the advent of Buddhism and the creation of the *Upanishads* in India, to the Socratic tradition in Greece. In these philosophies was first grasped the idea of the human in a more universal sense and the possibilities of equality glimpsed.[3]

Perhaps the earliest expression of a common humanity was in the work of one of China's forgotten philosophers, Mo Tzu, who lived in the fifth century BCE and whose influence at the time vied with that of Confucius. At the heart of his philosophy was the insistence that the wellbeing of strangers should concern us as much as those of our family, that one should "regard others' states as though regarding one's state, regard others' families as though regarding one's family, and regard other persons as though regarding one's person". It was a remarkable argument to make 2,500 years ago, centuries before similar ideas began to develop within Greek and Christian traditions.[4]

In the second century CE, the Greek Stoic philosopher Hierocles imagined, in his *Elements of Ethics*, every human as standing at the centre of a series of concentric circles. The first circle was the individual, next came the family, the local community, the country and finally all of humanity. To be virtuous, Hierocles argued, was to draw these circles together, constantly transferring people from the outer to the inner bounds, treating strangers as cousins and cousins as siblings, making all humans part of our concern. The Stoics called this process of drawing the circles together *oikeiosis*, an almost untranslatable word but which means something like "the process by which everything is made into your home".[5]

For all such early claims, it is in Christianity that many find the origins of the universalism underlying much modern secular thinking. "There is neither Jew nor Greek, there is neither slave nor free, there is no male and female: for you are all one in Christ Jesus." So wrote Paul, seen by many modern Christian thinkers as the man who laid the philosophical foundations of their faith, preaching, in the words of historian Tom Holland, of "a deity who recognized no borders, no divisions". Except, the deity did. Those that did not take shelter in the body of Christ were barred not just from the kingdom of heaven but often from universal brotherhood on earth, too. Well into the early modern period, there were debates as to whether non-Christians were to be seen as fellow human beings, whether they possessed souls.[6]

It was also a form of universalism that appeared not to apply to the everyday life of the present world. From the beginning, the historian of Christianity Diarmaid MacCulloch observes, there was an acknowledgement that "Christianity was not going to make a radical challenge to existing social distinctions". Status and hierarchy, inequality and privilege were all to stay. "Each one should remain in the condition in which he was called", as Paul himself put it.[7]

Most strikingly, virtually every Christian thinker until modern times accepted the legitimacy of slavery. The tension between preaching about human brotherhood and accepting the institution of servitude was "neatly resolved in Christian theology", Robert Fogel observes, "by treating slavery as a condition of the body rather than of the spirit. In the spiritual realm, 'all men were brothers in union with God', but in the temporal realm, slavery was 'a necessary part of the world of sin'". Augustine, a Roman citizen born to a Berber family in north Africa in the fourth century CE, became perhaps the greatest of all Christian theologians. Slavery, he insisted, was ordained by God's law which demanded "the preservation of the order of nature, and forbids its disruption." Jesus "did not say to [slaves]: 'Get rid of your master'... but rather 'Be a slave'".[8]

The cries of those who opposed slavery "fell like seed among thorns" in Holland's evocative words. At the dawn of the modern world, even those Christians self-consciously committed to equality accepted the necessity for, even legitimacy of, slavery. The Religious Society of Friends, the Quakers, emerged from the ferment of the English Civil Wars (1642–51) as one of the most egalitarian of Christian denominations. They are celebrated as the pioneers of abolitionism. Quaker voices against slavery were, however, a minority until the second half of the eighteenth century. There were Quaker planters in the West Indies and Quaker slave merchants in London. One early critic of slavery, Benjamin Lay, tells the story of his wife Sarah visiting a fellow Quaker in Barbados in 1718, the couple having recently arrived on the island from England. She was shocked to find outside the house a "hung up Negro stark naked, trembling and shivering, with such a Flood of Blood under him". The Quaker owner, with no sense of embarrassment that this might be a morally repugnant act, explained that it was punishment "for absconding a day or two".[9]

Not until the latter decades of the eighteenth century did Quakers and other Christians turn decisively against slavery. "Radical anti-slavery", Robin Blackburn observes, "required the existence of a secular public space" and a willingness to challenge the established social order. It required, too, a new conception of equality and of a common humanity.[10]

III

There is perhaps no period of history that has been more analysed, debated, celebrated and disparaged than the Enlightenment. An intellectual wind of change that blew through eighteenth-century Europe, placing great store on reason and tolerance and helping reset the meanings of concepts such as humanity, equality and

15

democracy, it is not simply a historical moment but one through which controversies about the contemporary world are played out. From the role of science to the war on terror, from free speech to racism, there are few debates today that do not engage with the Enlightenment, or, at least, with what we imagine it to have been. Inevitably, the imagining of the Enlightenment has become a historical battleground.

The story of the Enlightenment, of what it was and how it developed, began to be written by Enlightenment philosophers themselves. Immanuel Kant in his essay "What is Enlightenment?" answered that it was "Man's release from his self-incurred tutelage". Humanity had enchained itself through its own ignorance. Enlightenment thinkers had set it free by allowing the light of reason to shine upon human problems. This was, of course, a self-serving definition, one that airily dismissed the earlier intellectual traditions upon which Kant and his fellow-philosophers drew and was blind to the ignorance and unreason of many Enlightenment thinkers themselves. Yet, it also gave a sense of the historical significance of the era.

That significance has been challenged over the past century from different perspectives. Some historians developed national, rather than pan-European, accounts of the Enlightenment: the French Enlightenment, the German Enlightenment, the Scottish Enlightenment, each to be analysed in its own terms, often as a display of national pride. Others have stressed the social and cultural rather than intellectual aspects of the period, questioning, in the words of Robert Darnton, "the overly highbrow, overly metaphysical view of intellectual life in the eighteenth century". A third group of scholars challenged the very idea of the Enlightenment as a good. In 1944, in the shadow of Auschwitz, Theodor Adorno and Max Horkheimer, key members of the Frankfurt School of Marxist thinkers, published their seminal work *Dialectic of Enlightenment*. Like many radicals of the time, they asked themselves why it was that Germany, a nation with deep philosophical roots in the Enlightenment, should succumb so quickly and so completely to Nazism. The answer seemed to lie in the character of Enlightenment thought itself. Adorno and Horkheimer did not reject the Enlightenment in its entirety, but they saw it as not only lighting the way to emancipation but also as enabling the darkness of the

Holocaust. In recent decades this scepticism has been nurtured within postmodern and postcolonial theory. Enlightenment rationalism and universalism, long acknowledged as the foundation stones of progressive belief, are now, as we shall see in Chapter 9, often dismissed as Eurocentric, even racist.[11]

Conflicts between these various interpretations have been exacerbated by the "culture wars"; one's attitude to the Enlightenment has come to mark one's place on the culture-war map. On the one side are those who imagine that to be critical of the Enlightenment is not to believe in science and reason. On the other, many suggest that to defend the Enlightenment is to defend racism and imperialism. As in many such debates, there are elements of truth on both sides. One theme of this book is the need to comprehend both the immense significance of the Enlightenment and the depth of the contradictions and paradoxes that rent it.

From one perspective, what defined the Enlightenment was not a specific set of ideas, but a questioning attitude. Even Michel Foucault, one of its sternest postmodern critics, acknowledged that "the thread that may connect us with the Enlightenment is... a philosophical ethos that could be described as a permanent critique of our historical era".[12]

Beyond this attitude were also several philosophical themes which, while often fiercely contested, nevertheless provided a thread through much of the Enlightenment. The two most important motifs were the moral significance of equality and of a common human nature. Hand-me-downs from religious, especially Christian, thought, they were remade in the eighteenth century. "It is universally acknowledged", the Scottish philosopher David Hume wrote, "that there is a great uniformity among the acts of men, in all nations and all ages, and that human nature remains the same in its principles and operations". Similarly, the French *philosophe* Denis Diderot argued that manners or habits "are not African or Asiatic or European. They are good or bad." There are slaves "under the Pole where it is very cold, and a slave in Constantinople where it is very hot; but everywhere a people should be educated, free and virtuous."[13]

Linked to the belief in a common human nature and in universal values was the idea of equality. "If we would indicate an idea which throughout the whole course of history has ever more and more

17

widely extended its empire", wrote the Prussian philosopher, linguist and diplomat Wilhelm von Humboldt (1767–1835), "it is that of establishing our common humanity—of striving to remove the barriers which prejudice and limited views of every kind have erected among men, and to treat all mankind without reference to religion, nation or colour, as one fraternity, one great community." Von Humboldt expresses here beautifully the link, as many Enlightenment philosophers saw it, between the concept of a common humanity and that of equality, of "treat[ing] all mankind without reference to religion, nation or colour". The link was not, however, readily forged.[14]

The idea of equality required belief in a common humanity. But belief in a common humanity did not necessarily lead to an acceptance of equality, either as an ideal or as a practical possibility. That it did so in the minds of eighteenth-century European philosophers was, in many ways, remarkable. "In a Europe long dominated by kings, princes and nobles, saturated in the culture of courts and courtiers", the historian Jonathan Israel observes, "to speak of fundamental equality must have seemed... to be going against the grain of reality, to be lost in chimeras." If the Axial age was the first great turning point in human history, Siep Stuurman suggests, "the Enlightenment represents the second". It "radically changed the terms of the debate about common humanity and cultural difference". Henceforth, "equality received the benefit of the doubt while inequality had to be justified by rational argument".[15]

Enlightenment philosophers drew upon the claims of religious groups from the radical wing of the Reformation, groups such as the Levellers and the Diggers in England, who emerged through the Civil Wars, or the Anabaptists in the Low Countries and German-speaking lands. These groups all had different beliefs but were linked by a commitment to equality and democracy. Their Protestantism stood opposed not just to the Catholic Church but also to the Protestantism of mainstream leaders such as Martin Luther and John Calvin. The "magisterial Reformation" directed by such leaders was intensely conservative, appealing to monarchs and princes chafing at the constraints imposed by Papal power, but having no desire to create a more equal society. When, in 1524, German peasants revolted against oppressive taxes and laws, demanding the end to serfdom and the right to use common fields, forests and waters, they were championed by poorer clergy but condemned by mainstream clerics. Luther defended the slaughter of thousands in a brutal crackdown by the authorities on the grounds that the peasants had "become faithless, perjured, disobedient, rebellious, murderers, robbers and blasphemers, whom even a heathen ruler has the right and authority to punish".[16]

Luther and the radicals read the same Bible, were equally hostile to the doctrines of the Catholic Church, and were both adamant that faith was a matter of an individual's relationship with God unmediated by religious institutions. But these religious beliefs were given different meanings by distinct social and political views. What was essential to radical egalitarianism was not religious doctrine but political vision, the vision upon which Enlightenment philosophers drew, and which they transformed into a defining principle.

IV

And, yet, it is not so straightforward. Samuel Johnson's rhetorical question about American revolutionaries—"How is it that we hear the loudest yelps for liberty among the drivers of negroes?"—can be asked also of Enlightenment philosophers. Many combined a defence of liberty and equality with profoundly racist attitudes. Consider three of the most influential Enlightenment thinkers—David Hume, Immanuel Kant and Thomas Jefferson.

David Hume (1711–76), the leading light of the Scottish Enlightenment, whose naturalism, scepticism and moral theories have been highly influential, was a strong opponent of slavery, but nevertheless helped his patron Lord Hertford buy a slave plantation in Grenada. He argued that "human nature remains the same in its principles and operations" but also that "I am apt to suspect the negroes to be naturally inferior to the whites". The "uniform and constant difference" between whites and blacks, he insisted, "could not happen... if nature had not made an original distinction between these breeds of men".[17]

Immanuel Kant (1724–1804) is the towering figure of the Enlightenment. He synthesized rationalism and empiricism, setting the terms for much subsequent philosophy, and continues to exercise significant influence in a swathe of philosophical disciplines from metaphysics to ethics. Kant was also an important figure in the development of racial theory. Between 1775 and 1788, he published three major works that engaged directly with the question of racial difference. For Kant, humanity comprised one species but four races—Whites, Blacks, Hindustanic and Kalmuck—distinguished primarily by skin colour. The original human stock contained "seeds" that predisposed them to particular racial qualities, mental and physical, but which expressed themselves only in certain climatic or geographical conditions. Once the four basic types had emerged, they remained permanently fixed and could not further change. This allowed Kant to maintain both that human populations could change and that races were fixed.[18]

Kant not only established a taxonomy of race, but also imposed value judgments upon them. "Humanity", he wrote, "has its greatest degree of perfection in the white race. The yellow Indians have a somewhat lesser talent. The Negroes are much lower and the lowest of all is part of the [Native] American peoples." According to Kant, "The race of the American cannot be educated" because "it lacks affect and passion", while Negroes "can be educated but only as servants (slaves)". The "Moors", he believed, "like all inhabitants of the hot zones have a thick skin; when one disciplines them one cannot hit them with sticks but rather whip with split canes, so that the blood finds a way out and does not suppurate under the skin".[19]

Across the Atlantic, Thomas Jefferson wrote in 1787 of African slaves that they "have been liberally educated, and all have lived in countries where the arts and sciences have been cultivated to a considerable degree." Still, "never yet could I find that a black has uttered a thought above the level of plain narration; never seen even an elementary trait of painting or sculpture". The condition of Roman slaves, who were "of the race of whites", was "much more deplorable than that of blacks on the continent of America". They had, nevertheless, often been the "rarest [of] artists" and had "excelled too in science". "It is not their condition, then, but nature", Jefferson suggested, "which has produced their distinction".[20]

How can we reconcile the views of Hume, Kant and Jefferson with those of Humboldt and Diderot, and with the Enlightenment's attachment to equality? Many scholars believe we cannot. The late philosopher Charles Mills argued that for Enlightenment thinkers whiteness was "a prerequisite for personhood" and therefore a necessary attribute to be deserving of equality; non-whites were limited "to subperson status". Far from there being a contradiction between Enlightenment ideas of equality and the claims about racial differences, the two are fully compatible because "egalitarian theory's terms were never meant to be extended generally outside the European population". Similarly, Emmanuel Eze observes that in Enlightenment writings, "'reason' and 'civilization' became almost synonymous with 'white' people and northern Europe, while unreason and savagery were conveniently located among the non-whites, the 'black', the 'red', the 'yellow', outside Europe". The Enlightenment should be seen not as the source of modern ideas of equality but as the cradle of racism, helping articulate "Europe's sense not only of its cultural but also *racial* superiority".[21]

If Mills and Eze are right, we would have to rethink our whole approach to the idea of equality in the Enlightenment, indeed to the very idea of equality in the modern world. But are they right?

V

Paris, 25 May 1781. The Palais de la Cité, a magnificent cluster of buildings on the Île de la Cité. Home to the kings of France from the sixth to the fourteenth centuries, it now housed the treasury, the courts of justice and the *Parlement de Paris*, a judicial, not legislative, body. A crowd had gathered. And there, at the bottom of the splendid staircase that swept down from the *Parlement*, the public hangman was getting ready for work, to flog and to burn. Only, on this day, the victim was not a human but a book.

It was not uncommon for forbidden books to be publicly burnt in pre-Revolutionary France. It was, though, a special book the hangman held in his hands on that particular day: the *Histoire philosophique et politique des établissements et du commerce des Européens dans les deux Indes*, more commonly known as *Histoire des deux Indes* ("History of the Two Indies"). It was among the most read eighteenth-century books, with thirty (underground) editions in France, and many foreign translations. There were twenty English editions alone.

Originally published anonymously in 1770, the work came to be associated with Guillaume Thomas François Raynal, a former priest.

It was banned by the French government and placed on the Catholic Church's *Index Librorum Prohibitorum*, its list of forbidden books. The third and much expanded edition published in 1780 in Geneva caused the greatest outrage. The *Parlement* labelled the work "impious, blasphemous, seditious, tending to incite people against rightful authority" and ordered its incineration. Raynal was forced into exile, narrowly escaping imprisonment.[22]

The *Histoire* was not an easy read. The 1780 edition was a four-volume work of more than 3,000 pages, stuffed full of statistics and tables. How did it become such a bestseller, and why was it considered so dangerous?

The *Histoire* was an excoriation of European slavery and colonialism. The work of several authors, it has an uneven, sometimes contradictory, character, with mainstream views jostling with radical sentiments. The radicalism was infused primarily by Denis Diderot (1713–84), whom some believe contributed almost a third of the 1780 edition. Like Raynal, Diderot trained initially for the priesthood in a Jesuit college, but almost immediately abandoned the Church for a different kind of contemplative life—that of a writer. Disowned by his father, he made his way to Paris, where he lived a bohemian existence, always at the edge of poverty, yet became one of the most significant figures in the Enlightenment. His most remarkable achievement was the 28-volume *Encyclopédie*, which he created and edited with mathematician and philosopher Jean-Baptiste le Rond d'Alembert. Its goal was "to assemble all the knowledge scattered on the surface of the earth", and in doing so "change men's common way of thinking". Perhaps even more than the *Encyclopédie*, it was the *Histoire* that achieved that latter aim.[23]

The two "Indies" of the title referred to the Americas and the Caribbean islands (to the west) and to India and much of Asia (to the east). The book was a history of European exploration and conquest since the fifteenth century, combining quantitative data about trade and the world's material resources, and a panegyric to commerce, with a devastating denunciation of European colonialism. At its heart lay Diderot's moral universalism, his insistence that all humans possess "the same needs, pleasures, pains, strengths and weaknesses" and so are entitled to the same dignity, justice and consideration. European colonialists, Diderot argues, had no sense that different societies' common needs could be expressed in different ways. Any society unlike those of Europe was taken to be backward or unworthy of respect. The indigenous peoples of Mexico had created complex and highly structured societies. But the Spanish conquistadores "fancied that these people had no form of government because it was not vested in a single person; no civilization because it differed from that of Madrid; no virtues because they were not of the same religious persuasion; and no understanding because they did not adopt the same opinion." So blind were they to the lives of others they would have been "inclined... to consider Athens in the same contemptuous light."[24]

Europeans' "insatiable thirst for gold", Diderot argues, "has given birth to the most infamous and atrocious of all trades, that of slaves." The "majority of European nations are soiled by it, and a vile self-interest has stifled in human hearts all the feelings we owe to our fellow men". Colonialism, too, had brought little but disaster, as "ruins have been heaped upon ruins", and "vast tracts... cemented with blood". Whether writing of the Spanish in the Americas, the French in the Caribbean, or the English in India, Diderot is equally abrasive. He is not, he insists, being a moral relativist. He does not prefer "a savage to a civilized state". But, as he asks of the arrival of the conquistadores in the Americas, "Tell me, reader, do you see here civilised people arriving among savages, or savages received by civilised people?"[25]

If the writings of Hume, Kant and Jefferson represent one strand of Enlightenment thinking about race and equality, the *Histoire des Deux Indes* represents another. These two distinct strands, the "moderate" and the "radical", and the struggle between them, were key in shaping the character of the Enlightenment and of the post-Enlightenment world, and in framing subsequent debates about race, colonialism and identity.

The idea of the Radical Enlightenment remains contested among historians. Nevertheless, it is a useful way of looking at eighteenth-century debates, and at the paradox of an age which helped establish modern ideas of both equality and racial inequality. The Radical Enlightenment comprised not so much a fixed group as an approach to questions of democracy and equality, secularism and progress, an approach whose meaning was often fiercely debated by the radicals, but one that, for all the variety of perspectives, was fundamentally distinct from that of the mainstream. The mainstream Enlightenment consisted of the figures with whom we are most familiar and about whom historians have most written—not just Kant, Hume and Jefferson, but also Locke and Voltaire, Adam Smith and Benjamin Franklin. It was, however, the Radical Enlightenment, shaped by lesser-known figures such as d'Holbach, Diderot and Spinoza that endowed the Enlightenment with its heart and soul. Where the mainstream sought "to modify and effect repairs to the old structure, given us by divine providence, and hence basically good", argues Jonathan Israel, the radicals strove "to tear the old house of *ancien régime* society down and put another in its place".[26]

Many of the mainstream philosophers possessed rich patrons and official posts. The radicals operated largely in clandestine groups. The great names of the French Enlightenment—Voltaire, Montesquieu and Turgot—gathered in salons in splendid houses and in grand cafes. The lesser figures congregated in the seediest of taverns where "one only finds pimps, buggers and *bardaches*", to quote the notorious blackmailer and police spy Charles Claude Théveneau. They produced illicit pamphlets printed by hidden presses and sold, in the words of Philipp Blom, "*sous le manteau* (under the cloak) as secretly and often as expensively as hard drugs today, and with the same risk of being arrested and imprisoned". These pamphlets ranged from pornographic stories to atheist tracts. What they had in common was their challenge to conventional norms. And that they were forbidden.[27]

It was in these taverns and in these pamphlets, among the pornographers and the pimps, that the Radical Enlightenment first found its voice. It was where Diderot began his intellectual life, before eventually graduating to the grand salons. It was here, too, that ideas and concepts that have helped make the modern world first saw the light. While the great figures of the French Enlightenment "grew fat in Voltaire's church", Robert Darnton observes, "the revolutionary spirit passed to the lean and hungry men of Grub street, to the cultural pariahs who... hated the Old Regime in their guts, who ached with the hatred of it."[28]

The two most subversive themes in the underground pamphlets were the insistence on a Godless universe and a radical vision of equality, two themes that became inextricably linked. It was not that the radicals were all atheists. Not only were there many believers with varying degrees of faith, but the roots of the Radical Enlightenment lay, at least partly, in the religious movements that formed the revolutionary edge of the Reformation. But Christianity itself was changing.

From the late Middle Ages there had developed within the Christian tradition a new humanist sensibility as well as a greater willingness to accept a more naturalistic view and a growing desire to root faith in reason. The Radical Enlightenment pushed these arguments much further. For the radicals, to be human meant to have the power and capacity to be master of one's own destiny, independently of divine intervention. Whereas for previous generations nature made sense as God's order, many *philosophes* now insisted that only humans infused it with meaning. "The universe is dumb", Diderot declared; it is only "the presence of man that gives interest to the existence of beings".[29]

As the God-ordained order crumbled, so the argument for equality became both more necessary and more possible. Having dispensed with God, the radicals had, in Jonathan Israel's words, no "meaningful alternative" to articulating a new view of the human in which morality was grounded in a "generalized radical egalitarianism extending across all frontiers, class barriers and horizons". Egalitarianism became the moral anchor for radicalism, and would continue to be well beyond the Enlightenment. It was, ironically, in the fracturing of the God-ordained order that the moral universalism implicit in Christianity could become manifest.[30]

VI

On the morning of 28 October 1647, a group of soldiers met at St Mary's Church in Putney, in south-west London. They had come not to pray, nor to fight, but to partake in what might seem a very unsoldierly act—a political debate, among the most momentous in British history. All were regulars in the New Model Army, the most radical and significant of the Parliamentary forces waging war against Charles I, in the English Civil Wars that rent the nation through the 1640s. The Army had been established in 1645 as a body of professional soldiers committed to the Parliamentary cause and possessed an extraordinary degree of internal democracy—every regiment voted on representatives, called "Agitators", for an army council, and ordinary soldiers were vocal in their political opinions.

The issue at stake in what are now called the Putney Debates was the nature of England's constitution once Charles had been defeated. Dismayed by the timidity of the army officers' proposals, which would have retained the monarchy, rank-and-file soldiers produced their own constitutional plan. "An Agreement of the People" was written largely by Levellers, the name given by their enemies to a disparate movement of radicals who believed that "all degrees of men should be levelled and an equality should be established". The document called for biennial Parliamentary elections, for the rule of law to apply equally to everyone without reference to "tenure, estate, charter, degree, birth, or place" and for freedom of speech and worship. "The poorest he that is in England hath a life to live as the greatest he", argued Colonel Thomas Rainsborough, speaking for the radicals, and therefore "every man that is to live under a government ought first by his own consent to put himself under that government."[31]

The Levellers were not calling for universal suffrage; under their proposal, women, servants and paupers would be denied the vote. It took more radical groups, such as the Diggers, to argue for full suffrage. Nevertheless, it was still too far-reaching for the Grandees, or officer class. "Liberty", as Henry Ireton, a general in the Army and Oliver Cromwell's son-in-law, put it in the debate, "cannot be provided for in a general sense if property be preserved". What worried the Grandees was that, in the words of Colonel Nathaniel Rich, "If the master and servant be equal electors", then "there may be a law enacted, that there shall be an equality of goods and estate". To preserve the right to property, equality must be constrained and, Ireton insisted, the vote must be restricted to "persons in whom all land lies, and those in corporations in whom all trading lies". In response to which Rainsborough acidly asked, "I am a poor man, therefore I must be oppressed?"[32]

This tension between "equality" and "property" is one that shaped much subsequent history, particularly the Enlightenment battle between the moderates and the radicals. The birth of modernity embodied a series of tensions, that were, and remain, unresolved. In the latter decades of the eighteenth century, those tensions exploded to create what we now call the age of revolution, an age in which the old order, the *ancien régime*, unravelled. From those tensions emerged also the paradox of an age that laid the modern foundations both of equality and of inequality.

Between the sixteenth and the eighteenth centuries, a series of social and economic changes paved the way for modernity—the creation of more individualized societies, the beginnings of a market economy and of novel forms of manufacture, the emergence of new social forces, from the nascent bourgeoisie to the even more nascent working class. From the perspective of the twenty-first century, though, the eighteenth-century world seems more feudal than modern. There had been steady economic growth since the early 1600s. Nevertheless, Europe remained overwhelmingly rural, and life for the majority continued to be parochial, fragmented and inward looking. Of the new entrepreneurial class, the key figures were the merchant, the financier and the colonial planter, not yet the industrialist. Nation-states barely existed in the modern sense. Europe was a patchwork of empires, kingdoms, duchies and papal states, mostly ruled, with the exception of Britain, by absolute monarchs. Below them were hierarchies of landed nobles. Buttressing the whole system was an orthodoxy of churches and a clutter of institutions whose power seemed to derive from their very obsolescence.

Enlightenment philosophers aimed to free humanity from the grip of tradition and unreason, to abolish archaic institutions based on prescription and to establish society on a more rational foundation. It was the philosophy primarily of the embryonic bourgeoisie, of merchants and financiers, of intellectuals and artisans, whose aspirations to economic, political and social power required the undermining of feudal institutions. But those who were, in Hume's words, "plac'd in the Middle Station" of life lacked the social means to effect change. A relationship developed therefore between the educated classes and old rulers. "A prince needed the middle class and its ideas to modernise his state", Eric Hobsbawm observed. "A weak middle class needed a prince to batter down the resistance of entrenched aristocratic and clerical reaction to progress."[33]

Enlightenment ideals appealed, however, not just to rulers who wanted a more rational *ancien régime*, or to a middle class that wanted a society sufficiently reformed to afford it power. They appealed, too, to those who wanted more profound changes. There were bourgeois radicals such as the American patriots who sought to break free from the claims of political oligarchy, waging a Revolution to create a more democratic system. But those same revolutionaries wished also to limit the claims of equality, denying the most basic of rights to slaves, free blacks, women and workers. These were the groups—the poor, the dispossessed, the enslaved— who pushed the implicit logic of Enlightenment claims about equality and a common humanity to their conclusion, who recognized that to make good on these claims, a fundamental transformation of society was necessary. It was, as we shall see in later chapters, through the struggles of slaves to emancipate themselves, of colonial subjects challenging imperial rule, of the working class demanding decent wages and conditions, of women claiming the right to vote, that the idea of equality was given a fuller meaning.

All this only made moderates more fearful of the social consequences of equality. The conundrum they faced is well expressed in the work of Adam Smith. Moral philosopher and political economist, Smith's two great works, *The Theory of Moral Sentiments* and *The Wealth of Nations*, published in 1759 and 1776 respectively, spoke to the two sides of the challenge facing the moderates. *The Wealth of Nations* made the case for a free market economy, and for the "invisible hand" of the market as the means to social equity. *The Theory of Moral Sentiments*, written seventeen years earlier, recognized the importance of "sympathy" in social life and the necessity of an equitable society. It was not that the two books stood opposed to each other. It was rather that in both were exposed the moderates' dilemma.

Every individual, Smith wrote in *The Wealth of Nations*, exploits his capital in a fashion "most advantageous" to himself. But "the study of his own advantage... necessarily leads him to prefer that employment [of capital] which is most advantageous to the society". The rich are "led by an invisible hand to make nearly the same distribution of the necessaries of life which would have been made had the earth been divided into equal portions among all its inhabitants". Despite the division of society into rich and poor, the market ensured as great a degree of equality as if such equality had been enforced by the mandatory redistribution of wealth. And, yet, it was not so simple. The "disposition to admire, and almost to worship, the rich and the powerful, and to despise, or, at least, to neglect, persons of poor and mean condition", Smith wrote in *The Theory of Moral Sentiments*, is "necessary both to establish and to maintain the distinction of ranks and the order of society" but is "at the same time, the great and most universal cause of the corruption of our moral sentiments". Maintaining the distinction of ranks was "corrupting" because inequality was not a social good. "No society", Smith observed, "can surely be flourishing and happy, of which the far greater part of the members are poor and miserable". Nevertheless, it was "necessary" because inequality was a driver of social and economic growth. The existence of the rich led the poor to work harder to achieve what they did not have. This meant that "wherever there is great property, there is great inequality" and "the affluence of the rich excites the indignation of the poor". Since the rich man "is at all times surrounded by unknown enemies", so he necessarily must be protected "by the powerful arm of the civil magistrate continually held up to chastise" the poor.[34]

Smith accepted the ideal of equality in the abstract; that is, he acknowledged that at some level all human beings were of equal moral worth. He recognized, too, that too much inequality was not a social good. Nevertheless, he also thought it necessary to "maintain the distinction of ranks"—in other words, inequality—without which there could be no economic or social progress. The philosopher and historian Adam Ferguson, a fellow luminary of the Scottish Enlightenment, was even clearer. "It has pleased Providence for wise purposes", he wrote, "to place men in different stations, and to bestow on them different degrees of wealth. Without this circumstance there could be no subordination, no government, no order, no industry." For Ferguson, "Every person does good, and promotes the happiness of society, by living agreeable to the rank in which Providence has placed him". This is a premodern view of social order remade for a market economy. Over the following century, nature, not God, would come to sanctify the placing of "men in different stations". Why did different peoples occupy different places in the social hierarchy? Because they were naturally—racially—different.[35]

Jean-Jacques Rousseau disagreed. There are few thinkers so difficult to categorize politically or who so divide opinion. A key figure of the Enlightenment, Rousseau (1712–1778) nevertheless became alienated from what he regarded as its facile optimism. He was drawn to a darker view of civilization that cut against the predominant understanding of society as a tool of human improvement. He saw humans as naturally good, and society as having corrupted their original nature, introducing selfishness, inequality and evil. This led him eventually to break with his close friend Diderot and the radicals. On the question of equality, however, Rousseau was, with the significant exception of his traditionalist views on the role of women, among the most important eighteenth-century thinkers, who both shaped and was shaped by the ideals of Diderot's circle.

"The first man who, having enclosed a piece of ground, thought of saying 'This is mine' and found people simple enough to believe him, was the true founder of civil society. How many crimes, wars, murders; how much misery and horror the human race would have been spared if someone had pulled up the stakes and filled in the ditch and cried out to his fellow men: 'Beware of listening to this impostor. You are lost if you forget that the fruits of the earth belong to everyone, and the earth itself belongs to no one!'".[36]

The striking image with which Rousseau opens the second part of his *Discourse on Inequality* could not demonstrate better the difference between his and Smith's approach. For Smith, the needs of property compelled restrictions on equality. For Rousseau, the needs of equality demanded restrictions on property rights.

The cleavage between the radical and the moderate vision was visible not just on the question of equality but also on many other linked issues from democracy to poverty. "We no longer believe", Condorcet, one of the leading figures of the Enlightenment, wrote in 1786, "that nature has divided the human race into three or four orders... and that one of these orders is also condemned to work much and eat little." Many did indeed come to believe that in the century to come.[37]

VII

It was a warm summer night in July 1770, wisps of mist floating along the Thames in central London. Thomas Lewis, a young black man, was walking along the Chelsea Embankment. He was suddenly ambushed by two men, John Maloney and Edward Armstrong. They overpowered him, bundled him into a boat and ferried him down the Thames to Gravesend to a ship, the *Captain Seward*, where he was chained, ready to be transported to Jamaica to be sold. The two thugs had been paid to catch Lewis by the ship's captain Robert Stapylton, with whom Lewis had previously sailed, and who insisted that Lewis was his slave.

Lewis' screams for help were heard by residents of nearby houses. One contacted the abolitionist Granville Sharp who issued a writ of habeas corpus to free Lewis. The ship transporting him to Jamaica had already departed, with Lewis according to one account "chained to the mainsmast", but headwinds had kept the vessel off the coast of Kent, allowing the writ to be served. Sharp then brought a private prosecution against Stapylton. The case came before William Murray, Earl of Mansfield, the Lord Chief Justice of England. Himself a slave owner, Mansfield opened proceedings by noting that he respected the right to property in slaves, and that the issue at hand was not about whether slavery was legal in England but whether Stapylton could prove that he owned Lewis, so giving him the right to assault and kidnap him. The jury refused to accept Lewis as Stapylton's property. As the foreman gave his verdict, the public gallery, and according to Sharp, the jury itself, broke into shouts of "No property! No property!"[38]

On no issue was the conflict between equality and property more sharply expressed than in that of slavery. For radicals, slavery provided a case study in why equality should not be limited by considerations of property. For moderates, the need to protect property, and the fear of extending equal rights to wider sections of the population, often made them shrink from fully opposing slavery.

In May 1792, the historian Edward Gibbon wrote from Lausanne to his friend Lord Sheffield about a Parliamentary debate on the slave trade. Sheffield had opposed a motion for abolition proposed by William Wilberforce. The previous year, a similar motion had fallen. This time Wilberforce won, though with an amendment that the ban should be "gradual". Not till 1807 did the Slave Trade Act finally pass into law. Why, Gibbon wanted to know, had Parliament become more receptive to banning the trade? If opposition to the slave trade "proceeded only from an impulse of humanity, I cannot be displeased", he wrote. He worried, though, that it presaged deeper changes. "In this rage against slavery… was there no leaven of new democratical principles? no wild ideas of the rights and natural equality of man?", Gibbon asked, adding "It is these I fear".[39]

Gibbon was happy to restrict the slave trade out of an "impulse of humanity" but did not wish that impulse to stretch any further, to usher in "democratical principles" or "wild ideas of the rights and natural equality of man". It was a view common among moderate supporters of the Enlightenment. Edmund Burke, the founder of modern conservatism, is often portrayed as hostile to slavery. But as he became more fearful of radicalism in the wake of the French Revolution, he rowed back on his abolitionist view, suggesting to the Home Secretary Henry Dundas (the man who amended Wilberforce's abolition bill to make the changes "gradual"), that "the cause of humanity would be far more benefited by the continuance of the trade and servitude, regulated and reformed, than by the total destruction of both or either".[40]

Equally, many abolitionists insisted that rights should not be extended beyond slaves. William Wilberforce is celebrated as one of the great opponents of slavery. He was also a great opponent of working-class rights. Wilberforce saw the emancipation of slaves as a Christian duty not as an expansion of equality. He derided the possibilities of universal suffrage, was implacably hostile to trade unions, and supported the use of sedition laws and of internment without trial to supress radical dissent. He feared that "the lower orders" might "be tempted by the delusive and wicked principles instilled into their minds" to attempt "the overthrow of every civil and religious establishment".[41]

For radicals, on the other hand, the abolition of slavery, universal suffrage, uplift of the working class, and diminution of property rights were all wrapped together. The Scottish jurist George Wallace was unequivocal in his condemnation of slavery. "Men and their liberties", he declared, cannot be traded. Slavery should be abolished even if it meant economic loss; it was intolerable to abuse fellow humans so that "our pockets may be filled with money, and our mouths with delicates". Wallace's anti-slavery radicalism came more easily to him, Robin Blackburn reflects, because of "his unusual lack of respect for private property". "Property, that bane of human felicity", Wallace wrote, "must necessarily be banished out of the world before an Utopia can be established."[42]

Equality was reinvented in the modern form in the eighteenth century. But its boundaries were fiercely contested. The meaning of equality was tied up with myriad other concerns; not just property, but democracy, hierarchy, order, colonialism, individualism, working-class rights and the rights of women. It was out of these debates that the modern idea of race would develop.

2

THE INVENTION OF RACE

I

"It is on the degree of curliness or twist in the hair that the most fundamental divisions of the human race is based."[1]

So wrote William Sollas in his 1911 book *Ancient Hunters and Their Modern Representatives*. The professor of palaeontology and geology at Oxford University was not being ironic. He was simply, as he saw it, stating a fact. Racial differences were real, incontestable and profound. And, yet, scientists found it impossible to define what they were. Every measure of racial difference, from the shape of the skull to the character of blood types, was shown to be changeable and incapable of differentiating one race from another. "A race type", the British anthropologist Alfred Haddon acknowledged, "exists only in our mind". "With more complete knowledge", he added, "it becomes increasingly difficult to define a race". The French anthropologist Paul Topinard described race as "an abstract conception, a notion of continuity in discontinuity, of unity in diversity". It was "a real but directly unattainable thing." When Harvard anthropologist Ronald Dixon set out in the 1920s to write a *Racial History of Man*, he gave up on using objective categories. Instead, he decided, in his own words, to "set up arbitrary standards and, using these as our measure, determine the character and relationships of people in terms of our arbitrarily selected units". The acceptance of something that did not exist became the starting point for proving that it did. And with that, Dixon wrote a 600-page book.[2]

Races cannot be shown to exist, but many are compelled to believe and act as if they do. Why? That is the question I want to explore in this chapter, tracing the idea of race from its first glimmerings in the early modern world to its full flourishing in the late nineteenth century, to show how, and why, race became the medium through which many of the contradictions of modernity came to be understood.

II

"Geographers up to this time have only divided the earth according to its different countries or regions", French physician and traveller François Bernier wrote in 1684. He proposed "dividing it in a different way"—by race. Bernier's "A New Division of the Earth, According to the Different Species or Races of Men Who Inhabit It" is now regarded as the first scheme of racial classification in European scholarship. It was published at the very beginning of the Enlightenment. This was the age in which modern ideas of the self, and of the individual as a rational agent, began to develop; in which the authority of custom and tradition weakened while the role of reason in explaining the natural and social worlds expanded; and in which humans became seen as part of the natural order, and knowledge was secularized. Voyages of exploration enlarged the bounds of European understanding and heightened the sense of a technological and social gulf between Europe and the rest of the world. They also brought them face-to-face with new kinds of animals. Great Apes, in particular, beings that seemed so similar to humans and yet were not, caused astonishment and reflection.[3]

All these changes and discoveries raised new questions about human nature and human differences. Natural philosophers had begun classifying all of nature. Where did humans fit into this project? And how did differences between human groups slot into the new taxonomy of nature? The meaning of identity profoundly changed. In the premodern world, an individual's identity was intimately bound up with the community in which he or she lived, or with the faith that nourished that community. No one had self-consciously to reflect upon their identity; it was a given. Every individual possessed a fixed place in society from which derived his or her privileges, duties and obligations. In early modernity, the social and moral bonds that gave form to communities began to fray. The individual was beginning to emerge as a new kind of social actor, detached from the specifics of a community. What was one's identity, and how was it created, in this new world?

There were new puzzles, too, about the relationship between the present and the past—the nature of history—and between different human societies. History was seen less as static or cyclical, more as something that progressed. It was also seen as the product of humans and of human activity. So, questions arose as to how history progressed and why certain human groups seemed to progress more than others. Over time, "race" became a means of addressing some of these questions, a means of making sense of some of these changes.

The concept of race did not emerge out of nothing. Ideas about the inferiority and subhumanity of certain groups were already present. Antisemitism, long a feature of Christendom, intensified in the late Middle Ages, leading to pogroms and eventually, in 1492, to the expulsion of Jews from Spain, which had previously been one of the more tolerant countries in Europe. The Crusades had similarly hardened attitudes towards Muslims. Nor was it just Jews and Muslims who felt the lash of discrimination. Europe, from around the eleventh century, became in the words of medievalist Robert Moore, a "persecuting society", in which "deliberate and socially sanctioned violence" was directed against groups that ranged from heretics and Jews to lepers and sodomites. In Islamic societies, too, there developed new, less tolerant views of Christians and Jews. Muslim societies permitted slavery but, as in the Ancient world and in premodern Christian Europe, largely abjured racial distinctions in deciding whom to enslave. As the Islamic empire expanded into sub-Saharan Africa, however, and black Africans made up an increasing proportion of Islam's slaves, so new claims, such as blacks being descendants of Ham's cursed son Canaan, and enslavement a punishment for their ancestor's sin, found a foothold. These claims were later adopted by Christians, too.[4]

Such prejudices were, nevertheless, a long way from racial ideas in the modern sense. National and ethnic differences were viewed more in terms of customs, language and law than of blood or biology. In any case, as George Frederickson notes, "inequality based on birth was the norm for everyone from king down to peasant", and inequalities based on group differences were merely "special cases of a general pattern". Only in a world in which the principles of social equality and a common humanity had become accepted could ideas of inequality and racial difference gain meaning. That was the world that was slowly coming into being in eighteenth-century Europe.[5]

III

Above, how high, progressive life may go!
Around, how wide! how deep extend below?
Vast chain of being! which from God began,
Natures ethereal, human, angel, man,
Beast, bird, fish, insect, what no eye can see,
No glass can reach; from Infinite to thee,
From thee to nothing...

So wrote Alexander Pope in his philosophical poem "An Essay on Man", published in 1733–4. Its aim was to "vindicate the ways of God to man" and to lay out the natural order that God had decreed. At the heart of that natural order was the "*scala naturae*" or the "Great Chain of Being". An idea dating back at least to Ancient Greece, it presented the cosmos as a ladder of ascent from the inorganic world to the Supreme Being. In between came all the forms of life from angels through humans to other animals to plants to minerals. The Chain of Being was central to Christian theology, and to European conceptions of the world around them, shaping not just the natural world but human society, too. The hierarchical relationships between the slave, the serf, the nobleman and the king were all part of the Chain.[6]

A year after the final parts of Pope's "Essay on Man" appeared in print, another book was published that played a major role in cutting down the Chain of Being—Carolus Linnaeus' *Systema Naturae*. Professor of botany at Uppsala University in Sweden, Linnaeus believed that all living forms could be fitted into a rational pattern. He replaced the linear view of nature as imagined in the *scala naturae* with a nested structure of species, genera, families, orders, classes, phyla and kingdoms, a system we still use today. Over time, with much revision and rearrangement, Linnaeus developed a complex classification system for humans, too.

Linnaeus placed humans, apes and monkeys in the same order, which he first called "Anthropomorpha" and later "Primates"; humans were given their own genus, *Homo*. In the tenth edition of *Systema Naturae*, published in 1758, Linnaeus introduced the term *Homo sapiens* to distinguish true humans from human "monsters"—*Homo monstrosus*—such as the Patagonian giant, the Alpine dwarf and cone-headed Chinese, and *Homo ferus* ("feral man") a category of individuals such as the wolf-boy of Hesse and the wild girl of Champagne. *Homo sapiens* was in turn divided into four "varieties" (though Linnaeus never called them "races"): *americanus, europaeus, asiaticus* and *afar*, each defined by a mixture of observation and prejudice. So, *Homo sapiens europaeus* was "white, serious, strong. Hair blond, flowing. Eyes blue. Active, very smart, inventive", whereas *afar* was "black, impassive, lazy. Hair kinked. Skin silky. Nose flat. Lips thick… Crafty, slow, foolish".[7]

The *Systema Naturae* was celebrated as an astonishing feat of scientific classification. It was also criticized for its lack of rigour and flights of fantasy. The two most important eighteenth-century critics were the Frenchman Georges-Louis Leclerc, the Comte de Buffon (1707–88), and the German Johann Friedrich Blumenbach (1752–1840).

Buffon was a mathematician and naturalist whose most famous work, the 36-volume *Histoire Naturelle*, published over a span of forty years, aimed to bring together all the available knowledge on the natural sciences. Rather than force nature into a single classification system with a small number of categories, as Linnaeus sought to do, Buffon believed it better to describe nature's diversity and the complex patterns that such diversity created. He stressed continuity between groups and the absence of discrete boundaries.

Buffon's prejudices were revealed in his belief that all humans were originally white and that non-white peoples were degenerations of this primeval homogeneity. Nevertheless, his hostility to a rigid classification system, and his insistence that human differences were fluid, suggested an understanding of human groups notably different to that which would be embodied in the concept of race. Buffon, the anthropologist Jonathan Marks observes, "was not asking the questions How many races are there? and What are they? as Linnaeus and his intellectual descendants did and would". Rather, "he tried to ask the questions, How is variation in the human species patterned? And How did it come to be this way?" While the Linnaean system was a triumph for biology, it was, Marks argues, a disaster for anthropology. In pushing anthropologists to ask "how do we classify a race?" and "how many races are there?", it led them down "one of the blindest alleys in modern science".[8]

Blumenbach was also critical of Linnaeus, but in a significantly different way. He did ask the questions "How many races are there? and What are they?", and his answers still shape the world.

In 1775, the same year as Kant produced his first paper on racial categories, Blumenbach published his MD thesis *On the Natural Variety of Mankind*, one of the most influential works in the history of race. Blumenbach considered Linnaeus his mentor but thought his work on humans unscientific. Racial categories should be defined solely by "objective" physical characteristics. He put particular store on the features of the skull, amassing what was then the largest collection of crania in Europe.

It was Blumenbach who turned "Caucasian" into a key racial term, one of five races in his classification, the others being Ethiopians, the peoples of sub-Saharan Africa; Americans, the native peoples of the New World; Mongolians, the peoples of East Asia; and Malays, the peoples of Oceania. In Blumenbach's scheme, "Caucasian" included not just Europeans but also the inhabitants of North Africa, west Asia and the Indian subcontinent. It also quickly became a synonym for "white". In the history of race, such contradictions were quickly glossed over. Blumenbach's reason for using the label Caucasian exposes also the limits of his "objective" approach. "I have taken the name of this variety from Mount Caucasus", he wrote, "because its neighbourhood... produces the most beautiful race of men". Smuggling in the aesthetic in the guise of objective science became a hallmark of racial thinking.[9]

While Blumenbach declared his taxonomy to be scientific, he was ambivalent as to its meaning. The different human varieties, he observed, "so run into one another" that "you cannot mark out the limits between them". There were no fixed boundaries between races. Blumenbach accepted, too, that no characteristic was to be found in one race that could not be found in another. He argued that it was important to divide humanity into distinctive categories for the purposes of scholarship but also that the boundaries of such categories were, to a degree, arbitrary and fluid. This more subtle aspect of Blumenbach's argument was soon lost in the fog of race, while the categories themselves became a fixity. Over the next two centuries, anthropologists put forward various racial taxonomies in which the number of races varied from three to several dozen. Blumenbach's five-fold taxonomy, however, and his terminology— in particular, "Caucasian"—became established in both scientific and popular thinking, and remain so to this day.[10]

IV

By the end of the eighteenth century, the concept of race had found a foothold in European intellectual circles. The classification of human types, including the main system we still hold today, was established. Many leading Enlightenment figures, from Blumenbach to Kant, accepted the reality of racial categories and embedded them into well-developed theories. Yet, for all this, racial thinking remained marginal. Those who proposed racial explanations did so, with a handful of exceptions, *sotto voce*. Hume's comment about the inferiority of blacks appeared in a footnote. Jefferson wrote to a French correspondent that he had expressed his racial opinions "with great hesitation", adding that "whatever their degree of talents, it is no measure of their rights" (though, of course, in Jefferson's America, it did become a measure of their rights).[11]

Why such caution about openly expressing racial ideas? A key reason was the significance of equality as a defining feature of Enlightenment thought. The colonies, particularly those built on slavery, provided fertile ground for racial thinking. In Europe, however, not till the nineteenth century did such ideas truly take hold. In the eighteenth century, the understanding of the relationship between human unity and human differences was still being fashioned. What equality meant, to whom it applied, and how one should view the vast array of different human societies and ways of living, were matters of heated debate. Out of such debates, new ideas of race emerged, ideas that came to dominate in the nineteenth century.

There also emerged, as political philosopher Sankar Muthu shows, a sustained critique of ethnocentrism and colonialism. It was a critique that rested on three fundamental ideas. The first was an insistence that all "human beings deserve some modicum of moral and political respect simply because of the fact that they were human". Second, there was an understanding that the universal human capacity for speech, reason and sociability could be expressed in different cultural forms, each as valid as the other. This, Muthu suggests, provided the basis for a "more inclusive and meaningful moral universalism", an acceptance that peoples whose cultures and societies were unlike those of Europeans were, nevertheless, worthy of respect and equal consideration. And, third, there was the acceptance of a degree of "moral incommensurability", an acknowledgement that different peoples might desire different moral ends, that this could create a variety of cultural and social practices, and that "entire peoples cannot be judged as superior or inferior along a universal scale of value".[12]

Muthu picks out three thinkers as particularly significant in developing this strand of Enlightenment thought. The first is Diderot, whose arguments we have already explored. The second is Immanuel Kant, whose presence in this list might seem surprising given his views of race and difference. Kant's thought, however, underwent a transformation in the 1790s, and he had, as the title of a paper by philosopher Pauline Kleingeld puts it, "Second thoughts on race", seemingly rejecting his earlier views on racial hierarchies. In his 1795 essay "Towards Perpetual Peace", Kant condemns "the inhospitable conduct of the 'civilised' countries of Europe", whose ill-treatment "of the lands and peoples they visit... is terrifying in its extremes". Kant adds, in parenthesis, "'visit' = 'conquer'!". When Europeans "first came upon America, the Negro lands, the Spice Islands, the Cape etc., they regarded them as lands without owners, for they counted the inhabitants as nothing". In India, "under the pretence of intending to establish trading posts, they brought in foreign soldiers to oppress the natives" and "spread famine, rebellion, treachery, and the whole litany of evils that afflict mankind". It is a view, Kleingeld and Muthu note, significantly different from that of even a decade earlier.[13]

Why Kant changed his attitude, he never explains. He may have been radicalized by the French Revolution of 1789, or perhaps he was stung by the critique he faced from the third figure in Muthu's study, the most influential, complex and misunderstood thinker on ideas of cultural differences: the German philosopher Johann Gottfried Herder.

V

"Man has been the same in all ages: only, he expressed himself in each case according to the conditions in which he lived." That might have been written by Hume or Voltaire or any mainstream Enlightenment figure. But Herder, whose words they are, meant by them something significantly different than did more mainstream thinkers. And that something significantly different helped give shape to ideas both of race and of antiracism.[14]

Herder was born in the eastern Prussian town of Mohrungen (now part of Poland) in 1744. At 18, he enrolled at the University of Königsberg, where Kant taught. Herder became his greatest student. The two also became great rivals, with distinct answers to the question that Kant had raised: "What is Enlightenment?"

A seminal figure straddling the Enlightenment and the post-Enlightenment worlds, Herder sought through his philosophy to negotiate the terrain between moral universalism and cultural relativism; that is between the claim, on the one hand, that all humans possess a common essence, by virtue of which all enjoy the right to be treated with respect and dignity, and, on the other, the belief that one should understand and judge social norms and practices in terms of the cultures in which they are embedded, not of the norms and practices of one's own society.

Herder was as committed to social equality as any Enlightenment radical. He despised both colonialism and slavery. Addressing European slave traders, he thundered, "And what right have you, monsters! even to approach the country of these unfortunates, much less to tear them from it by stealth, fraud and cruelty?" He was also a strong opponent of racial ideas. "*All mankind*", he wrote, "*are only one and the same species*". This was not simply a statement of fact but also a moral commitment: "O man, honor thyself. Neither the pongo nor the gibbon is thy brother; the American and the Negro are; these therefore thou shouldst not oppress or murder, or steal, for they are men like thee."[15]

Fostering universalism, Herder insisted, required one to challenge the claim that European ideas were necessarily better by virtue of having come from Europe. Why, he asks, should we so "readily bestow 'our own ideal' of *virtue* and *happiness* on every remote nation, every ancient age of the world?" Is Europe to be the "only judge" of what is good, "assessing, condemning, or prettifying [other societies'] mores all by itself?" It was obvious to Herder that "One shape of mankind and one corner of the earth could not contain" all that constitutes the good, for the good is "distributed among a thousand shapes—an eternal Proteus!—strolling through all the parts and ages of the world."[16]

The fundamental unit of human existence was, for Herder, the *Volk*. This is usually translated as "the people" or "the nation", but has a deeper, more spiritual, connotation. What made each *Volk* unique was its *Kultur*: its particular language, literature, culture and modes of living. Herder's critique of the concept of race rested, at least in part, on the foundational character of the *Volk* to his worldview.

The unique nature of each *Volk* was articulated through its *Volksgeist*—the spirit of a people refined through history. The relationship between the individual and the collective was expressed not through a political contract but in a spiritual union. Herder was politically and philosophically dissimilar to Edmund Burke; nevertheless, he would have agreed with Burke that a nation was "a partnership between those who are living, those who are dead and those who are to be born". To be a member of a *Volk* was to think and act in ways given by the *Volk*.

Vital to the uniqueness of every *Volk* was language; not language in the abstract, but the specific language through which an individual and a people expressed themselves. "Every language", Herder wrote, "bears the stamp of the mind and character of a people", and "each nation speaks in accordance with its thought and thinks in accordance with its speech". Language linked the present to the past, and the individual to the whole. "Has a nation anything more precious than the language of its fathers?", he rhetorically asked. "In it dwell the entire world of tradition, history, religion, principles of existence: its whole heart and soul." A foreign language was something alien to the soul. He could "only stammer with intense effort in the words of a foreign language; its spirit will evade me."[17]

Herder saw himself as defending an authentic Germanness from imperialist designs, particularly of the perfidious French. But attachment to one's culture could blur into a detestation of others. In his poem "To the Germans", Herder bemoaned German intellectuals' embrace of French culture, and in particular of the French language:

Spew out the ugly slime of the Seine.
Speak German, O you German!

It is not difficult to see how such sentiments might appeal to ultranationalists and reactionaries.

Herder abhorred migration and mixture which were "strongly detrimental to… the beauty or uniqueness of a people". Only when a people stayed attached to the geographic region of their ancestors could they remain "whole". Only then could the Earth be "considered as a garden, where in one spot one human national plant, in another, another, bloomed in its proper figure and nature; where in this spot one species of animal, in that, another, pursued its course, according to its instincts and character".[18]

The philosopher Sonia Sikka draws a contrast between Herder's views and those of a contemporary figure like Salman Rushdie. While in hiding from the Ayatollah Khomeini's fatwa, Rushdie wrote a defence of his novel *The Satanic Verses*, seeing it as "a lovesong to our mongrel selves", a work that "celebrates hybridity, impurity, intermingling, the transformation that comes of new and unexpected combinations of human beings, cultures, ideas, politics, movies, songs". The most vociferous critics of *The Satanic Verses* are, he noted, "of the opinion that intermingling with a different culture will inevitably weaken and ruin their own. I am of the opposite opinion". Whether Herder would have applauded the burning of *The Satanic Verses* is impossible to say. He would certainly have been horrified by Rushdie's argument for "hybridity". Nothing, he believed, was more unnatural than "the wild mixture of various nations and races under one sceptre". In such societies "there is no life". This conflict between what Rushdie called "mongrelisation" and the "absolutism of the Pure" shapes much of the debate about identity today.[19]

Herder occupies an ambiguous role in modern political thought. In the eighteenth century, he stood in that part of the Enlightenment tradition that stressed the importance of equality, was deeply hostile to colonialism, and dismissed Eurocentric visions of universal values. Yet, his approach, paradoxically, both sharpened the meaning of equality and universalism and gave succour to those hostile to those very notions. In the twentieth century, his pluralism, celebration of cultural difference and insistence on the incommensurability of values became the root of much antiracist thinking, and the often-unacknowledged foundation of identity politics. Before that, in the nineteenth and early twentieth centuries, Herder's impact was to encourage, albeit unwittingly, the racial viewpoint. Once it was accepted that different peoples were motivated by different sentiments unique to themselves, that these sentiments inexpressibly imbued a people's history, tradition and consciousness, and defined every individual's being, it was not a great leap to view those sentiments as racial, and as giving validation to segregation, apartheid and worse. The German literary historian and Nazi Benno von Wiese found in Herder the vindication of the belief that "a people which does not keep its blood pure, falls into the danger of destroying its 'original form'".[20]

Herder would undoubtedly have loathed the Nazis. Yet, for all his attachment to equality, and disdain for racial ideas, his cultural relativism led him to deeply ethnocentric and repulsive views. He wrote of Africans that nature had been "obliged to deny [them] nobler gifts", such as a "finer intellect which the creature whose breast swells with boiling passions beneath this burning sun must necessarily be refused". To compensate, nature had provided Africans with a "sensual disposition", a people "for whom the sensual appetite is the height of happiness". Nature "formed of him what was most fit for his country, and the happiness of his life. Either no Africa should have been created or it was requisite that Negroes should be made to inhabit Africa."[21]

Herder gave life to ideas that would be at the heart of racial thinking over the next century and a half: the linking of physical traits to mental and moral attributes, the hostility to cultural and racial intermixing, the celebration of "equal but different". Sikka, a thinker deeply sympathetic to Herder, viewing him as an "enlightened relativist", acknowledges nevertheless that "Herder approaches an idea similar to that of a 'racial soul'".[22]

All this flowed from an unswerving defence of equality and an unflinching hostility to colonialism. It is a reminder that both universalism and relativism need to be handled with care. Universalist claims made many blind to European ethnocentrism and, as we shall see in subsequent chapters, were used to justify colonialism and imperialism; cultural relativism led many to embrace bigoted ideas and practices. It is a lesson as important today as it was in Herder's time.

VI

A young man—perhaps the artist himself—has fallen asleep at his table. From behind him flies out a flock of bats and owls. One owl lands on his desk, offering the sleeping man a chalk-holder. At his left shoulder perches a black cat, while on the floor there sits a lynx, perhaps with a hint of smouldering anger in its eyes. Written at the side of the table is the title of work—*El sueño de la razón produce monstruos*—"the sleep of reason produces monsters".

Francisco Goya painted his celebrated work—one of a series of prints he called *Los Caprichos* ("fantasies" or "follies")—in 1799. It is a dark, demon-haunted vision to mark the end of the century of light, the meaning of which is ambiguous. "El sueño" can be translated both as "sleep" and as "dream". Is it the sleep of reason or the dream of reason that produces monsters? That was a debate that possessed European societies at the cusp of the nineteenth century, especially in the wake of the French Revolution and the Terror.

Goya's second version of the print contains the caption: "Imagination abandoned by reason produces impossible monsters; united with her, she is the mother of the arts and source of their wonders." This might suggest that both the dream and the sleep of reason—reason alone, or no reason at all—can produce monsters. The ambiguity pointed also to the struggle at the end of the eighteenth century that later generations came to see as that between Romanticism and the Enlightenment.

Romanticism is one of those concepts that cultural historians find invaluable but almost impossible to define. It took various political forms, nurturing strands of both conservatism and of radicalism, and appeared in different national versions. It was not a specific political or cultural view but expressed a cluster of attitudes and preferences: for the unique over the universal, the organic over the mechanical, intuition over intellect, particular communities over abstract humanity. It expressed both a celebration of human agency and anxieties about the world the Enlightenment had unleashed.

Emerging capitalist societies had destroyed many old divisions, but had created new ruptures, not simply between Europeans and non-European peoples, but also fault lines of class, rank and status within European societies themselves. These divisions would have seemed unremarkable in the premodern world in which difference and inequality was stitched into the fabric of society. But they posed a fundamental problem in a new world built around the idea that "all men are created equal". Despite such a bold declaration, the social inequalities of the new world seemed as permanent as those of the old. Over time, they came to be seen as ineradicable, and hence as natural. By the second half of the nineteenth century, the naturalization of social divisions had acquired both the stamp of scientific truth and the status of common sense. It was out of the sense that inequality was natural that the modern concept of race became established, a way of explaining the persistence of social inequalities in a society that had proclaimed its belief in equality.

What concerned many was not simply the seeming permanence of divisions and inequalities. It was also fear of what may be the social consequences of equality—the unstitching of hierarchies, the upending of tradition, the empowering of the lower classes. Such fears gave birth to early forms of the Counter-Enlightenment and, as we saw in the last chapter, helped shape the moderate opposition to the Radical Enlightenment. The French Revolution, and the social turmoil it unleashed in the decades around the turn of the nineteenth century, from the Terror to the Napoleonic Wars, brought these fears to the centre of public debate.[23]

The "real object" of the Revolution, Edmund Burke lamented, was "to break all those connections, natural and civil, that regulate and hold together the community by a chain of subordination; to raise soldiers against their officers; servants against their masters; tradesmen against their customers; artificers against their employers; tenants against their landlords; curates against their bishops; and children against their parents". Democracy was contrary to nature.

"The occupation of an hairdresser or of a working tallow-chandler", sneered Burke, "cannot be a matter of honour to anyone." The lowly "ought not to suffer oppression from the state; but the state suffers oppression if the likes of them, either individually or collectively, are permitted to rule". "The levellers", Burke insisted, drawing comparison between the Jacobins in France and the radicals of the English Civil War, "only change and pervert the natural order of things."[24]

Here we can see the unease felt by figures such as Adam Smith ripened into florid fears. Order and stability, tradition and authority, status and hierarchy—such themes had always been present in the arguments of reactionary opponents of Enlightenment claims for whom the altar and the throne rather than Parliament and the ballot box were the pillars of a healthy society. Now they found an echo within the ranks of Enlightenment moderates, such as Burke, who saw the disorder and radicalism of the French Revolution as exposing the need to constrain the boundaries of equality and democracy.

Burke (1729–97) is regarded as the founder of modern conservatism. For conservatives, defence of inequality and hierarchy, and wariness of liberty and democracy, was inextricably woven into their ideology. Liberals could not forego their attachment to equality so easily. Yet, they too, feared the consequences of pushing the arguments too far. These fears became palpable after 1848, when a series of revolutions swept through Europe, from Paris to Vienna, Berlin to Budapest. The insurrections failed, most being brutally crushed by the old regimes, but all created profound anxieties about social order. Liberals had initially welcomed the barricades but many were shocked by the violence and disorder unleashed. Writing from Paris in 1852, the English liberal Walter Bagehot cheered a *coup d'état* by Louis Napoleon that, in restoring order, dissolved the National Assembly, killed hundreds of opponents, and imprisoned or exiled several thousand. "The first duty of society", Bagehot insisted, "is the preservation of society": "To keep up this system we must sacrifice everything. Parliaments, liberty, leading articles, essays, eloquence—all are good, but they are secondary." He warned against being "misled by any high-flown speculations about liberty or equality" and to recognize the need to protect society from the "dangerous classes". The echoes of Burke's fears after 1789 are unmistakable.[25]

After 1848, pessimism, one historian notes, "began to colonise liberalism". There was increasing talk of "degeneration" as a natural phenomenon, and of the racial separateness of the "dangerous classes". "Doctrines of decay", Hannah Arendt reflected, "seem to have some very intimate connection with race thinking".[26]

Liberals, even more than conservatives, needed to explain the persistence of inequalities and divisions that they had believed would be erased by social progress, a need that drew many towards racial ideas. Race was not a concept consciously forged to explain away social inequalities. Rather, as social divisions acquired the status of permanence, so differences presented themselves as if they were natural, not social. Racial ideology was the inevitable product of the persistence of differences of rank, class and peoples in a society that had accepted the concept of equality.

Two decades after Goya painted *Los Caprichos*, he produced another series, far darker, more tormented and pitiless. Composed in a small palette of sepulchral tones—ochre, brown, grey and black, with occasional flashes of green or blue—the "Black Paintings" were fourteen murals created between 1819 and 1823, and quite unlike Goya's previous work. Most are set at night. Humans are depicted as witches or ghouls, the world as monstrous and heartless. The most famous of the "Black Paintings" depicts Saturn devouring his son, drawn from the Roman myth. Perhaps the most expressive of Goya's feelings, though, is a painting that on the surface appears less dark. "Duel with Cudgels" shows two peasants fighting each other in an otherwise empty landscape. There are patches of blue sky and a shaft of sunlight illuminates the scene. The lower halves of the men's legs have, however, disappeared, as if stuck in a quagmire, or rooted in the ground like a tree. Unable to escape, they can only fight, the two men raining unending blows upon each other. In Goya's work, John Berger observes, "it is not the dark… that holds horror and terror. It is the light that discloses them".[27]

In many ways, Goya's darkness and despair were out of step with the tenor of the nineteenth century. It was an age that worshipped progress and in which, unlike in the eighteenth century, there was tangible evidence of advancement. This was the age of Edison and Benz, of railways and sewage systems, of the telegraph and the photograph, of pasteurization and the anaesthetic. The very process of progress, though, brought in its train a sense of trepidation. When Marx and Engels wrote, in *The Communist Manifesto*, published in 1848, the year of the failed revolutions in Europe, of how "the bourgeois epoch" was distinguished by "constant revolutionising of production, uninterrupted disturbance of all social conditions, everlasting uncertainty and agitation", and described their age as one in which "all that is solid melts into air, all that is holy is profaned", it was both a salutation and a warning.[28]

The speed of change exposed, too, the lack of change in, even decay of, sections of the population. The concept of race captured the two sides of nineteenth-century social consciousness. Implicit in it was the notion of progress, of certain peoples and nations and civilizations as having advanced and as being superior. But race expressed also the sense of the darkness within, of degeneration, of the barbarian and the brute gnawing away at the gains of civilization and eroding the promise of racial superiority.

VII

"Four generations had not sufficed to blend the hostile blood of the Normans and Anglo-Saxons, nor to unite, by common language and mutual interests, two hostile races." So begins Walter Scott's *Ivanhoe*, not just a swashbuckling novel within the Romantic tradition, but also perhaps, when it was published in 1819, the first novel of race. For Scott, the distinction between Norman and Saxon was not social or national but racial, William of Normandy's invasion of England in 1066 being a racial assault on a free people.

A central character in *Ivanhoe* is Robin Hood. The legend of Robin Hood had emerged in England in the Middle Ages as an early form of a class hero ("robbing the rich to feed the poor"). In Scott, he is a racial hero, too, a champion of the Saxons against Norman oppression. It is a story both of racial identity and of racial reconciliation, of the forging of a new nation, symbolized by Ivanhoe, the Saxon knight, pledging allegiance to Richard, the Norman king.

In the early decades of the nineteenth century, there emerged new interest in folk cultures and in peoples' histories. Today, we think of the Grimm brothers as creators of the folk tales we read to children. They were also philologists and historians who established a methodology for collecting and recording such tales. Influenced by Herder, the Grimms saw in folklore a pure form of national literature and culture. Their work inspired similar projects elsewhere, particularly in Britain.

As significant as the turn towards folk culture was the rethinking of history as the story of the people, not of elites; a rethinking, too, of history as a dynamic, creative force, rather than as the passive unfolding of progress. There emerged also new attempts to reinterpret such histories in racial terms. Epoch-defining was Prussian historian and diplomat Barthold Georg Niebuhr's *The History of Rome*, given first as a series of lectures in 1812–13, and later published as a book at the end of the1820s. In Niebuhr's hands, Roman history became a racial struggle between patrician and plebeian, each a distinct race. It was a retelling of the past, and also of the present. For Niebuhr, the Roman Empire had helped spread Christianity and provided the basis of law and civilization for Western Europe. Yet, it was only in the struggle against imperial rule that German tribes had been able to preserve the "noble peculiarities of our national genius", and to safeguard them not simply against Roman power but also against "secondhand, artificial spiritless Frenchified forms" which had "made us lukewarm and unnatural". The echo of Herder is palpable. For Niebuhr, and for those who followed, a people's identity was defined by its race, which had to be preserved unadulterated.[29]

This idea of the noble free tribes of the ancient German forests, from whom had descended modern Germans, Anglo-Saxons and Scandinavians, and who had led the resistance to "Frenchified forms", was popular—at least, outside of France. The English historian John Mitchell Kemble helped rewrite the story of England as a racial war between Saxons and Normans. He renewed interest in Anglo-Saxon culture, translating many Norse and Anglo-Saxon works of literature, including *Beowulf*. Following Kemble, many historians pursued the idea of the racial uniqueness of English history.

French historians, too, developed racial theories of history, but their conception of what each race represented was, unsurprisingly, the opposite to that of German and British writers. "We imagine that we are one nation", wrote Augustin Thierry, "but we are two nations on the same land, two nations hostile in their memories and irreconcilable in their projects", one of which "had conquered the other". Thierry (1795–1856) was a liberal and a fierce supporter of the French Revolution. A fan of Scott's, Thierry's *History of the Conquest of England by the Normans*, published in 1825, presented the Anglo-Saxons as heroic resisters of Norman tyranny. But Normans were not, in Thierry's eyes, French. The "two nations" that constituted France were Gauls, the original inhabitants, and Franks, a Germanic people who conquered much of Western Europe after the decline of the Roman Empire. The eastern Franks became German-speaking peoples, while those in the west gave their name to France. Normans had descended from the Frankish invaders. Thierry saw the French Revolution both as the revolt of the people against the aristocracy and also of indigenous Gauls against their Frankish conquerors.[30]

If, for Thierry, the French Revolution was a conquered people throwing off the yoke of racial oppressors, for Joseph Arthur de Gobineau (1816–82), it demonstrated the degeneration of the French race. A minor French aristocrat, Gobineau's starting point was the need to combat democracy and the "unnatural" idea of equality. Every society begins "by making inequality its chief political motto", the "origin of all systems of caste, of nobility and of aristocracy". Only as a race degenerates and "the majority of the citizens have mixed blood flowing in their veins" do they "feel it to be their duty to assert that all men are equal". Race was a phenomenon that "overshadows all other problems of history" and "holds the key to them all".[31]

There were, for Gobineau, three basic races, white, yellow and black, each with its own characteristics. "All civilizations derive from the white race", which combines a supreme intellect with "an extraordinary instinct for order". The yellows have a "longing for material pleasures" and can "appreciate and take over what is useful to him". Black peoples' "mental faculties are dull or even non-existent" but they possess "an intensity of desire". These differences existed not just across the globe, but within France itself. France was composed of three separate races that corresponded to the nation's class structure. Indeed, as George Mosse has observed, Gobineau's descriptions of the original races betrayed his class prejudices as much as his racism, with the whites possessing "virtues of the nobility", the materialistic yellows a perfect fit for the bourgeoisie, while the negroid lower orders are "a mob on the loose... eternal *sans culottes*".[32]

There is a numbing crudity to Gobineau's arguments and descriptions. Nevertheless, the main elements of his theory—history as a racial struggle; civilization as the preserve of whites; social classes as racially distinct—became staples of racial thinking in the second half of the nineteenth century. Race was a concept whose very lack of definition was its virtue. It could be applied to peoples, nations and language groups. It elucidated global trends and class relations. It revealed the superiority of the German peoples and of the French people. It demonstrated why the French Revolution was a necessity and why it was a catastrophe. Race, like God, was always on your side.

VIII

Through the late eighteenth and early nineteenth centuries, two distinct storylines emerged about human differences. One looked to classify biological races, as in Blumenbach's influential work. The other stressed the particularities of culture, language and tradition that imbued every people with a unique inner spirit or *Volksgeist*. In the middle decades of the nineteenth century, these two strands fused. Both midwife to, and child of, this fusion was racial science. It was also midwife and child to a new understanding of what it was to be human.

The discipline of biology, the very word, was a nineteenth-century creation. It emerged out of a number of disparate, often conflicting, developments. At the turn of the century, the Frenchman Georges Cuvier, whom some called the "new Aristotle", helped establish palaeontology and comparative anatomy as scientific disciplines. He refined the Linnaean system, incorporating fossils into the classification and, while remaining hostile to notions of evolutionary change, confirmed extinction as a fact. Meanwhile, in Germany, there developed *Romantische Naturphilosophie*, a form of biology influenced by Romanticism and idealist philosophy. Romantic biologists stressed the unity of nature, seeing every living form as a concrete manifestation of an ideal archetype or *Bauplan*.

They also saw the physical form as the outer manifestation of the inner spiritual being. It was a science infused with mysticism and wild speculation. Yet, intermixed with the metaphysics was often solid scholarship, and *Naturphilosophen* helped advance many areas of biology, including embryology, neurology and palaeontology. And then, in 1859, came the most significant development in biology—the publication of Charles Darwin's *On the Origin of Species*, in which he laid out his theory of evolution by natural selection, one of the great scientific breakthroughs of the past two hundred years.

These developments transformed the ways in which scientists looked at the relationship between humanity, society and nature, and helped create a new "science of Man". That transformation was leavened by changing political and philosophical sensibilities, too. Particularly important was the emergence of what the French thinker Auguste Comte called "positivism" (a philosophy related to, but not the same as, what came to be called "positivism" in the twentieth century).

Born almost a decade after the French Revolution, Comte spent much of his life addressing the dilemma that liberals faced in the tumultuous age that followed: How could society reconcile its belief in social progress with its desire for social stability? His answer was to look to science to legitimize social order. Comte was contemptuous of both the "metaphysicians" of the Enlightenment and conservatives who reacted against them, the former for believing that order and progress were opposing principles, the latter for wishing to return to a pre-Enlightenment order. "True liberty", he wrote, "is nothing else than a rational submission to the preponderance of the laws of nature".[33]

Comtian positivism helped generate a new "science of Man" that incorporated three themes central to the scientific racism of the second half of the century. The first was the belief in the continuity of the human and the non-human animal world. Traditionally, there had existed within European thought, shaped as it was by Christianity, a great chasm between humans and other animals. Humans were created in God's image, and uniquely possessed souls and free will. The Great Chain of Being linked all living forms while also emphasising the distinction between humans and beasts. Enlightenment naturalists challenged that view, recognizing humans as part of the natural world. Nevertheless, most also viewed them as fundamentally distinct, given their status as the only truly social and cultural beings.

Through the nineteenth century, that distinction became blurred, almost erased. Scientists began to see the origins of all human faculties in animal life, while also recognizing behaviours, such as instincts, which had been previously consigned to the animal world, as human properties, too. It was a trend accelerated by the publication of *The Origin of Species*, and in particular by Darwin's subsequent works, *The Descent of Man* and *The Expression of the Emotions in Man and Animals*. Against the background of a greater willingness to see human differences in racial terms, the erasure of the gap between humans and other animals gave scientific legitimacy to the view of Africans as being closer to animals than Europeans.

The image of a gradation of peoples, some closer to non-human animals, others further away, was strengthened by the second major theme of the new science of Man: a teleological view of history. Human development was seen as purposive, leading ever-forward to the triumph of civilization, defined as contemporary European society. Such social evolutionism had its roots in the Enlightenment. Many eighteenth-century thinkers looked upon history as the story of progress from savagery to civilization in a series of fixed stages, through which every people had to pass, their ascent following an unalterable blueprint.

For some, this conception of history suggested that no people was irrevocably backward, that all could subscribe to civilization. The idea of a history unfolding to an end that looked like contemporary European society also implied, however, that Europe was the measure of civilization by which the rest of the world should be judged—the view that philosophers such as Diderot and Herder had challenged. In the nineteenth century, this challenge drained away, and the progress of history was turned into the liberal argument for colonialism. European rule was necessary to allow the rest of the world to advance towards civilization. According to James Mill (father of the philosopher John Stuart Mill), societies that could not progress on their own, such as India, could "be shown how to do so" by colonial rulers, and would then "follow the same road which more advanced societies have taken before it".[34]

At the same time, "savage" societies came to be seen as historical throwbacks, windows into a past long vanished in Europe. "The least developed races", the Scottish ethnologist John Ferguson McLennan believed, revealed "the most ancient condition of man", representing "history at the farthest-back point of time to which… we can reach". For James Mill, "as the manners, institutions, and attainments of the Hindus" had "been stationary for many ages", so "by conversing with the Hindus of the present day, we, in some measure, converse with the Chaldeans and Babylonians of the time of Cyrus; with the Persians and Egyptians of the time of Alexander".[35]

As the critical aspects of Enlightenment thought were stripped away, many came to see "backward" societies as backward because the people were racially inferior and lacked the capacity to progress on their own. The naturalist Thomas Huxley—"Darwin's bulldog"—was one of the leading liberals of his age. His 1865 essay "Emancipation: Black and White" made a case against slavery and for women's rights. Yet, in comparing negroes with whites, he insisted that it was not possible to conceive of "our prognathous relative" ever being "able to compete successfully with his bigger-brained and smaller-jawed rival, in a contest which is to be carried on by thoughts and not by bites". For Huxley, "The highest places in the hierarchy of civilization will assuredly not be within the reach of our dusky cousins, though it is by no means necessary that they should be restricted to the lowest". Where Enlightenment radicals a century earlier had seen all peoples as capable of civilization, even staunch liberals were now sceptical.[36]

The third theme in the new science of human nature was the belief that mental abilities were related to physical characteristics, that there existed an intimate relationship between "inner Man" and "outer Man". An early expression of this view came in phrenology which claimed that the mind consisted of a number of distinct "faculties" or mental characters and aptitudes. These included the love of offspring, courage, ambition, the tendency to steal, kindness, mimicry and religion. The various aptitudes were located in twenty-seven "organs" on the surface of the brain, the size of which reflected the amount of the particular faculty they contained. Since the organs pressed upon the skull, the phrenologist could make an accurate analysis of an individual's personality and abilities by examining the shape of his head. Many phrenologists viewed it as a science not just of individuals but of racial groups, too. "The foreheads of negroes", Johann Spurzheim, one of the founders of the discipline, believed, "are very narrow" and "their talents of music and mathematics are also in general very limited", while "the heads of Kalmucks are depressed from above" making them "inclined to steal".[37]

By the 1840s, the popularity of phrenology had waned. Nevertheless, the fundamental principle of a correspondence between physical form and mental capacity became widely accepted. It gave weight to the insistence that *some* physical measure—cranial capacity, facial angle, cephalic index, brain weight—would provide a true indication of innate ability and allow human races to be placed on a scale of being. Phrenology validated also the idea that different peoples and nations—different *Volk*—could be distinguished by their physical attributes. The inner soul of a people—their history, language, culture and tradition—was intimately linked to their outer physical manifestation. The *Volksgeist* expressed both a racial essence and a distinct physical form.

James Cowles Prichard, the most renowned British anthropologist of the early nineteenth century, and a scholar who sustained something of the spirit of Enlightenment humanism in his work, dismissed writers whose "object is to portray national characters as resulting from combined influences, physical, moral, and political". They "abound in generalisations, often in the speculative flights of a discursive fancy". Scientists such as Prichard were, however, like ageing sheriffs in the Wild West of nineteenth-century science, their authority challenged by a new generation of gunslingers, for whom "race is everything" as the Scottish anatomist Robert Knox put it. Today, Knox is probably best known for his role in the Burke and Hare murder-for-dissection scandal. A rising star in the 1820s as an anatomist and lecturer in Edinburgh University, Knox bought bodies for dissection (£8 a cadaver, £10 in the winter—a handsome price at the time) from William Burke and William Hare, who obtained them at first through grave-robbing and later through murdering the city's poor. In 1828, Burke and Hare were caught and convicted of murder. Burke was hanged, and his body dissected, the skeleton and facial cast still displayed in Edinburgh University's anatomical museum. (Hare was spared after turning prosecution witness.)[38]

The scandal hung over Knox all his life. Driven out of Edinburgh and denied a professional post, he moved to London, making a living through hack journalism and public lectures. In Edinburgh, Knox had been a radical, scornful of religion and of the political elite, hostile to colonialism and slavery, sympathetic to the French Revolution. In the years after leaving the city, he renounced much of his radicalism, adopting a dark, fatalistic view of the human condition, and dismissing social reform as conflicting with the "iron-clad laws of human nature". The biography of the man mirrored the history of his age. In both man and age, race became the means through which this transformation from radical hopefulness to reactionary pessimism was felt and expressed. It was as his political mood darkened that Knox developed his arguments about race, summarized in his book, *The Races of Men*, first published in 1850.[39]

Knox's argument is set out in a single sentence in the preface: "Race is everything: literature, science, art, in a word, civilization, depend on it." Knox was a disciple of "transcendental anatomy". Derived from *Naturphilosophie*, it was a form of comparative anatomy that sought to find ideal patterns and structures common to living organisms. Also from *Naturphilosophie*, Knox borrowed the belief that as an embryo develops, it resembles successive adult stages in the evolution of the animal's ancestors—another mystical idea given scientific burnish. Different races were created through the arrest of embryonic development at different stages.[40]

Each race, Knox insisted, had "its own form of civilization, as it has its own language and arts". This was the *Volksgeist* given biological form. Since all history is a history of race war, so the strongest races must inevitably defeat the weakest, and destroy them. "Extinction" and "extermination" are words that crop up frequently in *The Races of Men*. "The aim of the Saxon", Knox wrote, "is the extermination of the dark races of men". "What signify these dark races to us?", he asks. "Who cares particularly for the Negro, or the Hottentot, or the Kaffir? These latter have proved a very troublesome race, and the sooner they are put out of the way the better."[41]

Many liberals found Knox's dark view of humanity repulsive. Yet, they agreed with many of his arguments, even if they expressed themselves in more subtle language. "The civilised races of man", Darwin wrote, "will almost certainly exterminate and replace throughout the world the savage races". Darwin was describing not what he desired, but that which he felt was inevitable, the playing out of a natural process. So, the "future fate" of New Zealand Maoris was akin to that of "the native rat now almost exterminated by the European rat". The line between what was seen as "inevitable" and what was deemed "desirable" was thin, and both rooted in a reoriented "science of Man".[42]

At mid-century, the main learned society in Britain for the scientific study of human differences was the Ethnological Society of London (ESL). Founded in 1843 by the anthropologist and liberal humanist James Prichard, among others, it was an offshoot of the Aborigines' Protection Society, a largely Quaker venture, and infused with an environmentalist view of human differences. In 1860, the anthropologist James Hunt, a disciple of Knox, and a polygenist—he believed that different races were different species—became secretary of the ESL. Chafing at its Quakerish ethos, he broke away three years later to set up the Anthropological Society of London. The new venture was a great success and when the two societies merged again to form the Anthropological Institute in 1871, it was clear that the "race is everything" viewpoint had triumphed. As Frederic Farrar, later to be Archdeacon of Westminster, observed, the idea that human diversity "might easily be accounted for from the effects of climate, custom, food and manner of life" had been "abandoned by the majority of scientific men". Enlightenment radicalism was no more.[43]

In America, too, in the middle decades of the nineteenth century, the equivalent of the Knoxes and the Hunts of anthropology took control. The leading polygenist of his age was the Philadelphia physician Samuel George Morton, of whom the *New York Tribune* wrote in his obituary that "probably no scientific man in America enjoyed a higher reputation among scholars throughout the world". Every race, for Morton, represented a "primordial organic form", a definition that betrayed his debt to Romantic biology and its concept of the archetype. And every race remained fixed and unchanging: "The Arabians are at this time precisely what they were in the days of the patriarchs; the Hindoos have altered in nothing since they were described by the earliest writers; nor have three thousand years made any difference in the skin and hair of the Negro".[44]

Morton's work was part of a wider movement, called the American School, that made a scientific case for polygenism and became increasingly influential from the 1840s. According to the American School, each race was adapted to a particular place and a particular climate. The surgeon and anthropologist Josiah Clark Nott and English-born Egyptologist George Robbins Gliddon set out the argument in their 1854 book *Types of Mankind*. The Earth, they wrote, "is naturally divided into several zoological provinces, each of which is a distinct centre of creation, possessing a fauna and flora" and "every species of animal and plant was originally assigned to its appropriate province". The "human family offers no exception to this general law", every race constituting "a primitive element in the fauna of its peculiar province." In a subsequent work, *Indigenous Races of the Earth*, Nott and Gliddon argued that "although boasting of reason", Man is "the most unreasonable of animals" because he is defying the laws of nature by migrating and "colonizing foreign lands... risking his life in climates that nature never intended him for".[45]

Once again, we can see the ghost of Herder. Unlike Morton, Nott and Gliddon, Herder was an egalitarian but he, too, believed that a people's attributes were defined by, and best expressed in, its place of origin, and opposed both migration and intermixing. For Herder, every people possessed a particular culture, language, history and tradition that defined it as a people, and distinguished it from every other people. For Knox, Morton, Nott and Gliddon, every racial type possessed a specific set of traits that defined it as a race, distinguishing it from every other. Whether cast in cultural or racial terms, it was a vision of fixed identities and rigid differences.

The journey from *Volksgeist* to race captured, nevertheless, a significant shift in perceptions of human beings, from a view of humans as primarily social creatures, governed by social laws, to one that saw them as primarily biological entities governed by natural laws. It was also a shift, as Nancy Stepan notes, "from an eighteenth-century optimism about man, and faith in the adaptability of man's universal 'nature', towards a nineteenth-century biological pessimism".[46]

Eighteenth-century *philosophes* sought to explain diversity. For nineteenth-century thinkers, diversity *was* the explanation. In the eighteenth century, philosophers tried to make sense of why humans appeared in diverse forms despite their underlying unity. In the nineteenth century, difference was taken as a given, and scientists sought to explain its origins and to analyse its consequences. In that change lies the coming of modern racial thinking.

IX

And then came Darwin.

The publication of *On the Origin of Species* in 1859 did more than any other scientific development to undermine the concept of race. It also did more than any other to confirm the existence of a racial hierarchy.

The traditional view of species presented them as designs of God, each adapted to its particular role in the order of creation and each defined by its essence. For Darwin, species were not fixed but continually changing through the selection of traits favourable for survival. Species were constantly adapting to shifting circumstances and new species forever forming out of old. In theory, Darwinism should have fatally undermined the idea of race, given that racial scientists were committed to a science of fixed and unchanging essences, to racial types whose stability allowed them to divide humanity into distinct groups. Initially, many racial scientists were indeed inimical to the idea of evolution. Soon, however, they adapted Darwin's theory for their own purposes and often in highly contradictory fashion.

When, in 1891, as President of the Royal Anthropological Society, John Beddoe gave a series of lectures on race, he finished with two conclusions. First, that "the physical characteristics of well-defined races of men are absolutely permanent"; and second that "Natural selection may alter the type". The two conclusions are clearly contradictory. If natural selection can alter the type, then the physical characteristics of racial types cannot be permanent. The contradiction did not bother Beddoe or any other racial scientist of the time because they developed a "two-stage" theory of human evolution, echoing the ideas of Kant a century earlier. Natural selection operated on early humans to establish racial types. Beyond a certain point, however, the human body was no longer subject to evolutionary forces and racial characteristics became fixed. Racial scientists could both commit themselves to Darwin's theory and view racial types as ancient and permanent.[47]

It was the intellectual and political climate of the late nineteenth century, not the theory of evolution itself, that shaped the application of Darwinism to human societies. The three themes of the new "science of Man"—the continuity of the human and animal worlds, a teleological view of history, and the outer physical form as the manifestation of inner mental capacities—had already helped validate the idea of a hierarchy generated outside of society and governed by natural laws. What racial science took from Darwinism were the two central metaphors associated with the theory—that of progress and struggle. Progress described the ascent of European Man, struggle the means by which he had achieved supremacy. Both ideas were, of course, part of the racial idiom well before Darwin published *The Origin of Species*.

When it came to race, Darwin changed everything—and nothing. Darwinism was not necessary to prove racial differences. The starting assumption of racial science was the reality of race. Racial scientists simply adapted Darwin's theory to suit their preconceived notions. The impact of "social Darwinism"—the application of Darwinian theory to the social and cultural realm—was paradoxically to reassert many of the traditional ways in which concepts such as "the survival of the fittest" had been used prior to Darwin.

In appropriating the concept of evolution by natural selection, racial science married the idea of a fixed hierarchy to that of progress—those at the top of the hierarchy arrived there on merit, because of their natural superiority in the struggle for existence. It resurrected the pre-Enlightenment Chain of Being in a form that made sense in a world that flaunted its attachment to both equality and science.

THE INVENTION OF WHITE IDENTITY

I

"When the first Africans arrived in Virginia in 1619, there were no 'white' people there." So declared Theodore Allen's groundbreaking 1994 study *The Invention of the White Race*. Both the statement and the argument of Allen's book have become celebrated since its publication. They also raise a puzzle. The Africans who arrived in Virginia in 1619, came not as free people but as slaves, having endured the horrors of transatlantic transportation, to be bought and sold by Europeans who had begun to colonize the Americas. In what sense, then, were there no white people in Virginia? In the sense, Allen observes, that the Europeans in Virginia did not identify themselves by their skin colour. They were English, and their children were English. Whiteness as an identity, just like race, had to be constructed, too.[1]

The construction of a white identity was not straightforward. The development of ideas of race paradoxically made the understanding of white identity more fraught. By the end of the nineteenth century the reality of race had been firmly established, but the question of who was white was deeply contested, far more so than a century earlier, when ideas of race were still in an embryonic form. Then, in the space of a few decades at the turn of the twentieth century, "whiteness" as we now understand it became consolidated, constructed as much out of fear as out of self-regard. This chapter tells the tangled story of the invention of white identity.

II

Sometime in August 1619, two ships, the *White Lion* and the *Treasurer* arrived at Port Comfort in Virginia, the former carrying as cargo

"20. and odd Negroes" whom the captain exchanged for "victuals". The "Negroes" probably came from the kingdom of Ndongo, in what is now Angola, and had been captured by Portuguese forces. They were being transported to the Spanish colony of Vera Cruz, in central America, when the slave ship was intercepted by the *White Lion* and the *Treasurer*, two English corsairs, and the slaves still alive confiscated as booty.[2]

The "20. and odd Negroes" were not the first slaves in America. The arrival of the *White Lion* has, however, come to be seen as the symbolic origin of slavery in the USA. In 2011, President Barack Obama inaugurated at Fort Monroe, Virginia, a National Monument, in part to commemorate "The first enslaved Africans in England's colonies in America". Eight years later the *New York Times* launched its "1619 Project", the aim of which was to establish the arrival of the slaves in 1619, not the Declaration of Independence in 1776, as the real starting point of American history. In response, the then President Donald Trump established the "1776 Commission" to insist on the significance of that year as America's true beginning, a commission that President Joe Biden subsequently dissolved.[3]

The complexities of history can never be captured by simplistic origin stories. Both slavery and the Revolution moulded the American nation and its self-image and both have shaped the ways in which we now think about its history. Slavery is important not as revealing the "true" origins of America but as a depraved practice that ineluctably imposed its stamp on the character of the nation and on the creation of both black and white identities.

Slavery was not invented by European colonists. It is an institution that reaches back into antiquity, and has been strongly embedded in most world cultures, including Christendom and the Islamic empire. The slavery introduced into the Americas through the transatlantic trade was, though, fundamentally different from that of the premodern world. First, the industrial scale of plantation slavery required unprecedented numbers of slaves and a degree of brutality that was new. Second, New World slavery was geographically distinct from Europe. In previous ages, slaves had laboured within the societies that regulated their treatment. New World slavers were far less restrained by the moral norms and social customs of the Old World societies whence they had come. And, third, slavery in the Americas was racialized in a way unseen before. Until the development of New World slavery, the distinction between slaves and masters had rarely been one of race. Christian and Islamic slavers both bought and sold African and European slaves.

The fall of Constantinople to Sultan Mehmed II in 1453, the end of the Byzantine Empire, and the march of Ottoman armies all the way to the gates of Vienna, transformed the geopolitics of Europe. It also transformed the character of slavery. The expansion of the Ottoman Empire cut off European slavers from their previous source of Balkan and Circassian slaves; these were now destined for Islamic markets. European traders turned to sub-Saharan Africa (as the Islamic Empire had, too) from which to procure human chattel. Christian Europe's slaves became almost entirely black. Slaves transported to plantations in the Americas were almost entirely African, too. But the early story of plantation labour was also more complicated.

By the end of the seventeenth century, American plantations were worked mainly by African slave labour. In the initial decades, however, the labour force comprised largely European indentured servants. The shift from servants to slaves was the result, David Brion Davis notes, "not of concerted planning, racial destiny or immanent historical design but of innumerable local and pragmatic choices made in four continents". Racial ideas did not lead to the use of African slaves. But as black slaves became the predominant labour force on New World plantations, it helped establish the categories of racial division.[4]

White indentured servants were tethered to masters for a fixed term, usually five or seven years. They may have been convicted prisoners, or prisoners taken in a conflict, such as during Britain's subjugation of Ireland. Many also came voluntarily, the prospect of exchanging a few years' hard labour for the possibilities of a better future more enticing than being poor and workless in England.

These bonded labourers could be bought and sold like livestock. It was a status as close to slavery as it was possible to get without formally enslaving people. Richard Ligon, traveller, writer and one-time Barbadian plantation owner, described what happened when a ship carrying indentured servants arrived on the island. Their journey would have been indescribably better than that of African slaves who had to endure the horrors of the "Middle Passage", chained together in a ship's hold, during which up to one in five—perhaps two million—would die. After arrival, however, the similarities in treatment were stark.

"The Planters go aboard", Ligon wrote; "and having bought such of them as they like, send them with a guid to his Plantation". There they built a shelter to house themselves out of "sticks, withes and Plantine leaves... that may keep the rain off." If there were no materials from which to construct a shelter, "they are to lie on the ground". Their supper was "a few potatoes... and water". The next day, "they are rung out with a Bell at work, at six a clock in the morning with a severe Overseer to command them". Their shift lasted at least twelve hours. If it rained during the day, "and wet them through, they have no shift but must lie so all night. If they put off their clothes the cold of the night will strike into them; and if they are not strong men, this ill lodging will put them into a sickness; if they complain they are beaten by an Overseer", often "till the blood has flowed".[5]

Servant life was similar in Virginia. It was common to be beaten, maimed, even killed with impunity. Elizabeth Abbott and Elias Hinton were servants, both of whom died after severe beatings from their masters, John and Alice Proctor. One witness testified that, after examining her while alive, he counted 500 lashes inflicted on Abbott; another that she had been "sore beaten" and her body "full of sores and holes very dangerously raunckled and putrified". The Proctors faced no punishment. A servant who stole a chicken faced the death penalty. For stealing oatmeal, "a man had a needle thrust through his tongue and was then chained to a tree until he starved".[6]

The fact that servants were white was of little significance to the authorities. What mattered was that they were poor and exploitable. They, too, were, in historian Edmund Morgan's phrase, part of "a system of labor that treated men as things". Half of Virginia's servants would die before their terms of servitude were complete; in Barbados, and other Caribbean islands, the figures were higher—three in four may have perished before they could free themselves.[7]

That "Virginia's labor barons" did not transform their servants into actual slaves was not, Morgan observes, "owing to any moral squeamishness". Rather, turning formally free people into slaves would have been a "tricky business". In any case, there already were enslaved people in Virginia—Africans. So, why did tobacco planters initially continue using indentured servants rather than switching to slaves, as they were eventually to do? Because bonded labour had advantages for planters. Servants were cheaper than slaves and could be worked as hard. If a servant failed to perform consistently or ran away, a court could extend the term of his servitude. Slaves were slaves for life and so could not be compelled to work harder by threats of extended enchainment.

Over time, as European economies revived, and as the authorities felt less of a need to decant sections of their population, fewer bonded servants began arriving. At the same time, more slaves were being imported, and at a cheaper price, from Africa. This transformed the brutal economics of plantation labour.

The substitution of slaves for servants also diminished the possibilities of revolt. Unlike African slaves, English bonded labour, as Barbara Fields observes, came not alone but "in company with the generations who had preceded them in the struggle; and the outcome of those earlier struggles established the terms and conditions of the latest one". Black slaves, however, "did enter the ring alone. Their forebears had struggled in a different arena, which had no bearing on this one. Whatever concessions they might obtain had to be won from scratch, in unequal combat, an ocean away from the people they might have called on for reinforcements."[8]

It was not that slaves did not revolt. They did, and often, and often in concert with servants. By the nineteenth century, slave rebellions, as we shall see in Chapter 6, would force emancipation. In the seventeenth century, it was different. Slaves were less organized and often divided by language and culture. Over time, slaves would build new traditions of resistance, often in union with poor whites. Because planters lacked the sanction of extending servitude, they resorted to forms of punishment even more grotesque than that faced by servants. A 1707 Virginia law authorized courts to punish runaway slaves "either by dismembring, or any other way... as they in their discretion shall think fit, for the reclaiming any such incorrigible slave, and terrifying others from the like practices".[9]

For much of the seventeenth century, blacks and whites, Morgan notes, "saw each other as sharing the same predicament". It was common for slaves and servants "to run away together, steal hogs together, get drunk together. It was not uncommon for them to make love together." Class distinctions, not racial divisions, were the means by which early colonial life was structured. There was no "white identity" across class lines.[10]

With the transformation of plantations into industrial complexes built on chattel slavery, all this changed. New arguments about the inferiority of blacks began to gain purchase in colonial communities. New laws established clearer distinctions between slaves and servants, blacks and whites. Virginia introduced legislation allowing for property belonging to blacks to be seized and sold with the profits used to support poor whites, a "highly effective device", Morgan observes, for sowing discord between servants and slaves. Miscegenation was now deemed a crime.[11]

Transatlantic slavery did not develop for racial reasons. European elites would have developed a slave system utilizing poor whites had it been practically possible. Attitudes to black slaves and white servants were, in the seventeenth century, similar. Over time, though, slavery became racialized. Partly, this was for pragmatic reasons— slaves were cheaper and easier to control. Partly, also, there developed deeper, more ideological motives. It was necessary to justify the acceptance of servitude in a society that proclaimed its fidelity to freedom and liberty. The racialization of slavery became a means of doing so.

III

In 1790, the US Congress ordained that "all free white persons" who had resided in America for at least a year "be entitled to the rights of citizenship". But who was "white"? That was an unresolved question. There is a Jewish meme that portrays Jews as "Schrodinger's Whites": simultaneously white and not-white. Many, perhaps most, whites in the nineteenth century were in a similar position of being white and not-white at the same time.

"What then is the American?", asked the soldier, farmer and diplomat Michel Guillaume Jean Crèvecoeur in his much-quoted *Letters from an American Farmer*. Published in 1782, the book was a eulogy to what later came to be called the American Dream—America as a land of self-determination and equal opportunity. An American,

Crèvecoeur answered, "is either an European, or the descendant of an European, hence that strange mixture of blood, which you will find in no other country". "He is an American", he continued, "who leaving behind him all his ancient prejudices and manners, receives new ones from the new mode of life he has embraced".[12]

Yet, many of those "ancient prejudices and manners" not only survived the transatlantic crossing, but also helped forge the new ones. Only whites could be Americans, but to be white, it was not sufficient to be of European descent. "Why", asked Benjamin Franklin, one of the great figures of the American Enlightenment, "should Pennsylvania, founded by the English, become a Colony of Aliens, who will shortly be so numerous as to Germanize us instead of our Anglifying them?" In his view the number of "purely white People in the World" was tiny: "All *Africa* is black or tawny. *Asia* chiefly tawny... And in *Europe*, the *Spaniards, Italians, French, Russians* and *Swedes*, are generally of what we call a swarthy Complexion; as are the *Germans* also." Only "the *Saxons*" and "the *English*" were truly white. "I could wish their Numbers were increased", Franklin lamented.[13]

A century later, Josiah Nott and George Gliddon, leading figures of the American School, which saw every race as a distinct species, questioned the very idea of a "Caucasian race". "Nothing short of *a miracle* could have evolved all the multifarious Caucasian forms out of one primitive stock", they believed. Instead, "there must have been many centres of creation, even for Caucasian races". According to Nott "the dark-skinned European races, as Spaniards, Portuguese, Italians, Basques, &c., mingle much more perfectly with the negroes than do fair races", thus proving both their difference and their degradation.[14]

Still later, in 1911, the Dillingham Commission, set up by the US Congress to investigate the state of immigration at a time of mass panic about the quality of migrating Europeans, published its 42-volume report. The Commission noted that the Bureau of Immigration "recognizes 45 races or peoples among immigrants coming to the United States, and of these 36 are indigenous to Europe". It noted also Blumenbach's "five great divisions of mankind" but broke down the "Aryan stock" (which it took as synonymous with "Caucasian") into a number of distinct races—Teutonic, Slavonic, Italic, Hellenic,

Lettic, Celtic, Illyric, Armenic and Indo-Iranic. Even to the US Congress Commission on Immigration, at the beginning of the twentieth century, what it was to be "white" was far from clear.[15]

From the early days of the Republic to the twentieth century, one group was without argument deemed white—"Anglo-Saxons". Who else belonged to the category was a matter of social negotiation. Belief in the racial superiority of Anglo-Saxons percolated through political and intellectual life in nineteenth-century America, often revealing a presence in the least expected of minds. Ralph Waldo Emerson is the towering figure of early nineteenth-century American literature, a personification of liberal values. He was also a tireless advocate of Anglo-Saxon whiteness.

Born in Boston in 1803, Emerson was a champion of transcendentalism, the American version of German Romanticism. During a trip to Europe, he met with Thomas Carlyle, the Scottish historian and polemicist, and the most influential promoter of German literature and philosophy in Britain at the time. The two struck up a lifelong friendship that shaped Emerson's views not just on Romanticism but also on race and Anglo-Saxonism.

Carlyle (1795–1881) occupies a strange niche in British intellectual history. "There is hardly a superior or active mind of this generation", George Eliot suggested "that has not been modified by Carlyle's writings". Among his friends, the "sage of Chelsea" could count the great and the good of British society, from Charles Dickens to Harriet Martineau. And, yet, he espoused some extraordinarily reactionary views. He had a fixation with order and duty, an obsession with moral degeneracy, and a morbid fear of anarchy. Both democracy and equality were affronts to the moral imperative to rule and be ruled. Carlyle's influence symbolized the paradox of an age that desired to be scientific and progressive but feared, also, the darkness and decay that lay just beneath.[16]

Germans were, for Carlyle, "the only genuine European people, unmixed with strangers". They had never been "subdued" thanks to "the masculine and indomitable character of the race". In time, Carlyle believed, "they must occupy or hold rule over the greater portion of the earth". The other European races were pale and effeminate in comparison. His greatest disdain was for the Celts, who were, in his eyes, the negroes of Europe. In his deliberately provocative "Occasional Discourse on the Nigger Question", Carlyle argued that freeing West Indian slaves was "to have 'emancipated' the West Indies into a *Black Ireland*—'free', indeed, but an Ireland, and black!" Blacks, the Irish, the working class—all had to learn to obey and serve the greater race—"to be servants to those that are born wiser than you, that are born lords of you". Carlyle was, Emerson acknowledged, deeply reactionary, but "his errors of opinion are as nothing in comparison with [his] merit".[17]

Though a staunch opponent of slavery, Emerson had little doubt about a hierarchy of races with Africans "stand[ing] so low" that "the difference... between themselves & the sagacious beasts [was] inconsiderable". Negroes were "so inferior a race" that they "must perish shortly like the poor Indians". What he most took from Carlyle was the belief in the genius and virility of the Saxon race. By "Germans", Emerson, like Carlyle, meant not just German-speaking peoples, but the descendants of ancient Germanic and Nordic tribes. The English often seemed to be better Germans than Germans themselves. As for Americans, they were in Emerson's words, "only the continuation of the English genius into new conditions". British colonialism was "carrying the Saxon seed, with its instinct for liberty and law, for arts and for thought... to the conquest of the globe". Emerson and Carlyle both imagined a transatlantic realm of "Saxondom", a concept that British politicians and historians enthusiastically pursued later in the nineteenth century.[18]

Through such complex transatlantic traffic, the racial myths and histories of whiteness developed. For Europeans, delineating the many races of the continent was an aid to nation-building and a means of making sense of social divisions within and between nations. For Americans, it helped nurture a myth of ancestry that would act as a foundation for their revolutionary story and justify the claim that America was built on freedom despite the millions enslaved and the majority denied suffrage. It also became a means of evaluating immigration and of policing relations between migrant groups.

The first group that posed the question for the American elite of "Who is white, and to what degree?" were the Irish. In the early decades of the nineteenth century, Irish immigrants were frequently referred to as "niggers turned inside out" and blacks as "smoked Irish". A joke of the time has a black man saying "My master is a great tyrant. He treats me as badly as if I was a common Irishman."[19]

The Irish were seen not just as socially and culturally but also as physically distinct, "low-browed", "brutish", even "simian". "To see white chimpanzees is dreadful", the English historian and clergyman Charles Kingsley observed of Ireland. Many American scientists agreed. In parts of Ireland, Samuel Morton claimed, "their physical traits, their moral character and their peculiar customs, have undergone little change since the time of Caesar", and "recall the memory of a barbarous age".[20]

The British anthropologist John Beddoe created an "Index of Nigrescence" which supposedly quantified the degree of blackness in a population. He even published a mathematical formula for deriving the index: $D + 2N - R - F$, in which D, N, R and F stood for the proportions of, respectively, dark-haired, black-haired, red-haired and fair-haired people in any locality. A high figure revealed a more backward race. Beddoe created a racial map which showed that the Irish, the Welsh and the highland Scots were more "Africanoid" than the English. There were, he thought, traces of the "Mongoloid" among the Welsh, while the Irish were close to Cro-Magnons, a prehistoric ancestor of modern Europeans.[21]

Over time, the panic about Irish immigration subsided in America, and they moved from being Cro-Magnon to being white, a process that historians such as Noel Ignatiev and David Roediger have mapped. The Irish began acquiring their whiteness in part because of their political influence as a group, and in part, also, through their role in the enforcement of workplace colour bars against blacks. The great abolitionist and African-American leader Frederick Douglass who, in the 1830s, had welcomed the solidarity Irishmen had shown blacks on Baltimore's wharves, was three decades later "at a loss to understand why a people who so nobly loved and cherished the thought of liberty at home in Ireland could become, willingly, the oppressors of another race here". But even as the Irish became drawn into whiteness, the whiteness of new groups of European migrants—mainly from southern and eastern Europe—now became questioned.[22]

IV

"They have seen the passing of the American Indian and the buffalo", reflected William Ripley in 1908, "and now they query as to how long the Anglo-Saxon may be able to survive." Ripley was one of America's most renowned academics, professor of political economy at Columbia University and of economics at MIT, and author of a landmark book, *The Races of Europe*. His chief preoccupation had become the fear that the Anglo-Saxon was destined to vanish like the buffalo and the Native American. "Whereas, until about twenty years ago, our immigrants were drawn from the Anglo-Saxon or Teutonic populations of northwestern Europe", he wrote, "they have swarmed over here in rapidly growing proportions since that time from Mediterranean, Slavic, and Oriental sources". He was particularly worried about Anglo-Saxons showing a "low and declining birth-rate" while "the immigrant European horde... has continued to reproduce upon our soil with well-sustained energy". He warned darkly that this "abnormal intermixture" of peoples might create "a physical type" that was a throwback to "an ancestral variety".[23]

Fear of racial degeneration became a central theme in academic and popular discourse on both sides of the Atlantic in the second half of the nineteenth century. In France, defeat by the Prussians in 1870, and the challenge of the revolutionary Paris Commune that seized power in the capital the following year, brought the issue of national dissipation to the fore. In Britain, initial defeats in the Boer Wars of the early 1880s and late 1890s led to similar foreboding. What many saw as the physical and mental deterioration of army recruits led to the belief that the British stock had declined.

In Europe, it was the wantonness of the lower classes that had introduced degeneracy into society. In America, the instruments of social corruption were what Edward Ross called "Caliban type" immigrants from southern and eastern Europe, who "belong in skins in wattled huts at the close of the Great Ice Age". There were among the new immigrants "so many sugar-loaf heads, moon-faces, slit mouths, lantern-jaws, and goose-bill noses that one might imagine a malicious jinn had amused himself by casting human beings in a set of skew-molds discarded by the Creator". This was no froth-at-the-mouth article in some scandal sheet, nor a marginal reactionary voice. Ross (1866–1951) was a leading sociologist, a professor at both Cornell and Stanford, his 1914 book *The Old World in the New* acclaimed as a serious work of social science. Ross would later be a supporter of Franklin D. Roosevelt and the New Deal, and even, most extraordinarily, a member of the Dewey Commission set up to defend Leon Trotsky from Stalin's charges. He was also, for a decade in the 1940s, chairman of the national committee of the American Civil Liberties Union. The argument and the language was not just mainstream but mainstream progressive.[24]

Ross coined the term "race suicide" to describe the differential birth rates of Anglo-Saxons and the newer migrants from southern and eastern Europe. The phrase was adopted and popularized by Theodore Roosevelt, who became US president in 1901 and, a decade later, founded the Progressive Party. Roosevelt was considered a "moderate" in his racial views. Moderate is, however, a relative term, and in the context of late nineteenth-century racial thinking, it could embrace some extreme beliefs. Roosevelt believed that the elimination by whites of inferior races was a moral good for "the benefit of civilization". It was a "warped, perverse and silly morality" to believe that the "waste spaces" of the earth "should be reserved for the use of scattered savage tribes, whose life was but a few degrees less meaningless, squalid, and ferocious than that of the wild beasts with whom they held joint ownership". Nor should one "apply to savages the rules of international morality which obtain between stable and cultured communities".[25]

Like most of the American elite, Roosevelt saw the Anglo-Saxon and Teuton as the greatest of all races, virile and manly like a mighty race should be, and quite unlike the French, who were "volatile" and "debauched". He boasted that "the English had exterminated or assimilated the Celts of Britain, and they substantially repeated the process with the Indians of America", adding that "of course in America there was very little, instead of very much, assimilation". In contrast, Spaniards, to their detriment, rather than "killing or driving off the natives as the English did... simply sat down in the midst of a much more numerous aboriginal population". Yet, for all their virility, Anglo-Saxons were not breeding fast enough. "Competition between the races", Roosevelt believed, reduced itself "to the warfare of the cradle". For a race to flourish it had to consist "of good breeders as well as of good fighters". Hence, "the man or woman who deliberately avoids marriage and has... a brain so shallow and selfish as to dislike having children is in effect a criminal against the race". Wilful childlessness was a "sin for which the penalty is... race death; a sin for which there is no atonement." It was, paradoxically, out of such fears that, as we shall see later, the modern idea of "whiteness" eventually became consolidated.[26]

V

It was 1840 and Francis Galton was a student at Cambridge University. He had been thinking about animal breeding. And from the breeding of cattle and horses, his mind wandered into the breeding of humans. "Could not the race of men be similarly improved?", he wondered. "Could not the undesirables be got rid of and the desirables multiplied?" And so were struck the first sparks of the "science" of eugenics, though it took another forty-three years before Galton coined the term from the Greek for "good" and "born".[27]

Galton was a polymath, whose work engaged with sociology and statistics, meteorology and psychology, geography and anthropology. He is, however, best known for his promotion of eugenics, "the science that deals with all influences that improve the inborn qualities of a race", as he put it, a programme for racial improvement through selective breeding. It was a science nurtured by, and that helped nurture, the growing fears of racial degeneration and race suicide. "Man has the choice of two methods of race improvement", the American lawyer and eugenicist Madison Grant wrote in his 1916 book *The Passing of the Great Race*, one of the most influential works of American scientific racism. "He can breed from the best, or he can eliminate the waste." The fear that the desirables were not sufficiently multiplying led to a determined attempt to rid society of the undesirables.[28]

The idea of certain human beings as "waste" had become a commonplace by the end of the nineteenth century. "The same words— 'residuum', 'refuse', 'offal'", Gertrude Himmelfarb observes, "were used to denote the sewage that constituted the sanitary problem and the human waste that constituted the social problem". The elimination of human waste was seen by many as progressive an act as the creation of a sewage system, a means of replacing *laissez faire* policies with social planning. "The superficially sympathetic man flings a coin to the beggar", the British social reformer Havelock

Ellis wrote in 1916; "the more deeply sympathetic man builds an almshouse for him so that he need no longer beg; but perhaps the most radically sympathetic of all is the man who arranges that the beggar shall not be born."[29]

It was in America that the desire to eliminate human waste was first turned into social policy. Charles Davenport, the wealthy scion of a New England family that could trace its roots back to the *Mayflower*, and a pioneer of biometrics, had met the elderly Galton during a visit to London in 1901, becoming a great admirer. In 1904, he was appointed director of the prestigious Station for Experimental Evolution in Cold Spring Harbor on Long Island, a project lavishly funded by the Carnegie Institution with a grant larger than the total endowment at the time for research in all American universities. The Station became the principal centre for the study of eugenics. Davenport also set up the Eugenics Record Office (ERO), again extravagantly funded, this time by Mary Williamson Harriman, whose money came from the railroad empire of her late husband. Davenport pioneered the collection of data on family histories as a means of demonstrating the inheritance of physical abnormalities and mental deficiencies. Conditions from alcoholism to pauperism to feeblemindedness were, he believed, the product of "bad blood". "The most progressive revolution in history", he wrote, could be achieved if "human matings could be placed upon the same high plane as that of horse breeding".[30]

There were two kinds of waste populations that eugenicists like Davenport wanted to eliminate. First, there were the "degenerates", the "idiots" and "imbeciles"—all standard medical categories—as well as the drifters and hardscrabble farmers, none of whom, in Davenport's eyes, could be regarded as meaningfully "white". Some scientists even saw "the idiot" as the missing link between humans and apes. It is "enough to compare the skulls of the chimpanzee, the Negro and the idiot", the zoologist Carl Vogt wrote, "to see that the skull of the idiot occupies in every respect an intermediate place between the two others". And then there were the waste immigrants, not just the clearly non-white races, but also European races, Ross's "Caliban types", that, too, were not truly white.[31]

From the beginnings of colonization, Nancy Isenberg notes in *White Trash*, her history of the lower orders in America, poor whites "were classified as a distinct breed". The language used to describe them—clay-eaters, crackers, waste people, trash, lubbers—"played off English attitudes toward vagrancy, and marked a transatlantic fixation with animal husbandry, demography and pedigree", the poor being "inferior animal stocks". It is one of the ironies of the American story that the depth of racism has allowed for the myth of a classless society to take root, the belief that in the New World, unlike in the Old, class plays little role in shaping society. Class and race are even more inextricably linked in the New World than in the Old, and out of that relationship, notions of whiteness have been forged and reforged.[32]

In 1877, Richard Dugdale, a New York prison reformer, published his study of *The Jukes*, "A Study in Crime, Pauperism, Disease and Heredity", as it proclaimed in its subtitle. Drawing on the work of European criminologists Cesare Lombroso and Martino Beltrani-Scalia, who saw criminality as an inherited trait, Dugdale traced the ancestry of a large group of criminals, prostitutes and misfits back through seven generations to a single set of forebears. Over seventy-five years, Dugdale calculated, the Jukes had cost the state $1,308,000.[33]

Dugdale's study was a sensation and spawned a new industry of family histories. The most influential of these was psychologist Henry Goddard's *The Kallikak Family*, published in 1912. "Kallikak" was a pseudonym constructed from the Greek words *kalós* (good) and *kakós* (bad). Goddard told the story of two families, or rather two branches of the same family, both descended from the same man, Martin Kallikak, but from two different women. One was his wife, "a respectable girl of good family". From this *kalós* line came progeny that "married into the best families in the state, the descendants of colonial governors, signers of the Declaration of Independence, soldiers and even founders of a great university". The *kakós* branch was the product of Kallikak's casual sex with a "feebleminded tavern wench". Of the 480 individuals in this line, "only forty-six have been found normal". Of a present-day member of the *kakós* branch, Goddard writes that she showed "no reasoning from cause to effect, no learning of any lesson... Her philosophy of life is the philosophy of an animal".[34]

The difference between the two lines was entirely the product of heredity—and of the women involved. The "degeneracy" of the *kakós* branch came from "bad blood having been brought into the normal family of good blood... from the nameless feebleminded girl". No amount of social improvement could change such people. "If all the slum districts of our cities were removed tomorrow", Goddard believed, "and model tenements built in their places, we would still have slums in a week's time" because "these mentally defective people... can never be taught to live otherwise than as they have been living." With the *kalós* line, too, "it was not the environment that made that good family" but "their own good blood".[35]

Influenced by such studies, Indiana became in 1907 the first state to introduce compulsory sterilization of the feebleminded, followed soon by fourteen other states. These early eugenic laws were often struck down by the courts. But, over time, the work of Davenport, Goddard, Ross and others helped change both the public and the judicial mood. In 1922, the ERO published a "model eugenical sterilization law" which sought "to prevent the procreation of persons socially inadequate from defective inheritance". These included the "feebleminded", the "criminalistic", the "blind" and the "deformed" as well as "orphans, ne'er-do-wells, the homeless, tramps, and paupers". In 1924, Virginia passed the first such law. Carrie Buck, who, with her mother Emma, had been committed to the Virginia Colony for Epileptics and Feebleminded in Lynchburg, was ordered to be sterilized. The case was challenged in court and went all the way to the Supreme Court. "Three generations of imbeciles are enough", concluded Justice Oliver Wendell Holmes, summing up the Court's support for forced sterilization. Over the next forty years, 65,000 people were forcibly sterilized in the war to eliminate human waste and to cleanse the white race of its degenerates.[36]

VI

And then there were the immigrants.

Like most American intellectuals of his age, Davenport's worldview was rooted in myths of Anglo-Saxonism. "The early immigrants to America" from England, he wrote, were "men of courage, independence, and love of liberty". Not so, later immigrants. The Irish brought with them "alcoholism... mental defectiveness and a tendency to tuberculosis". "Hebrew immigrants" were prone to "thieving and receiving stolen goods" and drawn to "offenses against chastity". Southern Italians possessed little "self-reliance, initiative, resourcefulness nor self-sufficing individualism" and tended "to crimes of personal violence". The new blood, Davenport warned, would make the American population "darker in pigmentation, smaller in stature... more given to crimes of larceny, kidnapping, assault, murder, rape and sex-immorality". To keep out "bad blood", Davenport suggested creating an army of field workers to "send to the other side of the ocean" to "visit the relatives of the person in question and learning his personal and family history".[37]

Before he could persuade the US government to set up such an army, a new technique emerged to help distinguish good blood from bad—intelligence tests. First developed in France by the psychologists Alfred Binet and Theodore Simon as a way of detecting "mentally deficient" children, Goddard began to use them as a means of sorting the population into groups of different innate capacity not just in intelligence, but also in all those other traits, the degeneration of which was causing such angst—morality, chastity, willpower. In 1913, Goddard was invited by the Commissioner of Immigration to test immigrants at Ellis Island. His conclusions were alarming. "The intelligence of the average 'third class' immigrant is low", his study suggested, "perhaps of moron grade". In Goddard's view, 87 per cent of Russians, 83 per cent of Jews and 79 per cent of Italians were "feeble-minded".[38]

Four years later, Harvard psychologist Robert Yerkes organized the testing of recruits to the US Army about to enter the First World War. It was a mammoth operation, involving some 1,750,000 men and generating a huge body of data. According to Yerkes, "the mental age of the American-born soldier is between thirteen and fourteen years" while "that of the soldier of foreign birth is less than twelve years".[39]

The Princeton psychologist Carl Brigham turned the data into a popular book, *A Study of American Intelligence*. In common with many racial scientists, Brigham divided Europe into three major races— the Nordic, the Alpine and the Mediterranean. The original European immigrants to America comprised "an almost pure Nordic type". The "next great movement" was of "Western European Mediterraneans and Alpines from Ireland and Germany". It is another of the oddities of racial thinking that Celts were often regarded as being of Alpine or Mediterranean origin. The third movement of European migrants, still ongoing, was of "the Alpine Slav and Southern European Mediterraneans". Membership of one or other European race was not determined by one's country of origin. Rather, the various nationalities of Europe, Brigham claimed, were made up of different proportions of Nordic, Alpine and Mediterranean blood. The English comprised 80 per cent Nordic and 20 per cent Mediterranean; the Irish 30 per cent Nordic and 70 per cent Mediterranean; Italians 5 per cent Nordic, 25 per cent Alpine and 70 per cent Mediterranean. And so on. All were invented figures but were given the stamp of scientific authority.

According to Brigham, the higher the proportion of Nordic blood, the more intelligent the nation. His calculations revealed that two-thirds of the "colored draft" were in the three lowest categories of intelligence, as were 63.8 per cent of Poles and 60.5 per cent of Italians, but only 8.8 per cent of English migrants, and 16.2 per cent of Germans. However absurd all this may seem now, it was, at the beginning of the twentieth century, taken seriously by many in America who would not see themselves as "idiots".[40]

The immigration panic led to a series of legal restrictions, culminating in the Johnson-Reed Immigration Act of 1924, which banned all immigration from Asia and set quotas for European migrants, based on the proportion of the American population already from a particular country. It was an attempt to freeze American demography. Before 1924, two-thirds of immigrants to America had come from southern or eastern Europe. After the Act, that fell to ten per cent. In the forty years during which the quotas existed, immigrants from Britain, Germany and Ireland made up nearly three-quarters of the total. As the eugenicist Harry Laughlin put it, "Henceforth... the hereditary stuff out of which future immigrants were made would have to be compatible racially with American ideals", making "American ideals" the "hereditary stuff" of race.[41]

VII

In August 1866, a banquet was held in the English port of Southampton in honour of Edward John Eyre, the governor of

Jamaica. That year, Eyre had put down an uprising on the island, the Morant Bay Rebellion, with the utmost ferocity. Several hundred (some claim several thousand) black Jamaicans were killed, and more than 350 summarily executed during a four-week rampage by British troops.[42]

Eyre's actions divided opinion in Britain. Liberals and radicals set up the Jamaica Committee to prosecute the Governor, its patrons including John Stuart Mill, Charles Darwin and Thomas Huxley. Eyre's supporters established a Defence and Aid Committee, backed by Charles Dickens, Alfred Lord Tennyson and John Ruskin, among others, which had organized the Southampton banquet. In response to the banquet, the Jamaica Committee held a counter-rally. Hundreds also thronged to a protest outside the banqueting hall. Reporting on the protest, the *Daily Telegraph* commented that "There are a good many negroes in Southampton, who have the taste of their tribe for any disturbance that appears safe". In fact, as historian Douglas Lorimer observes, "the *Daily Telegraph's* 'negroes' were... the very English and very white Southampton mob".[43]

The description of protestors as "negroes" was no slip of the pen. For the Victorian elites, the working class was as racially distinct from the middle class as blacks were from whites, while also possessing many of the same traits as blacks. The kind of view Americans imposed on European migrants, European elites imposed on their working class and poor. Much of the justification of Eyre's actions was grounded in the view that Jamaican blacks were little different from English workers. Edwin Paxton Hood, speaking for West Indian planters, claimed that the Negro "is in Jamaica as the costermonger is in Whitechapel; he is very likely often nearly a savage with the mind of a child". The construction of a white identity was even less straightforward in Britain than it was in America.[44]

In 1864, the London newspaper, *Saturday Review*, published an article on "Slaves and Labourers". "The Bethnal Green poor", it suggested, were "a race of whom we know nothing, whose lives are of quite different complexion from ours, persons with whom we have no point of contact". Slaves, the article acknowledged, "are separated from the whites by more glaring... marks of distinction". Nevertheless, "distinctions and separations, like those of English classes which always endure, which last from the cradle to the grave, which prevent anything like association or companion-ship... offer a very fair parallel to the separation of the slaves from the whites". This separation of classes was important because each had to keep to their allotted place on the social ladder: "The English poor man or child is expected always to remember the condition in which God has placed him, exactly as the negro is expected to remember the skin which God has given him. The relation in both instances is that of perpetual superior to perpetual inferior, of chief to dependant, and no amount of kindness or goodness is suffered to alter this relation."[45]

While the working class was seen as racially inferior, black people were often accorded greater respect than commonly imagined. Because race in the nineteenth century was an expression of social distinctions, rather than simply of colour differences, non-whites regarded as possessing a high social status were treated with more deference than lower class whites. In 1881, King Kalakaua of Hawaii visited England and was a guest at a party given by Lady Spencer. Also at the party were the Prince of Wales and his brother-in-law, the German Crown Prince, the future Kaiser. The Prince of Wales insisted that, in the seating arrangements, King Kalakaua should take precedence over the Crown Prince. "Either the brute is a king", he told his brother-in-law, dismissing his objections, "or he's a common or garden nigger, and if the latter what's he doing here?"[46]

This might seem to us insufferably racist. But it demonstrates, too, the degree to which, for Victorians, social status was as important, if not more so, than skin colour. When Arthur Hamilton Gordon was made governor of Fiji in 1874, he insisted that Fijian chiefs were his equals, possessed as they were of "undoubted aristocracy". "Nurse can't understand it all", Lady Gordon observed with amused condescension in her diary. "She looks down on them as an inferior race. I don't like to tell her that these ladies are my equal, which she is not!" David Cannadine, who recounts the story in his book *Ornamentalism*, observes that for the British elite, the Empire "seemed to be full of the dross and detritus of the British metropolis", the "poor rejects from the slums and backstreets of Birmingham and Glasgow", in contrast to whom "the native princes [and] ruling chiefs" seemed "better people, at the apex of a better world".[47]

Douglas Lorimer has shown the degree to which, until the middle of the nineteenth century, social status defined the manner in which black people were treated in Britain. A former white resident of the West Indies, on returning to London, was shocked to see a "black gentleman… enter a room on equal terms to myself". When he was introduced to her as a partner for a dance, she shuddered that "If the footman had presented himself for that purpose I could not have been more startled". African Americans were equally startled by their reception in Europe. Samuel Ringgold Ward, in his *Autobiography of a Fugitive Negro*, observed that "Englishmen do not expect servants to ride in first-class carriages; but a person of wealth or position, of whatever colour, has, in this respect, just what he pays for". When Frederick Douglass travelled to Britain in 1847, the shipping company Cunard refused to give him, as a black man, a first-class berth. When the same happened on his return from Liverpool to Boston, Douglass wrote a letter of protest to the *Times*. The newspaper was outraged that "A highly respectable gentleman of colour" should be so treated. Samuel Cunard himself was forced to issue a public apology.[48]

In the second half of the nineteenth century, however, as racial arguments became more entrenched, commentators became more sceptical about Negroes aspiring to high social status. As a result, Lorimer observes, "the conventional norms about the correct bearings towards one's social inferiors, whether black or white, were extended to include all blacks regardless of an individual's character or background. A white skin became on essential mark of a gentlemen."[49]

This did not mean, though, that the working class was now seen as "white". Rather, the lowly status of workers reinforced the sense both of their racial inferiority and of their possessing the same standing as colonial peoples around the world. As black people became consigned to the lower classes, the working class at home became viewed through a colonial lens. "As there is a darkest Africa is there not also a darkest England?", asked William Booth, the founder of the Salvation Army, in his 1890 book *In Darkest England*. Describing Henry Morton Stanley's travels in equatorial Africa, which that year had created headlines, Booth continued, "May we not find a parallel at our own doors, and discover within a stone's throw of our cathedrals and palaces similar horrors to which Stanley has found existing in the great Equatorial forest?" The answer was yes: "The Equatorial Forest traversed by Stanley resembles that Darkest England of which I have to speak... [in] its monotonous darkness, its malaria and its gloom, its dwarfish de-humanized inhabitants, the slavery to which they are subjected, their privations and their misery."[50]

Such analogies were common in the last decades of the nineteenth century. They exposed, as Gertrude Himmelfarb observes, middle-class terror that there existed, "in the most advanced city of the most advanced country in the world... the equivalent of Bushmen and Fingoes, tribes which resisted amelioration and acculturation", who "perversely persisted in a way of life and work that was an affront to civilized society". It was, Himmelfarb observes, "as if some primitive spirit, some vestige of primeval nature, were mocking the proud presumptions of modernity".[51]

It was not just in Britain that such fears emerged. Philippe Buchez was a physician and sociologist, and briefly president of the French National Assembly. He was a Christian socialist who strove "to recover a Christian tradition which would be in essential harmony with the revolutionary principles of 1789". He was, though, deeply troubled by the contemporary state of the nation, and especially of the lower orders.[52]

The people of France had been "placed in the most favourable circumstances", Buchez observed in a lecture in 1857; they were "possessed of a powerful civilization" and lived in a nation that was "among the highest ranking... in science, the arts and industry". How was it possible, then, "that within a population such as ours, races may form—not merely one, but several races—so miserable, inferior and bastardized that they may be classed as below the most inferior savage races, for their inferiority is sometimes beyond cure?" It was as if France had fallen asleep, and a monstrous bestiary had been conjured up on her own soil.[53]

The question that Buchez raised in his speech expressed the fundamental dilemma faced by men of his class and generation. He had a deep belief in equality that he had inherited from Enlightenment thinkers and which led him to his socialist beliefs. He trusted in progress and assumed that all humans could develop into a state of civilization. In practice, however, social divisions seemed so deep and unforgiving that they appeared permanent, as if rooted in the soil of the nation. As if they were natural. As if they were racial.

The argument that class divisions were in reality racial divisions, pioneered in the early nineteenth century by figures such as Niebuhr, Kemble, Thierry and Gobineau, now colonized the mainstream. For the Polish sociologist Ludwig Gumplowicz, early human societies were confronted with the question "Who was to work for whom?" The answer was settled through "the struggle of races" which imposed a "division of labour... in which inferior and difficult tasks fall to the dominated while the superior and easier occupations... became the prerogative of the dominant". This led to "the coincidence of occupational classes and castes with... racial differences". By this, Gumplowicz did not mean what we might suggest today— that blacks or Asians are over-represented in lower-paid or more menial jobs. What he meant, rather, was that what today we would call the "white working class" was working class because it was racially inferior.[54]

Lester Ward, the first president of the American Sociological Association, drew on the work of Gumplowicz to emphasize how "the genesis of society... has been through the struggle of races". "The conquering race looks down with contempt upon the conquered race and compels it to serve it in various ways", Ward believed. "The conquered race maintains its race hatred". Here lay the origins of social class. Over time, though, Ward suggested, the animosity between the races abated, creating a people, and eventually a nation. This was the plot of *Ivanhoe* turned into sociological theory.[55]

By the dawn of the twentieth century, more than a hundred years of constructing a white identity had made it more difficult to define its meaning. It was, however, at this moment that a slew of social developments coalesced to consolidate whiteness as an identity, most importantly the extension of democracy at home and of imperialism abroad. Both helped transform the way that people understood race and class, giving rise to the kind of racial thinking that still persists today.

VIII

In the latter decades of the nineteenth century, many countries gradually extended the vote beyond the hitherto magic circle of white propertied men to sections of the working class and women, too. By the early part of the twentieth century most Western nations had created something close to universal suffrage.

The extension of suffrage led to two conflicting responses within the middle class and ruling elites. On the one hand, it exacerbated fears about the lower orders and about democracy. The two main topics of her circle, the British Fabian socialist Beatrice Webb suggested, were "the meaning of the poverty of masses of men" and the "desirability of political and industrial democracy". "If the bulk of the people were to remain poor and uneducated", she wondered, "was it desirable, was it even safe, to entrust them with the weapon of trade unionism, and, through the ballot box, with making and controlling the government of Great Britain with its enormous wealth and far-flung dominions?"[56]

Such anxieties found scientific expression in the new discipline of crowd psychology. Its pioneer was Gustave Le Bon, for whom humanity was torn between the primal elements of instinct and reason. The elite was capable of suppressing the former and so being rational. The masses were controlled wholly by impulse and emotion. Sigmund Freud, describing Le Bon's "character sketch of the group mind" as "brilliantly executed", appropriated many of his ideas. The relationship between the ego and the id was, for Freud, akin to the relationship between the elite and the masses. The mind is like "the modern State in which a mob, eager for enjoyment and destruction, has to be held down forcibly by a prudent superior class".[57]

The lesson many drew from such studies was that liberty was too precious to be entrusted to democracy. Parliamentary democracy, Aldous Huxley believed, was a system in which "confidence tricksters, rich men, quacks may be given power by the votes of an electorate composed in great part by mental Peter Pans, whose childishness renders them peculiarly susceptible to the blandishments of demagogues and the tirelessly repeated suggestions of the rich men's newspapers". It was an argument that would return a century later in debates over "populism". And yet, the very developments that gave rise to such views also made them less politically palatable. It was more difficult to be so dismissive of people whose votes now mattered. The sense of the inferiority and irrationality of the lower orders did not disappear but it was expressed *sotto voce*, more dinner-table talk than public speech.[58]

The language of race became refocused more exclusively upon black and white, the West and the Rest. "The problem of the Twentieth Century", as WEB Du Bois put it, became "the problem of color line". That line was dramatically strengthened by the New Imperialism. Between 1870 and 1914, most of the world outside Europe and the Americas came under the direct rule or indirect control of a handful of European states, the USA and Japan. The most vivid expression of this was in the "Scramble for Africa". In 1870, ten per cent of Africa was under formal European control. By 1914, that figure had leapt to almost 90 per cent, Abyssinia and Liberia alone remaining independent. The Berlin Conference of 1884–5 parcelled out different parts of the continent as spheres of influence for different European states.[59]

By the eve of the First World War, the British Empire covered one-fifth of the world's landmass and included a quarter of its people. Such global sovereignty gave new resonance to a sense of racial superiority even as there developed anxieties about degeneration and decay. "I believe that the British race is the greatest of governing races", Colonial Secretary Joseph Chamberlain told a banquet in Australia. "I say that not merely as an empty boast, but as proved and shown by the success which we have had in administering vast dominions." As popular enthusiasm for Empire grew, so racial thinking ceased to be an elite ideology and became an element of mass culture. The racial superiority of the British people was celebrated in mass circulation newspapers and popular entertainment.[60]

It was not just in Britain that the New Imperialism generated mass enthusiasm. Germany only became a nation in 1871. By the end of the century, it had acquired the fourth largest empire in Africa as well as colonies in the Pacific. Imperialist expansion was driven by a desire to compete with other major powers. It also served domestic needs. The speed of industrialization combined with a population boom to create a *fin de siècle* preoccupation with new space for the excess people. The term *Lebensraum*—living space—which forty years later was to be brandished by the Nazis to justify their expansion through Europe entered the lexicon in the 1890s. It possessed not just physical but spiritual and racial connotations, too. Mass migration to America was one response to the lack of opportunities and room at home. Many deplored it as racial haemorrhaging and a loss of identity, the absorption of Germans into a different culture. Colonialism came to be seen as an alternative that would allow Germans to maintain their Germanness, while also demonstrating their superiority, both against other European nations and over "savage peoples".[61]

In America, the significance of slavery had ensured a colour line more sharply delineated than in Europe. The debate over who was white had, however, blurred that line throughout the nineteenth century. In the early twentieth century, new developments sharpened it. America elbowed its way into the league of imperialists, annexing the Philippines, Guam, Puerto Rico and Cuba in the wake of the Spanish-America war of 1898, as well as Hawaii and Samoa. The writer John O'Sullivan had coined the term "manifest destiny" in 1845 to describe America's right "to overspread the continent", justifying the seizure of California and other parts of Mexico. Conquest of territory beyond the American continent only strengthened belief in such destiny. There could be no stopping imperialist expansion, Indiana senator Alfred J. Beveridge insisted, because "the inherent tendencies of a race are its highest law. They precede and survive all statutes, all constitutions" and "are not to be stayed by the hand of man". Even opponents of imperialism often couched their opposition in racial terms, protesting, as three-time Democratic Presidential nominee William Jennings Bryan did, that "An empire suggests variety in race and diversity in government", which would only weaken America.[62]

Imperialism, nevertheless, also posed problems for the racial viewpoint. Until Japan joined the fray, the major imperialist powers were all white, and all with conflicting interests. The same kinds of distinctions between different European races were drawn in discussions of imperialism as they had been in the immigration debate. Franklin Giddings, professor of sociology at Columbia University, noted in 1901 the "superiority of the Anglo-Saxon and the decadence of the Latin race", adding contemptuously that "a people that idly sips its cognac on the boulevards as it lightly takes a trifling part in the *comédie humaine* can only go down in the struggle for existence with men who have learned that happiness... is the satisfaction that comes only with the tingling of the blood."[63]

Anglo-Americans did not have sole rights to bigotry. Most Filipinos, wrote the journal *Irish American*, "are in a state of barbarism but little removed from their condition at the time when Columbus revealed America to the eyes of Europe". *Kuryer Polski*, a Polish journal, identified Filipinos as a "half savage people" and suggested that independence would lead them to be as corrupt and uncivilized as "the negro republic of Hayti". But many also chafed at the pervasive Anglo-Saxonism. "The moment a Teuton or a Celt achieves fame", one Irish American lawyer and diplomat sardonically observed, "he is hailed as a new product of 'Anglo-Saxon' civilization! But if he winds up in the police court in the morning, he is regarded simply as a drunken German or Irishman".[64]

American debates over imperialism, unlike the ones in Europe, exposed a tension between expressions of Anglo-Saxon superiority, white supremacy and American exceptionalism. Over time, Anglo-Saxonism faded into the background, while the sense of white supremacy and of American exceptionalism became dominant and, to a degree, fused. That it did so was largely the result of two domestic developments. The first was the imposition of Jim Crow laws—a system of apartheid—in the South which, as we shall see in Chapter 7, had influence well beyond Southern states. The second was a series of racist immigration controls. The 1924 Immigration Act was the high point of Anglo-Saxonism, and of hostility towards southern and eastern Europeans. It was, paradoxically, also the moment at which a broader sense of whiteness became solidified. Partly, this was because the Act helped defuse the panic about the "wrong" type of European migrant. More importantly, the Act did not just set quotas on the not-quite-white races of Europe. It also barred all immigrants from Asia.

There had been more than seven decades of anti-Asian agitation leading up to this. The first Chinese immigrants had begun arriving in the 1850s. They were seen as a threat both to the livelihoods of white workers and to the racial purity of America. For Edward Ross, the theorist of "race suicide", "the yellow man can best the white man because he can better endure spoiled food, poor clothing, foul air, noise, heat, dirt, discomfort and microbes. Reilly can outdo Ah San, but Ah San can underlive Reilly." Africans, wrote Theodore Roosevelt, had been brought to America by a "transoceanic aristocracy" and had proved almost "fatal to the white race". American democracy, however, "with the clear instinct of race selfishness" has seen "the race foe" in the case of the Chinese, and "kept out the dangerous alien". A century later, immigration as an evil undemocratically foisted on the working class by a "cosmopolitan elite" would again become a major political theme.[65]

In 1875, following a panic about "Chinese prostitutes", America enacted the Page Act, the nation's first restriction on immigration, excluding anyone from an "Oriental country" who came for "lewd and immoral purposes". Seven years later came the Chinese Exclusion Act, banning all Chinese labourers. Finally came the bar on all Asians in 1924.

"Between the 1920s and the 1960s", Matthew Frye Jacobson notes, "concerns of 'the major [racial] divisions' would so overwhelm the national consciousness that the 'minor divisions' which had so preoccupied Americans during the period of massive European immigration, would lose their salience in American culture". Americans, in other words, became so obsessed by the threat of blacks and Asians that fears of the "not quite whites" faded away. This was not simply an American but a global phenomenon, too, particularly in Britain's "white Dominions". Australia inaugurated its White Australia policy in 1901 with the passage of the Immigration Restriction Act. It was soon followed by Canada, New Zealand and South Africa. Immigration restriction, wrote the American writer and eugenicist Lothrop Stoddard, "is a species of segregation on a large scale, by which inferior stocks can be prevented from both diluting and supplanting good stocks." The aim, in short, was to create a worldwide version of Jim Crow laws.[66]

Like much of the debate about race at the turn of the century, these global racial controls on movement embodied both a sense of racial superiority and an expression of fear. "The day will come, and perhaps is not far distant", the British-born Australian educationalist and politician Charles Henry Pearson wrote in his 1893 book *National Life and Character*, "when the European observer will... see the globe girdled with a continuous zone of black and yellow races, no longer too weak for aggression or under tutelage, but independent". And whites, "struggling among ourselves for supremacy in a world which we thought of as destined to belong to the Aryan races and to the Christian faith" would be "elbowed and hustled, and perhaps even thrust aside by peoples whom we looked down upon as servile, and thought of as bound always to minister to our needs".[67]

The book was a sensation, required reading by commentators and world leaders from William Gladstone to Theodore Roosevelt. It "shook the self-confidence of the white races", one critic observed, "and deprived them of the absolute sense of assured superiority which had hitherto helped them to dominate". Empire might have provided for a sense of racial superiority, but the growing challenge posed by the peoples of the empire could not but nurture trepidation and dread.[68]

The victory of Japan over Russia in the Russo-Japanese war of 1904–5 deepened such dread. "The echoes of that yellow triumph over one of the great white Powers reverberated to the ends of the earth", wrote Stoddard in his 1920 bestseller *The Rising Tide of Color*, and "signalled a body-blow to white ascendency". Then came the carnage of the First World War and the horror of the Russian Revolution. In the Great War, Stoddard reflected, "the colored world suddenly saw the white peoples which, in racial matters had hitherto maintained something of a united front, locked in an internecine death-grapple of unparalleled ferocity". Where once "the colored races [had] accorded to white supremacy a fatalistic acquiescence" and "the white man" had been "universally feared", it was no longer so. In response, the white world had to strengthen the dykes to "wall in" the "rising flood of color" by curtailing all immigration. Stoddard used an analogy that was both extraordinary and yet typical of the time. "Just as we isolate bacterial invasions, and starve out the bacteria by limiting the area and amount of their food-supply", he wrote, "so we can compel an inferior race to remain in its native habitat" to "limit its numbers and therefore its influence". Without such action the "white race" faced "final replacement or absorption by the teeming colored races".[69]

This was a new kind of white supremacy rooted not in a sense of superiority but in the terror of that superiority, and the world it had created, slipping away. Three centuries after the *White Lion* docked in Port Comfort, white identity was finally consolidated at the very moment that white supremacy was beginning to crumble.

4

THE REINVENTION OF JEW-HATRED

I

Central London. 22 March 2021. A march in support of Palestinian rights, following a week of Israeli bombing of Gaza in retaliation for Hamas firing rockets into Israel. And, on the march, a demonstrator holding a placard depicting Jesus carrying the cross on the way to crucifixion. Accompanied by the slogan "Do not let them do the same thing today again". It was, as I wrote on Twitter at the time, a "What the hell?" moment.

The placard, comedian and author David Baddiel wrote, depicted "the oldest negative myth about the Jews", that "Jews are Christ-killers". The message was clear: "Jews are… murderers of all that is good and innocent and sacred in this world". It was one placard in one demonstration but it was also an illustration of how many people, including "progressives", view Jews. The relationship between the left, Jews and antisemitism is an issue to which I will return in Chapter 9. Here, I want to explore a different question: how does antisemitism fit into the argument I have been making about the invention of race? If, as many, including Baddiel, argue, antisemitism is the oldest racism in the world, how does that square with the claim that the concept of race is a product of modernity?[1]

To speak of race as a modern invention is not to deny the existence of bigotry in the premodern world. Indeed, it was a world in which inequality was stitched into the social fabric and in which all manner of prejudices flourished, when persecution of those deemed "different" was the norm. That, paradoxically, is why premodern forms of hatred are distinct from contemporary ideas of race and practices of racism. Before modern notions of racial difference and inequality could develop, modern ideas of equality and a common humanity had to develop, too. The same is true of antisemitism. Modern antisemitism is distinct from premodern hatred of Jews because it is the product of an age in which the principle of equality, including the equality of Jews, had been accepted. In practice, however, bigotry and discrimination towards Jews was widespread. Antisemitism became not simply the expression of bigotry and discrimination but also the justification of why Jews were unworthy of equality.

When Salo Baron, perhaps the pre-eminent scholar of Jewish history, was asked, while testifying at the trial of Adolf Eichmann in Jerusalem in 1961, how he would explain the "negative attitude which had existed for so many hundreds of years... against the Jewish people", he replied: "dislike of the unlike". But, as he, and other great Jewish historians such as Bernhard Blumenkranz, have shown, what constitutes being "unlike", and how and whether Jews are regarded as unlike, has changed over time. Before the eleventh century, Blumenkranz suggests, Jews and Christians "Speaking the same language, dressing in the same manner, engaging in the same professions... intermingled in the same houses, just as they all came together under arms to defend the common homeland". All this began to change with the development of what historian RI Moore calls "a persecuting society" in the later Middle Ages when those deemed different in any way—Jews, heretics, lepers, sodomites, witches and many others—became targets for "deliberate and socially sanctioned violence" and subject to segregation, exclusion and discrimination.[2]

Most importantly, the meaning of "unlike" is necessarily different in communities in which difference is viewed as an unchangeable feature of the social landscape, and the acceptance of inequality an essential element of social consciousness, to what it is in societies in which ideas of equality and a common humanity have gained purchase. Just as through the Enlightenment, modern forms of both equality and of inequality were established, so the following century witnessed both the emancipation of Jews and the rise of ferocious new forms of anti-Jewish hostility. The formal recognition that Jews were entitled to full equality and citizenship rights transformed their relationship to the societies in which they lived.

A new phrase entered the lexicon in the late eighteenth century and came into widespread use in the nineteenth—"the Jewish Question". It referred to the "problem" of how to fit Jews into modern society, a problem that now seemed acute because the very act of emancipation raised new issues about their difference. Previously, distinct Jewish practices, rituals and occupations made sense in a world in which differences were viewed as natural and inevitable. Emancipation turned the issue on its head. The differences of Jews, and the barriers that still existed to full participation in social life, were now an anomaly, a challenge to the claims of equality.

That anomaly was seen by the end of the nineteenth century in racial more than in religious terms. If the persistence of inequalities in societies that had accepted the significance of human equality gave birth to the concept of race, the development of the racial concept, in turn, helped transform the hatred of Jews from a religious to a racial ideology. Jews were anomalous because they were racially distinct. This chapter looks at the emergence of the "Jewish Question" and at the creation of modern antisemitism.

II

On 2 January 1792, fourteen of Nancy's most notable Jews, including the grand rabbi, stood in the main square with the political leaders of the northern French town, to partake of a new ceremony. "The oath that we are about to take", announced Berr Isaac Berr, a lay leader of the local Jewish community, "makes us, thanks to the Supreme Being, and to the sovereignty of the nation, not men, but French citizens."[3]

Not far away, in the town of Bischheim-au-bourg, the same ceremony took place, but with a different outcome. Here, the town council insisted that every Jewish oath-taker cross himself to establish he was telling the truth. This, of course, the Jews refused to do. Both sides appealed to the Departmental Directory, the regional authority that spoke on behalf of the central government. The Directory agreed with the Jews. A new ceremony was set for 18 April. This time, Jews were told they had to remove their hats before they could take the oath. Again, they refused, it being vital to them never to make an oath in God's presence without covering their heads. Once more, both sides appealed to the Directory, and once more the Directory sided with the Jews. Finally, on 30 April, at the insistence of the Directory, the five most prominent Jews of Bischheim succeeded in swearing allegiance to the country, thereby winning full political rights.[4]

The ceremonies in Nancy and in Bischheim reveal the transformative impact of the French Revolution on the place of Jews in society. They reveal, too, the difficulties faced by the post-revolutionary society in trying to sweep away old prejudices, and the new conflicts now emerging between equality and identity.

The historical significance of Jewish emancipation is often overlooked. The shadows of two colossal events in the twentieth century, the Holocaust and the foundation of the state of Israel, have, historian David Sorkin observes, obscured the magnitude of emancipation which "was, and remains, the principal event". Similarly, David Vital argues that emancipation was "the principal engine of change" for Jews in modern Europe. Nothing else "would serve so powerfully to precipitate such revolutionary changes in their mores, their culture, their internal social structure".[5]

It was not just the Jewish world that emancipation transformed. Of the 28 million inhabitants of France at the start of the Revolution in 1789, fewer than 35,000 were Jewish. Most—around 30,000— were Ashkenazi Jews. The Ashkenazim had originally settled along the Rhine, and later migrated into Central and Eastern Europe. In France they lived in the north-east, in Alsace and Lorraine. Around 3,500 Sephardic Jews, whose roots were in the Iberian peninsula but who had been expelled from Spain and Portugal in the fifteenth century, lived in the south-west, around Bordeaux. There were also around 500 Jews, both Ashkenazi and Sephardic, in Paris. Given these tiny numbers, why did the question of Jewish emancipation become such a major and incendiary issue?

The emancipation debate was only partly about Jews themselves. Rather, Jews became "good to think [with]", a phrase originally coined by the anthropologist Claude Lévi-Strauss to describe the totemic use of animals in primitive societies, and subsequently appropriated by the historian Ronald Schechter to portray the place of Jews in late eighteenth-century France. The debate about Jews was the keystone to a wider set of arguments about the meaning of universalism, the boundaries of equality, the rights and duties of citizenship and the degree to which a nation could tolerate "difference".[6]

For radicals, to acknowledge as equal citizens a group that had faced such a history of bigotry and exclusion was fundamental to their project of transforming society and rooting it in the soil of equality. For their opponents, denying Jews equal rights was important for the same reason. They recognized that to accord full citizenship to such a shunned and despised group was to cement the belief in "equal rights for all", a belief to which they were deeply hostile. Radicals and traditionalists had fundamentally different visions of France; this led them to profoundly different attitudes to Jewish emancipation. The status of Jews became the means through which was played out a historic tussle over the meaning of the French nation and the desirability of Enlightenment ideals.

The liberalization of policies towards Jews had begun before the French Revolution. In January 1782, Habsburg Emperor Joseph II had proclaimed the *Toleranzpatent*, or Edict of Toleration, which aimed at "making the Jewish population useful and serviceable to the state". Jews would be allowed to send children to Christian schools and to universities. Many crafts and trades were now open to them, as well as the right to establish factories in certain areas. Just four decades earlier, in December 1744, Joseph's predecessor, Empress Maria Theresa, had ordered the expulsion of the long-settled Jewish communities of Bohemia and Moravia. Where Maria Theresa's actions looked back to a history of bigotry, Joseph II's edict looked forward to the incorporation of Jews into society, signalling the change in attitudes wrought through the Enlightenment. Yet, it was not emancipation in the sense of equal treatment. Toleration was conditional and piecemeal and driven by a desire to exploit "useful" Jews.

This is what made the French model so revolutionary: emancipation was unconditional, rooted in the insistence that all people, irrespective of background, could be citizens possessed of equal rights. It transformed the meaning of Jewish identity. It was an identity that in the premodern world had been ineluctably moulded by the history of the Jewish people, by its tragedies and its promises, by their incarnation as God's chosen people. It had been shaped, too, by the bigotry and isolation they faced. Jews had, in most European states, to live in designated Jewish areas, perform only the jobs open to Jews, abide by Jewish law, bend to the will of Jewish courts. With emancipation, participation in the Jewish community was, as Gary Kates puts it, "no longer a legal obligation, but became instead a moral duty. Only in this context could Jewish identity become a matter of intense personal concern." It was Jews, perhaps, above all other people, whose changing relationship to wider society helped frame the debates over the meaning of identity.[7]

Even in France, though, the process of achieving such equality was neither swift nor unambiguous. On 26 August 1789, the National Assembly adopted the Declaration of the Rights of Man and of the Citizen. Drafted by the Marquis de Lafayette, an aristocrat who had fought with the rebels in the American War of Independence, the echoes of the American Declaration of Independence, as well as of Enlightenment debates, are clear. "Men are born and remain free and equal in rights", reads the opening to Article 1. The Declaration is justly celebrated. It was also profoundly limited, rooted as it was in a defence of property as well as of equality. Property, according to Article 17, is "an inviolable and sacred right". The conflict between property and equality that ran from the Putney Debates to the debates over slavery, flowed through the Revolution, too. At its heart was the distinction between "active" and "passive" citizens. Only "active citizens"—men over 25 paying taxes and who were not servants—could vote or hold public office; just 4.3 million out of a population of 29 million. Excluded were women, the young, servants, the poor, the unemployed. And, to begin with, Jews, too.[8]

The first major National Assembly debate on the "Jewish question", on 23 December 1789, broke up in deadlock, the reactionary supporters of the *ancien régime*, and Jew-haters among the more revolutionary deputies, still too strong to be outmanoeuvred by liberals and radicals. It was not just the National Assembly rent by divisions. The Jewish community was, too, especially between the Ashkenazi Jews of the north-east and the Sephardic Jews of the south-west. The Jews of Alsace and Lorraine were among the poorest communities in France, forced, because of their exclusion from most crafts and guilds, into peddling, horse trading (literally) or money-lending. In Bordeaux, Sephardim merchants had prospered as mercantile capitalism emerged in the sixteenth century, and their wealth defined the local Jewish community.

As trade expanded in early modern Europe, many ports began developing colonies of foreign merchants. Sephardic Jews constituted one such colony. Cities such as Ancona, Livorno, Venice, Hamburg and Amsterdam were at the forefront not just of economic but of social and cultural development, too, centres of a new cosmopolitanism and tolerance. So it was in Bordeaux. Successive monarchs, from Henry II in 1550 to Louis XVI in 1776, had issued *lettres patentes*, special legal instruments that recognized Jews as "loyal subjects" to be treated like "all our other subjects", and accorded them rights including freedom of movement and the ownership of property. All these privileges were denied to the Jews of Alsace and Lorraine.[9]

Such differential treatment inevitably created friction. After the failure of the National Assembly to accord Jews active citizenship, Bordelais Sephardim submitted a petition (having presented a similar one the previous year) accusing their northern brethren of wanting to live "under a separate regime", whereas they were already "naturalised Frenchmen" enjoying "all the rights of citizens" and so should be treated differently. The Deputies agreed. On 28 January 1790, they declared that southern Sephardic Jews should "continue to enjoy the rights they have hitherto enjoyed" and so "shall enjoy the rights of active citizens". The National Assembly in effect renewed the corporate privileges awarded by the *ancien régime* and declared these to be the equivalent of active citizenship.[10]

Finally, on 28 September 1791, almost two years after the Declaration of the Rights of Man, the Assembly decreed that all Jews "duly qualified" could become active citizens. This was the decree under which Berr Isaac Berr and the Jewish notables of Nancy had acquired their citizenship, the decree which the town of Bischheim had attempted to deny.[11]

Other revolutionaries hailed the French decision. The Napoleonic Wars, which convulsed Europe from around 1799 to 1815, carried that model of emancipation across much of Western and central Europe. Yet, until at least the mid-nineteenth century, Joseph II's vision of conditional toleration held sway across much of the continent. The nineteenth century was an age in which emancipation was granted and then revoked, often many times over. Napoleon's defeat at Waterloo in 1815 led to Jewish advances being rolled back in most states, sometimes partially, sometimes totally. The Revolutions of 1848 again placed Jewish emancipation on its banners. But the revolutions were pitilessly suppressed, and many democratic gains reversed, including equality for Jews. Even in France, Napoleon rescinded many Jewish rights in 1808, though they were restored ten years later. In Russia and Poland, a number of reforms drew upon the tradition established by Joseph II, but repression rather than reform was the norm.[12]

Nevertheless, the very fact that in 1791 equality for all Jews had been proclaimed not as a reward for services rendered but on the basis of a moral vision—that Jews as human beings deserved the same rights as others—was itself a revolutionary moment. The claim in the American Declaration of Independence that "all men are created equal" was ignored by the framers of that declaration and the founders of the republic. Nevertheless, it inspired many to struggle for that equality and to extend it to all. French revolutionaries celebrated the Declaration of the Rights of Man but denied those rights to slaves and colonial subjects. Regardless, the Declaration became a weapon, as we shall see in Chapter 6, in the hands of those demanding universal rights. Similarly, the granting of equality to Jews on the moral basis of their humanity may have been abrogated at various times, but it served as a standard for those pushing for true Jewish emancipation.

And yet, however fundamental the French model, it was also ambiguous in meaning. "Jews should be denied everything as a nation but granted everything as individuals." So insisted Comte Stanislas de Clermont-Tonnerre, a liberal aristocrat and champion of Jewish rights, in the National Assembly debate of December 1789. It is a phrase that has since become much celebrated. Its implication, however, is far from clear. It can be read as a defence of individual as opposed to group rights, that Jews should not face any curtailment of their rights, but nor should they possess any special privileges. This is the classic liberal view. Clermont-Tonnerre's line could, however, also be read as meaning that Jews had, in Alfred Low's words, to "completely relinquish Jewish identity".

And this was how many non-Jews came to view the meaning of emancipation, that, in Germany for instance, the "Jew was to shed his Judaic heritage, cease to be a Jew, and eagerly embrace Germandom". The emancipation of Jews required also the emancipation of Jews from Judaism.[13]

The fact that Jewish emancipation was not simply, or even primarily, about Jews, but a process that turned Jews into "a visible symbol of human liberation", Hannah Arendt acutely observed, "proved the source of a great deal of mischief". Many Enlightenment supporters of Jewish emancipation ignored the lived experience of Jews, and indeed saw that lived experience, the attachment of Jews to Judaic customs, as an undesirable expression of a backward tribalism. Instead, Arendt acerbically noted, "Jews in all their concrete noxiousness are to be overlooked for the sake of *the* Jew, whose oppression is a disgrace to mankind". This, she argued, laid the ground for modern antisemitism which "turns this abstraction on its head by overlooking 'decent' Jews with whom one may be personally acquainted... in favour of *the* Jew, who has at last been discovered to be the evil principle of history". The very presentation of Jews not as flesh-and-blood humans but as symbols of the struggle for equality paved the way for antisemites to do the same—but reversing the symbolic meaning of "the Jew".[14]

III

As the walls, sometimes metaphorical, sometimes literal, that had separated Jews from the rest of society began crumbling, so new barriers and cleavages were created. Emancipation did not wash away the sense of Jews as alien to society. Rather, Jewish difference was understood in a different way. In the eighteenth century, Jews were often seen as an anachronism, a tribal remnant of superstition and backwardness, and hence as an obstacle to universal values. A century later, they came to be the embodiment of the very opposite: of cosmopolitanism and modernity, of the soullessness that seemed to define the capitalist world, of uprootedness at a time when many felt the need to cling on to the nation, the *Volk* and tradition. And what defined them as Jews was no longer religious faith as such but rather a form of "Jewishness" which eventually became understood in racial terms. The very process of assimilation, of shedding that which made Jews distinct, exposed the ineradicable "racial" quality of Jewishness.

This new perception of Jewishness was shaped by two other developments. One was the growth of cultural pessimism and of disenchantment with capitalism and modernity, the other the intensification of more strident and *volkish* forms of nationalism.

The germs of this new perception can be seen in the work of Herder. He was no antisemite; Arendt called him "an outspoken friend of the Jewish people". Nevertheless, just as his conception of pluralism, and of the *Volk*, led him to reactionary views about human differences and laid the groundwork for racial thinking, so it also pulled him into dangerous waters in his thinking about Jews.[15]

Herder rejected the old bigotry based on religion. "The writings of the Jews", he believed, "unquestionably have had an advantageous effect in the history of mankind." On reading the Tanakh and the Talmud, he exulted in "how holy and exalted these books are for me". But the Jews that Herder admired were not the Jews of the present but those of the past. He celebrated the Jewish culture expressed in "Hebrew when it was the living language of Canaan before it became mixed". In present-day Europe, though, Jews could be no more than "parasitical plants on the trunks of other nations". The character and values of Jews, their ways of thinking and living, their laws and practices, were formed long ago and in a different place. They could not but be aliens in nations to which they did not, and could not, belong.[16]

Here lies the tension between Herder's espousal of pluralism and his insistence that cultures could only be authentic if rooted in an exclusive *Volk*, a distinct place and an unbroken history. It is a tension that still lies at the heart of identity thinking today. In the nineteenth century it was a contradiction that allowed many to erase the promise of tolerance through the demands of the authentic *Volk*. It not only paved the way for racial thinking but allowed the most grotesque racists to purloin Herder as justification for their arguments. The Anglo-German writer Houston Stewart Chamberlain, whose theories of Aryan superiority led him to celebrate the Nazis, despised Herder's advocacy of equality. But, he observed, "in spite of his outspoken humanism", Herder believed that "the Jewish people is and remains in Europe an Asiatic people alien to our part of the world".[17]

In Herder's writings, we can see the first flickers of the modern idea of antisemitism. What made the new antisemitism distinct from the old hostility to Judaism is not just that it was parsed in the language of race rather than of religion. It was also that it was at its core a war against modernity—a racialized hatred of all that the modern world represented, from capitalism to equality, from consumer culture to democracy, from secularism to cosmopolitanism.

In the seventeenth and eighteenth centuries, a small number of Jews had become, either as merchants or as financiers, important cogs in Europe's economic machine as it cranked up in the era of mercantile capital. In both cases, they relied for their success partly on their capacity to forge international connections, many fashioned through centuries of forced expulsions and movements that had necessitated the creation of networks of succour and support. As restrictions on Jews eased in the nineteenth century, they were able to enter previously forbidden trades and professions. Nevertheless, many states continued to rely on Jewish financiers, often finding it difficult to persuade other sections of the population to lend money. Only a handful of Jews could, of course, play such roles. But the fact that they could allowed many to identify Jews with finance capital and with cosmopolitanism.

The latter decades of the nineteenth century were marked by pessimism and insecurity. There was unparalleled social change; Germany embarked on industrialization only in the second half of the century, and then at disorienting pace. At the same time, capitalism felt precarious, marked by financial crashes and recessions, unemployment and poverty. The old ways of life and culture disappeared. Jews became a symbol of much of what was wrong or had vanished.

It was in these decades that the term "antisemitism" was coined. Some attribute the term to the Jewish scholar Moritz Steinschneider, others to the German journalist Wilhelm Marr who, in 1879, founded the Anti-Semitic League. Whatever the etymology, the word, and the concept it denoted, became embedded in academic and popular debate. In both France and Germany, the last decades of the nineteenth century would see Jew-hatred turn into a social force.[18]

In France, defeat in the Franco-Prussian war of 1870 exacerbated a sense of national and racial degeneration, tipping the nation into a crisis of identity. Many damned the universalist values of the Revolution and the Enlightenment for having created a nation cut adrift from its moral moorings. In his 1897 novel *Les Déracinés* (*The Uprooted*), Maurice Barrès tells of a group of young men spiritually destroyed by their "rootless" teacher Paul Bouteiller, "a child of reason, foreign to our traditional local or family habits, completely abstract and truly suspended above the void". Bouteiller sought to "detach" his students "from the soil and from their social group, to take them out of their prejudices" and to imbue them with a sense of scepticism, even nihilism, leading them to tumble into the moral void above which he had placed himself.

Barrès was not just a novelist but also a key figure in late nine-teenth-century French politics, a Boulangist member of the Chamber of Deputies. Led by the charismatic general Georges Boulanger, Boulangism was a populist movement that initially drew support from the left but soon became a bastion of the reactionary right. Barrès was both an eloquent defender of workers' rights and a strident nationalist and merciless antisemite. He became a key figure in the Dreyfus Affair, in which France ripped itself apart in its response to a case of high treason, low farce, deep principle and profound Jew-hatred.

Captain Alfred Dreyfus was a French artillery officer from Alsace, upstanding, righteous and patriotic. He was also Jewish. In December 1894 he was sentenced to life imprisonment for treason for passing secrets to the Germans and sent to rot on the notorious Devil's Island in French Guiana.

Two years later, the new head of the army's intelligence unit, Georges Picquart, uncovered evidence pointing to another French military officer, Major Ferdinand Walsin Esterhazy, as the real trai-tor. The Army General Staff, furious at its previous judgment being questioned, dispatched Picquart to North Africa, later imprisoning him on trumped-up charges. Esterhazy faced a court martial in 1898, having been told beforehand that he would be found not guilty; he then fled the country. In an attempt to shore up the case against Dreyfus, Esterhazy's friend Major Hubert-Joseph Henry, created a childishly inept forgery naming Dreyfus as a traitor. When caught, he committed suicide. In 1899, Dreyfus was court-martialled for a second time and again found guilty but with "extenuating circumstances". Within days he received a presidential pardon. Finally, in 1906, Dreyfus was officially exonerated and reinstated in the army.

The bare bones of the story give little sense of its true dimensions. The Affair became the platform for a ferocious public debate on what it was to be French. Should the contract that bound citizens be civic or racial? Was one's loyalty to a set of ideals or was it forged out of a mythical heritage, shaped by history, tradition, place and race? It was not just Dreyfus but the republic itself, and republican notions of citizenship and national identity, that was on trial. And just as at the end of the eighteenth century Jews had been a means of "thinking through" wider issues of citizenship, equality and identity, so it was again a century later.

The most famous intervention was novelist Émile Zola's "J'Accuse" open letter, published, after Esterhazy's court-martial acquittal, on the front page of *L'Aurore*, a newspaper owned by Georges Clemenceau, a radical republican and future prime minister. The injustice of the Affair offended Zola's Enlightenment-wrought sensibilities. "It is a crime", he wrote in "J'Accuse", "to stoke the passions of reactionism and intolerance, by appealing to the odious antisemitism that, unchecked, will destroy the freedom-loving France of the Rights of Man". He deliberately named those he deemed responsible for the framing of Dreyfus and for the cover-up, challenging them to sue for libel. They did—and won. Zola was forced to flee France, returning only when the sordid story had finally unravelled.

For the anti-Dreyfusards, that which Zola celebrated—the Enlightenment, the Revolution, the Rights of Man—was the acid that had corroded the French nation. Kantianism, which symbolized the spirit of all they scorned, sought, in Barrès' words, to turn "our young Lorrainers, Provençaux, Bretons and Parisians... into an abstract ideal man, everywhere identical with himself, while our need is for men firmly rooted in our soil, in our history, in our national conscience". Jews were the most potent embodiment of everything they despised—a people unrooted, unFrench, cosmopolitan. They were different because they symbolized the lack of difference, the universal man.[19]

For the writer and journalist Édouard Drumont, the French Revolution itself had been a Jewish conspiracy. In 1889, on the centenary of the Revolution, he wrote bitterly that it was "their ceremony, the centenary of those foreigners who have chased away the brave native Frenchmen from their homes... The centenary of 1789 is the centenary of the Jew." Drumont became the most celebrated antisemite of his day, the impresario of mass-market Jew-baiting. His 1886 book, *La France Juive*, two volumes and 1200 pages dripping with antisemitic venom, sold over a million copies. He founded *La Libre Parole*, a newspaper defined by its Judaeophobia. Shortly after the conviction of Dreyfus, it published on its front page a cartoon of two hook-nosed Jews vainly trying to wash blood from their hands and clothes. The caption read: "Jews, for us in France, only blood can get out a stain like that". In another cartoon, Zola, a pig, smears his own excrement over the map of France. In the decades leading up to the First World War, George Mosse has observed, most people would have thought "it was France rather than Germany" that was most "likely to become the home of a successful and racist National Socialist movement".[20]

Germany, unlike France, did not have to dwell on reasons for defeat in the Franco-Prussian war. Nevertheless, the same kind of cultural pessimism and hostility to modernity that shaped French antisemitism did so in Germany, too. The pace of industrialization in Germany in the latter decades of the nineteenth century was without parallel until perhaps the Soviet Union the following century. Precipitous capitalist expansion was accompanied by wild speculation, reckless investment and bursting bubbles. The suddenness with which a new proletariat was created, the speed and ugliness of urbanization, and the transformation of traditional cultures and lifestyles, deepened the sense of social precariousness. Marx and Engel's celebrated description of capitalism as ensuring that "All that is solid melts into air, all that is holy is profaned" seemed a particularly apposite description of late nineteenth-century Germany.

These changes spawned two kinds of oppositional movements. On the one side, there were working-class anti-capitalist organizations, primarily trade unions and the Social Democratic Party (SPD). While hostile to capitalism, such groups embraced modernity and saw themselves as inheritors of the universal values of the Enlightenment and the French Revolution. They welcomed and defended Jewish emancipation and unequivocally opposed any attempt to undermine their rights. Sections of the left, especially romantic socialists despairing of industrialization, were drawn towards antisemitic ideas. But the dominant working-class organizations, the SPD in particular, were implacably hostile to such bigotry.

There is today a widely-held view that Marx helped foment antisemitic ideas, in particular through his essay "On the Jewish Question". In fact, as Robert Fine and Philip Spencer have observed, Marx both played on antisemitic tropes, particularly the identification of Jews with finance capital, and "supported Jewish emancipation unequivocally and without conditions". What critics fail to recognize, Marx's biographer Francis Wheen observes, is that the essay was "written in defence of Jews", against those who "argued that Jews should not be granted full civic rights and freedoms unless they were baptised as Christians". "We do not tell the Jews", Marx wrote, "that they cannot be emancipated politically without radically emancipating themselves from Judaism". But, he added, "the fact that you can be emancipated politically without completely and absolutely renouncing Judaism shows that *political emancipation* by itself is not *human* emancipation".[21]

For Marx, it was important to defend the right of Jews to full political rights but also to recognize that human emancipation required the transcendence of religion, too, and not just for Jews. Later Marxists often failed to make this distinction and helped stoke antisemitic ideas. In the nineteenth century, however, Marx's work acted as a firewall against leftwing antisemitism. "The strong influence of Marxism on the labor movement in Germany", Arendt observed, "is among the chief reasons why German revolutionary movements showed so few signs of anti-Jewish sentiment".[22]

Rightwing anti-capitalism was different. It was rooted in a conservative outlook shaped by Romanticism and fuelled by a hatred of modernity, the Enlightenment, and liberalism. It was in this milieu that the new antisemitism was nurtured. Even more than French reactionaries, German Romantic conservatives perceived the modern world as a realm of putrefaction. "The spiritual life of the German people is in a state of... rapid decay", bemoaned the philosopher and art historian Julius Langbehn, whose anonymously published 1890 book *Rembrandt als Erzieher* ("Rembrandt as Teacher") was a hugely successful critique of German culture. "We shall all sink into nothingness", lamented Paul de Lagarde, another influential conservative. Theirs was, as historian Fritz Stern puts it in the title of a book, the politics of cultural despair, an existential howl against modernity.[23]

Liberalism, with its attachment to democracy, equality, individualism and the free market, had, such critics feared, stripped German culture of its authenticity and soul. Constitutionalism and the rule of law had eroded the power of tradition and custom. Equality had undermined the organic loyalties of a hierarchical society. The nation-state had sapped the strength of the *Volk*.

Liberals and conservatives were both nationalists, but of different stripes. For liberal nationalists, drawing on Enlightenment ideas of modernity and progress, the nation was constituted through the state and people bound together through a civic concept of national identity. Conservatives rejected the nation state because, for them, the meaning of the nation was carried in the history of the people, not in artificial political constructions. They looked to Herder, not Kant, for their cultural vision.

Jews symbolized for German conservatives, as they did for French intellectuals like Barrès and Drumont, all that they detested— modernity, democracy, equality, liberalism, cosmopolitanism. Langbehn saw Jews as "a poison" because "they are democratically inclined" and "have an affinity with the mob". For the philosopher and diplomat Konstantin Frantz, "Nothing suits the Jewish point of view better than the idea of the so-called constitutional state" under which "all institutions and laws are measured entirely by abstract concepts of law" and which consequently "recognizes neither Jews nor Christians, only citizens". Jews were the ultimate urban intellectuals who abominated the *volkish* peasant life, having, according to Lagarde, "as a matter of principle, an aversion from the occupations which seem to me to be important above all others, agriculture and stockbreeding". This supposed Jewish hostility to the soil and to nature was a constant theme for the Romantic conservatives. The converse was also true for them: that the peasant, the *Volk*, was untouched by liberalism, modernity and Jewish corruption.[24]

Most conservatives believed with Langbehn that "a Jew can no more become a German than a plum can turn into an apple". Many were not in the least reticent in suggesting how the issue had to be resolved. "With trichinae and bacilli one does not negotiate", Lagarde insisted; "they are exterminated as quickly and as thoroughly as possible". Given what was to happen half a century later, it is a viscerally shocking comment. Yet, it was a sentiment neither peculiarly German nor uniquely anti-Jewish. It is, after all, little different from the views of Theodore Roosevelt or Robert Knox on how to deal with "troublesome races".[25]

At the time of German reunification in 1870, antisemitism was, Peter Pulzer writes, "accepted by only a small minority of the politically dominant groups". By the turn of the century it was more pervasive, but not preponderant. Only in the wake of the First World War did brutal hatred of Jews seize the popular imagination and turn into a social movement. What Romantic conservatives did was to nurture these ideas, make them respectable, and create the intellectual and social material upon which the Nazis could later draw. "All the movements most fashionable in the 1920s and 1930s... had their intellectual roots in the prewar years", Pulzer reflects. "The main difference between the political antisemitism of the post- and pre-war period", he adds, "lies not in its content, but in its success".[26]

IV

"The Sanscrit [sic] language is of a wonderful structure; more perfect than the Greek, more copious than the Latin, and more exquisitely refined than either." So claimed William Jones in his annual discourse to the Asiatic Society of Bengal in 1786. Jones was an Anglo-Welsh lawyer and one of the great scholars of ancient and non-European languages. Appointed a judge at the Supreme Court in Calcutta in 1783, Jones founded the Asiatic Society of Bengal, which became the focus for much research into Indian history, philosophy and languages. For Jones, the significance of Sanskrit lay not only in its exquisiteness and perfection, but also in its relationship to European languages. There was a "greater affinity" between Sanskrit, Latin and Greek "than could possibly have been produced by accident". All three were likely "to have sprung from some common source, which, perhaps, no longer exists". That common source became called "Proto Indo-European", and most European, Persian and north Indian languages were thought to be members of the same Indo-European family.[27]

The emerging discipline of philology—the study of languages and their historical development—became a particular passion for European Romantics, animated as they were both by an obsession with language as the soul of the *Volk*, and by an enchantment with, even idolatry of, ancient Indian cultures and religions. Romantics projected onto Indian philosophies and religions a sense of the wonder and mystery they felt had been expunged by the mechanistic methods of Enlightenment rationalism. For poet and philosopher Friedrich Schlegel, one of the founding figures of German Romanticism, affinities of language and mythology, of architecture and philosophy, revealed that "the greatest empires and most noble nations" of antiquity, including Egypt and Israel, were colonies founded by Indian priests. He identified Germans as one of several "descended nations" that had originated in India.[28]

Philologists described the Indo-European language family as "Aryan", derived from the Sanskrit word *Ārya*. The Herderian concept of the *Volk*, in which a language and a people were tightly identified, became the bridge between Aryan as a description of a language family and as a label for a race. Schlegel's brother, the poet and professor of Sanskrit, August Wilhelm Schlegel, argued that the Indian "nation" was the fusion of two distinct races, dark-skinned "savages" and Sanskrit-speaking Aryans, members of a "white race" that had migrated south from central Asia, bringing the "first rudiments of civilization" to India. Another group of Aryans had moved north to Europe. Soon, Indians were expelled from their own Aryan myth. Instead of an Indian, or central Asian, origin for European cultures, many now insisted on Europe as having given birth to the Aryan civilization, and Aryans as having migrated from west to east, not east to west.[29]

Jews, too, were eventually expunged from the Aryan race, coming to be seen as "Asiatics"—Semites. When Gobineau wrote his *Inequality of Races* in 1853, "Aryan" had become a settled term synonymous with "white", but Jews were still part of that race. Within two decades, Aryans and Jews had been separated into distinct races. Yet, scientifically demonstrating that distinction proved elusive.

In 1871, the German Anthropological Society organized a physical survey of almost seven million schoolchildren, to determine how Jews and non-Jews were racially differentiated. The survey, or "Schulstatistik", was directed by Rudolf Virchow, one of the most eminent scientists of his day, a founder of modern pathology and of social medicine, a key figure in the development of cell biology, and the first to describe and name many medical conditions from leukaemia to thrombosis to spina bifida. He was politically active, a passionate advocate of social and political reform. He had taken part in the 1848 Revolution, for which he lost his hospital post, and was a founder member of the liberal German Progress Party. But, like many of his day, he was deeply invested in ideas of racial difference.

Acknowledging it impractical to measure skulls in a mass survey, there being too few people trained to do so, Virchow decided to catalogue eye and hair colour, which an untrained surveyor could ascertain. In common with most German anthropologists of the time, he believed that there were two pure physical types in the nation, the blond-haired and the dark-haired, the one providing "the classical appearance of the Teutons" and being the foundation of the "German race", the other associated with a number of races including Czechs, Walloons, Slavs, Franks and Jews. The blond and the brunet were also associated with distinct skull-types, the former being "dolichocephalic" or long-headed, and the latter "brachycephalic", or short-headed. The two groups were separated by skin colour, too. All blue-eyed blonds were deemed "white", while any child with brown eyes or dark hair was automatically listed as "brown skinned". As with much racial anthropology, skin colour was not determined by the actual physical shade but denoted an interior essence that defined racial type.[30]

Virchow's survey showed that Germans were, unsurprisingly, a mixed-up population. Just 32 per cent of German children were blond-haired and 42 per cent of Jews dark-haired, while 54 per cent of the former and 47 per cent of the latter were of a "mixed type". These findings, George Mosse observes, "should have ended controversies about the existence of pure Aryans and Jews". Of course, they didn't. For Virchow, the survey demonstrated "sharp oppositions... between the races". Race was a given, and scientists simply read any data as confirming what they already knew existed. They saw what they wanted to see. The "Schulstatistik", Andrew Zimmerman reflects, "taught Germans not so much to *think* as to *experience* themselves in terms of whiteness and brownness and to recognize distinctions between 'Jews' and 'Germans'".[31]

More important than science in the experience of race was the mysticism and irrationalism that became a feature of late nineteenth-century culture, especially German culture. There was a resurgence of spiritualism and occultism, with the flourishing of movements such as theosophy and of notions such as the "race soul". Not just mysticism but myth, too, became embedded in *fin de siècle* consciousness. The old Romantic vision of songs and sagas being the medium through which the spirit of the *Volksgeist* could be sustained across history found new meaning in an age in which ideas of the collective unconscious and the racial soul blossomed. A pivotal figure in the remaking of old myths for modern racial needs was Richard Wagner who, from mid-century onwards, had been in his operas reworking old Germanic and Norse lore to give substance to the Aryan ideal.

The young Wagner had been a Utopian socialist. In 1848, he had stood on the barricades in Dresden, watching the Royal Dresden Opera House, of which he was musical director, burn down. He viewed the revolution in Promethean terms as destroyer and regenerator. "I will destroy the domination of one over many, of the dead over the living, of matter over spirit", he apocalyptically wrote in a newspaper article. "I am the one God whom all creation acknowledges".[32]

Forced into exile after the revolution was crushed, Wagner maintained his messianic vision but abandoned his optimistic humanism for *volkish* notions of racial identity. His hatred for the power of money and for the commercialization of art led him, like many others, into the vortex of antisemitism. He began work on his *Ring* cycle, based loosely on the medieval German epic *Nibelungenlied*. The revitalization of myth was, for Wagner, a form of spiritual redemption, and a means of allowing common folk to apprehend more profound truths. The Bavarian town of Bayreuth, where Wagner organized an annual Festival, became the focal point for those who despaired of the cultural degeneration fostered by liberal modernity and sought to reinvigorate German culture on *volkish* lines. Through mystery and myth, the racial distinction between Aryan and Jew became firmly established.[33]

In this spirit, Houston Stewart Chamberlain (1855–1927) warned that "one of the most fatal errors of our time is... to give too great weight in our judgments to the so-called 'results' of science". There was no point to scientific investigations of race because "It is a fact of direct experience that the quality of the race is of vital importance". The province of science "is only to find out the how and the wherefore, not to deny the facts themselves in order to indulge your ignorance". We know what is true, and it is the job of science to provide the evidence for our intuitive truth.[34]

Chamberlain was a British-born writer so enraptured by Wagner's music that his early love of French culture gave way to a new obsession with Germany, and with *volkish* Romanticism. He became a naturalized German, coming to live in Dresden and in 1908, twenty-five years after Wagner's death, he married the composer's daughter Eva von Bülow. Chamberlain's colossal, trenchant *Foundations of the Nineteenth Century*, published in 1899, became the foundation of twentieth-century German racial thought, synthesizing racial history, folk psychology, Aryan myth and eugenics. "Nothing is so convincing as the consciousness of the possession of Race", he wrote; it "lifts a man above himself: it endows him with extraordinary—I might almost say supernatural—powers". Races, though, were not ready-made but had to be created. "A noble race does not fall from Heaven", Chamberlain believed, "it becomes noble gradually, just like fruit-trees, and this gradual process can begin anew at any moment."[35]

In Chamberlain's history, out of the "chaos" of antiquity, two pure races emerged—Teutons and Jews. Teutons were the most Aryan of the Aryans, and Germans the most Teutonic of the Teutons. The Teutonic spirit had been aroused by the birth of Christ, who may have been Jewish by "religion and education" but not by race, for he was Aryan. In the Middle Ages, the Teutonic peoples came to recognize their "all-important vocation as the founders of a completely new civilization and culture". And in the Reformation they overthrew the "dead hand" of Rome, both ancient and modern.[36]

Chamberlain did not think Jews inferior—he admired them for their singlemindedness in maintaining their "purity of blood"—but viewed them as a racial threat, seeking "to infect the Indo-Europeans with Jewish blood" and turn Europeans into "a herd of pseudo-Hebraic mestizos, a people beyond all doubt degenerate physically, mentally and morally". In Chamberlain's version of history, "The Indo-European, moved by ideal motives, opened the gates in friendship", at which point "the Jew rushed in like an enemy, stormed all positions and planted the flag of his, to us, alien nature". The aim of the Jew was to "put his foot upon the neck of all the nations of the world and be Lord and possessor of the whole earth". Already "our governments, our law, our science, our commerce, our literature, our art... practically all branches of our life have become more or less willing slaves of the Jews".[37]

Chamberlain drew on a host of existing prejudices, expressed by figures from Herder to Langbehn, from Gobineau to Barrès, and repackaged them into a vast, racial history that caught the imagination of turn-of-the-century Europe. History became reframed not simply as a racial struggle but as an existential conflict between the only two pure races left in the world—the German and the Jew. Chamberlain became the Nazis' favourite philosopher, and Hitler Chamberlain's idol.

Redemption, for Chamberlain, could come only through the elimination of Jewish blood and the Jewish spirit from the German people and German culture. How that elimination would come about, Chamberlain did not specify. He was, he demurred, "a modest historian" who could "neither influence the course of events nor possess the power of looking clearly into the future". But elimination there must be. "No arguing about 'humanity'", he concluded, "can alter the fact that this means a struggle", a struggle that "is above all others a struggle for life and death".[38]

5

BARBARISM COMES HOME

I

"There was no Nazi atrocity—concentration camps, wholesale maiming and murder, defilement of women or ghastly blasphemy of childhood—which the Christian civilization of Europe had not long been practicing against colored folk in all parts of the world in the name of and for the defence of a Superior Race born to rule the world." So wrote the great African American leader WEB Du Bois. Hannah Arendt agreed. "African colonial possessions", she observed, "became the most fertile soil for the flowering of what was later to become the Nazi elite. Here they had seen with their own eyes how peoples could be converted into races and how... one might push one's own people into the position of the master race."[1]

It is difficult not to think of the malevolence of Nazism, and of the horrors of the Holocaust, as uniquely evil. Yet, neither the Nazis, nor the Holocaust, emerged out of nothing. They were made possible by the ideas of race that had become deeply rooted in Western societies and by the practices of colonialism. When a "moderate" American politician, Theodore Roosevelt, a decade before he became President, could talk of the extermination of Native Americans as "moral" because their lives were "but a few degrees less meaningless, squalid, and ferocious than that of the wild beasts"; when an English Liberal, Charles Wentworth Dilke, could write that "nature seems to intend the English for a race of officers, to direct and guide the cheap labour of Eastern peoples"; when, in 1933, the Nazis could borrow the American Model Eugenical Sterilization law almost in toto for their own eugenic law; then, it is not difficult to see how the Nazis, for all the uniqueness of their crimes, drew upon decades of racial theory and practice. What was unique about the Nazis was the zeal with which they pursued their Aryan dreams, and their willingness to import colonial practices into the heart of Europe. This chapter explores how Western racial thinking in the age of empire can illuminate our understanding of Nazism and its legacy.[2]

II

"The Herero people must now leave this land. If they do not, I will force them to do so by using the great gun [artillery]. Within the German border, every male Herero, armed or unarmed, with or without cattle, will be shot to death. I will no longer receive women or children, but will drive them back to their people or have them shot at."[3]

So proclaimed General Lothar von Trotha, Commander in Chief of German South West Africa, the colony that is now Namibia, in October 1904. It came to be known as the "extermination proclamation". Six months later, Trotha issued another proclamation, this time to the Nama people: "The Nama who chooses not to surrender and lets himself be seen in German territory will be shot, until all are exterminated." If they continue to rebel against German authority, "it will fare with them as it fared with the Herero... I ask you, where are the Herero today?"

The Herero and the Nama were peoples that occupied much of southwestern Africa. Both were pastoralists, semi-nomadic cattle herders, the Herero occupying the north of the region, the Nama living further south. Germany officially declared the region a Crown Colony in 1890, taking over from a German adventurer Adolf Lüderitz, who had first arrived there in 1883, and found no European power in charge. Abuse of local peoples led to a series of rebellions, culminating in the Herero and Nama wars that erupted in 1904. When the governor, Theodor Leutwein, failed to make sufficient headway against the uprising, Berlin dispatched 14,000 new troops under von Trotha, an experienced colonial soldier known for his sadistic brutality. He viewed every struggle between Europeans and colonized peoples as part of a global race war, which could be won only through the annihilation of the racial enemy.

Otto Danhauer, a retired soldier who had become the military correspondent of a German newspaper, wrote of a conversation with the general in his new post. "Against *Unmenschen* ["nonhumans"] one cannot conduct war 'humanely'", von Trotha had told him. "And he allowed me to publish these words", Danhauer added.[4]

In the summer of 1904, the greater part of the Herero, some 50,000 people, migrated northwards, making camp at the foot of a large plateau, known to Europeans as Waterberg. Surrounded by sheer sandstone cliffs, it was the last source of water before the vast desolate wilderness of the Omaheke, the western extension of the Kalahari desert. It was also a place of deep spiritual meaning, central to the Herero creation myth. It was here that von Trotha decided, in his own words, "to annihilate them with an instantaneous blow". He surrounded the encampment with seven thousand soldiers. On the morning of 11 August, with the Herero still asleep in their huts, the Germans poured down barrage after barrage of artillery fire. The only escape route was into the Omaheke. "We had been explicitly told beforehand", wrote one of the commanders, that the aim "was the extermination of the whole tribe". As the surviving Herero fled into the desert, a German private, Adolph Fischer, described the scene: "The greater part of the Herero nation and their cattle lay dead in the bush, lining the path of their morbid march… Wherever we dismounted, our feet would hit against the human bodies… Whoever took part in the chase through the Sandveld lost his belief in righteousness on Earth."[5]

Having killed a large proportion of the Herero, and forced the survivors into a pitiless landscape, von Trotha ordered his troops to cut off the waterholes, and to patrol the perimeter of the desert. "The eastern border of the colony will remain sealed off and terrorism will be employed against the Herero showing up", he explained to Leutwein. "That nation must vanish from the face of the earth." The official German history of the battle of Waterberg boasted of genocide. "The hasty exit of the Herero to the southeast, into the waterless Omaheke, would seal his fate", it crowed.[6]

But it did not. Not yet, anyway. Thousands of Herero survived even in the unforgiving Omaheke, barely alive, yet not dead. They foraged for roots and hunted small game, even scorpions. There were also several thousand Herero who had not been at Waterberg but still lived in their own communities. They were attacked by German forces and killed on sight. "Shoot, kill, hang. Whatever you liked. Old or young. Men, women, children", wrote one German soldier about his orders. Many German politicians, including the Chancellor Bernhard von Bülow, a fervent advocate of imperial expansion, worried that this campaign might "demolish Germany's reputation among civilized nations and indulge foreign agitation". They feared, too, that the elimination of the Herero would deprive the colony of its labour force. So, now, began the next phase of the extermination plan. The Germans established forced labour camps—which they called *Konzentrationslager* or "concentration camps"—in which any Herero still surviving was interned. When the Nama people rebelled, in October 1904, they, too, were incarcerated. The camps came to serve both the economic imperative and the desire for extermination.[7]

The term "concentration camp" was first used to describe Britain's policy in the Boer War of creating large encampments to detain some 30,000 Boer women and children and more than 100,000 African and "coloured" people. Britain had drawn on the experience of Spanish colonial forces in Cuba where, in 1896, General Valeriano Weyler imposed a policy of "reconcentración"— relocating hundreds of thousands of Cubans into barbed-wire camps in an effort to isolate rebel fighters. The *New York Times* condemned the move as making "war like a savage". No "savages" had ever created such camps. It was, however, to become a favoured twentieth-century tactic among colonial administrators battling insurgents.[8]

In Cuba and South Africa, the camps were part of a military strategy to isolate insurgents from the wider population. In South West Africa, they were established after the Herero had already been defeated. They served as work camps and as death camps.

There were five main camps in South West Africa, each near a colonial settlement requiring labour. The prisoners were treated with merciless cruelty. "From early morning until late at night, on weekdays as well as on Sundays and holidays", wrote Heinrich Vedder, a missionary in Swakopmund, where one of the camps was located, the prisoners "had to work under the clubs of raw overseers until they broke down." The only food they received was raw rice. "Like cattle hundreds were driven to death", Vedder mournfully observed, "and like cattle they were buried".[9]

In Swakopmund, 40 per cent of prisoners died within four months; few prisoners lasted more than ten. Worse was the camp on Shark Island, just off the town of Lüderitz. Prisoners were so afraid of it, Vedder reported, that "a man slit his own throat with a pocket knife" rather than be transferred there. A scene witnessed by another missionary, August Kuhlmann, might explain why: "A woman, who was so weak from illness that she could not stand, crawled to some of the other prisoners to beg for water. The overseer fired five shots at her. Two shots hit her: one in the thigh, the other smashing her forearm... In the night she died." Shark Island, David Olusoga and Casper Erichsen conclude in their history of "Germany's forgotten genocide", "was a death camp, perhaps the world's first."[10]

When the camps were closed in 1907, up to three-quarters of the Herero and around half the Nama population had been exterminated. Lothar von Trotha returned to Germany and was awarded the Pour Le Merité, the highest military honour. His "devoted service and self-sacrifice... deserves the warmest gratitude of the fatherland", noted the German High Command in its official history of the Herero War.[11]

III

Shake any nineteenth-century European discussion about colonialism and tumbling out come expectations, even celebrations, of extermination:

Rev. Frederic Farrar, 1867: "They are without a past and without a future, doomed, as races infinitely nobler have been before them, to a rapid, an entire, and perhaps for the highest destinies of mankind, an inevitable extinction... these races—the lowest types of humanity, and presenting its most hideous features of moral and intellectual degradation, are doomed to perish."[12]

Edmond Perrier, 1888: "Just as animals disappear before the advance of man, this privileged being, so too the savage is wiped out before the European, before civilization ever takes hold of him. However regrettable this may be from a moral point of view, civilization seems to have spread throughout the world far more by dint of destroying the barbarians than by subjecting them to its laws."[13]

Benjamin Kidd, 1894: "Neither wish nor intention has power apparently to arrest a destiny which works itself out irresistibly. The Anglo-Saxon has exterminated the less developed peoples with which he has come into competition even more effectively than other races have done in like case."[14]

E. Caillot, 1909: "The Polynesian race did not manage to scale the rungs of the ladder of progress, it has added not the slightest contribution to the efforts that humanity has made to improve its lot. It must therefore make way before others that are more worthy, and disappear. Its death will be of no loss to civilization."[15]

Von Trotha's views about the Herero and the Nama were far from being uniquely monstrous. Across the Western world, in every lecture room, government department and dinner table could be heard talk of extinction of "the lowest types of humanity". For some it was a source of regret, for others of celebration; but virtually all thought it inevitable.

Nor was it just talk. The practice of treating "primitive peoples" as *Unmenschen* was not confined to German South West Africa. Perhaps the most monstrous practices were those in the so-called "Congo Free State"—the personal fiefdom of Belgium's King Leopold II. Leopold acquired the territory in the 1880s under the banner of the "International Association of Congo", and under the guise of a "philanthropic mission" to stop slave trading and bring progress to Africa. At the 1884 Berlin conference, the King persuaded other European states to support his venture. America, too, announced its "approval of the humane and benevolent purposes" of Leopold's project.[16]

What Leopold wanted from the colony that he named, with great chutzpah, *État Indépendant du Congo* ("Congo Free State"), was profit beyond measure. To achieve that, he created a system of forced labour more grotesque than most systems of slavery. Initially, the profits came from ivory. Then came the invention of the pneumatic tyre, creating a global fever for rubber, a fever inflamed by its use in myriad new functions, from tubing to electrical insulation. Rubber transformed Leopold's Congo into a truly fabulous cash machine.

Rubber vines grew wild in the equatorial rainforest that carpeted almost half of Leopold's fiefdom. Unlike rubber trees, vines required no cultivation or expensive nurturing. What they did call for was a huge labour force that had to work in dangerous, back-breaking conditions in the most inhospitable of environments. "The native doesn't like making rubber", wrote an officer in the Force Publique, Leopold's private army that brutally enforced his rule. "So he must be compelled". A detachment of the Force Publique would arrive at a village, kidnap the women, children and the elderly, and hold them hostage until the men had collected the requisite amount of rubber. That, though, was not the most monstrous feature of Leopold's system of compulsion.[17]

Those who did not produce sufficient rubber were shot, and their hands or feet chopped off as evidence to head office that the bullet had been wisely spent. Sometimes hands and feet were chopped off the living. And sometimes off children, too—it was a common practice to kill the children of men who failed to meet the rubber quota, and to return to the parents an amputated hand or foot.

Figures are difficult to compile with certainty in a country in which there was little record-keeping, especially, historian Adam Hochschild notes, "about something… considered so negligible as African lives". Nevertheless, both an official Belgian government commission in 1919, and modern academic studies, suggest that between 1880 and 1920, the population of Congo collapsed by a half, from around twenty million to less than ten million. Ten million Congolese probably lost their lives to Leopold's dreams of progress. It was not genocide, in that the Belgians were not seeking to destroy a particular group. It was, though, as Hochschild puts it, "a death toll of Holocaust dimensions".[18]

At the turn of the twentieth century, the indefatigable work of European and American campaigners, such as ED Morel, George Washington Williams, Alice Seeley Harris and William Sheppard, helped expose the malevolence of Leopold's Congo. To dampen down the scandal, in 1908, the Belgian government bought Congo from its king, at a handsome profit for Leopold, who had all his debts paid off and fifty million francs on top "as a mark of gratitude for his great sacrifices made for the Congo".[19]

And, then, the whole affair virtually disappeared from public consciousness until the twenty-first century. Forced labour did not disappear from the Congo. The more barbaric features, such as the mass killings and the amputation of feet and hands, were phased out. But

L'Union Minière du Haut-Katanga (UMHK), the corporation Leopold had created to exploit Congo's mineral resources—copper, cobalt, tin, gold, diamonds—maintained a more sophisticated version of the old method of compulsion, forcing village chiefs under threat of punishment to round up sufficient labourers who were then placed in chains to send to the mines. Historian John Higginson estimates that, prior to the Second World War, some quarter of a million people were press-ganged in this fashion, a coerced rural exodus that destroyed Congo's agricultural production.[20]

None of this disturbed the public conscience in Belgium. By the end of the century, twenty-six statues of Leopold graced Belgian squares and parks, most built since the 1920s, one as late as 1997. Despite the public conversations about Belgium's colonial legacy prompted by the Black Lives Matter movement in 2020, an opinion poll organized by Brussels' Africa Museum that same year found that 50 per cent of Belgians still believed that their country had done more good than harm in the Congo.[21]

A different cloak of amnesia has fallen over the British Empire. Irrespective of that 2020 poll, there is widespread acceptance by historians of the malignancy of Leopold's Congo. Many scholars, on the other hand, still view the British Empire as a force for good, a "civilizing mission" in the words of the political scientist Bruce Gilley. The British Empire, too, however, was built on brutal violence and racial contempt. From the crushing of resistance to British rule in Bengal in the 1750s to the repression of the Mau Mau rebellion in Kenya 200 years later, neither the contempt nor the violence was ever far from the surface.[22]

One of the favourite punishments meted out in British India was "cannonading". A British officer, Lieutenant George Cracklow, described, in a letter to his mother, what happened to Indian rebels captured during the so-called "Indian Mutiny" in 1857:

> The prisoners were marched up to the guns... and lashed to the muzzles with drag ropes... The guns exploded... I could hardly see for the smoke for about 2 seconds when down came something with a thud about 5 yards from me. This was the head and neck of one of the men... On each side of the guns, about 10 yards, lay the arms torn out at the shoulders. Under the muzzle and between

the wheels lay the remainder of the bodies with the entrails scattered about.[23]

A few weeks later, he wrote again to his mother that he had got so used to the killings that he thought "no more of stringing up or blowing away half a dozen mutineers before breakfast than I do of eating the same meal". This was the price of the "civilizing mission".

Some of the most grotesque expressions of the compulsion to civilize came in Australia, where civilization required the eradication of the indigenous people who already lived there. In Tasmania (or Van Diemen's Land as it was called until 1857), Edward Curr, director of the Van Diemen's Land Company, a farming corporation granted 250,000 acres under a royal charter, insisted that colonists had to "undertake a war of extermination" against local Aborigines, or else face abandoning the island. All conflicts between colonists and local peoples had "ended in other parts of the world by the extermination of the weaker race".[24]

When Britons arrived in Tasmania in 1803, there were between 4,000 and 17,000 Aborigines on the island, depending on which estimate one believes. Thirty years later, by the end of the Black War, the name given to the conflict between colonists and Aborigines in the 1820s, there were barely 200. They were rounded up and sent to Wybalenna, a specially created settlement on Flinders Island in the Bass Straits. It was not a death camp by any stretch of the imagination but it was, in historian Henry Reynolds' words, "a place of death". In 1847, the 47 who remained were again relocated, this time back to Tasmania, to a former convict settlement, Oyster Cove Station.[25]

Some historians, such as Robert Hughes and Lyndall Ryan, describe what happened in Tasmania as "genocide". Others, including Reynolds, disagree, pointing out that there was no intention on the part of the authorities to eliminate the Aboriginal population. However we describe it, there is little question that what Tasmania witnessed was the destruction of its indigenous population, a destruction made possible by the perception that they were "savages" and by extermination being thinkable, even if not morally acceptable to all.[26]

While Tasmania was the site of the worst expression of such destruction, it was not an isolated case. Throughout Australia, there was widespread insistence that extermination was a necessary solution. The *Perth Gazette*, in an editorial in 1837, insisted that "either the white inhabitants or the aborigine must obtain the mastery... it is the order of nature that, as civilization advances, savage nations *must* be exterminated sooner or later." On the other side of the continent, the editor of Queensland's *Peak Downs Telegram* similarly insisted that "a war of extermination is the only policy to pursue, the alternative being an abandonment of the country which no sane man will advocate for an instant".[27]

There were, of course, many who viewed such arguments with moral repugnance, including many officials in London, but they also felt isolated and pessimistic about the outcome. John West, the editor of the *Sydney Morning Herald*, was one of the most distinguished Australian historians of his age, a social reformer who had spent many years in Tasmania. "The evidence is irresistible", he wrote, "that the destruction of the blacks is the aim as well as the result of our colonial policy: that we have undoubtedly acquiesced when we have not participated, and that the guilt of these horrible massacres must finally rest with the Government, which is too weak to prevent [it] because it is unwilling to punish them".[28]

In the nineteenth century, the murderous consequences of the racial divide between the "civilized" and the "primitive" was confined largely to the non-Western world. In the twentieth century, that barbarism came home to Europe.

IV

"It is not possible to treat European countries as colonies", Benito Mussolini complained of his ally Adolf Hitler's war policy in 1941. Mussolini had no problem in dealing with non-Europeans in the most savage fashion. Six years earlier, Italian troops had waged a brutal war against Ethiopians, Il Duce ordering his commanders to "pursue a systematic policy of terror and extermination". That they did, using mustard gas, mass killings and torture. In February 1937, at least 20,000 civilians in Addis Ababa, around 20 per cent of the city's population, were killed in the Yekatit 12 massacre. A quarter of a million Ethiopians perished in the war. The Italian minister for the colonies, Alessandro Lessona, dreamed of an "Ethiopia without

Ethiopians". Europeans, though, Mussolini believed, should not be treated in the same way. That, however, is just what the Nazis set out to do. Not all Europeans, just those that were not considered truly European.[29]

The National Socialist German Workers' Party—the NSDAP, or the Nazis—was forged in the debris of the First World War. It drew upon the wellspring of Romantic nationalism, reactionary anti-modernism and ferocious antisemitism that had long watered the radical right in Germany. But "unlike their spiritual precursors, who had theoretical or philosophical pretensions", the historian Arno Mayer observes, "the early Nazis were engaged in political struggle, not in intellectual disputation. The old social critics had spoken to educated and elite audiences, with pedantic books, abstract arguments, and sober voices. By contrast, the fledgling Nazis and their ilk addressed popular audiences with fiery words and pamphlets", creating "an ideology of political combat".[30]

What defined the NSDAP was its ferocious hatred of Jews. It was also its equally ferocious hatred of Marxism and Bolshevism. The Bolshevik and the Jew were both incarnations of modernist decadence, social disorder and cultural defeat. Marxism, Hitler wrote in *Mein Kampf*, his 1925 autobiographical manifesto, was "a Jewish doctrine" that "rejects the aristocratic principle of Nature and replaces the eternal privilege of power and strength by the mass of numbers and their dead weight" and "contests the significance of nationality and race". It "systematically plans to hand the world over to the Jews", who had found in it a "weapon [with] which... to subjugate and govern the peoples with a dictatorial and brutal fist". The Russian Revolution was a Jewish conspiracy, "*the attempt undertaken by the Jews in the twentieth century to achieve world domination.*" The "next great war aim of Bolshevism" was Germany. The Jew was the embodiment of the grasping capitalist. He was also the embodiment of the menacing Bolshevik.[31]

None of this was new. The idea of the "Judeo-Bolshevik" was a common trope in Western debates. Winston Churchill distinguished between "national" and "international" Jews, the former being worthy, the latter members of a "sinister confederacy" that had "been the mainspring of every subversive movement during the Nineteenth Century". Jews held an "evil prominence" in the Russian

127

Revolution, and had "become practically the undisputed masters of that enormous empire".[32]

In Germany, the association of Jews and Bolsheviks emerged from the long-standing view among conservatives that the SPD was a Jewish front. In 1912, the War Ministry circulated a lengthy memo to senior officers and private organizations outlining how "Social Democracy is truthfully nothing more than the brainchild [*Geistesarbeit*] of the Jews". "Coolly, and with an iron fist", the memo concluded, "this foreign race must be removed".[33]

For much of the 1920s, despite the political humiliation and economic misery inflicted on Germany by the victorious Allies through the Versailles Peace Treaty of 1919, the NSDAP remained a tiny, barely consequential organization. Its stormtroopers, the SA, caused mayhem on the streets. But as late as 1928, the NSDAP won just 2.6 per cent of the electoral vote. Then came the Wall Street crash, the impact of which was felt more in Germany than elsewhere, leaving six million unemployed and mass desperation. The only people to flourish were loan-sharks and street fighters. In the elections of July 1932, the Nazis' share of the vote surged to 37.3 per cent, transforming it into the largest party in the Reichstag.

The Nazis drew from the traditional source of antisemitic movements: the lower middle class, small businessmen, artisans, farmers and white-collar workers who reviled ideas of equality, despised Jews, feared disruptions to the social order, and were drawn to nationalist rhetoric. But the NSDAP was able to call on wider sources of support, too, especially the affluent middle class and the business elite. The elite, both political and economic, would undoubtedly have preferred more orthodox authoritarian conservatism. But what it truly feared was working-class revolution. The end of the First World War had been marked by an attempted communist revolution, brutally supressed. The communist party, the KPD, had rebuilt itself and grown to become the largest in the Western world. In the Reichstag elections of November 1932, it took 17 per cent of the vote. Many saw the Nazis as the only force capable of crushing the communists. On 30 January 1933, Adolf Hitler was invited by President Paul von Hindenburg to become Chancellor of Germany.[34]

V

In September 1935, at the Nazi party's annual rally in Nuremberg, Hitler announced two new race laws directed at Jews. Beginning in April 1933, Jews had already been excluded from the civil service, and subsequently from many professions, and their numbers in schools and universities restricted. Jewish doctors were banned from treating non-Jews, Jewish actors from performing on stage or screen, and Jews excluded from the military. From the autumn of 1938, Jewish passports were stamped with the letter "J". The aim, in Hitler's words, was to force Jews "into a ghetto, enclosed in a territory where they can behave as becomes their nature, while the German people look on as one looks at wild animals". It was the language of von Trotha or Roosevelt faced with the "savage peoples" of the world.[35]

The Jewish community was not the immediate target when Hitler first acceded to power. It was, rather, the organized working class. Trade unions were crushed, political parties banned and civil liberties suspended. In March 1933, less than two months after taking power, the Nazis set up on the grounds of an abandoned munitions factory outside the medieval town of Dachau, near Munich, what Heinrich Himmler, commander of the SS, called "the first concentration camp for political prisoners". Interned there were Communists, Social Democrats, trade unionists, and other political opponents.[36]

The Nazis were in a minority in the cabinet, having only four of the twelve seats. The non-Nazis, nevertheless, accepted the terror unleashed against the working class and the left. Not only did the legitimation of Nazi brutality help destroy the staunchest opponents of Hitler's regime, but the creation of a public sphere saturated by violence also helped numb people into accepting the far greater terror that was to be unleashed against Jews. And buttressing the terror were the legal restrictions, the most important of which were the Nuremberg Laws.[37]

The Nuremberg Laws formalized the racial distinction between Jews and Aryans, declaring non-Aryans to be neither Germans nor citizens. The Reich Citizenship Law established that "A Reich citizen is exclusively a national of German blood, or racially related blood". The Law on the Protection of German Blood and German Honour declared that "Marriages between Jews and citizens of German or racially related blood are forbidden" as was "Extramarital intercourse between Jews and nationals of German or racially related blood." The prohibitions applied not just to Jews but also to blacks, Asians, Slavs, Roma, Sinti and any other group deemed non-Aryan.

The spirit of the Nuremburg laws reached back into the *volkish* antisemitic history of German Romantic conservatism, from Herder to Wagner to Chamberlain. Nazi thinking was also, however, influenced by a different tradition. In the period leading up to the Nuremberg Laws, Nazi legal experts and race specialists had conducted a debate about how to formulate in legal terms the racial distinction between Aryan and Jew, searching for similar laws elsewhere. The most useful source the Nazis found was America, whose racial concepts both intrigued and excited them. They intrigued them because a nation built on the idea of equality nevertheless was suffused with laws and practices that denied such equality on racial grounds. They excited them because US law had found a way of circumventing a problem with which Germans were wrestling: how to define racial distinctions in law when in science such distinctions seemed impossible to delineate. Nazi lawyers, James Q. Whitman notes in his study of American influence on Nazi racial jurisprudence, "regarded America, not without reason, as the innovative world leader in the creation of racist law".[38]

"The dominant political ideology in the USA must be characterized as entirely liberal and democratic", Herbert Kier wrote in an article on "Volk, Race and State" in the 1934 *National Socialist Handbook for Law and Legislation*. "With an ideology of that kind, which starts from the fundamental proposition of the equality of everything with a human countenance, it is all the more astonishing how extensive race legislation is in the USA". Kier listed thirty US states that "forbid mixed marriages between white and colored races". He added, in a tone almost of surprise, that "extramarital sex between members of different races is also forbidden in several states, even subjected to criminal punishment". He seemed astonished, too, at the lengths to which Southern states had gone to segregate races, "even in prisons". The American case, he concluded, demonstrated "The necessity of segregating humans according to their racial descent" even in a nation in which the dominant "political ideology... denies that human beings have different worth depending on their racial descent."[39]

Nazis were intrigued, too, by the looseness with which Americans defined races. Heinrich Krieger, the most important Nazi scholar of American law, observed that Americans created racial distinctions through "artificial line-drawing, partly by statute, partly by the courts". The problem that the Nazis were debating—how to deal with "mongrels" or mixed-race individuals—was not an issue for Americans because they reduced everything into "two population groups: *whites* and *coloreds*" and arbitrarily assigned people to one or the other. Similarly, the lawyer Roland Freisler pointed out that every state had a different definition of what constituted "colored" or "black". The courts did not bother about strict definitions but were happy to live with what Whitman describes as an "easygoing, open-ended, know-it-when-I-see-it" attitude to racial difference. Why, Freisler wondered, should not German law also simply distinguish between Aryans and coloureds? "Every judge", he pointed out, "would reckon the Jews among the coloreds, even though they look outwardly white".[40]

The Nazis were not the first Germans to look to America as a racial model. From the 1890s, many saw in Jim Crow laws a template for the colonies. In 1906, the Imperial Colonial Office launched a worldwide search to ascertain how different countries and empires had dealt legally with mixed-race marriages. The German consul in New Orleans thought colonialists "could draw lessons for their native populations from the experience Americans have gained with Negroes". Hans Tecklenburg, vice-governor of German South West Africa, wrote to Berlin about the need for a miscegenation policy in the colony, contrasting "the degradation of the European race in the former Spanish colonies in Central and South America" with the "strict separation between Caucasians and colored Africans" imposed in "the United States and England's African colonies". German South West Africa imposed a miscegenation ban in 1905, German East Africa a year later, and German Samoa in 1912. This led to a debate in the Reichstag. When SPD deputies protested that racial laws would be a stain on Germany's reputation, one MP responded, "I have never heard that the United States' reputation has suffered even the slightest bit because of it".[41]

Ironically, the arbitrariness of American race laws led to one feature that seemed harsh even to Nazis. The "one drop" rule, which ensured that one drop of "negro blood" damned you as black, was described by a Nazi commentator as "unforgiving hardness". In the Nuremberg Laws, Jews were defined as those having three Jewish grandparents, or two Jewish grandparents while also practising the Jewish religion, or having married a Jewish spouse. *Mischlinge*, "half Jews", could be counted as Aryans, unless they were religiously observant or married to a Jew. "For Nazis of the early 1930s", Whitman notes drily, "American race law sometimes looked *too* racist".[42]

If the Nuremberg Laws, and the drive to exclude Jews from the national community, was one pole of Nazi race laws, the other was its "race hygiene" programme, eugenic laws aimed at improving the Aryan stock by eliminating the "unfit". Here, too, the American influence was important. In July 1933, the Nazi Law on Preventing Hereditarily Diseased Progeny permitted compulsory sterilization of the "unfit" including the "feeble-minded", the "physically deformed", manic depressives, alcoholics and the blind and the deaf. It was based on the American eugenicists' Model Eugenical Sterilization Law. In 1929, Harry Laughlin, who had drawn up the Model Law, published an article in the journal *Archiv für Rassen und Gesellschaftsbiologie* ("Archive for Race and Social Biology") in which he described "eugenic sterilization as the effort of the state 'organism' to get rid of the burden of its degenerate members". Four months after the first sterilization law, the Nazis moved to rid themselves of more of the nation's "degenerate members" with the Law Against Dangerous Habitual Criminals that permitted the detention and compulsory castration of certain types of "asocial" individuals. They were defined as those who "will not adapt themselves to the natural discipline of a National Socialist state", including "beggars, tramps, Gypsies, whores", as well as those whose behaviour "gives offence to the community". All could be taken into "preventive custody", a euphemism for concentration camps. Some 400,000 Germans, two-thirds of them women, were sterilized between 1934 and 1939.[43]

The eugenic policy eventually turned into the mass murder of those deemed unfit. The programme began by transferring children with congenital deformities to special "paediatric clinics" where they were either starved to death or given lethal injections. Conservative estimates suggest that some 10,000 children were killed this way, their corpses providing "research material" for scientists. In the summer of 1939, the plan expanded to include adults, too. In occupied Poland, the SS *Einsatzgruppen*, or special action groups, began shooting, then gassing, patients in mobile units. From these programmes emerged the methods of genocide used against Jews, Roma, homosexuals and other groups in the coming years.[44]

Despite all this, Nazi eugenics received considerable support from the German scientific establishment. NSDAP deputy leader Rudolf Hess's dictum that "National Socialism is nothing but applied biology" was enthusiastically embraced by scientists and other academics. Germany's most important scientific centres, in particular Berlin's Kaiser Wilhelm Institutes, coordinated much of the work. "The card indexes, charts, diagrams, maps, books, articles and statistics, which they produced", Michael Burleigh and Wolfgang Wippermann point out, "were partly responsible for the clinically comprehensive and devastatingly effective manner in which Nazi racial policies were carried out".[45]

The eugenics programme also had, until the late 1930s, considerable support from international scientists. *Eugenic News*, the publication of Charles Davenport's Eugenic Record Office, praised Nazi sterilization law as "clean cut, direct and a 'model'", from which "nothing more could be desired". In 1935, the International Congress for Population Science took place in Berlin, attended by a glittering array of international scientists. Clarence G. Campbell, president of the American Eugenic Research Association, hailed Hitler for having constructed a "policy of population development and improvement that promises to be epochal in racial history", setting "the pattern which other nations and other racial groups must follow if they do not wish to fall behind in their racial quality". American philanthropic organizations such as the Rockefeller and Carnegie Foundations poured money into German research programmes and institutes, the Nazi takeover doing little to give them pause. Not till 1939 did Rockefeller cease funding for German projects.[46]

By the end of the 1930s, distaste for Nazi policies had stemmed the influence of more hardline eugenicists outside Germany, giving greater hearing to "reform eugenicists". The latter believed in the sterilization of the unfit but, while accepting ideas of racial superiority and inferiority, were often hostile to Nazi racial practices, especially towards Jews. Many, the historian Stefan Kühl notes, expressed "simultaneous criticism of Nazi antisemitism and enthusiastic support for the Nazi eugenic programme".[47]

Even the outbreak of the Second World War did not sever all links, especially with American racial thinkers. The geneticist TUH Ellinger visited the Kaiser Wilhelm Institutes in the winter of 1939–40, and on his return wrote an article for the *Journal of Heredity* in which he insisted that the treatment of Jews was not persecution but "a large-scale breeding project, with the purpose of eliminating from the nation the hereditary attributes of the Semitic race". The journalist and white supremacist Lothrop Stoddard, whose works, especially *The Rising Tide of Color* and *The Revolt Against Civilization*, were widely read in Nazi circles, visited Germany in late 1939. Stoddard met Himmler and had an audience with Hitler. "At that moment I was bidden to the Presence", he rhapsodizes about his encounter with the Führer. He was also invited to sit on the bench in one of the Higher Hereditary Health Courts that made the final decisions on whom to sterilize. Appearing before the court, Stoddard wrote, was a man "rather ape-like in appearance", another "obviously unbalanced mentally", and a "deaf-mute girl... not feeble-minded, but [with] a poor family record". Stoddard would have sterilized all three and seemed disappointed that the court reserved judgment until it received further details, a stance he thought "too conservative".[48]

VI

"What India was for England, our territories of Russia will be for us... Like the English, we shall rule this empire with a handful of men." So insisted Hitler as German tanks rolled towards Moscow in September 1941.[49]

The German desire for its own empire was deep-rooted in its history. On unification in 1871, driven both by a sense of wanting to act as a Great Power and by the call of *Lebensraum*, Germany flexed its muscles in Africa and the Pacific. Having arrived late on the imperial scene, however, there was little chance of carving out more than a briar patch to the grand English garden. Even that briar patch was snatched away under the Versailles Treaty of 1919.

In the years after the First World War, eyes turned east rather than south. "For Germany... the only possibility of carrying out a healthy territorial policy lay in the acquisition of new land in Europe itself", Hitler wrote in *Mein Kampf*. Yearnings for a "Greater Germany" and demands for colonies in the east also ran deep in history. They were usually wrapped in racial contempt for Slavs, a contempt that seeped across the political spectrum. For Heinrich von Treitschke, one of the most influential nineteenth-century German historians, and a liberal turned reactionary nationalist, "hatred of Slavs... is deep in our blood". The Slav "seems to us a born slave". Friedrich Engels, for very different reasons, saw Slavs as "reactionary peoples". He welcomed the possibility of Germans, Austrians and Magyars "gaining their freedom" by taking "bloody revenge on the Slav barbarians". And for many German liberals of the 1848 generation, nationalist aspirations often took on colonialist and anti-Slavic forms. "Our right is that of the stronger, the right of conquest", one delegate at the Frankfurt Parliament thundered about Germans living under Slavic rule. "Legal rules appear nowhere more miserable than where they presume to determine the fate of nations."[50]

For Hitler, Jews and Slavs were "Asiatics" who "had to be driven out of Europe". Just as the persecution of Jews was viewed by Nazis as analogous to America's treatment of its black population, so it was with Slavs. "We are here in the midst of negroes", a German official said of Ukraine in 1942. Hitler looked upon Ukrainians "as Redskins". "We'll supply the Ukrainians with scarves, glass beads and everything that colonial people like", he contemptuously remarked. The colonial character of the eastern conflict was reinforced by the use of Africa veterans. Viktor Böttcher, deputy governor of Cameroon before the First World War, became the administrator of the Polish lands of Posen. Franz Ritter von Epp, who had participated in the Herero and Nama genocide, was in 1933 appointed Governor of Bavaria, presiding over the construction of the Dachau concentration camp. The following year, he became head of the Nazi Party's Colonial Policy Office.[51]

The perception of the war in the east as, in Hitler's words, "a brutal racial war which would admit no legal restrictions" intensified its savagery. There was an extraordinary divergence in casualty figures on the Eastern and Western fronts. While Britain and America lost fewer than half a million combatants, at least eight million Soviet soldiers perished. By the end of 1941, six months into the invasion of the Soviet Union, an astonishing two million Soviet prisoners had died in German hands; by the end of the war the figure stood at around 3.3 million—more than half of all Soviet POWs. As a group, only Jews suffered a greater loss or more brutal treatment. In contrast, of the 231,000 British and American prisoners held by the Germans, around 8,300—3.6 per cent—died in German custody. The Germans fought on the Western Front as if in a "normal" war against civilized nations. The Eastern Front, on the other hand, was more like the kind of conflict they had waged in South West Africa. The war against the Soviet Union was for Hitler a *Vernichtungskrieg*, or "war of annihilation", just as the suppression of the Herero and Nama had been.[52]

The savagery evolved into deliberate mass killings both by the Wehrmacht, the German army, and the SS *Einsatzgruppen*, the latter often staging their operations as public spectacle. In the first nine months of the war, the *Einsatzgruppen* are thought to have exterminated more than half a million people, mostly Jews. Here lie the origins of the "Final Solution". The question of when the Nazis set out to exterminate all Jews has been the focus of much historical debate. Recent research suggests that what began as the racial hatred and persecution of Jews was eventually transformed through the chaos and savagery of war, and in particular of the invasion of the Soviet Union, into the Final Solution as the "answer" to the "Jewish question". A determination to force Jews out of Germany, and more broadly Europe, through emigration, became, as Hitler's forces pushed eastwards, a plan to physically eliminate them.

In the autumn of 1941, the SS and officials in the "General Government", the name for German-occupied Poland, launched an extermination programme that was later codenamed "Operation Reinhard" in honour of assassinated SS leader Reinhard Heydrich.

Three concentration camps—Belzec, Sobibor, and Treblinka—were specially constructed, run largely by personnel from the earlier eugenics programme. Other concentration camps, most notably Auschwitz, were transformed into death camps.[53]

In January 1942, at the infamous Wannsee conference on the outskirts of Berlin, senior SS figures and government officials met to map out the implementation of the Final Solution. "Step by step we have forced Jews out of all levels of German life", Heydrich told the meeting. "We have forced them out of the *Lebensraum* of the people partly by transfers to concentration camps... We have seen since the beginnings of the war the liquidation of hundreds of thousands of Polish, Baltic and Russian Jews... The Jews remaining in the Reich and all Jews in our present and future spheres of influence will be evacuated to the east for the final solution".[54]

VII

Filip Müller's account of his time as a prisoner in Auschwitz is barely readable, not because it is poorly written, but, to the contrary, because so profoundly, intensely tormenting is its depiction of the horror:

> The damp stench of dead bodies and a cloud of stifling, biting smoke surged out towards us. Through the fumes I saw vague outlines of huge ovens. We were in the cremation room of the Auschwitz crematorium. A few prisoners, the Star of David on their prison uniforms, were running about. As the glow of the flames broke through the smoke and fumes, I noticed two large openings: they were cast-iron incinerators. Prisoners were busy pushing a truck heaped with corpses up to them. Stark pulled open another door. Flogging Maurice and me, he hustled us into a larger room next door to the cremation plant. We were met with the appalling sight of dead bodies of men and women lying higgledy-piggledy among suitcases and rucksacks. I was petrified with horror... A violent blow accompanied by Stark yelling: "Get a move on! Strip the stiffs!" galvanized me into action. Before me lay the corpse of a woman. With trembling hands and shaking all over I began to remove her stockings... I was like one hypnotised and obeyed each order implicitly... It took some time before I began to realize that there were people

lying there at my feet who had been killed only a short while before. But what I could not imagine was how so many people could have been killed at one time.[55]

However much one accepts Roman playwright Terence's celebrated line *Homo sum, humani nihil a me alienum puto*—"I am human, and I think nothing human is alien to me"—it is difficult not to imagine Auschwitz as completely alien to the human experience. The savagery of the Nazis, and of the Final Solution, seems beyond the grasp of humanness.

Yet, not only were Nazis human, but so also was their barbarism. Ideas of racial inferiority, the depravity of punishments imposed on "savages", the celebration of the extermination of whole peoples—all were stitched into Western culture long before 1933. Shark Island was not Auschwitz, but it was a step along the way to the creation of the death camps. Some of the most grotesque features—such as forcing prisoners to clean up after the killings—were to be found in South West Africa. There, captives were even forced to boil the severed heads of the dead—many of whom would have been a son, a daughter, a mother, a father, a friend—and "scrape the flesh, sinews and ligaments off the skulls with shards of broken glass" so they could be packed in crates to be shipped to German museums and universities.[56]

Many worry that to "historicize" the Holocaust—to attempt to understand it using the same historical tools that would be applied to other periods or societies—is to degrade the sense of the uniqueness of the Final Solution, and to normalize the Nazi period. This question became the central theme of the *Historikerstreit*, or historians' debate, that raged in Germany in the 1980s. In a response to Martin Broszat, one of the most eloquent advocates of the historicization of Nazism, Saul Friedländer recalled Hannah Arendt's observation that the Nazis had tried to "determine who should and who should not inhabit the world". "*This*", he insisted, "*is something no other regime, whatever its criminality, has attempted to do.*"[57]

It is true that historicizing Nazism opens up the possibility that we lose the sense of the depth of its malevolence; the possibility, too, that we come to see the Holocaust as just another atrocity among many in the twentieth century. There is a danger, too, of erasing the specific character of antisemitism—its rootedness in

ideas of global conspiracy and in hostility to modernity and cosmopolitanism. In trying to avoid this peril, we should not, however,
fall into the opposite trap of failing to recognize how much the Nazis
drew upon pre-existing cultural attitudes and practices; that ideas
about extermination and about "who should and should not inhabit
the world" were commonplace in discussions of colonialism and
"primitive peoples". If we fail to recognize this, we not only
entrench historical amnesia about colonialism, but also face the
jeopardy of normalizing colonial behaviour and attitudes. There is
a thin line to navigate and a danger of falling off on both sides.

The truth that Europeans have to face about Nazism, the
Martinique poet and statesman Aimé Césaire wrote, is that "before
they were its victims, they were its accomplices; that they tolerated
that Nazism before it was inflicted on them, that they absolved it,
shut their eyes to it, legitimised it, because, until then, it had been
applied only to non-European peoples."[58]

6

WHOSE UNIVERSAL?

I

"The freedom you and I enjoy to-day", Frederick Douglass told the audience at Chicago's Quinn Chapel in 1893, during the World's Fair being held in the city, "is largely due to the brave stand taken by the black sons of Haiti ninety years ago… Their swords were not drawn and could not be drawn simply for themselves alone. They were linked and interlinked with their race, and striking for their freedom, they struck for the freedom of every black man in the world."[1]

Douglass, one of the great figures of nineteenth-century America, a former slave and abolitionist who acquired an almost sage-like status in the post-Civil War nation, was not alone is his understanding of the significance of the Haitian Revolution. Throughout the century, and well into the twentieth, it became an inspiration for those struggling for their freedom, not just in America, but throughout the world. Yet, today, that Revolution, and its significance, is almost forgotten, certainly in Europe and America.

The Haitian Revolution, which began in August 1791 and culminated in the independence of Haiti on 1 January 1804, was the third of the great Enlightenment revolutions following the American and the French, in 1776 and 1789 respectively. It began as an insurrection by slaves and ended as a national liberation struggle. It was in Haiti, Aimé Césaire reflected, that the colonial knot was first tied when Christopher Columbus landed in 1492. It was also the place, Césaire added, where the knot of colonialism began to unravel as "black men stood up in order to affirm, for the first time, their determination to create a new world, a free world".[2]

141

The significance of the Haitian Revolution lies far beyond the fact that it was perhaps the first successful major slave revolt in history or that it was the first successful challenge by a black nation to the might of Europe. It also reframed the meaning of the "Rights of Man", wrenching it from the interpretation accorded in eighteenth-century Europe to the one that we accept today. Most Europeans were able both to proclaim the "Rights of Man" and accept the tyranny of servitude. The Haitian revolutionaries made such accommodation far more difficult, and in so doing transfigured the significance of the Enlightenment and of universalism.

Supporters and critics of the Enlightenment have both tended to view it as a uniquely European phenomenon. For the one, it is a demonstration of the greatness of Europe; for the other, a reminder that its ideals are tainted by racism and colonialism. Yet, as we shall see, global struggles and movements infused Enlightenment ideals with new meanings. The relationship between Enlightenment ideas and the practice of racism and colonialism was, as the Martinique-born Algerian revolutionary Frantz Fanon, observed, complex. "All the elements of a solution to the great problems of humanity have, at different times, existed in European thought", he wrote in his 1961 masterpiece *The Wretched of the Earth*. "But Europeans have not carried out in practice the mission which fell to them".[3]

Yet, the tension between Enlightenment ideals and the reality of racism and colonialism, raised new questions. From the late eighteenth to the early twentieth centuries, radicals, whether anti-colonialists or campaigners for women's suffrage, took for granted that their struggles were rooted in the universalist ideals of the Enlightenment. Through the twentieth century, however, European barbarism led many to question the very idea of universalism. Europeans, as Fanon observed, "are never done talking of Man, yet murder them everywhere they find them... in all corners of the globe". And they do so "in the name of the spirit of Europe". If Europe was responsible for the subjugation of more than half the world, what worth could there be in its political and moral ideas, which at best had had failed to prevent that subjugation, at worst had provided its intellectual grounding? Did not those challenging European imperialism also need to challenge European ideas? Such ideas, the critics argued, were tainted because they were a means of effecting European power. They grew out of a particular culture, history and tradition, and spoke to a particular set of needs, desires and dispositions. Non-Europeans had to develop their own ideas, beliefs and values rooted in their own cultures and histories. These arguments would lay the ground for those challenging injustice and oppression to cleave to what we now call the politics of identity.[4]

The next four chapters explore the shifting place of the Enlightenment, and of universalist ideals, in radical struggles and the consequences for the ways in which we think of race and identity, beginning with a look in this chapter at the significance and legacy of the Haitian Revolution.

II

Leclerc was a plantation owner in Limbé, in northern Saint-Domingue, the French colony renamed Haiti after independence. In August 1791, the slaves on his plantation, like on many across the island, rose in revolt, setting alight the cane fields, the buildings and the machinery—anything that symbolized the oppression under which they laboured. A few weeks later, after the rebels had temporarily retreated, Leclerc returned to his estate. Just one building was left standing, in which had lived the insurgents' commander. Inside, on a mahogany table, he had placed the single book that had survived the incineration of Leclerc's library—Raynal and Diderot's *Histoire des Deux Indes*. It was open on the page that warned of the "terrible reprisals" that colonists would face if slaves were not emancipated.[5]

It was revolutionary trolling at its best. It is also a reminder of the complex relationship between the radicalism of the Enlightenment and the obscenity of slavery, of both the willingness of French revolutionaries to maintain human bondage and the inspiration that Enlightenment writing could provide for slave insurrectionists.[6]

Saint-Domingue was among the richest colonies in the world, its dizzying profits built on slavery and sugar. In 1697, Spain had ceded to France the western part of the island of Española. Known by the Gallicized name of the main town on the island, Santo Domingo, it became a hub for slave plantations. Initially producing indigo, and later coffee, many planters soon turned to sugar, "the economic miracle of the eighteenth century". A raw commodity requiring much processing, sugar production created the most "industrialized" slave plantations in the Americas. They were also among the most brutal. Between 850,000 and a million slaves were brought to Saint-Domingue; almost ten per cent of the entire transatlantic slave trade consumed by French planters in the space of a century. Yet, such was the death rate, there were fewer than half a million slaves on the island in 1789. They were worked literally to death, then replaced by more slaves who, too, were worked to death.[7]

Caribbean brutality transformed France. By the eve of the French Revolution, the livelihood of as many as a million of the 28 million inhabitants of France depended directly on colonial trade. Slavery helped foment the challenge to the old order. "A new distribution of wealth involves a new distribution of power", as Antoine Barnave put it. Barnave was the most influential of the moderate deputies in the National Assembly who sought to usher out the old regime without turning the world upside down by undermining the propertied classes, including those for whom property meant fellow human beings. "This regime is absurd", Barnave said of slavery, "but it is established and one cannot handle it roughly without unleashing the greatest disorder". The National Assembly's Committee on Colonies, under the supervision of Barnave, decreed in March 1790 that neither the French constitution nor the Declaration of the Rights of Man applied to the colonies. Colonists and their property were put under the "special safeguard of the nation"; those who sought "to foment risings" against the plantation regime would be "guilty of treason". The Committee had ensured, as Laurent Dubois sardonically notes, that "the colonies were safe from the dangers of universalism".[8]

The Assembly could not even agree that free people of colour in the colonies should have the vote. Saint-Domingue had a significant proportion of freed slaves and so-called "mulattoes"—people of mixed African and European ancestry. Many were rich and themselves owned plantations and slaves. But, in a society in which white colonists were terrified of blurring the distinction between black slaves and free whites, all were denied social and political equality, often in the pettiest of ways. They were not just excluded from suffrage but banned even from "affect[ing] the dress, hairstyles, style or bearing of whites".[9]

An uprising by free people of colour in 1790 had been brutally suppressed. Its leader, Vincent Ogé, was tortured, publicly broken on the wheel, and his head displayed on a pike. The fate of the slave rebellion the following year was different. Beginning as a struggle to enforce reforms to the slave system, it turned in the course of a twelve-year-long insurrection into a demand for emancipation and, eventually, for national self-determination. Without that insurrection, Dubois observes, "the French Revolution would probably have run its course, like the American Revolution, without destroying the massive violation of human rights at the heart of the nation's existence".[10]

In September 1792, 6,000 soldiers and three new Commissioners, led by Léger Félicité Sonthonax, arrived from France, to restore order to the colony. By the time they landed, Spain and Britain had invaded Saint-Domingue, both hoping to grab a slice of the plantation riches and restore slavery. Realizing that the only way to save the colony was with the support of the rebel armies, Sonthonax issued a decree in August 1793 outlawing slavery. Six months later, on 4 February 1794, France, now under Jacobin control, officially abolished slavery in all French territories. The slaves of Saint-Domingue had forced French revolutionaries to take seriously their own revolutionary ideals.

Toussaint Louverture, a former slave who had emerged as the most audacious military commander, now pledged allegiance to the new France. Within four years, he defeated the armies of both Britain and Spain and, in August 1800, was installed as Saint-Domingue's Supreme Commander-in-Chief. Though the island was still a French colony, Louverture unveiled in July 1801 a new constitution that decreed that "servitude has been forever abolished".

In response, Napoleon Bonaparte, who had seized power in France, sent an expeditionary force, eventually reaching 100,000 troops, to restore metropolitan control and reimpose slavery. The French captured Louverture, who was to die in a prison in mainland France. But they unleashed a new insurrection, under a new rebel leader, Jean-Jacques Dessalines, who once more defeated the French. On New Year's Day 1804, Dessalines proclaimed the new, independent nation of Haiti, named after the original inhabitants of the island. In the space of twelve years, Saint-Domingue slaves had defeated, in turn, the local whites and the soldiers of the French monarchy, a Spanish invasion, a British expedition of some 60,000 men, and an even larger French force, sent by Napoleon. "The transformation of slaves, trembling in hundreds before a single white man, into a people able to organize themselves and defeat the most powerful European nations of their day", CLR James wrote, "is one of the great epics of revolutionary struggle and achievement."[11]

The Haitian Revolution was both an inspiration for those seeking freedom and a warning for those denying it. Slave revolts and freedom struggles in both America and the Caribbean found their mettle in the victory of Saint-Domingue slaves. Slave-holding nations were desperate to isolate the Revolution and prevent the spirit of freedom from spreading. The newly independent USA refused to recognize Haiti until the American Civil War of the 1860s. As the price of recognition, France blackmailed Haiti into paying it 150m francs (eventually reduced to 60m) "to compensate former colonists", a debt that crippled the Haitian economy.[12]

There were also darker lessons to be gleaned from the Revolution. Fearing that without plantation production, a liberated Saint-Domingue would not have sufficient economic heft to sustain itself, Louverture had established during the Revolution a militarized labour system in which workers were banned from leaving their plantations and faced severe punishment for slacking at their jobs. The people of Saint-Domingue were no longer slaves, and yet it was sometimes difficult to see the difference between the old order of slavery and Louverture's new wage labour system. A major uprising against Louverture's plantation regime, led by his nephew Moïse, in October 1801, had been brutally suppressed and Moïse executed.

Louverture's plantation edicts, and his authoritarian rule, were maintained by his successors after independence. These policies echoed the conflict between equality and democracy, on the one hand, and property, on the other, a conflict that, as we have seen, runs as a thread through the modern world. Even a nation born from the struggle for equality could not escape that conflict. The labour regimes and repressive rule threw light, too, on the relationship between race and class. Louverture and the new rulers of Haiti were of the same "race" as those over whom they ruled. Many had been slaves. That did not prevent them from consolidating into a new elite that could be almost as oppressive as the racialized ruling class it had replaced. That, too, is a thread that runs through the modern world.

III

Slaves had revolted against their condition throughout history. The character of those revolts profoundly changed with the coming of modernity. By the end of the eighteenth century, the historian Eugene Genovese argues, the aim of slave rebellions shifted decisively from seeking personal escape to attempts "to overthrow slavery as a social system". Early historians of the Haitian Revolution, most notably CLR James in his ground-breaking *The Black Jacobins*, placed much emphasis on the French Revolution and the Declaration of the Rights of Man, as providing, in Genovese's words "the conditions in which a massive revolt... could become a revolution in its own right". More recent accounts have downplayed or ignored the revolutionary ideology, stressing instead factors such as religion and the African cultures from which slaves had been snatched. This contrast reflects in part the accumulation of new research, and the trawling of new archives. It reflects also the broader aims of historians and the changing relationship of radicals to the Enlightenment.[13]

CLR James published *The Black Jacobins* in 1938, in a period of intense anti-colonial struggles when radicals still looked to Enlightenment ideals as the foundation of progressive movements. In the decades that followed, disenchantment with the Enlightenment became more deeply entrenched and a defining feature of many strands of radicalism. To talk of the Enlightenment as having shaped the consciousness of the Saint-Domingue rebels was, many insisted, to deny the rebels their agency. The Haitian scholar Michel-Rolph Trouillot argued that "the search for external influences on the Haitian Revolution" derives from the need to view the insurrection as having "been 'prompted', 'provoked' or 'suggested' by some higher being than the slaves themselves". Similarly, the French philosopher Louis Sala-Molins mocked the idea that Louverture "needed Raynal and Diderot to tell him in some big fat book to set himself free before he could think of doing just that".[14]

The mob that stormed the Bastille in 1789 were prompted not by a careful reading of the Declaration of the Rights of Man but by a fierce hatred of the old regime. Nevertheless, the Declaration provided a frame for the action. The assault by the dispossessed of Paris on that most hated symbol of tyranny became part of the process by which the *ancien régime* was overthrown and the principle of universalism took root as more than an abstract claim. Without the Declaration of the Rights of Man, without the ideals of the Revolution, without the writings of Spinoza or Diderot, the Bastille may still have been stormed, but it would likely not have been a historic moment in a process that brought about fundamental intellectual and social change.

Similarly, the slaves who rose up in Saint-Domingue in August 1791 did not need *philosophes* to remind them of their oppression. Against the background of the French Revolution and the Declaration of the Rights of Man, however, new possibilities were open to the insurrectionists and the revolt took on a life of its own. As the slave rebels pursued their early aims to reform the system of slavery, they were drawn to a wider and more expansive social vision, recognizing eventually in the emancipatory logic of the Rights of Man a tool more powerful than any sword or musket or cannon, and in the process transforming the meaning of universal rights. For the "emancipatory promise" of the Declaration of the Rights of Man to be fulfilled, Robin Blackburn argues, what was necessary was the "independent action of the previously excluded, oppressed and exploited social layers", the action of "radicalized *sans culottes* and slave rebels who understood that there should be no peace with slavery or slaveholders".[15]

Most Saint-Domingue slaves had grown up in Africa. The social and spiritual values of their previous lives were still deeply impressed upon them. Religion, Carolyn Fick observes, was "one of the few areas of totally autonomous activity for African slaves". For some, such as Louverture, that religion was the new faith they encountered in the New World—Christianity. Others found solace in vodou, an amalgamation of West African Vodun spirituality and Catholicism that was particularly strong on Saint-Domingue. At the same time, as Julius Scott has shown, slaves had established underground communications networks and were aware of political developments in Europe, from Parliamentary debates in London to the storming of the Bastille in Paris. The French authorities on both sides of the Atlantic were terrified about news of revolutionary developments in France reaching her colonies. The governor of Saint-Domingue, Antoine de Thomassin, comte de Peynier, confided in a letter to the French secretary of the navy, shortly after the fall of the Bastille, that "Our primary concern is for the impression this news makes on the Negroes." As early as autumn 1788, the French authorities issued orders "to abolish every press" in the French Caribbean, "in order to keep the flame of liberty from spreading to the Colonies". The colonial government ordered the seizure from any ship of "slaves coming from France, unknown passengers... papers, books, engravings and other objects capable of fomenting trouble".[16]

Despite such desperate measures, there was no staunching the transatlantic flow of ideas or news. Slaves were caught with "pamphlets printed in France, filled with commonplaces about the Rights of Man and the Sacred Insurrection" and individuals imprisoned for having read the Declaration to slaves. The adoption by insurrectionists of Enlightenment ideals was illustrated perhaps most strikingly in a July 1792 letter by three slave leaders, Jean-François, Biassou and Gabriel Belair, a letter many historians believe was actually written by Louverture, addressed to the Colonial Assembly and the citizens of Saint-Domingue. "You Gentlemen who pretend to subject us to slavery—have you not sworn to uphold the French Constitution?", the letter asks. "Have you forgotten that you have formally vowed the Declaration of the Rights of Man which says that men are born free, equal in their rights?" "The revolution which has taken place in the Motherland" had "opened for us the road which our courage and labour will enable us to ascend, to arrive at the temple of Liberty".[17]

If it is to deny the agency of Saint-Domingue insurgents to suggest that their struggle was shaped by Enlightenment ideals, it is surely even more so to claim that they were oblivious to the ferment in Europe or to deny them the capacity to push through the logic of the Rights of Man in a way that Europeans had failed to do. The insurgents helped create, in the words of Louverture's biographer Sudhir Hazareesingh, "a lively and fertile milieu in which ideas and practices were exchanged between Europe and the Caribbean, as well as between Africa and the Caribbean, where universal concepts such as freedom, justice and brotherhood were appropriated and given specific meanings" while "local ideals—such as the abolition of slavery, the rejection of racial hierarchy, and the definition of blackness" were given "universal significance".[18]

IV

On 23 July 1866, 200,000 people smashed through the railings of London's Hyde Park to hold a gathering. They had been called out by the Reform League, a campaign for extending the vote to working-class men. The League harnessed the spirit of the Chartists, the mass working-class movement for political reform that had faded by the 1850s, and of the rising power of trade unionism and socialism. A Reform Bill to extend suffrage to the "respectable" working class had been voted down by Parliament. In response the League organized nationwide protests. The government banned a proposed rally in Hyde Park. The demonstrators marched anyway, to be confronted by police. Three days of rioting followed.

"The conduct of the police in Hyde Park", Edward Beesly, a friend of Karl Marx, wrote in the working-class journal *Bee-Hive* a few weeks later, has "illustrated Jamaica on a small scale. In both instances wealth and respectability employed the executive apparatus to put down the lower orders."[19]

"Jamaica" was a reference to the brutal suppression of the Morant Bay rebellion by the island's governor John Eyre the previous year. There was little comparison between the violence meted out to Jamaican rebels and to the Hyde Park protestors. Nevertheless, working-class radicals had from the beginning condemned Eyre's actions and drawn parallels between the treatment of black people abroad and the working class at home. In December 1865, shortly after news of Eyre's brutality had reached this country, a *Bee-Hive* columnist with the nom de plume "Plain Dealer" insisted that the repression was an issue for British workers because black Jamaicans were as working class as they were: "Though their skin is black, their hair woolly, their noses flat, and their lips thick, they are entitled to the same consideration and sympathy as working-men of fair complexion". It was a theme to which he continually returned through the following year. "It makes no difference", he wrote in

September 1866, "that what Governor Eyre did was in Jamaica and not in England... The tragedy enacted at Morant Bay is not a whit more justifiable, by any reasons known to British law, than it would have been had the space before the Mansion House and the Royal Exchange been the theatre of the exploit." "Those of our countrymen who, in any dispute between black and white, confine their fellow-feeling to that side where they find complexions like their own", he added, "are not to be trusted".[20]

Eight years before the Morant Bay rebellion there had been another, even more historically significant, uprising—the so-called Indian Mutiny of 1857. For most Indians, it was not a mutiny but the first Indian independence revolt. Its brutal suppression was largely ignored by the British press. Politicians and journalists whipped up hysteria instead about the supposed barbarism of the rebels. There were, however, radical working-class voices who backed the insurgents. An editorial in the Chartist *The People's Paper*, insisted that "the Revolt of Hindostan" was no different to struggles for freedom by European peoples. Many Britons had supported Poles in their conflict with Russia and Hungarians with Austria. They should equally support the struggle of Indians against Britain. Another editorial acknowledged that "we have avowedly shown ourselves on the Indian side" because support for "democracy must be consistent". Again making the comparison with European struggles, it observed that anyone who says "'I am for Hungary, and against India'... lies against himself, against principle, against truth, against honour". "Right is right and truth is truth", it concluded, and "the Hindhus have both on their side".[21]

What we are seeing here is the development of two distinct, indeed antagonistic, notions of universalism, the liberal and the radical. The kind of universalist sympathy expressed by Plain Dealer and by *The People's Paper* stood in opposition to the kind of universalism that could justify that which they were opposing. Liberals, as we saw in Chapter 2, viewed European rule as necessary to allow the "barbarian" world to advance towards civilization.

John Stuart Mill was the great liberal philosopher of the Victorian era, whose book *On Liberty* is still seen as one of the foundational works of liberalism. A staunch abolitionist and opponent of hardline racism, Mill was a key figure in the Jamaica Committee, set up to prosecute Eyre for his murderous policies in Jamaica. He was also a strong proponent of colonialism. Mill, who spent much of his life working for the East India Company, saw colonialism, like his father James Mill, as obligatory in bringing civilization to the less advanced peoples of the world. He believed, like all classical liberals, that "over himself, over his own body and mind, the individual is sovereign", and that such sovereignty could be curtailed only "to prevent harm to others". This doctrine, applied, however, "only to human beings in the maturity of their faculties". Children could not be afforded such freedom. Nor could "childish" peoples. "Despotism", Mill believed, "is a legitimate mode of government in dealing with barbarians, provided the end be their improvement". Until a people or a society shows itself "capable of being improved by free and equal discussion", liberty "has no application". For such peoples "there is nothing... but implicit obedience to an Akbar or a Charlemagne". Or a Britannia.[22]

Mill did not view the backwardness of a "backward" people as necessarily racial or unchangeable, as Carlyle or Gobineau did. He believed, at least implicitly, that all peoples could become civilized and worthy of liberty. But many could do so only through enlightened despots guiding them to a higher place. Mill's opposition to Eyre was rooted in his belief that the Governor's actions were incompatible with the "improvement" of his colonial subjects.

Where The People's Paper saw the Indian Mutiny as a "national insurrection" that all those defending liberty should support, Mill wrote a long memorandum, in the wake of the rebellion, defending the East India Company's rule, and listing all the improvements it had brought to India, in tax reforms, educational advancements and infrastructure. It was not that Mill supported the violence meted to the Indian rebels. It was rather that in his view the beneficence of colonial rule outweighed any atrocity or denial of rights.[23]

For radicals, liberty and equality were the prerogative of all rather than the privilege of the civilized few. They did not just oppose tyrannical rule in the colonies; they also celebrated those who rose up against colonial tyranny. "We are the savages" wrote the English poet and abolitionist Percival Stockdale about Haiti revolutionaries, echoing the views of Diderot about conquistadors; "the Africans act like men; like beings endowed with rational and immortal minds". It was not a view that Mill, for all his liberalism, could come close to accepting.[24]

The radical hostility to colonialism that figures such as Diderot and Stockdale had expressed in the eighteenth century had largely disappeared by the nineteenth. Liberal imperialism became the dominant view. Radicalism, and the expansive, inclusive vision of the universal that it embodied, was not, though, entirely expunged. From the backing of *The People's Paper* for Indian rebels to the support of Lancashire mill workers for the boycott of Southern cotton during the American Civil War, despite great hardship to themselves, that strand of international solidarity was sustained. Only in the twentieth century would it fully flourish, and then largely in the voices of the colonized themselves.

V

George Padmore called it "an inspiration to Africans and other colonial peoples still struggling for their freedom from the yoke of white imperialism". For Ngũgĩ wa Thiong'o, it was the "one book" he would make "every black person read". Anti-apartheid activists in South Africa tore the book "into clusters of a few pages, to be circulated a little at a time"; they would "study each fragment closely and then pass it on to the next eager reader". Stokely Carmichael was "moved and inspired" and "overwhelmed by it". Martin Luther King Jr., was delighted to receive a copy via Louis Armstrong.[25]

If the Haitian Revolution was a beacon for those struggling against enslavement and colonial rule, *The Black Jacobins*, CLR James's magnificent, poetical portrait of the Revolution, became an inspiration to a new generation of radicals leading struggles against colonial rule and white supremacy. An almost seamless synthesis of novelistic narrative, factual reconstruction and polemical argument, *The Black Jacobins* (1938) helped transform both the writing of history and history itself. Three decades before historians such as Christopher Hill and EP Thompson began producing "history from below", James told of how the slaves of Saint-Domingue had been not passive victims of their oppression but active agents in their own emancipation. And, in telling that story, he created a work that was to become indispensable to a new generation of Toussaint Louvertures, a new cadre of anti-colonial leaders in Africa, Asia and the Caribbean. Louverture was significant to James not just because he had led the first great slave revolution; it was also that in so doing, he had made concrete the distinction between the immorality of European colonialism and the moral necessity of the ideas that flowed out of the Enlightenment. Most importantly for James, Louverture had shown how a struggle for emancipation could transform the meaning of universalism.

Born in Trinidad in 1901, Cyril Lionel Robert James is one of those towering figures of the twentieth century who, like the Revolution he so eloquently depicted, is all too rarely recognized as such. Novelist and orator, philosopher and cricketer, historian and revolutionary, Trotskyist and Pan-Africanist—there are few modern figures who can match his intellectual depth, cultural breadth or sheer political contrariness.

Black Jacobins was written at the end of a six-year sojourn in Britain in the 1930s during which a man who described himself as having "lived according to the tenets of Matthew Arnold, spreading sweetness and light and the best that has been thought and said in the world" was transformed into a herald of world revolution. London was then one of the vortices of the African and Caribbean diaspora, a city where writers and activists, poets and radicals, politicians and intellectuals, could meet, exchange ideas and forge alliances. It was here that Kwame Nkrumah met Amy Ashwood Garvey, where Jomo Kenyatta confided in George Padmore, where CLR James dined with Ras Makonnen. And at the heart of this intellectual ferment was the debate about race, class, imperialism and identity.

It was not in London that James' transformation from Arnoldian to revolutionary began but in the tiny Lancashire town of Nelson, home to his friend Learie Constantine. A legendary cricketer who had taken the West Indies' first wicket in Test cricket against England in 1928, Constantine had become tired of racism and the lack of opportunities for black players in the West Indies. So, he accepted an offer to play for Nelson, a team in the Lancashire League.

Nelson was a small Pennines town built around cotton with a tradition of working-class activism and municipal socialism. Decades later, James remembered that the radicalism of the mill workers made him question his gradualist views, helping "to educate" him, teaching him that social change could not be imposed from above but must surge up from below, that only through mass movements, and the continual extension of democracy, could real change come about.[26]

What also educated James was reading Leon Trotsky's *History of the Russian Revolution*. A magnificent, passionate account that interwove drama and polemic, Trotsky's work pushed James towards a decades-long fraught but profound engagement with Marxism. It also helped shape James' thinking about the Haitian Revolution, leading him to view it in some senses through the lens of a more modern revolution.

It was not just Trotskyism to which James was drawn. He became also a key leader of the Pan-Africanist movement. The belief that peoples of African descent had a common set of interests, Pan-Africanism sought to establish unity within the African diaspora. Trotskyism and Pan-Africanism may not seem the most compatible of bedfellows, the one viewing social relations primarily through the lens of class, the other defining solidarity in racial terms. James himself was clear where he stood on this issue. "The race question is subsidiary to the class question in politics, and to think of imperialism in terms of race is disastrous", he wrote in *The Black Jacobins*. "But to neglect the racial factor as merely incidental [is] an error only less grave than to make it fundamental."[27]

Given this unambiguous view on the relationship between imperialism, race and class, why was James drawn to Pan-Africanism? In part, the answer lies in the various meanings that Pan-Africanism possessed in the 1930s, and meanings different to those we might attribute to the term today. In part also the support of communists for Pan-Africanism expressed the significance of empire in shaping both global and class politics. Today, decades after decolonization, it can be difficult to grasp the degree to which a brutally naked form of imperialism dominated the globe. It can be difficult also to conceive the depth of often violent opposition to imperial rule, from mass strikes to national liberation movements. "Decolonization" is often imagined as a process by which the colonial powers "granted" independence to their colonies as a benevolent gesture. The decades of fierce struggle, and the ferocious suppression of such struggles, have been largely erased from public consciousness and left to moulder in archives and historians' texts.

Pan-Africanism in the 1930s stitched together two distinct political outlooks. For the "essentialists", there was an unbreakable thread running through the history and needs of the peoples of Africa. For the anti-capitalists, Pan-Africanism only had meaning in the struggles against imperialism and oppression, struggles defined by class as much as race, and which could pit African against African, as much as black against white. It was a distinction between those who drew on Herder's philosophy and those who were inspired by Louverture's actions. That tension was to shape the politics of anti-racism not just in the 1930s but ever since.

VI

Slavery had created the conditions for a sense of a common black identity spanning the Atlantic. From the eighteenth century on, black sailors, wharf-workers and fishermen, many of them enslaved, who criss-crossed the ocean, helped create what later came to be called the "black Atlantic". It is a resonant phrase that Paul Gilroy in particular has used to reflect on the nature of "black internationalism" and of the black diaspora. Having been snatched from their homelands and living in enforced degradation without dignity or hope, the identities of Africans, both those enslaved and those who had acquired freedom, had to be recreated and stretched across continents. Olaudah Equiano was a former slave who became a writer and abolitionist. In his autobiography, his "identity" is one that continually changes. He begins his narrative as an Eboe from Benin, becomes "almost an Englishman", after having spent so much time on a ship with English company, before beginning to see himself as an "African". The term "African" was first used by European explorers and slavers, erasing the various identities that existed on the continent. It became appropriated by those whose identities had been erased. "Africa" was an idea as much as a place; to be "African", an attempt to wrest a sense of belonging from a condition in which belonging had been denied first by slavery and then by the refusal of equality and true citizenship.[28]

Until the nineteenth century, such diasporic consciousness was more a felt sense than an articulated view. Through the nineteenth century, black writers began establishing a philosophical and political case for what came to be called Pan-Africanism. Perhaps the most influential was Edward Wilmot Blyden. Born in 1832 in the Danish West Indies (now the US Virgin Islands), he emigrated to Liberia after having been refused admission into American theological colleges because of his race. Established by the American Colonization Society to solve the "Negro problem" by finding black Americans somewhere to live outside of the USA, Liberia was welcomed by those who dreamed of a "return to Africa". As a newspaper editor, an academic at, and eventually president of, Liberia College, the nation's first university, and ambassador to both Britain and America, Blyden played a major part in the nation's development.

Blyden's philosophy changed considerably during his time in Liberia. He began by supporting political independence for "Negro states" but viewing with contempt African traditions. He came eventually to value traditional African mores and cultures but thought colonialism necessary for the development of the continent. Every race, Blyden wrote, "has developed for itself such a system or code of life as its environments have suggested", each "*distinct* but equal". Racial mixing led to degeneration and "no mongrel state can succeed". The echoes of Herder are unmistakable, as is the Jim Crowish "equal but different" claim. Many of these ideas became woven into Pan-Africanist thought. Blyden's claim of a distinct "African Personality", for instance, was adopted by Kwame Nkrumah, leader of post-independence Ghana, and perhaps the most significant Pan-Africanist figure of the postwar years.[29]

Blyden's ideas were cemented, too, into the foundations of Marcus Garvey's worldview. As the most important "back to Africa" polemicist of the early twentieth century, Garvey's ideas shaped the essentialist wing of Pan-Africanism. Born in Jamaica in 1887, he moved to the USA in 1916, after spells living in Central America and in England. In 1914, he had established his Universal Negro Improvement Association (UNIA) which sought "to improve the condition of the race" by "establishing a Nation in Africa where Negroes will be given the opportunity to develop by themselves". He set up chapters in America, beginning in Harlem, and here it flourished, transforming Garvey into the commanding black leader of his age.[30]

Garvey was an extraordinary man, a great orator and someone who spoke to the anxieties and aspirations of black people in America and the Caribbean. He was, though, as much a demagogue

157

as a visionary, a fantasist as well as a moral guide. For all his Afrocentrism, he never set foot in Africa and knew little about it. "He talks of Africa as if it were a little island in the Caribbean Sea", the Jamaican-born American poet and radical Claude McKay derisively observed, "ignoring all geographical and political divisions" on the continent. This would become a theme in much essentialist writing about Africa. Farcically, the UNIA elected Garvey "Provisional President of Africa".[31]

Garvey's vision was not only unrooted in reality but also, in the words of the historian of black nationalism Wilson J. Moses, "authoritarian, elitist, collectivist, racist, and capitalistic". He did not want all Black Americans to emigrate to Africa, just the most talented and the "pure bred". Garvey, like Blyden and many black nationalists, opposed "race-mixing" and was contemptuous of "mulattoes" whom he thought should be left in America to "die out". His "Race First" separatism drew him towards Ku Klux Klan leaders whom he regarded as "better friends of the race than all other groups of hypocritical whites put together". "We were the first Fascists," he told the popular historian JA Rogers. "Mussolini copied Fascism from me".[32]

Garvey's principal rival as a voice for black communities, particularly in America, in the early decades of the twentieth century, was WEB Du Bois. Born in Great Barrington, Massachusetts, in 1868, Du Bois' life spanned a century of extraordinary transformation, of the world and of the place of black people in it. He was born three years after the end of the Civil War, and sixteen years before European powers carved up Africa at the Berlin conference. He died on the day of the March on Washington in 1963—the day Martin Luther King Jr. gave his famous "I have a dream" speech; by the time of his death twenty-seven African states had gained their independence. A founder of the National Association for the Advancement of Colored People (NAACP), and author of some of the most profound works on race, imperialism and American politics, Du Bois was among the most influential and significant intellectuals of the twentieth century. The old cliché of an intellectual embarking on a "journey" is probably truer of Du Bois than of most. His views continually evolved from his early liberalism to the Marxism of his old age. At the beginning of twentieth century he was a driving force behind the Pan-Africanist movement, a convenor of the First Pan-African Congress in 1919, deliberately held at the same time and in the same city as the Paris Peace Conference, and of the three other Congresses that followed in the 1920s.

His views of race, of Africa and of the meaning of black solidarity were very different to Garvey's. As a young man, Du Bois wrote in his 1940 autobiographical work *Dusk of Dawn*, he had held a rigid, biological view of race. Over time, his views shifted. "Human beings", he observes in an imagined debate with a white supremacist, "are infinite in variety, and when they are agglutinated as groups, great or small, the groups differ as if they, too, had integrated souls. But they do not." When his fictional antagonist asks him how then could he talk about "black people", Du Bois responds, "the black man is a person who must ride 'Jim Crow' in Georgia". It is a remarkably perceptive view, one that links the notion of race to the contingent practices of racism rather than to any essential quality of blackness or other forms of identity; and one that is as meaningful, and as necessary, today as it was in the days of Jim Crow.[33]

Du Bois was equally nuanced in his views of Pan-Africanism. "What is Africa to me?", he asked. "Once I should have... said 'fatherland' or perhaps better 'motherland' because I was born in the century when the walls of race were clear and straight; when the world consisted of mutually exclusive races". But, again, over time, his views had become more sophisticated. "The physical bond is least", he now believed, "and the badge of color relatively unimportant save as a badge; the real essence of this kinship is its social badge of slavery; the discrimination and insult; and this heritage binds together not simply the children of Africa, but extends through yellow Asia and into the South Seas. It is this unity that draws me to Africa." It also had to embody "a unity of the working classes everywhere". "The Color Problem and the Labor Problem", were to Du Bois, "two sides of the same human tangle". Blackness, for Du Bois, meant more than having a black skin; to be African meant more than coming from a particular continent. These were political identities, not racial or geographic.[34]

VII

Lovett Fort-Whiteman was born in 1889 in Dallas, Texas, the son of a former slave. Fifty years later, on 13 January 1939, he died in prison. Not in Texas, or even the USA, but in the Sevvostlag Prison Labour Camp in Kolyma, in the wilderness of Siberia.

In 1919, Fort-Whiteman had become perhaps the first African American to join the fledgling US Communist Party, arriving there through union activism and agitation for black rights. He soon became a full-time communist organizer. Travelling to the Soviet Union, Fort-Whiteman, like many African Americans who had grown up knowing only segregation, disenfranchisement, public humiliations and lynchings, romanticized the communist state as a land from which "every trace of racial friction has been removed". He eventually abandoned America to live in his communist utopia.[35]

It was, however, the worst time to decamp to utopia, the era of purges and famine, of unrestrained Stalinism and the Great Terror. Fort-Whiteman became entangled in Stalin's poisonous web, his criticism of black American poet and writer Langston Hughes' *The Ways of White Folks* being denounced as "counter revolutionary". His real crime was being too friendly with Stalin's enemies, in particular Nikolai Bukharin, who was arrested in 1937, endured a show-trial and was executed the following year. Fort-Whiteman was sentenced to five years' hard labour and dispatched to the depths of Siberia. There in the frozen tundra where temperatures fell to sixty degrees below zero, he toiled building the Kolyma highway. Condemned for working insufficiently hard, he was severely beaten and his rations cut. Before he starved to death, his teeth were knocked out. The first black American communist became also the only African American to die in Stalin's gulags.[36]

Fort-Whiteman's extraordinary and tragic story sheds light on one of those almost forgotten but significant episodes in the history of race—the role of black communists in challenging racism. In 1919, following the Russian Revolution the previous year, the Bolsheviks created the Third Communist International, or Comintern. (The First International had been the International Workingmen's Association established by Marx and Engels; the Second International had foundered at the start of the First World War as many of its constituent national parties supported the war, and on opposite sides.) At its second congress in 1920, the Comintern proclaimed that its task was to "liberate the working people of the entire world. In its ranks the white, the yellow, and the black skinned peoples—the working people of the entire world—are fraternally united." Two years later, at its fourth congress, Comintern declared it vital to "fight for the racial equality of blacks and whites, for equal wages and equal social and political rights" and to "force the trade unions to admit black workers".[37]

For black radicals, Comintern provided a means of locating their specific struggles within an international framework. It allowed those leading national liberation movements in Asia to make common cause with compatriots in Africa and the Caribbean, enabled activists combating racism in the metropolitan countries to reach out to anti-colonial fighters, and encouraged black militants to link their struggles to wider working-class movements. Such connections were already being made, of course, but with Comintern sporadic associations became transformed into constant exchange. The kind of universalism that the Haitian Revolution had first nurtured was now flowering across the globe.

There were major debates over how the relationship between race, class and nation should be conceived, perhaps the most contentious being the question of whether African Americans constituted a distinct "nation". There was also much criticism of national communist parties in Europe and America. Nguyen Ai Quoc (better known by his later nom de plume of Ho Chi Minh) castigated the French Communist Party, the PCF, for its failure to take seriously colonial liberation struggles and wondered whether it understood that the fate of the working class "in aggressive countries that have invaded colonies is closely tied to the fate of the oppressed peoples of the colonies". Across the Atlantic, Claude McKay commended the work of Comintern but was highly critical of American communists who had "to emancipate themselves from the ideas they entertain towards the Negroes".[38]

Comintern policies were designed to further the interests of Moscow rather than necessarily those of black workers or colonized peoples. The organization was opportunist, sectarian and often made abrupt, absurd changes to its dictates. For all the romanticization of Soviet policy, Moscow's treatment of its own minorities became increasingly deplorable. And, as Fort-Whiteman discovered, Stalin's policies could be deadly. Yet, at a time when racism was deeply rooted in labour movements, when many trade unions barred black members, when few socialist parties or labour organizations opposed colonial rule, and many supported it, Comintern's uncompromising stance on racism, imperialism and the "Negro question" gave voice to many anti-colonial movements, knitted together struggles across continents and, as we shall see in Chapter 8, helped create new forms of antiracist solidarity in America that foreshadowed the postwar civil rights movement. Stalin's policies were murderous and destructive, his "socialism in one country" helped strangle principled forms of international solidarity. Yet, paradoxically, for a short period, Stalin's Soviet Union helped sustain those who aspired to maintain more radical forms of universalism and give concrete form to such radicalism.

VIII

As dawn broke on 3 October 1935, 100,000 Italian troops crossed the shallow, sluggish Mareb River that marked the border of Eritrea, then an Italian colony, and Abyssinia (what is now Ethiopia). There were regular Italian soldiers, Eritrean volunteers and fascist Blackshirts. A smaller invading force moved into Abyssinia from Italian Somaliland to the east. Above the main force were hundreds of aircraft, behind it was a mass of artillery guns, and following them another 400,000 soldiers. Leading the cavalcade were tanks and the cavalry.[39]

Mussolini called the Italian invasion of Abyssinia "a war of civilisation and liberation", echoing British, French, German and American justifications for their foreign incursions. It was in reality, like most colonial wars, a brutal, barbarous conflict. The major powers were reluctant to confront Italy for both pragmatic and racial reasons. British Foreign Office minister Lord Stanhope insisted that to back Ethiopia "would be going back on the White Man everywhere" while the *Daily Mail* insisted that the sympathy of the British public was "wholly with the cause of the white races which Italy is so finely upholding". The League of Nations voted down Abyssinian Emperor Haile Selassie's call to deny recognition of the Italian conquest; but it did deny Abyssinia a loan with which to finance a resistance movement. The Soviet Union continued selling oil to Italy to fuel Mussolini's war machine. Many on the right hailed the magnificence of Mussolini's fascists. Few on the left took the war seriously.[40]

For those on the left committed to anti-imperialism, however, the Italian invasion of Abyssinia had a galvanizing effect. CLR James set up, with Amy Ashwood Garvey, the first wife of Marcus Garvey, the International African Friends of Abyssinia (IAFA) to mobilize opposition to the Italian invasion. The IAFA gave way in 1937 to a broader solidarity organization, the International African Service Bureau for the Defence of Africans and People of African Descent (IASB). "The Abyssinian invasion", Robert Hill, historian and James' literary executor, suggests, "marked a turning point" in black nationalism, paving "the way for the emergence of an explicitly political Pan-Africanism". James himself was more cautious. "There are some amongst our society, including myself, who believe that the only final guarantee for Africa, and for the rest of the world, is the international socialist order". Others, however, "believe that Ethiopia must be supported because God said so in the Bible". And yet others for whom racial unity was their only concern.[41]

For James, the idea of "black internationalism" made sense only as an aspect of working-class politics and of global class struggle. So it did to George Padmore, too. A fellow-Trinidadian, and a child-hood friend of James', Padmore had become a leading figure in Comintern as organizer of the International Trade Union Committee of Negro Workers (ITUCNW). He broke with Soviet Communism in disgust when, in the mid-thirties, Moscow, in one of its frequent handbrake turns, moved to close down in the name of "anti-fascism" any anti-imperialist activity directed against "democratic" imperialist nations such as Britain, France and America. Though he left the Soviet orbit, Padmore did not abandon his dedication to working-class struggles. Moving to London, he and James became close friends and comrades.

James and Padmore viewed blackness much as Du Bois did. For Du Bois, as we have seen, "the badge of color [was] relatively unimportant". What mattered was the history of "slavery... discrimination and insult", which bound together "not simply the children of Africa" but all oppressed peoples, and the working class, too. "Modern imperialism and modern industrialism", Du Bois wrote, "are one and the same system". For all three, blackness was not something to be embraced in itself, but challenged as a mark of oppression and discrimination; and if class politics meant little if it did not take seriously questions of race and imperialism, the struggle for black rights was equally devalued if not viewed through the lens of class politics. As Padmore put it in his *Life and Struggles of Negro Toilers*, his aim was not just to expose "the conditions of life of the Negro workers and peasants in different parts of the world" and to "enumerate some of the struggles" in which they were engaged, but also "to indicate... the tasks of the proletariat in the advanced countries" to help create a joint struggle.[42]

For other Pan-Africanists, there was something special about "the children of Africa" that needed to be embraced. Jane Nardal was a Martinique-born writer and philosopher who laid the foundations for what became the Négritude movement, a largely Francophone assertion of black consciousness. "Blacks of all origins and nationalities, with different customs and religions, vaguely sense that they belong in spite of everything to a single and same race", she wrote in 1928 in a celebrated essay on "L'Internationalisme Noir" in the first issue of the journal *La Dépêche Africaine*. She thought it important to encourage "pride in being black, in turning back towards Africa, cradle of the blacks, in recalling a common origin". The Negro, she added, "will have to do his part in the concert of races, where, until now, weak and intimidated, he has been silent". The black individual "must not be the copy of another race" but must "be himself... affirm his personality". This was black internationalism not merely as a means of establishing solidarity with all those suffering from racism, but as reclaiming an essentialist black identity.[43]

In the 1930s, and in the immediate postwar decades, the strength of working-class movements and anti-imperialist struggles allowed Herder to live with Louverture. Over time, the tensions between the two worldviews became less resolvable. From Algeria to Zimbabwe, from Cuba to Vietnam, as former colonies gained independence, once-radical leaders turned into authoritarian, often despotic, statesmen, many creating one-party states, and exhibiting a disregard for the poor and the oppressed. Liberation movements became senile and corrupt. The politics of class disintegrated. The kind of radical internationalism that James and Padmore championed no longer seemed plausible. All that was left eventually was the husk of identity.

"I am a man, and what I have to recapture is the whole past of the world. I am not responsible solely for the revolt in Santo Domingo." So wrote Frantz Fanon in his first masterpiece, *Black Skin, White Masks*, published in 1952. Perhaps of all the mid-century black intellectuals who engaged with the political and moral implications of colonialism and its overthrow, none more wrestled with the dilemmas of racism and universalism than Fanon. In the 1960s he became a hero of Black Power and Third-Worldist movements, embraced for his embrace of violence. The Black Panthers' Eldridge Cleaver reportedly said that "every brother on the rooftop can quote Fanon". In the decades since he has become an icon of postcolonial theorists, lauded as a critic of Enlightenment universalism and Eurocentric humanism. As Fanon's biographer David Macey sardonically notes, "the 'post-colonial Fanon' is in many ways an inverted image of the 'revolutionary Fanon' of the 1960s". Where "the Third Worldist Fanon was an apocalyptic creature", the post-colonial Fanon "worries about identity politics and often about his own sexual identity, but he is no longer angry". The real man was a lot more nuanced and conflicted than either the apocalyptic or the identitarian Fanon.[44]

Born in 1925 into a middle-class family in the French colony of Martinique, Fanon attended the most prestigious school on the island where his teachers included Aimé Césaire, one of the founders of the Négritude movement. In 1944, he enlisted with the Free French forces. Hoping to join the fight to free the world from racism and fascism, Fanon found instead that the French army itself was racially defined, with "white Europeans at the top and North Africans at the bottom" and West Indians in an "ambiguous" place in between. That ambiguity was underscored when, as Allied troops were poised to cross the Rhine into Germany, Fanon's regiment was "whitened"—the word used in official documents—by the removal of all African soldiers and turned into a "European" unit. The Martinican soldiers were retained—not white but sufficiently less "black" than the Senegalese to be acceptable. It was an experience deeply burnt into Fanon's consciousness. Before leaving Martinique, he had insisted that "freedom is indivisible", which is why he had to join up. In the dying days of the war, he wrote to his parents, that if he should be killed "never say: he died for the good cause". He had been "deluded" into helping "defend an obsolete ideal". "*I was wrong!*", he thundered in fury.[45]

But he wasn't. He remained attached to the idea that freedom was indivisible; only, he now recognized that those who most proclaimed their fidelity to freedom were often also the ones who viewed it as indelibly partitioned by race.

After the war, Fanon studied medicine and psychiatry at the University of Lyon. In 1953, he was appointed a psychiatrist at the Blida-Joinville hospital, Algeria's largest psychiatric facility, arriving just as the colony was exploding into a bloody war for independence. Realizing that he had to take sides, he resigned from his post, was expelled by the colonial authorities, and moved to Tunis where he became a figurehead for, though never part of the leadership of, the FLN, the Algerian liberation movement. Suffering from leukaemia, he died in December 1961, three months before Algeria finally gained its independence.

His first book, *Black Skin, White Masks*, explored the psychological effects of racism and attempted to explain the roots of the feelings of dependency and inadequacy that black people experienced in a white world. A black man (and Fanon primarily addresses men) in a colonial society is, he argued, only "an object in the midst of other objects". He lacks an identity because white society—which defines what is and isn't—refuses to give him one. So, he internalizes the cultural values of the colonizer and becomes alienated from himself. To "disalienate" himself, the colonized had to reject both the culture and the language of the colonizer: "To speak means above all to assume a culture, to support the weight of a civilisation". Colonial subjects had to create their own cultures, to reclaim their own histories, to be recognized on their own terms.[46]

There is an echo here of Du Bois' celebrated line in *The Souls of Black Folk* about the "double consciousness" that black people possess, "this sense of always looking at one's self through the eyes of others". There is more than an echo of Herder's argument about the disjuncture than comes when unable to view the world through one's own culture. But if Fanon demanded recognition of black people as black people—"He who is reluctant to recognize me opposes me", he wrote, and seals me "into thingness"—he was also deeply critical of essentialist arguments about blackness and black culture. In mid-twentieth-century France such arguments found greatest expression in Négritude, a movement that emerged in the 1930s, drawing on many strands of thought: the "Internationalisme Noir" of Jane Nardal, the "New Negro" movement in America, better known as the Harlem Renaissance, the "back to Africa" views of early pan-Africanists such as Edward Blyden and Marcus Garvey, and the concept of culture and language embedded in European Romantic thought.[47]

Three figures, all poets and politicians, are usually seen as the founders of Négritude: the French Guianese Leon Damas, Léopold Senghor, later to be president of Senegal, and Aimé Césaire, who all met as students in Paris. They rejected arguments for assimilation and asserted instead a pride in blackness and in black culture and history. The movement, Césaire wrote, was a means of answering the questions that Senghor had asked of him when first they met: "Who am I? Who are we? What are we in this white world?" And in trying to answer those questions they were led to viewing black people as a singular whole, whose thoughts, beliefs and ways of life were distinct to that of whites. With "its deportation of populations, its transfer of people from one continent to another, its distant memories of old beliefs, its fragments of murdered cultures", the history of black people was the history of a community whose experience was "unique". How, Césaire asks, "can we not believe that all this, which has its own coherence, constitutes a heritage?" For Senghor, this heritage had established distinct black and white forms of thinking. "From our ancestors", he wrote, "we have inherited our own method of knowledge". So, while "European reasoning is analytical, discursive by utilization... Negro-African reasoning is intuitive by participation". Senghor probably saw these as tendencies rather than as absolute distinctions. Nevertheless, it was a racialized view of cognition and of political values. It was, as Jean-Paul Sartre wrote in "Black Orpheus", his preface to an anthology of Négritude poetry, a form of "anti-racist racism", which for Sartre was "the only road that will lead to the abolition of racial differences".[48]

Fanon disagreed. Though Césaire was by now a close friend and mentor, and Sartre a great influence on his work, Fanon disdained such thinking, rejecting what he saw as the trapping of black people within a fantasy carapace of culture and history. The African cultures that Pan-Africanists and advocates of Négritude celebrated as authentically African were, he observed, "mummified" objects. Under colonialism, any indigenous culture, "once living and open to the future, becomes closed, fixed in the colonial status, caught in the yoke of oppression". Rather than supporting living cultures, constantly being made and remade through struggle, essentialists sought cultures that had been "put into capsules", embracing them as "authentic".[49]

Fanon wanted to be encased by an imagined black history no more than by a mummified black culture. "The discovery of the existence of a Negro civilization in the fifteenth century", he observed, "confers no patent of humanity on me". He would not make himself "the man of any past", nor "exalt the past at the expense of my present and of my future". "I am", he insisted, "not the Slave of the history that dehumanised my ancestors."[50]

Fanon rejected the very idea of a singular black identity. "There is nothing, a priori", he maintained, "to warrant the assumption that such a thing as a Negro people exists." Nor do all blacks have a single set of experiences. "The Negroes of Chicago only resemble the Nigerians or the Tanganyikans in so far as they were all defined in relation to the whites" but their "objective problems were fundamentally different". All were deemed "black" only because they were so categorized by racists. "The Negro is not", he added. "Any more than the white man."[51]

What gives black people their beliefs and ideals cannot derive from their blackness: "My black skin is not the wrapping of specific values". His solidarity is not with those who share his skin colour but with all those who share his ideals and will defend the rights and dignity of all people. "Every time a man has contributed to the victory of the dignity of the spirit", he wrote, "every time a man has said no to an attempt to subjugate his fellows, I have felt solidarity with his act. In no way should I derive my basic purpose from the past of the peoples of color."[52]

Fanon's dismissal of essentialist arguments was inextricably linked to his scorn for the racist ideas that undergird colonialism, for the chasm between Enlightenment ideals and colonial practice. He was contemptuous of Europeans who "are never done talking of

Man" and yet "murder men everywhere they find them, at the corner of every one of their own streets, in all the corners of the globe. For centuries they have stifled almost the whole of humanity in the name of a so-called spiritual experience." It was "in the name of the spirit of Europe that Europe has made her encroachments, that she has justified her crimes and legitimized the slavery in which she holds four-fifths of humanity". For the peoples of the colonized world to resurrect their humanity they must "not imitate Europe", nor "pay tribute to Europe by creating states, institutions and societies which draw their inspiration from her".[53]

Nevertheless, for all his disdain for European culture, for all his insistence that European ideas had helped enslave the non-European world, Fanon also accepted that, "All the elements of a solution to the great problems of humanity have, at different times, existed in European thought". The problem was that "Europeans have not carried out in practice the mission which fell to them". The non-Western world would have to "start a new history of Man", a new history that, while not forgetting "Europe's crimes", will nevertheless "have regard to the sometimes prodigious theses which Europe has put forward", a history that aimed "to create the whole man, whom Europe has been incapable of bringing to triumphant birth".[54]

What makes Fanon important is his attempt to wrestle with the duality of the European legacy, with the universalist ideals of the Enlightenment and with the depravity of racism and colonialism. It is also his attempt to reclaim the significance of universalist values for all of humanity. When Fanon writes "I am not responsible solely for the revolt in Santo Domingo", what he means is that it is not just the Haitian Revolution that defined him. It was also the American, French and Russian Revolutions, the Indian Mutiny and the Boxer Rebellion.

There was, however, a duality in Fanon's own thought. His universalist perspective could itself be blinkered. He saw homosexuality as a sexual perversion and the product of white racism; "the Negrophobic man is a repressed homosexual", he wrote in *Black Skin, White Masks*. This became the mindset of many postcolonial nations which regarded homosexuality as the product of morally degenerate colonial cultures, as a phenomenon alien to black or indigenous history, leading in many cases to the merciless persecution of gays. To view cultures as organic, to regard differences as unyielding, to understand colonialism as the product of white culture, to celebrate an all-encompassing black culture—to do so is to open the way to reactionary views about what is authentic and who "belongs". Fanon might have believed that "My black skin is not the wrapping of specific values"; he might have dismissed the "exalt[ing of] the past at the expense of my present and of my future". Yet the conflict in his thought between the pursuit of a universalist perspective and an almost Herderian desire for former colonial subjects to reclaim their own particular cultures created contradictions and blind spots.[55]

Nevertheless, Fanon's universalist perspective was vitally important, though often forgotten after his death. However constrained and conflicted his universalism, he recognized that for the ideals of the Enlightenment to be made concrete it had to be wrenched away from European hands and made the possession of all humanity.

7

SOLIDARITY FRACTURED

I

In October 1892, New Orleans came to a standstill. Three unions, the Scalesmen, the Packers and the Teamsters—the so-called "Triple Alliance"—came out on strike for a ten-hour working week, overtime pay and a union closed shop. The Scalesmen weighed commodities for shipment, the Packers loaded them onto ships and trains, while the Teamsters were drivers and general labourers. The New Orleans Board of Trade offered to negotiate with the predominantly white Scalesmen and Packers but not the mainly black Teamsters—under no circumstances, it declared, would it talk with "niggers".[1]

The three unions scorned the racially divisive tactics, refusing the employers' offer. Instead, the city's Workingmen's Amalgamated Council, a united front of forty-nine unions created that summer under the aegis of the American Federation of Labor (AFL), escalated the fight, calling for a general strike. On 8 November, 25,000 workers downed tools. Streetcars stopped running. The gas supply failed. The electricity grid shut down. No newspapers were printed. Food deliveries came to a halt.

The governor of Louisiana, Murphy J. Foster, called out the militia. Employers attempted to create an army of strike-breakers. Both failed. Within four days, the employers agreed to a ten-hour day and overtime pay (though not a union shop). "With one fell swoop, the economic barrier of color was broken down", a beaming Samuel Gompers, founder and president of the AFL, declared in a letter to John Callahan, one of the strike leaders. "The white wage-workers of New Orleans" had shown that they "would sacrifice their means of livelihood to defend and protect their colored fellow workers".[2]

The New Orleans General Strike was indeed a remarkable example of working-class solidarity in the face of racial provocation. It was also the exception rather than the rule. Even as the AFL helped build working-class unity across the colour line, it was willing to tolerate affiliated unions that barred African Americans, as virtually every union did. One of the tragedies of the American labour movement is how, despite the examples of successful cross-racial action, race became the great dividing line, among workers as in the rest of society, and in the failure of more universal solidarity, both black and white workers—most especially blacks—were grievously damaged. This chapter tells of the fraught relationship between black and working-class struggles in nineteenth-century America, and of the battle to sustain a universalist vision in the face of opposition from both without and within.

II

"What, to the American slave, is your Fourth of July?", asked Frederick Douglass in 1852 in perhaps his most famous speech. The answer was "a day that reveals to him more than all the other days of the year, the gross injustice and cruelty to which he is the constant victim". For the slave, he told his white audience, "your celebration is a sham... your denunciations of tyrants, brass fronted impudence; your shouts of liberty and equality, hollow mockery", all "a thin veil to cover up crimes which would disgrace a nation of savages".[3]

The principles contained within the Declaration of Independence, he acknowledged, were the "saving principles" of the nation; the US Constitution "a glorious liberty document". Both documents had been read, however, in such a way as to deny many peoples their rights. The "rich inheritance of justice, liberty, prosperity and independence, bequeathed by your fathers is shared by you, not by me". And, so, "this Fourth of July is *yours*, not *mine*. *You* may rejoice, *I* must mourn."

A quarter of a century later, in April 1876, Douglass gave another talk which has become equally celebrated, at the dedication to the Emancipation Memorial in Washington DC, honouring Abraham Lincoln. Attending the ceremony was President Ulysses S. Grant together with members of his cabinet, Congress and the Supreme

Court. Douglass, the keynote speaker, was bracingly honest. "Truth compels me to admit", he told his audience, that Lincoln was not "either our man or our model". He was "pre-eminently the white man's President, entirely devoted to the welfare of white men" who was "no less ready than any other President" to "protect, defend, and perpetuate slavery in the states where it existed". And yet, "while Abraham Lincoln saved for you a country, he delivered us from a bondage".[4]

Both speeches expressed the contradictions with which Douglass wrestled all his life, between the universal ideals on which the American nation had seemingly been founded and the reality of the oppression faced by black people. The very statue that topped the Emancipation memorial embodied those contradictions. It depicted Lincoln standing upright, holding the Emancipation Proclamation in his right hand, while at his feet kneels a shirtless, liberated slave, his shackles broken. Days after he had spoken at the dedication, Douglass wrote a letter to the *National Republican* newspaper expressing his misgivings. "What I want to see before I die", he concluded, "is a monument representing the negro, not couchant on his knees like a four-footed animal, but erect on his feet like a man."[5]

Almost a century and a half later, during Black Lives Matter protests in June 2020, there were unsuccessful attempts to topple the statue of Lincoln. Like Douglass, the protestors detested the message of a memorial that depicted a black man "couchant on his knees like a four-footed animal". Unlike the protestors, though, Douglass viewed the statue not simply as demeaning freedmen but also as celebrating their freedom. In his speeches and writing he expressed the tension of the contemporary "1619 vs 1776" argument long before that argument was articulated.[6]

Born into bondage as Frederick Bailey in 1817, or possibly 1818—the dates and familial milestones so important to the rest of society being one of the many humanizing features denied to slaves—Douglass escaped enslavement when he was about twenty, and took on a new name, to afford himself a certain protection as a fugitive slave. He soon became a central figure in the abolitionist movement, working closely for many years with William Lloyd Garrison, one of the most influential leaders of the struggle against slavery. The son of an immigrant seaman, and a printer by trade, Garrison founded his newspaper *The Liberator* in 1831 in frustration at the timidity of mainstream critics of slavery. It became a platform for radical abolitionists, such as Douglass.

Between Douglass' "Fourth of July" speech in 1852 and his address at the Emancipation Memorial in 1876 lay the Civil War, the defining event of nineteenth-century America. The Southern states seceded from the Union in 1860 to be free to pursue their own enslavement policies. For Abraham Lincoln, though, just elected as President, the war was not a struggle to abolish slavery. Horace Greeley, editor of the *New York Tribune*, had, in an editorial in August 1862, excoriated the President's faintheartedness. In response, Lincoln acknowledged that slavery was not his concern: "If I could save the Union without freeing any slave I would do it... What I do about slavery and the colored race, I do because I believe it helps to save this Union."[7]

Lincoln abhorred slavery but was no abolitionist. He staked his moral ground on there being no extension to slavery beyond where it already existed. And once slaves had been emancipated, he believed, they should leave America and colonize another land— preferably in Africa. It was a strain of thought that harked back to Jefferson, at the heart of which was the belief that blacks and whites could not comfortably live together. Yet, as Douglass observed in the midst of the conflict, even if Lincoln "did not recognize it", nevertheless "the 'inexorable logic of events'" would ensure that the war was "a war for and against slavery". The incipient universalism of the Declaration of Independence and the explicit universalism embodied in the struggles of slaves and of abolitionists warranted that the Civil War became a war about emancipation.[8]

In the early decades of the nineteenth century, racism and segregation became more entrenched, not just in the slave states of the South, but also in the Northern states that had abolished slavery. In 1800, no Northern state formally restricted the vote by race. In the nineteenth century, every state that entered the Union, except for Maine, did so. New York, Connecticut and Pennsylvania, which previously had a non-racial franchise, either narrowed or eliminated the right of blacks to vote. "Racial prejudice", the French philosopher and diplomat Alexis de Tocqueville noticed, "seems to me stronger in those states which have abolished slavery than in those where slavery still exists and nowhere is it as intolerant as in those states where slavery has never been known".[9]

In response, a new, militant form of abolitionism emerged in the 1820s, reframing the idea of freedom as a truly universal entitlement. Forging a radical inter-racial movement, the new abolitionists recognized that the struggle to abolish slavery was inextricably linked to wider currents of social change. They were few in number but their influence, both at the time and historically, was immense. They infused American politics with the spirit of the radical Enlightenment and helped redefine what it was to be American, demanding, for instance, birthright citizenship—the right of citizenship for everyone born in America, unconstrained by race or gender.

The new abolitionists were "immediatists", insisting on the instant, unconditional emancipation of slaves at a time when many opponents of slavery imagined it as a gradual process. They developed the concept of "human rights", which, Douglass argued, "are supported, maintained and defended for *all* the human family; because all mankind have the same wants, arising out of a common nature". The influence of the radical Reformation and the radical Enlightenment are unmissable.[10]

Abolitionists were affronted by the claim, often made by working-class campaigners, that "wage slavery" was analogous to chattel slavery. Nevertheless, many recognized that, in the words of the black newspaper *Colored American*, "The cause of the poor laboring man, white or colored, and the cause of the slave, is ONE and the SAME", because "The same aristocratic feeling—the same greediness of gain—the same disregard of their interest, and the same want of sympathy for them, are ALIKE, trampling the white labourer and the slave, INTO THE VERY DUST." Many were at the forefront, too, of the campaign for women's suffrage, and women were central to the abolitionist movement. All this led to many proslavery writers seeing behind abolitionism another spectre haunting the modern world. "We treat abolitionism and socialism as identical", wrote the social theorist and supporter of slavery George Fitzhugh, "because they are notoriously the same people, employing the same arguments and bent on the same schemes. Abolition is the first step in Socialism".[11]

III

"They work little, and that little, badly; they earn little, they sell little, and they have little—very little—of the common comforts and consolations of civilized life", wrote Frederick Law Olmsted of poor whites in the South. "Their destitution is not material only; it is intellectual and it is moral", he added. Olsted was an architect and social critic whose dispatches for the *New York Daily Times* in the 1850s were collected into a series of books that revealed to Northerners a world of which many had no comprehension. In the North, to talk of "wage slavery" was to wield a metaphor. In the South, large sections of the working class "dwelt in a shadowland enjoying a status neither fully slave nor entirely free", in the words of Richard B. Morris, one of the first historians to cast light on the lives of white workers in the antebellum South.[12]

Indentured servitude survived into the nineteenth century as white paupers, vagrants and debtors were compelled to serve years of unpaid labour. Such regulations, introduced to corral poor whites within their "shadowland", became, Morris notes, the basis for the "Black Codes" which Southern states introduced after the Civil War to maintain black former slaves in as close to a condition of slavery as possible. Pauper orphans or children whose parents were deemed too poor or incapable of bringing them up decently were bound into "apprenticeships"—a euphemism for servitude. In many Southern states, fathers of illegitimate children could also be forced into bonded service, a practice that in North Carolina ended only in 1939.[13]

Poor whites not bound into servitude lived the most degraded of lives, a "strange, cadaverous, shuffling, miserable race", as the *New York Times* described them at the beginning of the Civil War. They were "white trash", a phrase popularized by Harriet Beecher Stowe, in her less remembered novel *Dred*. They formed the pool of dispensable labour that could be drawn upon to do the most dangerous or dirty jobs deemed "too hazardous for Negro property", in Morris' words, or who could be used seasonally, as at harvest time when there was no spare slave labour. They were hired piecemeal on a daily or weekly basis, on wages depressed by their lack of economic leverage and by the ever-present possibility of using slaves for no wages at all. They lived not at the edge of but inside the void of desperate poverty, inhabiting pitiful hovels, and often suffering from hookworm because they ate dirt or could not afford shoes.[14]

No life could be worse than that of slaves, denied the most basic of human needs, and living without redemption under the shadow of the whip, of rape and bestial violence, an unfreedom that seeped into their very bones. Nevertheless, black slaves and poor whites often recognized, as they had in colonial times, the common threads of their lives, of their mutual poverty and deprivation. And, however deep-set the racial divisions, there were also "cordial and even intimate and loving relationships" across that divide, relationships that "challenged southern racial boundaries".[15]

In 1835, the South Carolina Supreme Court ruled that an individual's race "is not to be determined solely by the distinct and visible mixture of negro blood, but by his reputation, by his reception into society, and his having commonly exercised the privileges of a white man". It was "proper", the court concluded, "that a man of worth, honesty, industry and respectability, should have the rank of a white man, while a vagabond of the same degree of blood should be confined to the inferior caste". Until the "one drop rule" became institutionalized later in the nineteenth century, even in the Southern slave states "whiteness" and "blackness" were categories defined as much by property, respectability and class as by skin colour. "White privilege" was as circumscribed by class as by race.[16]

IV

The setting was magnificent: the Church of the Puritans, on Manhattan's Union Square, the design inspired by the Abbé Saint Denis in Paris, the resting place of French kings. The meeting was joyous, opening with a rendition of Julia Ward Howe's "Battle Hymn of the Republic", written three years earlier and already a patriotic Union anthem. The American Anti-Slavery Society, meeting on 10 May 1865 for its thirty-second annual gathering, had much about which to be joyous. The previous month, Confederate general Robert E. Lee had surrendered to Ulysses S. Grant, commander of the Union forces. The day before the abolitionists assembled, Andrew Johnson, who had become President after the assassination in April of Abraham Lincoln, officially declared the end of the Southern insurrection.

And yet, for all the celebration, the meeting was unexpectedly divisive. The grand old man of the abolition movement, William Lloyd Garrison, told the meeting, to gasps, that, with the victory for the Union, "My vocation as an Abolitionist, thank God, is ended". He proposed a resolution that "further anti-slavery agitation is uncalled for" and the Society be extinguished.[17]

Wendell Phillips and Frederick Douglass, two abolitionist leaders who now matched Garrison in their influence, took exception. "Absolute equality before the law and civil equality for the negro is what we demand", Phillips told the meeting, and that was a long way from being achieved. Douglass agreed. "Slavery is not abolished until the black man has the ballot", he insisted. Phillips put forward a counter-resolution to Garrison's, calling for the Society to continue its work until "the liberty of the negro [was put] beyond peril".[18]

The discord that rent the air, even within a congregation radically united in its hostility to slavery, reflected the depth of disagreement within the nation, as the Civil War ended, about the meanings of "freedom", "equality" and "citizenship", and about the kind of society America should be. As different classes and groups jostled over the values, laws and institutions that should shape the future nation, the banner of universalism became frayed, and new ruptures emerged between African Americans, white workers and women.

For African Americans, both former slaves and those who had been free, the mere removal of chains was necessary but sorely insufficient. What they wanted was the right to be treated equally in every sphere of life, from schooling to voting, from the workplace to the public square. They desired, too, sufficient economic autonomy and independence to have control over their lives. Especially for former slaves, that meant owning a plot of land— "forty acres and a mule" in the phrase of the day. Only then could one be sure of not having to work for a master.[19]

For the Southern elite, freedom meant the freedom to carry on much as before, to craft a new order that resembled that of a slave state but with wage labour. Equality and freedom were privileges not rights, to which blacks were not entitled. The elite view did not necessarily percolate throughout the South. Southern society was deeply stratified, with smaller yeoman farmers and poor whites possessing distinct views, often contrary to those of the elite. Not just racial divisions but class conflict, too, as we shall see, shaped Southern society.

For much of the Northern elite, the ending of slavery expressed the triumph of the "free labour" ideology. Drawing upon the ideas of classical eighteenth-century political economists such as Adam Smith, this stressed social success as deriving from individual effort and self-discipline, and the freedom to buy and sell one's labour on the market and to make contracts. A free market ensured untrammelled economic and social mobility and warranted social harmony between farmers, manufacturers and workers.

The rise of industrial capitalism was, however, already devouring the myth of social harmony. For Northern workers, class conflict not market idyll defined their lives. The end of Reconstruction was marked by the greatest explosion of industrial conflict in the nation's history. Among many sections of white workers, that conflict expressed itself, though, as much in hostility towards black workers as towards employers.

"Reconstruction" is the name given to the period following the war and to the attempt to remake American laws and institutions to redress the inequities of slavery, guarantee the rights of the nation's black citizens and reframe the relationship between the federal state and the South. It cleaved into three distinct periods. In 1865–6, in the immediate aftermath of the war, came "Presidential Reconstruction" when, at a time in which Congress was not sitting, Andrew Johnson defined the policies. Then came Radical Reconstruction, when Congress, enraged by Johnson's acquiescence to Southern elite sensibilities, challenged presidential authority and pushed through some of America's most consequential laws. Finally, from 1877 onwards, came the end of Reconstruction, the restoration of white supremacy, and the South's shift towards an apartheid society.

Johnson was born in North Carolina and represented another Southern state, Tennessee. He saw himself as the voice of the yeoman farmer opposed to the "slaveocracy". He was also a white supremacist. It is, he boasted in his State of the Union Speech in 1867, to "the glory of white men" that he has "the qualities... to build upon this continent a great political fabric". "Negroes", on the other hand, had "shown less capacity for government than any other race of people" and "wherever they have been left to their own devices they have shown a constant tendency to relapse into barbarism". To extend suffrage to blacks would be "to degrade it and... to destroy its power". It was, historian Eric Foner suggests, "probably the most blatantly racist pronouncement ever to appear in an official state paper of an American President".[20]

Johnson dismissed the desire of freed blacks for land and restored most plantations to prewar owners. He rejected, too, the claim that emancipation required social and political equality, readily accepting the Southern states' so-called "Black Codes" under which many states forced black workers to sign yearly labour contracts. Those who failed to do so, or to keep to their contracts, could be arrested as vagrants and auctioned off to an employer for whom they would have to work for free. Labourers leaving an employer before the end of their contract would forfeit wages already earned and, again, could be sold in auction. Several states introduced a system of apprenticeships under which courts could declare black parents incapable of raising their children and those children be assigned to employers to work for free. These measures were enforced through a system of coercive violence of state militias, private vigilante terror groups and white supremacist courts.[21]

Johnson's betrayal of black emancipation led to a fierce struggle with the new Congress, elected in 1866, in particular with the Radical Republicans, the faction of the party tempered by the moral sensibility of radical abolitionism. Through the conflict—which culminated in an impeachment trial that Johnson survived by a single vote—Congress pushed back against Southern reaction and gave life to a series of landmark laws and Constitutional amendments.

The Civil Rights Act of 1866 defined as citizens all persons born in America, except for Native Americans, all having the same right "to the full and equal benefit of all laws... enjoyed by white citizens". The Act gave practical meaning to the Thirteenth Amendment which, the previous year, had abolished slavery. The Fourteenth Amendment, approved by Congress in 1866 and ratified two years later, wrote birthright citizenship and equal treatment, as defined in the Civil Rights Act, into the Constitution. It was, however, constrained by moderation. The Amendment implicitly acknowledged the ability of states to deny the franchise to blacks. It excluded both Native Americans and women, protecting the right to vote only of "male inhabitants", the first time a reference to gender had been inserted into the nation's founding document.

Two years later came the Fifteenth Amendment which declared that the right to vote "shall not be denied or abridged... on account of race, colour, or previous condition of servitude". It, too, was a compromise that curtailed radical hopes. Congress voted down a broader proposal banning voter restriction not just on race or previous servitude but also "nativity, property, education, or religious beliefs". Ohio Representative Samuel Shellabarger protested that the law allowed states to restrict suffrage on the basis of "intelligence or want of property, or any other thing than the three things enumerated", allowing blacks to still be "excluded from the elective franchise". That was exactly what was to happen.[22]

The Fifteenth Amendment also ignored once more the demands for women's suffrage, banning restrictions based on race but not gender. The American Equal Rights Association (AERA) had been founded in 1866 to link the campaigns for black and women's voting rights. In the debate over the Fifteenth Amendment, that link was shattered in bitterness and rancour. At its 1869 convention, Douglass, for decades a prominent advocate of women's suffrage, justified giving priority to blacks. The violence and terror being rained upon African Americans made black suffrage "an urgent necessity", a matter of "life and death". Feminists, he suggested, should view the Amendment as a first step towards universal suffrage. Elizabeth Cady Stanton, a leading advocate of votes for women, eviscerated such arguments in her keynote address to the convention but did so in a deliberately elitist and racist manner. "The old anti-slavery school say that women must stand back and wait until negroes shall be recognized", she snorted. "But we say, if you will not give the whole loaf of suffrage to the entire people give it to the most intelligent first. If intelligence, justice and morality are to have precedence... let the question of woman be brought up first and that of the negro last".[23]

Earlier that year, in a speech to the first women's suffrage convention in Washington, Stanton had been even more contemptuous of foreigners and "Sambos". "If American women find it hard to bear the oppressions of their own Saxon fathers, the best orders of manhood, what may they not be called to endure when all the lower orders of foreigners now crowding our shores legislate for them and their daughters?", she asked in disgust. "Think of Patrick and Sambo and Hans and Yung Tung... making laws for... [leading women' rights campaigners] Susan B. Anthony or Anna E. Dickson."[24]

These were not, Stanton's biographer Lori Ginzberg observes, "merely figures of speech, thoughtless slips of the tongue and the pen." Rather, "Stanton was drawing upon a powerful sense of her own class and cultural superiority". And, yet, the battle lines were messy. Stanton, Anthony and countless other women were deeply invested in the abolitionist movement at a time when the public conversation was steeped in lurid myths of black male sexuality and the fragility of white women. It took considerable courage and depth of belief for white women to continue to speak up about abolitionism. That solidarity was tested, however, by the willingness of radicals to check their support for women's right to vote. Radical abolitionists had viewed emancipation not as a stand-alone demand but as part of a struggle for universal rights unconstrained by race, sex, religion or class. When the time came, however, there was little support from many of their allies to extend the demand for suffrage, or other rights, to encompass women. The racism was indefensible, but the anger generated by the betrayal was almost inevitable.[25]

The conflict over the Reconstruction Amendments was, in today's language, a conflict over competing identity claims, and perhaps the first significant such conflict at a national level. It ended, again in today's language, with the politics of identity taking precedence over the values of universality. "Mrs. Stanton will, of course, advocate the precedence for her sex, and Mr. Douglass will strive for the first position for his, and both are perhaps right", as activist Lucy Stone put it in the AERA debate. What the fallout revealed was both the fragility of the universalist vision and the ease with which a single-minded identitarian view could unleash sectarianism and bigotry. It is a lesson as important today as it was in the wake of the American Civil War.[26]

V

It was the first integrated hotel in Washington DC, and the first with a telephone. Jefferson Davis, later president of the Confederate

States, and the Radical Republican Charles Sumner had both been guests. And it was here that Reconstruction came to die.

Wormley House, not far from the White House, was owned by one of Washington's first black businessmen, James Wormley, and patronized by the nation's white elite. In February 1877, five Republicans and five Democrats met there to thrash out what came to be called the "Wormley Agreement" to fix the disputed 1876 Presidential election. The election had ended in a stalemate, with both Republican Rutherford B. Hayes and Democrat Samuel Tilden claiming victory. The Agreement was a shabby compromise under which the Democrats agreed to accept Hayes as winner on condition that all federal troops in the South returned to barracks. This would be to abandon the main protection against racist terror and allow the Democrats, in the nineteenth century the party of slavery and segregation, to consolidate their power in the region. The Republicans paid for the Presidency with the termination of Reconstruction.[27]

The retreat from Reconstruction had, in fact, begun well before the Wormley House meeting, and its roots lay, paradoxically, in changing attitudes to class as much as to race. In 1873, the economic expansion that had marked the previous decade came to a juddering halt. One of the nation's leading banking houses, Jay Cooke, collapsed after over-extending itself investing in railroads, the main driver of expansion. This triggered a financial crisis, leading to what became known as the Great Depression until that label was attached to an even deeper economic breakdown in the 1930s.

More than half the railroads fell into receivership. Some 54,000 businesses went bankrupt. Working-class life became a struggle for survival from day to day. The Great Railroad Strike of 1877, which began after the Baltimore and Ohio Railroad cut wages for the third time in a year, spread throughout the industry, and well beyond, as factory workers and brick makers, tram drivers and sewer workers, came out in sympathy or to address their own grievances. In the bitter conflict, $5m worth of property burnt down, thousands were jailed, and at least a hundred workers killed as private militias and federal troops violently crushed the strikes.[28]

A decade earlier, Republicans had embraced free labour ideology as the means to an equal and democratic society. Now, the working class was seen as a threat to social order. The Paris Commune of 1871 had excited much debate in America, revealing to many the barbarism of the common people, the reason they "were unfit to have a hand in government". It was a spectre that hung over the conflicts provoked by the depression, generating headlines such as "Commune in Chicago" and "The Red Flag in New York". A *New York Times* editorial on "Communism in America" in December 1873 cautioned workers against "listening to the violent socialistic statements of foreign agitators". A month later, another editorial on "The Communists" warned that "there is a 'dangerous class' in New York quite as much as in Paris, and they want only the opportunity or the incentive to spread abroad the anarchy and the ruin of the French Commune".[29]

The heightened fear of the working class not only eroded free labour ideology but also led many to question the ideals of equality and democracy it embodied. In a period in which racial ideas became dominant, and both social Darwinism and the American School of racial science gained purchase, perceptions of emancipation and Reconstruction were reframed. The journalist James Shepherd Pike had long campaigned against slavery. He also possessed, like many liberals of the time, racist views and a contempt for the lower orders, black and white. As Reconstruction unravelled, the racism and the contempt came to the fore. Pike's 1874 book, *The Prostrate State*, based on a series of reports he had filed for the *New York Tribune* on life in South Carolina, set the tone. Reconstruction had failed, Pike claimed, because of the "barbarism" of blacks. "Races of men", he wrote, "exhibit the same general characteristics from age to age" and "the black is a child of vice and ignorance and superstition in South Carolina as well as in Africa". Emancipation had replaced the "old aristocratic society" of the South with "the most ignorant democracy that mankind ever saw". It was "the dregs of the population habilitated in the robes of their intelligent predecessors, and asserting over them the rule of ignorance and corruption", the "slave rioting in the halls of his master, and putting that master under his feet". Pike was scornful of attempts to provide education for blacks. "They have to be taught not to lie, not to steal, not to be unchaste", he insisted, so as "to revolutionize their whole moral nature". Teaching blacks "reading and writing... merely lends a cutting edge to their moral obtuseness". Blacks had to be taught to work hard and to know their station in life.[30]

As elite attitudes shifted, so did interpretations of the law and of America's founding ideals. In a series of judgments, the Supreme Court emasculated Reconstruction legislation. In 1873, white New Orleans butchers whose livelihoods had been threatened by a Louisiana law sued; the "Slaughterhouse cases" they brought ended with the Court restricting the application of the Fourteenth Amendment. The Court insisted that the Amendment protected only rights that owed their existence to the federal government, not to the states, so legitimizing the ability of Southern states to curtail black freedom. Three years later the Supreme Court set free three white perpetrators of the Colfax massacre. On 13 April 1873, a large mob of former Confederate soldiers and Ku Klux Klan members, armed with rifles and a cannon, attacked black Republican freedmen and state militia protecting the courthouse in Colfax, Louisiana. Up to 152 black men were killed, most after they had surrendered, in the "bloodiest single instance of racial carnage in the Reconstruction era". Just three men were eventually convicted of murder. The Supreme Court overturned those convictions, insisting that federal authorities could act only against violations of citizens' rights by states, making federal prosecution of individuals who had committed racist crimes almost impossible, and giving a green light to acts of terror by vigilante groups.[31]

In 1883, the Supreme Court declared much of the Civil Rights Act of 1875, which banned racial discrimination in public transport and accommodation, to be unconstitutional. It again insisted that the Fourteenth Amendment had banned states, but not individuals or corporations, from discriminating. "When a man has emerged from slavery", Justice Joseph Bradley concluded in the majority opinion, "there must be some stage in the progress of his elevation when he takes the rank of mere citizen, and ceases to be a favorite of the laws". To be treated as "mere citizens", and not be discriminated against because of their race, was just what African Americans wanted. In the eyes of the nation's highest court that desire amounted to a demand "to be a favorite of the laws".[32]

The lone dissenter on the Supreme Court bench, John Marshall Harlan, observed that the Reconstruction Amendments "did something more than to prohibit slavery as an *institution*". They "decreed universal *civil freedom* throughout the United States". To achieve such universal freedom, Harlan insisted, Congress had the right to "enact laws to protect people... against deprivation *because of their race*". The idea of "universal civil freedom" was precisely what was now being challenged and what the end of Reconstruction foreclosed. The "Redeemers"—those that sought to redeem the region through the reimposition of white supremacy—took control throughout the South, pushing it into a new path at the end of which was the construction of a system of apartheid enforced by Jim Crow laws.[33]

"The slave went free", WEB Du Bois elegiacally lamented; "stood a brief moment in the sun; then moved back again toward slavery".[34]

VI

Frank Ferrell was an engineer, a socialist, and a lifelong trade unionist. He was also black. A leading member of the New York District 49 of the Knights of Labor, a cross-racial radical labour movement, in 1886 he was a delegate to the Knights' annual conference, held that year in the South, in Richmond, Virginia. The District 49 delegation was due to stay at Murphy's Hotel, owned by the Confederate veteran Captain John Murphy. He told them that only white people were permitted in the hotel, so Ferrell was barred. The delegates refused to segregate themselves. Instead, they came to Richmond carrying tents. Several boarded with black families. "The delegates", the *New York Times* reported, "are determined to fight the battle on the color line right in the midst of that part of the country where race prejudice is the strongest, and they will insist on carrying on what they claim is a fundamental principle of their order—that the black man is the equal of the white socially as well as politically."[35]

Ferrell was chosen to introduce Terence Powderly, the Knights' president or "Grand Master Workman", to the 800 delegates, sitting on the same platform as Virginia's Governor Fitzhugh Lee. And in the evening Ferrell joined white delegates to watch a performance of *Hamlet* at Richmond's Mozart Academy of Music, the first black man to sit in the "white" seats in the town's history.

All this created a national sensation, dividing opinion across the land and among the Knights. The *New York Herald* called District 49 delegates "anarchists" and told the Knights that "they must take the world as it is". The Raleigh *News and Observer* thought it "well that our people should be warned in time of the new and vile use to which the Knights of Labor organization is to be put". But the Philadelphia *Press* praised the stance of the New York delegates, insisting that "Laboring men struggling to better their condition have a common cause which binds them together in a common brotherhood. There can be no color line."[36]

A leader of the Knights in Richmond told the Richmond *Dispatch* that the actions of District 49 delegates were "an outrage upon the people of this city, and an insult to the Knights of Labor of the United States". A letter from a "white Virginian Knight" in the *New York Tribune* criticized, however, Virginia's "political aristocracy... which has no sympathy for the workingman, and which seeks to perpetuate its political control by appeals to race prejudice". The *Boston Herald* cited "a conservative and influential citizen of Richmond" who acidly told Northern Knights to get their own house in order: "New York and Massachusetts lodges have been the most persistent in their refusal to admit colored Masons into their lodges, and yet a party of New Yorkers undertake to force a social equality upon us that they do not practice themselves." Powderly himself wrote a letter to the Richmond *Dispatch* insisting that he had "no wish to interfere with the social relations which exist between the races of the South", but simply wanted "to encourage and help to uplift [the Negro] race from a bondage worse than that which held him in chains twenty-five years ago—viz., mental slavery".[37]

The events of Richmond illustrated the divisions and tensions that rent the labour movement. There were many organizations that recognized the importance of cross-racial solidarity and equality as a necessity not just for blacks but for white workers too. The Knights of Labor had been founded on that very basis, with its slogan "An injury to one is the concern of all". But segregation and the exclusion of black workers was common even within the Knights and the leadership was unwilling to antagonize its racist members nor wider sentiment in the nation. The New York *Freeman*, a black newspaper, accused Powderly of "craven deference to the yell of the Southern white press and the demands of white Southern Knights of Labor" and attempting to "straddle" what could not be straddled.[38]

Before the Civil War, not one trade union, in Philip Foner's words, "allowed a black worker, skilled or unskilled, male or female, to join its ranks". The war changed little. An infamous case of black exclusion during Reconstruction was that of Lewis Douglass, Frederick's son. In the summer of 1869, he was working at the Government Printing Office in Washington DC. A skilled and experienced typographer, he had learned the craft in his father's own shop at an early age. When he applied for a union card, the Typographical Union refused on the spurious grounds that Douglass had previously worked in a printing office without having been a union member. The reason, Douglass protested, was that the union barred black members. Lewis, thundered Frederick Douglass, "is denounced for not being a member of a Printer's Union by the very men who would not permit him to join such a Union". "There is no disguising the fact", he added, "his crime was his color".[39]

It was against this background that the Knights of Labor was created. Formed initially in 1869 as a secret society by Philadelphia garment workers whose union had been crushed by employers, it became within two decades the largest labour organization in America with up to a million members. Unlike previous such organizations, the Knights opened its doors to black workers and, in 1881, to women, too. There were limits to its inclusiveness—it supported the exclusion of Chinese workers from America, though the degree of its hostility is still a matter of debate. Nevertheless, the Knights established a degree of organization and unification of the American working class previously unseen.

Yet, while local organizations often put up heroic resistance to racist violence, the depth of racism within its own ranks, and the failure of the national leadership to challenge it, doomed the organization. Perhaps the most egregious betrayal was that of Louisiana sugar workers. Their conditions had barely changed since the days of slavery. Not only were they paid starvation wages, but wages not in cash but as "scrips" which had to be redeemed in plantation stores that inevitably inflated their prices. In 1886, the Knights began recruiting among the sugar workers. The following year they came out on strike for a wage rise and union recognition. The employers and the state met them head-on with terror, with state militias gun-ning down strikers, and vigilantes burning them out of their homes. The worst violence happened in Thibodaux, when vigilantes killed at least 35 people.[40]

Despite this, the strikers held firm. When the employers offered to meet most of their demands if they dropped their insistence on unionization, the workers flatly turned them down. But, strikers having put their lives on the line for the union, the union refused to provide national help. In the end most strikers were forced to return to work on the old terms. For black workers, Philip Foner and Ronald Lewis write, it was "a terrible lesson". It was a turning point for the Knights. Within a decade as blacks deserted the union, and radical whites were expelled, it had become a reactionary husk of its old self. By 1894, the Knights of Labor was arguing that the solution to the "Negro problem" was to deport blacks to the Congo Basin, Liberia or "some other part of Africa".[41]

This became a common story. Frustrated by the timidity and sectionalism of existing labour movement organizations, a new one would be established on radical principles and with the aim of sur-mounting the racial and other divisions that rent the working class. Over time, the desire of the leadership to maintain and enlarge the organization would lead it to accommodate to racist workers and unions and to betray its original principles.

By the time the Knights of Labor had succumbed to racism, it had already been supplanted as the main labour movement organization by the AFL. Founded in 1886, the AFL was, like the Knights in its early days, committed in principle to racial equality and to challenging the exclusion of black workers from unions and workplaces. The New Orleans General Strike of 1892 demonstrated what could be achieved with solidarity between black and white workers. But within four years of that strike, the AFL had dropped its ban on allowing unions that barred black workers from affiliating. Instead, it set up black-only unions in parallel with white-only unions—effectively warranting a labour movement built on segregated lines.[42]

The fact that employers often used non-unionized black labour to break strikes became the excuse to legitimize racial exclusion by unions. Black workers "have allowed themselves to be used with too frequent telling effect by their employers to injure the cause and interests of themselves as well as of white workers", claimed an AFL statement in 1901. The very racial divides that employers exploited to weaken the labour movement became the justification for entrenching those same divides within organized labour, thus weakening the movement even further.[43]

There continued to be heroic attempts at grass roots level to organize across racial lines. The work of the Industrial Workers of the World (the "Wobblies"), founded in Chicago in 1905, the most radical of union federations, the Communist Party in the American South in the 1930s, and, as we shall see in Chapter 8, the emergence of "civil rights unionism" in the interwar years that married black and working-class struggles, all demonstrated what might have been possible. But the failure of the main labour movement organizations to challenge racial divisions allowed those divisions to fester and to undermine solidarity across racial lines.[44]

VII

They came mob-handed, around 500-strong, armed with rifles and rapid-fire guns, led by an upper-crust former Congressman Alfred Waddell. Early on the morning of 10 November 1898, they marched through the centre of Wilmington, North Carolina, to the community centre where the *Daily Record* was published, said to be the only black-owned daily newspaper in America. They torched it. By now, the mob was around 2,000-strong. They marched into black neighbourhoods, destroying businesses and property, assaulting black inhabitants, and killing many in the most barbarous of ways. The death toll remains unknown but is estimated at between 60 and 300. Hundreds more were forced to flee the town to take shelter in nearby swamps. While most of the mob continued to riot and kill, a small group, led by Waddell, seized the mayor, the board of aldermen and the police chief, forced them to resign at gunpoint and drove them out of town. The mob installed a new city council that elected Waddell to take over as mayor. America had witnessed what many regard as its first coup.[45]

The Great Depression of 1873, and the class conflict that followed, signalled the unravelling of Reconstruction, and eventually the entrenchment of Democrats in city halls, state legislatures and governors' offices throughout the South. Twenty years later, in 1893, came another economic crisis and another watershed, bringing an end to the "Gilded Age", unleashing economic turmoil and social conflict, and resetting political norms. Factory workers, black and white, were thrown on the scrapheap, and farmers, black and white, turned into sharecroppers. In response, new political parties emerged, most significantly the People's Party, or the Populists, through which small farmers took a stand against the predatory practices of industrial capital. In many regions, particularly the South, blacks (who mainly supported the Republicans) and whites (many of whom backed the People's Party) came together to create "Fusion" tickets to oppose the ruling Democrats. Fusion candidates promised local self-government, free public education, regulation of monopoly capitalism and electoral reforms to protect black suffrage. Few white Fusionists were racial egalitarians; most held racist views. Many, however, saw the importance of cross-racial solidarity. "You are kept apart that you may be separately fleeced of your earnings", Tom Watson, leader of the People's Party in Georgia, told a multiracial audience. "You are made to hate each other because that hatred is the keystone of the arch of financial despotism that enslaves you both".[46]

In 1894, Fusion candidates in North Carolina won two-thirds of the seats in the state legislature. Two years later, a Republican, Daniel Russell, was elected governor after decades of Democratic rule. The new administration capped interest rates, increased public-school funding, shifted the burden of taxation from individuals to corporations, and allowed symbols to be put on ballots to enfranchise those unable to read.

The Democrats responded with a ferocious propaganda campaign to drive a wedge between African Americans and white workers, warning of the horrors of "Negro Rule". Newspapers whipped up hysteria with a stream of lurid stories and cartoons about the uncontrollable lust of black men for white women. One of the most notorious cartoons was by Norman Jennett, specially hired by the Wilmington *News and Observer* to create racist caricatures. It depicted a huge vampire with a black man's face and "Negro rule" inscribed on its wings, white women fleeing in terror from beneath its menacing claws. "The Vampire That Hovers Over

North Carolina", read the caption. The reason the mob torched the *Daily Record* office was that its editor, Alexander Manly, had openly challenged such sexual myths. "Tell your men that it is no worse for a black man to be intimate with a white woman than for a white man to be intimate with a colored woman", he wrote in response to a speech by Rebecca Latimer Felton, one of the South's leading women's voices, who had called for "lynching to protect women's dearest possession from the ravening human beasts". Latimer's speech was regarded as unexceptional; but Manly's editorial was seen as incendiary, deriding as it did primeval racial myths and mocking white sexual insecurities. It was inevitable that the truth would be met with violence.[47]

The Democrats created a terrorist militia, the Red Shirts, to wreak carnage on black communities across the state, disrupting church services and political meetings, and forcibly preventing black men from voting; that was how the Democrats won the 1898 state election. To pay for the campaign, the chairman of North Carolina's Democratic Party, Furnifold Simmons, made secret deals with railroad companies, banks and industrialists, promising to slash corporate taxes in exchange for funding. "The business men of the State are largely responsible for the victory", crowed the *Charlotte Daily Observer* after the election.[48]

Wilmington, with its large and politically engaged black population, was the heart of the Fusionist threat. It became also the focus of the Democrats' campaign. The coup was organized over several months by a group of wealthy businessmen and politicians called by their admirers "The Secret Nine". The group created armed militias to take control of the streets and drew up lists of black and white Fusionists to be banished or killed. At a rally, the day after the election, Waddell unveiled a "White Declaration of Independence". The Constitution, according to the Declaration, "did not anticipate the enfranchisement of an ignorant population of African origin", nor did the nation's founders "contemplate for their descendants a subjection to an inferior race". It demanded an end to "the rule by Negroes", the resignation of the mayor, the chief of police, and the board of aldermen, the *Daily Record* to "cease to be published" and "its editor banished from the city". The following day, Democrat insurgents launched their attack on the town.[49]

The Wilmington coup was the most dramatic illustration of the social transformation the 1890s betokened, marking in the South the full flowering of the age of Jim Crow. Why the practice of noxious segregation came to be named after a character in a minstrel show, no one seems to know. Ironically, though, it was Reconstruction that introduced segregation into the South. The decadence of antebellum society, where rich whites relied on slaves to cater to their every need, necessitated, in Joel Williamson's words, "a constant, physical intimacy". Because enslaved blacks possessed the status only of property, and this status was fixed and irrevocable, so there was, as C. Vann Woodward observes, "little occasion or need for segregation". There was, though, almost total exclusion. Both slaves and free blacks were debarred from most areas of Southern life, from schools to hospitals, hotels to militias. After the war, federal laws required not just the end of enslavement but equal treatment, too. "Equal treatment" came to be expressed through a policy of "separate but equal". Schools were opened to African Americans for the first time, but in most states there were separate institutions for blacks and whites. Hospitals, orphanages, care homes and poor houses were all segregated, as was much public transport. Even the dead were sorted by race—most cities had segregated cemeteries.[50]

The social structure bequeathed by the Republicans was adopted by the white-supremacist Redeemers, with little desire for Jim Crow-like apartheid. As late as 1898, the *Charleston News and Courier*, the oldest Southern newspaper, and deeply conservative, mocked a proposal for the enforced segregation of trains. "If there must be Jim Crow cars on the railroads", an editorial observed,

There should be Jim Crow waiting saloons at all stations, and Jim Crow eating houses... There should be Jim Crow sections of the jury box, and a separate Jim Crow dock and witness stand in every court—and a Jim Crow Bible for colored witnesses to kiss. It would be advisable also to have a Jim Crow section in county auditors' and treasurers' offices for the accommodation of colored taxpayers... Perhaps the best plan would be, after all, to take the short cut to the general end... by establishing two or three Jim Crow counties at once, and turning them over to our colored citizens for their special and exclusive accommodation.[51]

The editorial was written as satire. It turned out to be prophecy. All these satirical suggestions, with the exception of Jim Crow counties and Jim Crow witness stands, became reality—even separate Bibles for blacks and whites to kiss in court.

In the decade from the mid-1890s, in response to the success of cross-racial movements, a rush of laws imposed apartheid upon the South. With segregation came also disenfranchisement. The Fifteenth Amendment forbade disqualification by virtue of race. So Southern legislatures got creative, crafting laws to disbar blacks without mentioning their race. In many states, voters were now compelled to provide proof of age, date of birth and place of birth, evidence that those born into slavery were unlikely to possess. In many states, too, the majority of blacks, denied education, were illiterate. So literary tests were introduced to exclude them. Property qualifications and poll taxes—which required voters to have paid a tax that few blacks could afford—also became common. When laws were insufficient, there was always fraud and terror. In some districts more whites voted than lived there, while vigilante groups ensured that blacks hoping to vote were dissuaded by lethal violence. In 1896 more than half of Louisiana's registered voters were black; by 1904 it had fallen to less than one per cent. In Alabama, the black electorate fell from over 100,000 to less than 4,000.[52]

Accompanying segregation and disenfranchisement was a level of violence scarcely imaginable. One recent study estimates more than 4,000 African Americans were lynched in twelve Southern states between 1877 and 1950. Lynching was not simply an act of killing. They were public spectacles designed to humiliate and terrorize blacks and to provide a collective experience of sadistic supremacy for whites. Picnics were held at lynchings. When Thomas Brooks was lynched in Fayette County in Tennessee in 1915, the local paper reported that school lessons were delayed so that "pupils could get back from viewing the lynched man". Nor was the victim simply killed or hanged. They were tortured, set alight, their body parts hacked off, which were then "treasured" as trophies and souvenirs—teeth, ears, toes, fingers, genitals, bits of charred skin and bone—and often publicly displayed. It is a level of depravity as difficult to comprehend as that meted out by Nazis

to Jews. It is difficult to comprehend, too, the degree of courage
it took for investigative journalists, most notably Ida B. Wells, one
of the great leaders of both black rights and women's rights movements at the turn of the century, to document lynching and to
challenge the narrative about them.[53]

For all the vicious racism and the terror visited upon African
Americans, it was not "Negro rule" that worried the Southern elite.
In no sense did black people possess power or have the chance to
rule. Even in Wilmington, with a majority black population and a
relatively prosperous one, only three of the ten aldermen were
black. What really frightened the elite was the challenge to traditional rule posed by a coalition of workers and farmers, black and
white, who cast aside their sectional differences to create parties and
administrations that put the interests of ordinary people first. Jim
Crow did not emerge because of the peculiarities of Southern bigotry. It was imposed to thwart the threat of cross-racial solidarity.
Racial divisions had, from the days of colonialism, been created and
exploited as means of fracturing the solidarity of people at the bottom of society, and of derailing political and economic opposition.
So it was now.

It is not difficult to see what planters and industrialists gained
from erasing class solidarity in favour of white identity. But what
about white workers and small farmers? How did they gain from
abandoning their class interests and from forsaking their coalition
with black workers to ally themselves with rich whites in the imposition of Jim Crow? They were, Du Bois suggests, "compensated in
part by a sort of public and psychological wage". White workers
were "given public deference" and "admitted freely with all classes
of white people to public functions, public parks and the best
schools". There is truth to this, but it is far from being the whole
story. The balance sheet was far less comfortable, especially when
looked at in material terms. Poor whites lost more than they gained
from Jim Crow.[54]

It was not just blacks who were disenfranchised. Because the laws
that took the vote away from blacks could not formally be framed in
racial terms, most applied to working-class whites, too, who were
also poor and often illiterate. Some states applied runarounds such
as the "grandfather clause", which enfranchised individuals whose

grandparents had been eligible to vote, a provision applying to many whites, but excluding all blacks. In many cases, though, politicians welcomed the disenfranchisement of lower-class whites. Mississippi law, the congressman Eaton Bowers noted with pride in 1904, "disenfranchised not only the ignorant and vicious black but the ignorant and vicious white as well, and the electorate in Mississippi is confined to those and those alone who are qualified by intelligence and character for the proper and patriotic exercise of this great franchise".[55]

In Louisiana, after a new registration law was introduced in 1898, the black vote dropped by 90 per cent—and the white vote by almost 60 per cent. In Texas, the introduction of a poll tax in 1904 saw the percentage of whites voting fall from eighty to twenty-nine a decade later. In Mississippi, the Vicksburg *Commercial Herald* suggested that a poll tax had prevented 6,000 blacks from voting—and ten times as many whites. Since middle-class whites faced no problem from voting restrictions, all those denied the vote would have been lower class.[56]

Employment segregation under Jim Crow meant that white workers faced less competition from blacks. But, here too, matters were not so straightforward. The Faustian bargain white workers struck with employers was that in return for the elimination of blacks as competitors, they would forswear the protection of unions, and accept low wages and execrable conditions. CC Houston, editor of the Atlanta *Journal of Labor*, told a Congress Commission in 1898, that "Colored labor in the South is held over the head of white labor to the extent of holding down wages." In many trades, "the wages paid to white labor are based primarily on the wages paid to colored labor."[57]

Clare de Graffenried, an investigator with the US Bureau of Labor assigned to research the condition of wage-earning women and children, described the conditions of poor whites, or "crackers", in Georgia. It was not unusual to find three generations of women working side by side in the cotton mills, from sunrise to sunset, six days a week. "Sickly faces, stooping shoulders, shriveled flesh... stained lips, destitute of color and revealing broken teeth—these are the dower of girlhood in the mills", Graffenried observed. Legislators refused "to prevent the employment of children under ten and twelve", she angrily wrote, because "this curtailment, the manufacturers feel, would be disasterous [sic] to their interests". So, poor whites remained "always poor though always working".[58]

"There probably are not today in the world", Du Bois despairingly observed in 1935, "two groups of workers with practically identical interests who hate and fear each other so deeply and persistently and who are kept so far apart that neither sees anything of common interest."[59]

VIII

"If one of them white Southerners gets to the moon first, COLORED NOT ADMITTED signs will go up all over heaven as sure as God made little green apples, and Dixiecrats will be asking the man in the moon, 'Do you want your daughter to marry a Nigra?'".[60]

The weekly satirical stories that the African American poet and novelist Langston Hughes wrote for the *Chicago Defender* from 1943 for two decades picked away at the absurdities of America's racial divides and the ugliness of Jim Crow. In the decades since Southern apartheid was dismantled, Jim Crow and the South have become inextricably linked. And, yet, however much the South was the land of Jim Crow, and however much that may be a reality even on the moon, Jim Crow cannot be understood simply as a Southern phenomenon. "The wave of Southern racism" in the 1890s, Woodward notes, "came in as a swell upon a mounting tide of national sentiment and was very much part of that sentiment". It was a tide that led the Supreme Court, in 1896, to declare Jim Crow constitutional because, as it reasoned in the infamous *Plessy v Ferguson* case, "If one race be inferior to the other socially, the Constitution of the United States cannot put them upon the same plane". A tide that sanctioned scientific racism, social Darwinism and eugenics, engrained hysteria about "Caliban-like" immigrants, embraced an aggressive form of Anglo-Saxonism and birthed a new, belligerent patriotism.[61]

The same year as the Wilmington coup, the Spanish-American war confirmed the USA as a global imperialist power, with new territories stretching from the Caribbean to the Asia Pacific. Imperialist adventure fed into the themes of the new racism. The domination of non-white peoples by whites, and the bringing of civilization to barbarians was accepted as a fact abroad. Why not at home? "If the stronger and cleverer race is free to impose its will upon 'new-caught, sullen peoples' on the other side of the globe", the *Atlantic Monthly* wondered, "why not in South Carolina and Mississippi?" The White Man had to shoulder his Burden at home as well as abroad.[62]

The voices of the old radical abolitionists such as Frederick Douglass and William Lloyd Garrison had lost the resonance they once possessed. The voices that now held sway were those of men like Theodore Roosevelt and Lothrop Stoddard, men whose unabashed white supremacy reflected a nation transformed far beyond the boundaries of Dixie.

As the old politics unravelled, African Americans not only became the principal victims of that unravelling but also the scape-goats for it. Populists, driven out of office by the Democrats' white supremacy campaign, blamed former black allies for their setbacks. In the early 1890s Tom Watson had been a courageous advocate of cross-racial solidarity. By the early years of the new century, he had become an unyielding sponsor of white supremacy. "This is a white man's civilization, and the white man must maintain it", he wrote. He celebrated lynchings as revealing that "a sense of justice yet lives among the people".[63]

Black leaders themselves became more accommodating to the new climate. The death of Frederick Douglass in February 1895 symbolized the extinguishing of one tradition. Seven months later, Booker T. Washington's "Atlanta Compromise" speech marked the beginnings of another. Seven years old when President Lincoln announced his Emancipation Proclamation, Washington belonged to the last generation of African American leaders born into slavery. He was adamantly opposed to radical movements and to confrontation as a means of bringing about change. He did not believe that blacks were ready for full social equality and insisted that to agitate for such would only antagonize whites. Rather than seek influence as writers or academics or politicians, they should find hope in basic vocations, such as being mechanics or domestic servants. From his base as principal of the Tuskegee Institute, a black college in Alabama, Washington made the case that the best hope for blacks was to learn a trade, work hard, stop complaining and show to white society that they were fit to be treated as fellow human beings and citizens.

In his 1895 speech in Atlanta that brought him to national attention, Washington told white America that slaves had "proved our loyalty to you in the past, in nursing your children, watching by the sick-bed of your mothers and fathers, and often following them with tear-dimmed eyes to their graves". Free blacks would equally "stand by you with a devotion that no foreigner can approach, ready to lay down our lives, if need be, in defense of yours" because they were "the most patient, faithful, law-abiding, and unresentful people that the world has seen."[64]

Unsurprisingly, these conservative, non-confrontational themes of racial uplift found a hearing within the highest echelons of American society, celebrated by industrialists and politicians from Andrew Carnegie to Theodore Roosevelt. Washington's critics saw his approach not as pragmatism but as surrender. Du Bois had initially supported Washington, but the two became increasingly estranged. His programme, Du Bois snorted, "practically accepts the alleged inferiority of Negro races". It was not possible for African Americans to "make effective progress in economic lines if they are deprived of political rights, made a servile caste, and allowed only the most meagre chance for developing their exceptional men". It was a debate that would reappear, in many different forms, throughout the twentieth and twenty-first centuries.[65]

8

FROM CLASS SOLIDARITY TO BLACK LIVES MATTER

I

It was 25 March 1931. A cold spring day. A couple of dozen young men, mostly teenagers, were hoboing on a freight train between Chattanooga and Memphis, Tennessee. Some were black, some white. Riding freight trains was a common pastime in the Depression. For some, it was a free way to move from one often-futile job search to the next, for others a bit of adventure to enliven their dreary lives. On this day, as happened quite often, a fight broke out between the blacks and the whites, the latter insisting that this was a "white man's train". The black youngsters refused to back down, eventually pushing most of their antagonists off the train. Hearing about the humiliation, an armed posse stopped the train at Paint Rock, Alabama. They hauled nine black youngsters, all aged between thirteen and twenty, out of their box car and into jail. Haywood Patterson, Clarence Norris, Charlie Weems, Olen Montgomery, Ozie Powell, Willie Robertson, Eugene Williams, and Andrew and Roy Wright became the "Scottsboro Boys".[1]

The posse then discovered two young white women, Victoria Price and Ruby Bates, also on the train. Unemployed millworkers searching for jobs, they had been travelling with the white men and were not in the same box car as the black teenagers. Fearing that they might otherwise be charged with vagrancy or prostitution, Price and Bates accused the black men of rape. (Bates subsequently retracted her allegation.) Suddenly, the nine youngsters were facing not just jail time but the electric chair.

The prosecution divided the Scottsboro Boys into four groups, based on age, to face separate trials. All four trials were concluded within three days. Every jury was all-white. Medical evidence suggested that no rape had taken place. Every defendant was found guilty. In the case of the youngest defendant, 13-year-old Roy Wright, a mistrial was declared after a majority of the jury refused to accept the prosecution's recommendation that he be spared the death penalty on account of his age. The other eight defendants were sentenced to death.[2]

And that, normally, would have been that. Legal lynchings were not uncommon in the South. This time, though, into the maelstrom stepped an unexpected body—the Communist Party. Its intervention saved the boys from execution and helped put on trial not black sexuality but white supremacy.

This chapter tells the story of the changing character of the struggle for black rights in America, from the 1930s to the twenty-first century, from Scottsboro and the Communist Party to Ferguson, George Floyd and Black Lives Matter. This was the century in which many nations, especially in the West, took their cultural cues from America, and in which racial debates in the USA set the frame for similar debates elsewhere, even when the social and historical contexts were very different. Civil rights, Black Power, Black Lives Matter, culture wars, identity politics—all were themes exported globally. At the same time, the issue that is often taken to represent the uniqueness of the American model—the relationship between race and class, and the seeming significance of race as compared to class—is more complex and nuanced than often considered. In twentieth-century America, we glimpsed the possibilities of cross-racial solidarity in defence of black rights and in the face of ferocious racism; we saw also how, paradoxically, the more that racial equality was attained, the more that race and class became detached and the relationship between them obscured. Both sides of this equation have relevance far beyond America.

II

In the 1920s, the US Communist Party (CPUSA) was largely Northern and urban. In 1928, at its Sixth Congress, Comintern—the Communist International—passed its "Resolution on the Negro Question", declaring that African Americans had the right "to national self-determination in the southern states where the Negroes form a majority of the population". It was a highly controversial stance, but it pushed the "Negro Question" to the centre of the CPUSA's work. Comintern also directed the Party to take up the issues confronting black workers, to challenge segregation and racial terror and to recruit in the South. Communists began organizing sharecroppers and millworkers, the homeless and the unemployed. They faced terror and violence, bombings and beatings, arrest and imprisonment. Nevertheless, they demonstrated the possibilities of organizing across the racial divide in the most inauspicious of places.[3]

Where the Party in the North was comprised largely of leftwing intellectuals and working-class activists well-versed in radical causes, in the South, its black cadre, historian Robin Kelley notes, consisted of "unskilled and semiskilled industrial workers, sharecroppers, domestics, and housewives" with "no previous experience with radical movements". Because "the movement was built from scratch by people without a Euro-American left-wing tradition", so black party members in the South "interpreted Communism through the lenses of their own cultural world". What the Party offered was "a framework for understanding the roots of poverty and racism", linking "local struggles to world politics" and creating "an atmosphere in which ordinary people could analyze, discuss, and criticize the society in which they lived". It inevitably led to clashes with the black community's self-appointed leaders. In Birmingham, Alabama, Charles McPherson, local secretary of the NAACP, the pre-eminent African American organization, dismissed the Communist Party as full of a "large number of our own non-reading classes"; it would never become a political force because "intelligent and informed people cannot be swept off their feet by the propoganda [sic] of a questionable organization".[4]

McPherson's scornful dismissal of "our own non-reading classes" exposed the elitism and exclusivity of the NAACP. In contrast, the communists afforded poor blacks a "new kind of politics that required the self-activity of people usually dismissed as inarticulate". The black elite saw the distinction between themselves and the communists as one of race, ignoring the black cadre within the Party. Working-class and rural blacks recognized more than most the impact of racism and terror. They also recognized that the black elite may be of the same race, but they lived in a different world of class privilege.[5]

The NAACP had initially been reluctant to get involved with the Scottsboro Boys for fear of damaging its reputation. Communists had no such worries. James Allen, the party's organizer in the South, was fortuitously based in Chattanooga, home to four of the defendants. He quickly built trust with their parents and launched a campaign on two fronts. Through the communist-led International Labor Defence (ILD), he hired new lawyers to challenge the verdicts in court, eventually taking the case to the Supreme Court. The ILD also organized mass protests and a major publicity campaign. Days after the initial verdict, thousands demonstrated in Cleveland and New York. And in Berlin and Buenos Aires, Shanghai and Sydney. What made the Scottsboro campaign so dramatic and effective was the worldwide scope of the protests.

In 1932, after an appeal to the Alabama Supreme Court had failed, the ILD organized a European speaking tour for Ada Wright, mother of two of the defendants, Andrew and Roy. Criss-crossing sixteen countries in six months and speaking to half a million people, Wright faced obstruction from the authorities but electrified her audiences. The tour impressed on Wright "the presence of solidarities [she] could not have previously imagined".[6]

The success of the ILD campaign forced the black elite to change tack. The NAACP tried to strong-arm itself into the case, appealing to both the parents and the defendants, warning them against being associated with communists. The parents refused the overtures, recognizing that without the ILD campaign, the young men would all have been executed, and their deaths another statistic in the ledger of legalized lynchings. It was "the Russians", Ada Wright insisted, who had saved her sons.[7]

The NAACP was hostile to the very idea of appealing to working-class solidarity against racism. Even a figure as radical as Du Bois dismissed the communists' "attempt to show the Negro that his interest lies with that of white labor", noting that "Throughout the history of the Negro in America, white labor has been the black man's enemy, his oppressor, his red murderer". Communists had, he acknowledged, "made a courageous fight against the color line among workers". But they had lost even before they had started: "Whatever ideals white labor strives for in America, it would surrender nearly every one before it would recognize a Negro as a man".[8]

Du Bois' pessimism was rooted in part in the history of American labour relations; of unions that excluded blacks and enforced workplace segregation, of white workers who supported Jim Crow laws and participated in the KKK. There were certainly counterexamples of cross-racial solidarity, of organizations such as the Knights of Labor, in its early years, and the IWW that, often with great courage, promoted the rights of black workers. And though, as we have seen, these tended to be the exception rather than the rule, they pointed nevertheless to the possibilities of a different kind of working-class politics that too rarely was pursued.

The pessimism expressed also an elitist disdain for the working class and its capabilities, a disdain whose target was not just white workers. When the Scottsboro parents refused to recant their support for the ILD, William Pickens, a leading NAACP activist, excoriated them as "the densest and dumbest animals" he had ever met. Walter White, the organization's executive secretary, dismissed the parents as "pathetically ignorant and poor", the "type of Negro who would believe anything said by a white man". Mamie Williams Wilcox, mother of Eugene Williams, retorted that "we are not too ignorant... to know that if we let the NAACP look after our boys, they will die".[9]

What the ILD provided was more than simply legal support and global publicity. They also gave poor blacks something that elite black organizations could, and would, not: a political voice and a sense of their own agency. The Communist Party was undoubtedly cynical and opportunist. The constantly changing directives from Moscow hobbled solidarity work on the ground. The Scottsboro campaign fell in the midst of Comintern's "Third period" during which it was at its most sectarian, dismissing others on the left as "social fascists". The "Popular Front" period that followed in the mid-thirties reversed much of this, as the Party sought to build wide coalitions against fascism. Then came, in 1939, the Molotov-Ribbentrop non-aggression pact between Germany and the Soviet Union. Now, the line was that fascists were no longer a threat, so there should be no war against Nazi Germany. Two years later, as German tanks rolled into the Soviet Union, the Nazis were once more a menace, so much so that the struggle for racial equality at home in America had to be set aside to maintain a common front against Hitler.

The Party was not, however, simply Moscow's creature, especially in the South. It was a Stalinist sect tied to a vicious regime. It was also the most dynamic organization within the American left in the 1930s and 1940s, indispensable to the struggle against racism and for workers' rights. It embraced black members and promoted internally a degree of social equality previously unseen in American political parties. And despite Du Bois' cynicism, it played a major role in helping create cross-racial solidarity and in linking struggles for black political rights with working-class demands for improvements in wages, conditions, housing and welfare. Its campaign eventually freed the Scottsboro boys too.

Nevertheless, the clash between the communists and the NAACP during the Scottsboro case prefigured many of the themes that would be used in the 1940s and 50s to undermine black radicalism: the promotion of the red scare, the demand that only certain organizations had the right to speak for "their community", the attempt to traduce dissenting black working-class voices as "ignorant", the contempt for white workers as inherently racist, the insistence on racial unity over class solidarity.

III

He was a legend of African American history. Its most important leader of the first half of the twentieth century. The founder of the most influential black organization prior to the modern civil rights movement. The author of some of the most prescient works about race and racism. And he was in handcuffs. In February 1951, the 82-year-old WEB Du Bois became a victim of the red scare.

By the late 1940s Du Bois was no longer the harsh critic of communism that he had been a decade earlier. He was impressed by the willingness of communists to "challenge the color line". He had come to recognize the importance of class in the struggle for black rights. His anti-imperialism, and involvement in campaigns against nuclear weapons, pushed him closer to the Soviet Union. Indeed, even as many communists later left the party, especially in the 1950s after the Soviet suppression of the East German and Hungarian uprisings, Du Bois stubbornly maintained his support.

In 1950, Du Bois became chairman of the US Peace Information Center, and helped promote the Stockholm Appeal, an international petition against nuclear weapons organized by the Soviet-backed World Peace Council. The US Justice Department saw it as communist propaganda and demanded the Center register itself as "an agent of a foreign principal". This Du Bois refused to do. He and four other officers of the organization were themselves charged with being "foreign agents". An international defence committee was established to support them. In America, though, the black elite, with a handful of notable exceptions, such as Langston Hughes, kept its collective head down. The NAACP, historian Manning Marable observed, "was especially conspicuous in its moral cowardice", its executive secretary Walter White spreading rumours about Du Bois' treachery. Six months later, a white federal judge, more liberal than most black leaders, threw the case out for lack of evidence. It was one of the few victories in the tumult of red scare hysteria.[10]

America had come out of the Second World War as the most powerful nation on Earth, economically, politically and militarily. It was reshaping the postwar world to its requirements through agreements and institutions from Bretton Woods to the International Monetary Fund. Yet, as World War gave way to Cold War, the nation was sweat-drenched in fear and convulsed by McCarthyite hysteria.

On 25 March 1947, President Harry S. Truman issued Executive Order 9835—the so-called "Loyalty Order"—authorizing the FBI to investigate the beliefs and associations of all federal employees, launching, in the words of one study, "a purge of the federal civil service" that "inspired imitative purges at every level of American working life". By 1955, forty-four states had anti-communist laws. Tennessee made the espousal of revolutionary Marxism punishable by death. In Michigan "writing or speaking subversive words" could lead to life imprisonment. Connecticut criminalized the printing of "scurrilous or abusive matter" against "the United States, its military forces, flags or uniforms".[11]

The anti-communist hysteria, its causes and consequences, has been endlessly addressed in the decades since. Less discussed has been its bearing on the civil rights movement. The Cold War had a double-edged impact on racial inequality in America. The US authorities were aware of the propaganda value that segregation provided to the Soviet Union, especially among the newly independent nations of Africa, Asia and the Caribbean. "The moral influence of the United States", Secretary of State George C. Marshall warned in 1947, "is weakened to the extent that the civil rights proclaimed by our Constitution is not fully confirmed in actual practice". This fear helped nudge forward official attempts to break down Jim Crow. At the same time, McCarthyite paranoia led to a generation of black radicals being ostracized and isolated, not only delaying the possibilities of civil rights but also reshaping the character of black struggles.[12]

African Americans had, since the 1930s, made the link between the South's brutality towards blacks and the Nazis' treatment of Jews. Once America entered the war, it became difficult to reconcile a struggle waged against the Nazi's obscene racial ideology with a nation unwilling to challenge apartheid laws and lynchings at home. African Americans still recalled how, in the First World War, many black leaders, including Du Bois, had supported the war effort in the hope that they would later reap the rewards of equality and democracy. What they reaped was the "red summer" of 1919, when racial terror poured down on black communities, and segregation intensified. This time, equal rights at home was at the fore of African American demands. The "Double V" campaign, for victory over fascism abroad and racism at home, began as a letter to the *Pittsburgh Courier*, the largest circulation black newspaper, in 1942 and turned into a national movement.[13]

The veteran black union activist A. Philip Randolph, leader of the Brotherhood of Sleeping Car Porters, organized the March on Washington Movement, to pressure the federal government to desegregate the armed forces and provide opportunities for African Americans in the defence industry from which they had largely been excluded. The march, planned for 1 July 1941, was called off after President Roosevelt set up the Fair Employment Practices Committee (FEPC) and banned discrimination in the defence industries. The FEPC was more symbolic than transformational, having no powers of legal enforcement. The committee took "no position on the question of segregation", its chairman Mark Ethridge declared, adding that there was "no power in the world... which could now force the Southern white people to the abandonment of the principle of social segregation".[14]

But that was not true. Whatever federal administrators might have believed, on the ground there were working-class organizations that sought to break down the barriers of Jim Crow segregation. Through the 1930s and 40s, there developed what historian Robert Korstad calls "civil rights unionism"—the linking of working-class demands to the struggle for black rights. Building on the work of communists in the South, civil rights unionism challenged race bars in workplaces, led struggles for equal pay, battled for decent housing and fought political disenfranchisement. The centrepiece of Korstad's important study is the story of Local 42, a branch of the United Cannery, Agricultural, Packing and Allied Workers of America (UCAPAWA), in Winston-Salem, North Carolina.[15]

The town was dominated by the RJ Reynolds Tobacco Company, a corporation deeply hostile to unions. It took years of determined organization by UCAPAWA activists to gain recognition, and even more determination to improve wages and conditions that, in a plant in which most workers were black women, were atrocious. Local 42 did not limit itself to workplace activism. "Even before it gained recognition", Korstad notes, "it had taken up broader civic issues", including "helping to defend William Wellman, a black North Carolina man, against a death sentence on a false rape charge; backing a black candidate for the Board of Alderman; and joining forces with the city's dynamic young ministers to help blacks register to vote." Once established, "the union put voting rights and education for active citizenship at the top of its agenda".[16]

By the early 1940s, Local 42 had become an alternative social world. The union hall housed meetings and plays as well as history and current affairs classes. The union sponsored sports teams, sewing circles and swimming clubs. Its library was a revelation. At the city library, one worker remembered, "you couldn't find any books on Negro history. They didn't have books by Aptheker, Dubois [sic], or Frederick Douglass. But we had them at our library."[17]

The very fact that black workers, often women, were taking part in radio discussions, commenting on national affairs in the newspapers, even appearing before congressional committees, transformed the image of both black and working-class culture, in the eyes of the workers themselves and of the outside world. As blacks and whites organized side-by-side as equals, so "the aura of naturalness and inevitability that surrounded segregation" cracked. The activists created an "oasis of genuine inter-racialism" in which "the 'Negro problem' was transformed into the problem of how white racism could be overcome". Communist Party members did much of the hard graft, but the political culture flourished because it appealed to many outside communist circles.[18]

Local "community leaders" objected to working-class blacks taking the lead in struggles for equality. A 1943 letter to the *Winston-Salem Journal* from six "colored leaders" called on the workers to reject union radicalism and to rely on racial betterment through "good will, friendly understanding, and mutual respect and cooperation between the races". One worker acidly noted that black leaders "have always told us what the white people want, but somehow or other are particularly silent on what we want".[19]

The postwar red scare shredded this form of civil rights unionism. As radicals were marginalized, so that spirit of unapologetic inter-racialism and mass action against segregation was, if not extinguished, contained. "The democratic upsurge of black people which characterised the 1950s", Manning Marable observed, "could have happened ten years earlier". The playbook of the postwar civil rights movement was written in the early 1940s by Pauli Murray, one of the most important and extraordinary civil rights activists in America, but whose name barely registers now in public consciousness. Murray stirred up a storm in 1938 by applying to be a student at the segregated University of North Carolina (UNC), a quarter of a century before James Meredith provoked mass riots when in 1962 he became, in a landmark case, the first African American to enrol in the University of Mississippi. In 1940, she was arrested for refusing to sit in the "colored" section of a bus fifteen years before Rosa Parks. In 1943, she led sit-ins in segregated restaurants and lunch counters, successfully desegregating them, two decades before the Freedom Riders organized similar protests in the early Sixties.

Each time she appealed to the NAACP for support. What the NAACP was looking for, though, were "model" citizens around whom to build campaigns. Murray was outspoken, argumentative, and dismissive of conventional norms. Her uncompromising opposition to Jim Crow was anathema to the organization. "Its successes", Murray wrote of the NAACP, "came through cautious and modest advances within the framework of the 'separate but equal' principle". Murray was also what we now call "non-binary" or perhaps "transgender"—her gender identity was fluid and she was open about it. Murray would go on to become one of the most important postwar legal scholars, influencing the work of figures such as the lawyer Thurgood Marshall, and Supreme Court judge Ruth Bader Ginsburg. In the 1940s, though, the NAACP thought her so toxic that its executive secretary Roy Wilkins insisted that the organization should have "no record anywhere as having anything to do with Miss Murray's application [to UNC]". The sparks she created did not catch light for another fifteen years. [20]

Historians talk of the "long civil rights movement" to describe the significance of the prewar struggles for the later civil rights movement. The relationship between the prewar and postwar movements is not, however, a straightforward one. The decay of civil rights unionism decoupled the economic and the political. Where, for Local 42, the struggle for equal political rights was inseparable from that for decent wages, conditions, welfare and housing, when the civil rights movement re-emerged in the late 1950s, it concentrated mostly on the former. While this made sense for middle-class blacks, it was a blow for working-class African Americans. One of the tragedies of the politics of race and class in America was that, as the movement reset itself in the late Fifties, one of the most important lessons of the prewar struggles—the necessity of linking the battle for black rights to that for working-class improvement—became more obscured. [21]

IV

The two men met only once. It was on 26 March 1964, on the steps of the US Capitol in Washington DC. The Senate was debating the Civil Rights Act, the most momentous for a century. Watching

211

proceedings were the two figures who more than any others symbolized the struggle for black rights in 1960s America. Martin Luther King Jr. and Malcolm X. Both were ministers, though of different religions. Both were great orators, who used their eloquence to excoriate racism and lay out a new vision for the nation. Both would be assassinated, both turned into myths. And, for the first and only time, the two men met on the Capitol steps, briefly chatted, then went their different ways.

MLK and Malcolm X, both then and in historical memory, have come to symbolize opposing visions of the struggle for black rights. King, the reasonable, even conservative, figure, an advocate of integration and non-violence, a crusader for universalism and a champion of the American Dream; Malcom, the revolutionary firebrand, an unyielding Muslim and black nationalist, a purveyor of conflict and division, a sponsor of "race first" ideology. The story, though, is much more convoluted. The differences were real but revealed only a fragment of the picture. Both men constantly reworked their visions and reinvented themselves, such that, by the end of their foreshortened lives, each was possibly closer to the other than they were to their original selves. The differences between MLK and Malcolm X expressed the tension between universalist and identitarian perspectives, between the idea that black Americans are an integral part of American society and the belief that equality could come only through separation. Those tensions were expressed not simply between the two men but also within the worldviews of each. It was as each man wrestled with these conundrums that he journeyed to a different place.

They were born within four years of each other, on the cusp of the Great Depression, but into different circumstances. King came from a middle-class family in Atlanta, Georgia, his father a Baptist preacher. After graduating from the prestigious Morehouse College, King attended a theological seminary in Pennsylvania and then Boston University, before returning to the South in 1954 to be a pastor in Montgomery, Alabama. It was a propitious time to be taking up his new post. On 1 December 1955, Rosa Parks was arrested after refusing to give up her seat on a bus to a white passenger, sparking a boycott of Montgomery buses which was to last for 381 days. King became the spokesman for the campaign, a role that thrust him into the national spotlight. After a decade-long hiatus, largely the consequence of the anti-communist hysteria, the civil rights movement began reasserting itself in the late 1950s. The church had always played an important role in African American life, providing both a place of refuge and a space within which black communities could express their collectivity. The McCarthyite ostracization of radicals enlarged the space open to religious figures to assert political authority. King became the figurehead of the new movement, largely through the Southern Christian Leadership Conference (SCLC) that he helped found in 1957.

Four years older than King, Malcolm X was born as Malcolm Little in Omaha, Nebraska. His parents, Earl and Louise Little, were followers of Marcus Garvey, and organizers for the UNIA. Their political activity drew the wrath of racial terrorists, the family constantly harassed and forced to move again and again. Earl Little died in 1931 in what was described as a streetcar accident, though his family always believed it was a racist murder. A decade later, Malcolm dropped out of high school, despite excelling in his studies, after a teacher told him that his aspiration to be a lawyer was "no realistic goal for a nigger". Drifting around, he eventually ended up a drug dealer and pimp in Harlem. In 1946 he was given an eight-to-ten-year sentence for larceny and breaking and entering.[22]

It was prison that turned Malcolm Little into Malcolm X. He discovered the Nation of Islam (NOI). Founded in Detroit in 1930 by Wallace Fard Muhammad, the Nation preached an almost psychedelic mix of black nationalism, Pan-Africanism, mysticism, and an origin story in which the first god was black and the white race was conjured up in a eugenic experiment by a malevolent scientist. And all wrapped up in a warped form of Islam. What mattered was less the absurdities of the myths than the sense of black pride the Nation inculcated, the expression of solidarity in the face of ferocious racism. "I had never dreamed of anything like that atmosphere among black people who had learned to be proud they were black", Malcolm exulted after attending a Temple service in Detroit. He became a minister in the NOI. His dazzling oratory, meticulous organizational skills and a jeweller's eye for publicity, saw the organization soar in membership and become a national news item. Where elite black organizations, such as the NAACP, looked for model citizens around which to build their campaigns, the NOI swept up at the other end of the alley, recruiting those on the fringes of society, the hungry and the poor, the hustlers and the pimps, the unemployed and the incarcerated. The ones who burned with pride and resentment but possessed little hope. The ones like Malcolm. He had come from such a place and could reach out to those who still inhabited it.[23]

At the heart of Malcom's philosophy was an unbending rejection of compromise with oppressors. He opposed segregation, but also integration. Segregation was forced separation. He advised blacks to freely disconnect themselves from white America. Integration was "invented by a Northern liberal" to confuse African Americans. Malcolm had little time for that other shibboleth of the civil rights movement, non-violence. "It's a crime", he insisted, "for anyone who is being brutalized to continue to accept that brutality without doing something to defend himself". "You don't have a turn-the-other-cheek revolution", he taunted MLK.[24]

By the time Martin Luther King and Malcolm X met on the Capitol steps, both men were already well into their journeys of change. Three weeks earlier, Malcolm X had announced his break with the Nation of Islam. He chafed at NOI hostility to involvement in politics, a rule that Malcolm constantly broke. His fame as the leading advocate of black radicalism nurtured jealousies. He also found it increasingly difficult to justify the hypocrisies of the Nation's leader, Elijah Muhammad, especially his sexual abuse of women in the organization.[25]

After leaving the NOI, Malcolm remained critical of arguments for integration and non-violence but began working with broad-based civil rights campaigns. His influence, especially on young activists in the Student Nonviolent Coordinating Committee (SNCC), set up in 1960 by those irked by the conservatism of King and the SCLC, laid the foundations for the Black Power movement that was to come.

Malcolm converted to Sunni Islam, changing his name to El-Hajj Malik El-Shabazz, and travelled to Saudi Arabia to perform the Hajj. He witnessed there the possibilities of a multiracial society, "of people of all races, colors, from all over the world coming together as *one*". He saw that "men with white complexions were more genuinely brotherly than anyone else had ever been". Islam, he wrote, is the "one religion that erases from its society the race problem". There is an echo of the utopian naivety that black communists of an earlier generation had felt about the Soviet Union. Malcolm then travelled through Africa, meeting a swathe of postcolonial leaders. Everywhere he was feted almost as a foreign head of state. His journey strengthened his incipient Pan-Africanism. It also made him rethink his ideas about race. He met revolutionaries who were not black but were as hostile to racism as he was.[26]

In Ghana, Malcolm recalled, the Algerian ambassador, who was white, had asked, if Malcolm defined his objective as the victory of black nationalism, "where does that leave him? Where does that leave revolutionaries in Morocco, Egypt, Iraq, Mauritania?" Malcolm realized that he "was alienating people who were true revolutionaries". John Lewis, the chair of SNCC, recalled a conversation in which Malcolm "talked about the need to shift our focus... from race to class. He said that was the root of our problems, not just in America but all over the world".[27]

On 16 February 1965, Malcolm was assassinated by members of the Nation of Islam while giving a talk in New York. Up to thirty thousand people viewed his body as it lay in a glass-topped coffin in Harlem; ten thousand attended his funeral. Where on his journey Malcolm X might have ended had his life not been cut short is impossible to say. He had been forced, he acknowledged shortly before his death, "to *re-arrange* much of my thought patterns previously held, and to *toss aside* some of my previous conclusions". But in the decades following his murder, it was the old Malcolm rather than the one he was becoming that came to be fixed as the "real" X, both by those who despised him and those who embraced him.[28]

For King, Malcolm's murder seemed to accelerate his own journey to a more radical place. Initially reluctant to publicly oppose the Vietnam War, much to the disdain of Malcolm X and other radicals, by 1967 he recognized the necessity of doing so. "Our nation, which initiated so much of the revolutionary spirit of the modern world, is now cast in the mold of being an arch anti-revolutionary", he told an audience in Los Angeles in February 1967. "We have engaged in a war that seeks to turn the clock of history back and perpetuate white colonialism". Apart from the line about America initiating "the revolutionary spirit of the modern world", this might have been Malcolm X talking. Almost three-quarters of Americans disapproved of King's stance. *Life Magazine* called his speech "a demagogic slander that sounded like a script for Radio Hanoi". Mainstream black leaders distanced themselves. FBI Director J. Edgar Hoover told President Lyndon B. Johnson that King was "an instrument in the hands of subversive forces seeking to undermine our nation". Many of those who now hail King almost as a modern-day Founding Father fail to mention that at the time he was among the most reviled figures in the nation.[29]

King recognized, too, that equality meant more than simply civil and political rights. "What does it profit a man", he asked, "to be able to eat at an integrated lunch counter if he doesn't earn enough money to buy a hamburger and a cup of coffee?" In late 1967, he launched his "Poor People's Campaign", telling a reporter that "we are dealing... with class issues, the gulf between the haves and the have nots". His plans for a huge civil disobedience demonstration in Washington to pressure Congress to improve the lives of the have nots did not go down well with liberal supporters, the *New York Times* calling it a "formula for discord".[30]

King's new turn led him to support the Memphis sanitation workers' strike of 1968, perhaps the most important industrial struggle of the Sixties, and one that began and ended in tragedy. On 1 February 1968, two workers, Echol Cole and Robert Walker, were killed, chewed up by the garbage compacter in a refuse truck in which they had been forced to take shelter from the rain. Sanitation workers in Memphis were nearly all black, the management all white. Pay was abominably low and conditions atrocious—no breaks, no restrooms, no place to clean up after a shift, nowhere to shelter from the rain apart from in the back of the truck with the garbage. Four years earlier two other men had been crushed to death in almost the same way as Cole and Walker. When workers tried to unionize, they were sacked. In 1966, the city had taken out a court order banning sanitation workers from striking.[31]

This time, though, there was no staunching the anger. Eleven days after the deaths of their colleagues, virtually every sanitation worker came out on strike. They marched with placards bearing the now-iconic legend "I Am A Man". They were met with police violence and brutality. A month into the strike, King came to speak to a rally of 25,000 workers and supporters. On 28 March, he returned to lead a chaotic protest that disintegrated into rioting and violence, the police shooting dead sixteen-year-old Larry Payne. At a third visit on 3 April, he gave his final, haunted, apocalyptic sermon at the Mason Temple: "I've been to the mountaintop... And I've seen the promised land. I may not get there with you. But I want you to know tonight, that we, as a people, will get to the promised land." The following day, on 4 April 1968, he was assassinated at the Lorraine Motel in Memphis by James Earl Ray. The motives for, and the background to, the killing remain obscure, spawning a thousand conspiracy theories.

Public anger eventually forced Memphis mayor Henry Loeb to compromise with the sanitation workers. Almost two weeks after King's death, the city recognized the right to unionize, promised wage rises and brought an end to the strike.

As with Malcolm X, it is impossible to say where King might have ended up had his journey not been curtailed. By the end of their lives, the two men had drawn closer to each other's views. Their differences were, however, real and spoke to an inherent tension within the struggle for racial equality, both men a fusion of the conservative and the radical. King expressed a universalist ethos, but one rooted in a liberal vision of American society that, until his last few years, denied the necessity for more radical transformation. Malcolm X provided a radical critique of American democracy, but one, at least initially, rooted in a reactionary view of race, and of the kind of social change necessary.

In the 1960s, the tension between these two approaches, both within and between the two men, was fruitful. It created a dialogue about race, class and social change that shaped the political journeys of both King and Malcolm X. In the context of wider social ferment, it was the radicalism that came to the fore, and both men began to see the issue of class as a bridge towards a new kind of movement. In the succeeding decades, as radical possibilities slipped away, the conservative elements of both men's thinking came to dominate public discourse—on the one hand, a liberal, colourblind view of universalism, on the other, an increasingly racialized view of equality and identity.

V

Stokely Carmichael had just been released from a police holding cell in Greenwood, Mississippi. He was taking part in the "March Against Fear", originally launched on 6 June 1965 by maverick activist James Meredith as a lone walk along Highway 51 from Memphis, Tennessee to Jackson, Mississippi, through some of the most ferociously segregationist counties in the South. Meredith's aim was to stand up to a tidal wave of racist violence in the Mississippi delta and to encourage black voter registration. On the second day of the march, Meredith was shot and wounded by white supremacist Aubrey James Norvell. Carmichael, Martin Luther King and other civil rights leaders agreed to continue the walk in Meredith's stead. By the time it entered Jackson, some 15,000 people had joined in. In Greenwood, Carmichael was arrested for trespassing on public property. "This is the twenty-seventh time I have been arrested", an angry Carmichael told a rally after his release. "I ain't going to jail no more. What we gonna start saying now is 'black power'." The crowd picked up the phrase and turned it into a chant.

It was not the first time the phrase had been heard. As long ago as 1954, Richard Wright had written a book entitled *Black Power* about his journeys in West Africa. But here, on the march through Mississippi, it caught the moment, and fired the imagination. The mid-Sixties was a moment of inflexion. The civil rights campaigns had dismantled Jim Crow and raised expectations within black communities that their lives would truly change, that they would be able to break the shackles of poverty, low wages, racist violence and police brutality. Median income for African American families rose through the decade, there were fewer black families living in poverty, and the income gap between blacks and whites narrowed. But change was relatively modest. The quality of life for most black people living in the cities deteriorated. Rat-infested housing and inadequate education, high rates of crime and higher rates of infant mortality, all became even less tolerable. As did black people's experience of policing and of the justice system. In a searing essay about the "Harlem Six"—a sensational and sensationalized case in which six black teenagers, beaten and coerced by the police, were convicted of two murders before, over the space of several years, most of the convictions were overturned—James Baldwin wrote of "every Northern city with a large Negro population" being "policed like occupied territory". The sense of rage and frustration and thwarted hopes that flowed from all this unleashed a firestorm of inner-city rebellions. Between 1964 and 1972, the riots cost 250 lives, 10,000 serious injuries and 60,000 arrests.[32]

The riots were physical expressions of frustrated rage. Black nationalism gave it a political language. Even before his death, Malcolm X had found a hearing among civil rights activists vexed by the strategy of relying on democratic levers and non-violent protest, disenchanted by the seeming failure of integration. After his assassination, Malcolm became, in Manning Marable's words, "the fountainhead of the modern renaissance of black nationalism in the late 1960s". Within three years of his death, Marable writes, "Black Power had become the dominant ideological concept among a majority of black youth, and significant portions of the black working class and middle strata".[33]

But what did "Black Power" mean? What did it represent? And who did it represent? Today, most people identify "Black Power" with those organizations that proposed revolutionary remedies, in particular the Black Panthers. The Black Panther Party for Self-Defense was founded by Huey Newton and Bobby Seale in October 1966 in Oakland, California. In the years since, it has been both mythicized and demonized, celebrated as "the center of a revolutionary movement in the United States" or vilified as "a sixties group of thugs with Marxist revolutionary pretensions who successfully cowed middle-class, well-educated North American Negroes".[34]

Newton and Seale, both from poor, working-class backgrounds, had met at Merritt community college in Oakland. Frustrated by the accommodationist character of mainstream civil rights groups, they created the Panthers to provide protection, particularly from police violence. Armed members would shadow police patrols to intervene when officers crossed the line. Twinned with armed self-defence was the Panthers' community outreach work, beginning with a free breakfast programme for school children in Oakland, and expanding in different areas to include free health clinics, clothing, ambulance provision, house maintenance and pest-control. The

Panthers called these "survival programmes" before they could "bring about meaningful change in [black people's] social, political and economic status".[35]

Like many black nationalists, the Panthers saw the battle against racism in America as part of the global anti-colonial struggle. The late 1950s and the 1960s was the era of decolonization, of wars for freedom in Algeria and Vietnam, of the Cuban revolution, and of the anti-apartheid struggle in South Africa. The determination of the peoples of Africa, Asia and the Caribbean to free themselves from colonialism, and their many successes, lit the imagination of those struggling against racism and apartheid in America. Many, including the Panthers, came to see African Americans as comprising a special kind of colony. The only solution was "self-determination", though what that meant in practice for black Americans, nobody spelt out.

From one perspective, the Panthers were following in the tradition of radical Pan-Africanists such as CLR James, George Padmore and Frantz Fanon. There had, though, been a significant shift in the meaning of black internationalism. For a figure like James, Pan-Africanism was a stage on which to link the struggles of working-class people in the colonies with those in the metropolitan heartlands. The Panthers, on the other hand, were drawn to the international stage not just by the vibrancy of the anti-colonial struggles but also by disillusionment with white workers at home. Unlike many other black nationalist organizations, the Panthers often worked closely with inter-racial and white groups. They were also open to class politics in a way that later black nationalists were often not. Yet, they also felt that racism ran so deep in American society that the possibilities of black and white solidarity were illusory. This was a key reason for seeking international support. The Panthers' internationalism placed the struggles of African Americans in a broader context only by discounting the promise of homegrown working-class solidarity of the kind that had been so important in the development of civil rights unionism in the Thirties and Forties.

The dilemma with which the Panthers wrestled was how to effect social change when the agency for such change seemed to be diminishing. If white workers were too devoured by racism and subdued by consumerism, and if the democratic process was too feeble to bring about the social transformation necessary to revolutionize the lives of African Americans, what strategy should one pursue? They were wrestling, too, with the conundrum of how to relate the specific injustices faced by black communities to the wider struggles for social change. Both were questions that had faced antiracists throughout modern history, and which would be posed in an even sharper fashion in the last decades of the twentieth century.

It was a conundrum that would tear the Panthers apart. Violence, for some, became not a means of resisting racism but an end in itself. "What is necessary now is a party to advance and expedite the armed struggle", Kathleen Cleaver told the *Guardian* in 1971. Cleaver was the Panthers' Communications Secretary and, at the time, exiled to Algeria after her husband, Eldridge Cleaver, had been charged with attempted murder. "We need a people's army and the Black Panther vanguard will bring that about", she claimed. Having discounted the possibilities of working-class solidarity, there seemed little left for the Panthers apart from, on the one hand, community action, and, on the other, the cosplay of armed insurrection. They were, at the same time, the target of ferocious state repression. The FBI launched a programme of surveillance, sabotage, misinformation, agent provocateurs and lethal killings in an attempt to eviscerate the organization. Faced with crushing hostility from the state, as well as constant surveillance, raids and violence, internal faction fighting, and feuds with rival nationalist groups, the Black Panthers fragmented in the early 1970s and dismantled itself a decade later. Only the myths remained.[36]

VI

The mythmaking surrounding the Panthers—both the romanticization and the demonization—has helped obscure the other side of Sixties Black Power: its conservatism. Harold Cruse, a Communist Party member who became a trenchant black nationalist, observed that Black Power was *"nothing but the economic and political philosophy of Booker T. Washington given a 1960s militant shot in the arm"*. The confrontation between integrationists and nationalists was the latest expression of a battle that tailed back more than a century, to the disagreements between Frederick Douglass and Edward Blyden over the "back to Africa" projects, and to the debates between WEB

Du Bois and Booker T. Washington, and later between Du Bois and Marcus Garvey. What Washington had recognized, Cruse wrote, was that "the Negro had to achieve economic self-sufficiency before demanding his political rights". Garvey had added "the racial ingredient of black nationalism to Washington's ideas with potent effect". From Garvey to Malcolm X to Stokely Carmichael, "the Negro nationalist ideology", Cruse concluded, "regards all the social ills from which the Negroes suffer as being caused by the lack of economic control over the segregated Negro community."[37]

There was truth to this view of Sixties black nationalism. US politics, Malcolm X wrote, "is ruled by special-interest groups and lobbies". "What group", he asked, "has a more urgent special interest, what group needs a bloc, a lobby, more than the black man?" Similarly, Stokely Carmichael insisted that "*Before a group can enter the open society, it must first close ranks*... group solidarity is necessary before a group can operate effectively from a bargaining position of strength in a pluralistic society". For all the revolutionary bravado, this was the stuff of community brokerage, of machine politics and Tammany Hall, of the exercise of group power in a plural society. At its heart were two deeply conservative themes. The first was an argument about group identity that can be traced back to Herder; the view of black people as a self-contained group with its own culture, values and ways of living. The second was a claim about ethnic capitalism, the insistence on replacing white capitalists with black ones.[38]

"In Africa they speak of Negritude", wrote Julius Lester, a leading figure in SNCC. "It is the recognition of those things uniquely ours which separate us from the white man". And what separated blacks from whites was culture. Drawing on the argument of Léopold Senghor, Lester insisted that "the uniqueness of black culture" was that its "emphasis is on the nonverbal... it is the experience that counts, not what is said". Black people "have a language of their own". The words may be English "but the way a black person puts them together and the meaning that he gives them creates a new language". Black people have another language too: "that language is rhythm". Lester not only draws on Herderian arguments about culture and difference but embraces racist tropes about African Americans as "nonverbal" and possessing a love of "rhythm" to define them as uniquely black. Black people's unique culture, Lester feared, was under mortal threat. "Since the earliest days of slavery", he wrote, whites had enforced "a program of cultural genocide". Black nationalism was about resisting that genocide.[39]

The poet and critic Amiri Baraka was a founder of the Black Arts movement which was to the Sixties as the Harlem Renaissance was to the Twenties. A member of the Beat Generation in the 1950s, the influence of Malcolm X led him to embrace black nationalism, and to change his name from LeRoi Jones. The Black Arts movement was "the aesthetic and spiritual sister of the Black Power concept" that aimed to create a "Black aesthetic" and sought "the destruction of the white thing, the destruction of white ideas, and white ways of looking at the world". "Black Culture is alien to the white man", claimed Baraka. Black people were, for Baraka, "a race, a culture, a Nation" and "In order for the Black Man in the West to absolutely know himself, it is necessary for him to... seek a Black politics, an ordering of the world that is beneficial to his culture, to his interiorization and judgment of the world". This was raw racial thinking remade as cultural nationalism.[40]

Baraka shed his nationalism for Marxism in the 1970s. He recognized the dangers of appropriating racial thinking even for the cause of equal rights. He recognized, too, the importance of class in any struggle for equality. And he came to realize that simply having black faces in positions of power did little to combat racism or empower working-class blacks. He had spent many years trying to transform the politics of his hometown Newark by ensuring that there were black city officials in large numbers and in the highest positions. But, he wrote despondently, "Newark, the desolate wasteland of 1967, is now the desolate wasteland of 1976". It was "a city where a Black Muslim is head of the Board of Education, and collaborates with the capitalists in mashing budget cuts on the people of all nationalities by trying to fire 20 per cent of the city's teachers... and condemning the cafeteria workers, security guards and maintenance men, who are on strike now, to wages of $3,000 and $4,000 a year." "The solution is not to become the enemy in blackface", as he put it in his autobiography.[41]

The tendency to "become the enemy in blackface" was exacerbated by the second conservative theme in Sixties Black Power—

the celebration of black capitalism. Baraka, before his epiphany in the 1970s led him to reject black nationalism, had helped organize the first major Black Power conference, a three-day jamboree in Newark in July 1967. It took place immediately after almost a week of rioting had burnt down the city centre and left twenty-six people dead. Baraka's co-organizer was Nathan Wright, a Republican who would later serve in the Nixon and Reagan administrations. "The basic cause" of the riots, Wright suggested, was "pathology in the experience of black people". The conference, Manning Marable notes, "was housed in a plush, white-owned hotel" with "a stiff registration fee" to reduce the number of working-class activists. "The general concensus [sic] of this gathering", Julius Hobson, one of the more leftwing delegates, noted approvingly, "was that we need to transfer the economic power wielded by white men in the Black ghettoes of America to Black men". Not tear down the ghettoes, or provide decent housing and conditions, but ensure that those who controlled and profited from them were black capitalists.[42]

The next Black Power conference the following year, in Philadelphia, was co-sponsored by Clairol. Most remarkably, given the general impression of Black Power as a revolutionary movement, Richard Nixon, on the Presidential trail, endorsed it. "Much of the black militant talk these days", he observed, "is actually in terms far closer to the doctrines of free enterprise than to those of the welfarist thirties—terms of 'pride', 'ownership', 'private enterprise', 'capital', 'self-assurance', 'self-respect'". Federal policy "ought to be oriented towards more black ownership, for from this can flow the rest—black pride, black jobs, black opportunity and yes, black power".[43]

VII

The historian Robin Kelley has recalled how, in 2002, he was invited on to talk shows to discuss the case of the "Central Park Five". On 19 April 1989, a 28-year-old white woman, Trisha Meili, had been beaten and raped while jogging in New York's Central Park. She was in a coma for twelve days and had no recollection of the events. That same night, five young men—four of whom were African American and one Hispanic—were arrested and charged with rape, assault, attempted murder, robbery and riot. No forensic evidence linked any of the suspects to the crime. Under coercion, they confessed to being accomplices to the rape, confessions they later retracted. All were convicted and received sentences of between five and fifteen years. In 2002, murderer and rapist Matias Reyes confessed to the crime, DNA and other evidence confirming his guilt. The Central Park Five—Antron McCray, Kevin Richardson, Raymond Santana, Yusef Salaam and Kharey Wise— having spent up to thirteen years behind bars, were released and their convictions vacated.[44]

The media were interested in Kelley's take because of the echoes of the Scottsboro Boys. "Some of the comparisons", Kelley writes, "were strikingly obvious: the press demonized the defendants, calling the Scottsboro boys 'brutes', 'animals' and 'savages', just as the Central Park Five became known as a 'wolfpack'. The press demonized the mothers, as well as blaming single parenting and dysfunctional families for their behaviour... They were falsely convicted thanks to forced confessions, media hysteria, an overzealous prosecutor, and a longstanding racist discourse that presumes all black and brown men to be violent sexual predators." There was, however, "one fundamental difference... the presence of the left"; or rather, in the case of the Central Park Five, its absence. Where, in the 1930s, the activities of the left allowed both blacks and whites to recognize the significance of antiracism to working-class struggles, and to witness first-hand the relationship of antiracism to wider movements for social justice, the retreat of the left in recent decades has made such comparisons and such campaigns far more difficult. In the case of the Scottsboro Boys, it was the Communist Party and the ILD that were able to give voice to working-class blacks ignored even by the elite leadership of black organizations. There was no equivalent for the Central Park Five Today there is a new set of elite gatekeepers, but their authority is rarely challenged. Meanwhile, the meaning of antiracism has shifted from demands for political rights and material improvements to calls for the recognition of identity.[45]

The phenomenon that perhaps best illuminates these trends, and the dilemmas of contemporary antiracism, is Black Lives Matter, the most resonant movement challenging racism since "Black Power".

It began as a hashtag created in response to the acquittal in 2013 of George Zimmerman, who had the previous year shot dead an unarmed black teenager, Trayvon Martin, claiming "self defence". Around the hashtag, Alicia Garza, Patrisse Cullors and Opal Tometi created an online network. It became a national campaign during the three-month-long street protests in Ferguson, Missouri, that erupted after the shooting dead in August 2014 of unarmed black teenager Michael Brown by police officer Darren Wilson. And it exploded into international consciousness during the worldwide protests that followed the killing of George Floyd by Minneapolis police officer Derek Chauvin in 2020, for which he was eventually tried and convicted of murder. And as the movement expanded, it also expanded its remit, not just challenging police brutality but, for example, calling also for the removal of statues deemed racist and the "decolonization" of the educational curriculum.

For some, the movement represents a critical reawakening of antiracist consciousness and of black self-expression. For others, it is a divisive, even racist, organization that betrays the legacy of the 1960s civil rights struggle. In fact, what the movement, and the debate around it, gives voice to is the tension I have traced through this book, between a desire to push out and create a more universal perspective and a retreat into a narrow, racialized sense of identity.

Mike Brown and George Floyd were but two in a long list of African Americans killed by the police. Since the Ferguson protests, the *Washington Post* has gathered annual statistics for the numbers of people shot dead by police. That number barely changed between 2015 and 2021, remaining at around a thousand every year, rising slightly to 1,050 in that last year. The Mapping Police Violence (MPV) project collates figures for all deaths caused by the police. The figures broadly match that of the *Washington Post*, virtually all those who died at the hands of the police being shot dead; according to the MPV, 1,144 people were killed by police in 2021. The data also reveal a disproportionate number of African Americans killed. The *Washington Post* suggests that you are more than twice as likely to be a black victim as a white victim, while the MPV database suggests a disproportionality of almost three to one.[46]

Some studies, such as those of Harvard economist Roland G. Fryer, claim that the disparities are the products not of a racist reality but of poor statistical techniques. "Rates of crime, violent crime, hostile police encounters, and arrests vary dramatically between Blacks and whites", the criminologist Wilfred Reilly observes, "and adjusting for any of those rates eliminates the apparent disparity in police shootings". It is, however, not so simple. Many studies have shown that crime rate figures, or police encounters, are not independent variables—they themselves can be shaped by racial bias. African Americans are, as the Sentencing Project observes, "more likely than white Americans to be arrested; once arrested, they are more likely to be convicted; and once convicted, they are more likely to experience lengthy prison sentences". There is considerable evidence, for instance, that blacks and whites use and sell drugs at remarkably similar rates. But black men are arrested, convicted and imprisoned at far higher rates than whites—in some states black men being imprisoned at between twenty and fifty times the rate of white men, an issue to which I will return in the next chapter. One cannot simply adjust for the fact that crime figures, or the rate of hostile police encounters, are higher for blacks, without taking into account that those rates themselves may be distorted by racism.[47]

There are, nevertheless, questions to be asked about the BLM narrative. It is not just African Americans whose lives are devastated by police killings. More than half of those killed by US police are white; and while, proportionately, police killings of African Americans have fallen in recent years, those of white people have risen. While racism might be involved in the disproportionate numbers of black people killed by police, that disproportion cannot be explained simply as the product of racism. Studies show, unsurprisingly, that police violence is correlated with poverty—the poorer a neighbourhood, the greater the risk of an individual being killed by the police. African Americans are disproportionately poor and working class; poverty and class location must also play a role in their being victims of police violence.[48]

A 2020 study by the social epidemiologist Justin Feldman provides evidence for this while also suggesting that the correlation between income and police violence is stronger for whites than for blacks; it suggests, too, that while poorer whites are more susceptible to police violence than wealthier blacks, at any income level, blacks are more likely to be killed than whites. Other analyses suggest that once income levels are considered, the racial disproportion disappears. Such contradictory findings are almost inevitable—these are early studies, not all peer-reviewed and all wrestling with complex and fragmentary data. What all point to, however, is the significance of both race and class in defining whom the police kill.[49]

Black people have suffered grievously and disproportionately from police violence, but paradoxically not simply because of racism. Nor is it just African Americans who have suffered grievously and disproportionately. Working-class people—black, white, Hispanic, Native American—have, too. In viewing police violence primarily in racial terms, there is a danger both that we ignore much of the police violence meted out to working-class whites and that we miss out on significant shifts in policing strategy.[50]

US policing has always been violent and deadly. Many of the current issues with policing derive, however, from changing attitudes and policies towards the urban poor over the past fifty years. "Lower-class culture is pathological", claimed American political scientist Edward Banfield in his 1974 book *The Unheavenly City Revisited*. An influential conservative voice, Banfield played a significant role in transforming the liberal ethos of Sixties' social policy to the conservatism of the 1980s. Banfield divided society into four classes—upper, middle, working and lower. The upper-class individual is "self-respecting, self-confident and self-sufficient" and highly "future-oriented". The middle-class personality is a paler version of this, "less future-oriented" and without "as strong a sense of responsibility to the community". The "working-class individual does not 'invest' as heavily in the future" and is "little disposed to either self-improvement or self-expression". The nadir is reached with "the lower-class individual" who merely "lives from moment to moment", his behaviour controlled by "impulse" because "he cannot discipline himself" and "has no sense of the future." His "bodily needs (especially for sex) and his taste for 'action' take precedence over everything else—and certainly over any work routine". He lives in poverty because he is "not troubled by dirt and dilapidation".[51]

In many ways, Banfield was a voice from the past, echoing the arguments of early 20th-century eugenicists and racial scientists.

But his thinking was shaped also by the "culture of poverty" thesis that came to dominate the 1960s. It was an idea originally put forward by liberals such as the anthropologist Oscar Lewis, and the political scientist Michael Harrington, founder of the Democratic Socialists of America, whose book *The Other America* provided inspiration for President Johnson's "War on Poverty". Lewis described the culture of poverty as "a way of life", a set of "basic values and attitudes", that constitute an "adaptation" to poor people's "marginal position" and "is passed down from generation to generation along family lines". While it began as a liberal notion, and an argument for state intervention, the conservative spirit of the "culture of poverty", the view of social problems as the fruit of individual pathology rather than of a failure of policy, soon came to the fore. The lower class was, for Banfield, beyond redemption. "Owing to the nature of man and society", he wrote, "we cannot 'solve' our serious problems by rational management". The 1960s call for government action had transmuted by the 1980s into an insistence that any such intervention would only make matters worse.[52]

Banfield did not see African Americans as necessarily part of the lower class. It was, in his view, segregation, not the black mentality, that was responsible for the lowly place in which African Americans found themselves. "The movement of the Negro up the class scale", he believed, "appears as inexorable as that of all the other groups". Banfield combined a reactionary view of the lower class with a more liberal view of African Americans. The liberalism had far less influence than the reaction.[53]

In 1965, Daniel Moynihan, sociologist and Assistant Secretary of Labor in President Johnson's administration, published his report on "The Negro Family", which would become the touchstone for the "War on Poverty". Drawing on the "culture of poverty" thesis, Moynihan argued that the problems faced by African Americans were not simply political or economic, but also cultural. The consequence of "the incredible mistreatment to which [they have] been subjected over the past three centuries" was the making of a "tangle of pathology", the most significant being the creation of a "matriarchal structure" that had imposed "a crushing burden on the Negro male" and led to "the breaking of the family structure on the urban frontier". By the 1980s, with the rise of Reaganism, and the turn to neoliberal policies, the "tangle of pathology" thesis led to the argument that, as with the lower class, little could be done to alleviate African American life. The problem lay within. The only solution was sufficient law enforcement to keep the lower class in its place.[54]

Banfield's student James Quinn Wilson became the godfather of the "broken windows" approach. The smallest infraction—loitering, drinking, jaywalking—should, he insisted, be aggressively restrained. The police must target not just criminals but also "disreputable or obstreperous or unpredictable people". This became the heart of the "zero tolerance" policy of police chiefs such as New York's William Bratton. From Ronald Reagan to Bill Clinton and beyond, social issues were reframed as matters of law and order, and of managing the disruptive effects of the social inequalities.[55]

From the 1960s, many politicians also made a concerted effort to racialize crime, to paint criminality as a black pathology. Southern segregationists in the 1960s used the spectre of black crime to attack civil rights. "This exodus of Negroes from the South" into Northern cities, one Democratic Congressman claimed, "has been accompanied by a wave of crime". What, he demanded, "has civil rights accomplished for these areas?". By the 1970s such arguments had become part of mainstream Republicanism. HR Haldeman, presidential aide to Richard Nixon, noted in his diary that for Nixon "the whole problem is really the blacks. The key is to devise a system that recognizes this while not appearing to." The "war on drugs", which began in the 1970s, sharply reinforced the criminalization of African American communities.[56]

Yet, while the law-and-order drive was deeply imbued with racism, there was also more to it than that. Class, as sociologist Ronald Weitzer observed, was "an important, but often overlooked, factor shaping citizens' attitudes and experiences". Weitzer and his colleagues studied three neighbourhoods in Washington DC: white middle class, black middle class and black working class. The experiences of policing in the middle-class neighbourhoods, whether black or white, were remarkably similar. In both there was a positive view of the police, and in neither were residents bothered by the use of excessive force. For working-class blacks, police abuse was a daily feature of life. As one observed of the policing of middle-class black areas, "they don't treat them like [they treat us]... They know who they can push around and who they can't".[57]

As policing became a matter of containing the "dangerous classes", so the police "came to think of themselves as soldiers in a battle with the public". Militarized units such as Special Weapons and Tactics (SWAT), with full body armour and automatic weapons, initially created to deal with rare acts of exceptional violence, such as barricaded suspects or armed confrontations, became increasingly deployed to serve drugs warrants and even take part in routine, inner city patrols. In 1997, the Clinton administration launched its "1033" programme under which the Pentagon handed over to police forces surplus military equipment, from armoured vehicles to grenade launchers. Since the programme was inaugurated, US police departments have received $7.4bn worth of hardware this way. Policing was not just militarized but moved into new areas, such as schools. In her book *Lockdown High*, Annette Fuentes describes a talk by a trainer to school police: "You should be walking around in school every day in complete tactical equipment, with semi-automatic weapons... You must think of yourself as soldiers at war." In 1967, James Baldwin had written about "every Northern city with a large Negro population" being "policed like occupied territory". By the twenty-first century the police were boasting that they were just that, and right across the country.[58]

This history is important because it allows us to see contemporary police violence in a different context, not just as the product of racism, but also as the consequence of a long campaign to contain the "lower class", and of the shift to policing, rather than assuaging, poverty. To ignore the wider context and consequence of the law-and-order drive, is both to rewrite the history of militarized policing and to disregard many—indeed the majority—of the victims of police violence. Neither approach allows us to understand, or to challenge, the disproportionate numbers of African Americas being killed by the police.

VIII

On 5 May 2020, sanitation workers in New Orleans formed the City Waste Union and walked out on strike, deciding that they had had enough of poverty wages, lack of safety equipment during the Covid epidemic and the refusal to recognize unionization. And in so doing, they exposed the conundrum of a campaign like Black Lives Matter. New Orleans privatized its sanitation services in 1996. Virtually all the sanitation workers are black. The company that now runs the city's sanitation services, Metro Service Group, is black-owned. "Black Lives Matter" meant something different on the two sides of the class divide.[59]

BLM leaders are not oblivious to the importance of class to the struggle against racism. Alicia Garza has long been a campaigner for low-paid workers and was the special-projects director in the Oakland office of the National Domestic Workers Alliance. The organization's approach, nevertheless, cut against the possibilities of class-based politics. In a "What we believe" statement published in 2016, BLM noted that "We see ourselves as part of the global Black family" but did not mention class. (The statement was subsequently taken down after a controversy over one of the demands to "disrupt the Western-prescribed nuclear family structure".) The trouble is, the "global Black family" is a confected unity that serves only to obscure divisions with black communities and makes the creation of solidarity across racial lines more difficult. That is why Claude McKay a century ago derided Marcus Garvey for "ignoring all geographical and political divisions" among black people. It is what led Frantz Fanon to write of the black middle class in newly independent African nations that "we observe a permanent see-saw between African unity, which fades quicker and quicker into the mists of oblivion, and a heart-breaking return to chauvinism in its most bitter and detestable form". It is what prompted Malcolm X at the end of his life to talk "about the need to shift our focus… from race to class". It is the reason Amiri Baraka broke with black nationalism, condemning a "'blackness' that in many ways was bogus", its principal aim that of "carping at the black masses to follow the black middle class because this black middle class knew how to be black when the black workers did not".[60]

What was true a century ago, and half a century ago, is truer now. Many who have taken up the BLM banner, like many within the race consciousness movements it historically follows, conflate the necessity of challenging racism with the building of racial solidarity. Pursuing the second aim makes achieving the first more difficult. Even within America there is no single identity or set of interests that bind together all black people, and only black people; still less, all people of colour. To assume that there is only reinforces the power of the black elites and diminishes the voices of black workers, making it more difficult to tackle the problems facing those at the sharp end of racism.

New Orleans originally privatized its services under the excuse of helping local black businesses. Black bosses are, however, little different from white bosses and treat their workers with no more consideration. It does not matter to them that they and their black workers are supposedly part of the same global family. The strikers were fully aware that they stood in a long tradition of black working-class action. They saw themselves as inheriting the spirit of the famous 1968 Memphis sanitation workers' strike, even adopting the "I Am A Man" slogan. But they did not see theirs as simply a "black" cause. "Black exploitation does not end because the company is Black," Daytrian Wilken, spokesperson for the City Waste Union observed. "Their bottom line needs them to exploit Black men." When their workers went on strike, Metro responded by employing prison labour to do the work, a sordid strike-breaking tradition that goes back to the days of slavery.[61]

The New Orleans sanitation workers came out on strike three weeks before George Floyd was murdered in Minneapolis. They remained on strike throughout the swathe of protests that swept the nation and the world that summer, a summer that brought racism and black lives to the forefront of global consciousness. Yet, by September, they had been forced back to work having won few of their demands. They were grateful for the support they had received but it was insufficient to sustain the strike. The lesson is that challenging racism, and defending the rights of black workers, requires solidarity beyond that rooted in racial identity.

9

STAY IN YOUR LANE!

I

Kanye West knew how to tweak liberal tails. The rapper embraced
Donald Trump, calling him "my brother" and insisting that "the mob
can't make me not love him". Then, in a 2018 interview explaining
why he was all in with the president, West also suggested that slavery must have been "a choice" on the part of black people because it
had lasted four centuries.[1]

There was a swift backlash. From 50 Cent to Spike Lee to
Roxane Gay, celebrities, scholars and seemingly half of Twitter
pushed back. What outraged many critics was not simply the idiocy
of West's comments but also that he was a black man saying it. His
was an act of betrayal of the black community, indeed of his very
blackness. In an acerbic tear-down entitled "I'm not black, I'm
Kanye", the essayist Ta-Nehisi Coates recalled his mother's
response to Michael Jackson. He "was dying to be white", she had
observed; he was "erasing himself, so that we would forget that he
had once been Africa beautiful and Africa brown". Thirty years on,
Coates has a similar response to West as someone attempting to
escape black history and the black community, to be not-black.
West, Coates claimed, championed "a white freedom", a "freedom
to be proud and ignorant". All blacks "suffer for this, because we
are connected". When Jackson "destroyed himself, he was destroying part of us, too". And so it was with West. He needed, Coates
insisted, to embrace the "black freedom that called him back".
What is being imposed here are what the philosopher Kwame
Anthony Appiah has called "life-scripts" which establish the only
"proper ways of being black".[2]

While some cast out West into the pale beyond the boundaries of blackness, others insisted that whites should butt out of the debate. "If you think that you get to criticise black people for selling out to the system of anti-blackness that you as a non-black person benefit from and help maintain", wrote Ijeoma Oluo, a Seattle-based writer, "you need to check your privilege and be quiet for a while". Whites, she added, should "stay in your own lane".[3]

"White freedom". "Black betrayal". "Stay in your lane". To be antiracist in the twenty-first century is to view political values in racial terms; to insist that if one is reactionary, one has lost the privilege of being black; to erect racial boundaries beyond which certain people should not step. Where once antiracists might have seen these as prescriptions to challenge, now they are regarded as edicts to embrace. And where once antiracists saw their mission as combating racism, now many see it as confronting whiteness. This chapter tracks the trajectory of this racial somersault.

The first part of the chapter explores a complex set of changes in the postwar decades that transformed our understanding of race and identity and allowed for the recasting of antiracism. These changes include the growing estrangement of many on the left from the Enlightenment and ideas of universalism, on the one hand, and from the working class and class politics, on the other; the increasing significance of culture as a lens through which to understand social relations; and the breakdown of the postwar order and the rise of neoliberalism. The second part looks at how these changes fundamentally shifted the narrative about race, ushering in identity politics, giving birth to Critical Race Theory, and enabling new debates around whiteness and white privilege. Again, I look primarily at the race debate in America. It is here that many of the new themes about race and identity appeared in their sharpest forms. Understanding their flaws and weaknesses allows us to understand also the failings and limitations of the paler reflections of these ideas exported elsewhere.

II

"There is no document of civilization that is not at the same time a document of barbarism." So reads the inscription on Walter

Benjamin's tombstone in Portbou, in Girona, on the Spanish-French border, a quotation from his final work, "Theses on the Philosophy of History". A German Jewish philosopher and essayist, Benjamin was associated with the Institute for Social Research, better known as the Frankfurt School, an eclectic group of Marxists that became influential in the postwar world. He was forced, like other members of the School, to flee Germany when the Nazis came to power. Hoping to travel to America via Portugal, he was caught by Franco's police while crossing from France into Spain. Fearing that he would be transported to a German concentration camp, Benjamin committed suicide with an overdose of morphine.[4]

The tragedy of Benjamin's death was accentuated by the fact that in his intellectual life, too, he was wrestling with the question of how humanity could escape barbarism. If the impact of Nazism was eventually to discredit old-style racial thinking and to tarnish sections of the right, it was also to disorient the left, leading many to interrogate their most fundamental assumptions about history and progress. The question that haunted Benjamin was how Germany, a modern, scientific, advanced nation, deeply nourished by the Enlightenment, and with the strongest working-class movement in Europe, could so capitulate to Nazism. His answer was that barbarism was stitched into the fabric of modernity.

This was the argument, too, of *Dialectic of Enlightenment*, a pivotal 1944 work by Theodor Adorno and Max Horkheimer, two leading members of the Frankfurt School, both of whom had successfully found refuge in America. The fingerprints of Benjamin's "Theses" (which Adorno and Horkheimer had received from Hannah Arendt, another Jewish intellectual forced to flee Germany, and to whom Benjamin had entrusted his copy of the manuscript) can be found throughout the book. Enlightenment rationality, Adorno and Horkheimer argued, created new possibilities of discipline, control and annihilation. As another Frankfurt school exile in America, Herbert Marcuse, who became a guru of the 1960s student revolt, explained: "Concentration camps, mass exterminations, world wars and atom bombs are no 'relapse into barbarism' but the unrepressed implementation of the achievements of modern science, technology and domination." It was a thesis that, over time, would become more widely embedded on the left. So would the despair about human possibilities that it expressed.[5]

237

Nazism, as we have seen, did not emerge from nowhere but drew upon ideas and practices that already flourished, from colonialism to eugenics. Racial thinkers wrapped around themselves the cloak of science; liberal imperialists often claimed to be acting in the name of progress. This was, though, as the philosopher Tzvetan Todorov has observed, "to replaster the façade of a building constructed for quite a different purpose". Radical universalists from Toussaint Louverture to CLR James would have agreed. They not only recognized the importance of Enlightenment ideals in challenging racism and colonialism, but understood, too, that racial barbarism sprung from the denial of such ideals to all of humanity. In presenting Nazi savagery as the logical, indeed necessary, outcome of Enlightenment rationalism, Frankfurt school thinkers, and those that followed in their wake, signalled their abandonment of that radical tradition.[6]

It was not just the Enlightenment with which many on the left became disenchanted. It was also the other traditional shibboleth of the left, the proletariat. The postwar boom, the growth of living standards, and the rise of the consumer society and of mass culture, all seemed to have drawn the teeth of the working class. "Why should the overthrow of the existing order be of vital necessity", Marcuse asked, "for people who own, or can hope to own, good clothes, a well-stocked larder, a TV set, a car, a house, and so on, all within the existing order?" In his "Letter to the New Left", C. Wright Mills, the social theorist who was a major influence on Sixties radicalism in America, derided those who "cling so mightily to 'the working class'" as the agent of change; that was "a labour metaphysic", a "legacy from Victorian Marxism that is now quite unrealistic". The real change-makers were the "young intelligentsia". For large sections of the left there was, in the mordant words of historian H. Stuart Hughes, disappointment that "the class which Engels had celebrated as the 'heirs of classical philosophy' had failed to perform in the style expected of it", preferring "creature comforts to heroism, and kitsch to the elevation of its intellect."[7]

The "New Left" that emerged in the late 1950s was a loose association of groups and individuals self-consciously opposed to the "old left" of the communist parties and trade unions. It found expression in many parts of the world and there were different local flavours, in Britain, America, many European nations, many nations in Latin America. There were also many common themes and attitudes. The New Left developed partly in response to the tyranny of Stalinism, and sought to restore humanism into Marxist thinking, addressing issues from free speech to feminism that were often marginalized on the traditional left. It also embodied the disaffection with the Enlightenment and the working class. Where the old left had looked to the working class as the motor of change, the New Left found new, surrogate proletariats in the New Social Movements—third-world liberation movements, civil rights organizations, feminist groups, campaigns for gay rights. Where the old left had talked of class and sought to raise class consciousness, the New Left talked of culture and sought to strengthen cultural identity. It was not that New Left thinkers entirely abandoned their attachment to class politics. EP Thompson, one of the founding figures of the British New Left, was also the author of one of the finest studies of working-class history in *The Making of the English Working Class*. Nevertheless, central to the outlook of the New Left was not class but culture.

In Britain, this change was institutionalized through the academic discipline of "cultural studies", the original home of which was the Centre for Contemporary Cultural Studies in Birmingham University, founded and inspired by Richard Hoggart and Stuart Hall. The cultural perspective opened up new ways of telling stories about people and groups who had previously been ignored. It also distorted both the past and the present. The working class came to be defined as much by its cultural attributes as by its economic or political aspect, a shift that gathered momentum as its economic and political power declined.

Then, in the late 1970s and 1980s, an even more momentous transformation took place as the postwar order rooted in consensus politics and Keynesian economics gave way to a new era of "neoliberalism", exemplified by the economic and social policies of Margaret Thatcher and Ronald Reagan: the unleashing of free-market economics, deregulation and globalization, privatization and reductions in state spending, and more individualized and unequal societies. It was the period in which the labour movement and trade unions were gravely weakened, the left lost political influence, and the new social movements themselves disintegrated; the period in which the possibilities of radical social transformation seemed to fade. And it was the period in which social conversations about politics and class gave way to increasingly fraught exchanges about culture and identity.

III

The significance of culture in the postwar world was not merely that it provided a new perspective on class differences. It was also that it acted as a synonym for race, the concept that had oxygenated the prewar world, but was now all but unusable, at least in polite circles. Culture came to the rescue, becoming, as race had been previously, the marrow of the new age.

The hard graft of turning culture into a surrogate for race had already been accomplished in the early twentieth century, largely by a new breed of anthropologists, led by the German American Franz Boas and his circle of students, that included such stellar names as Margaret Mead and Ruth Benedict. Influenced by both German Romanticism and liberal egalitarianism, and repelled by racial science, Boas took the Herderian vision of a plurality of cultures and turned it into an anthropological concept. It was a notion of culture functionally equivalent to that of race, except in rejecting any sense of one group being inferior or superior to another, and in which the essence of a people was rooted in history rather than in biology. In the postwar world, as ideas of human differences were remapped on to the terrain of culture, concepts such as "multiculturalism" and "ethnic pluralism" became the new language of social policy and political debate.[8]

The Boasian understanding of culture embodied three key elements that came to shape the worldview of large sections of the left. First, it was both egalitarian and relativist; no culture was better or worse than another, just different. Second, one's relationship to a specific culture was so deeply rooted that it was difficult to excise that culture from our being. Every culture, in Boas' view, moulded an individual's behaviour to such an extent that, "we cannot remodel, without serious emotional resistance, any of the fundamental lines of thought and action that are determined by early education, and which form the subconscious basis of all our activities". Leslie White, one of Boas' students, insisted that the individual was not "the initiator and determinant of the culture process" but "a tiny and relatively insignificant part... of a vast socio-cultural system that... extends back to their remote past". Humans do not make culture, culture makes humans. As the historian George Stocking observed, "The idea of culture which once connoted all that freed men from the blind weight of tradition, was now identified with that very tradition".[9]

These all became signature themes for many postwar thinkers. The political philosopher Will Kymlicka insists that it is difficult to move from one culture to another and that "the choice to leave one's culture" is "analogous to the choice to take a vow of perpetual poverty and enter a religious order". Since cultures are essential to people's lives, if any "is threatened with debasement or decay, we must act to protect it". Where, in the prewar world, the desire was to protect the "purity of blood", in the postwar era, many sought to preserve the "authenticity" of a culture. And where once intellectuals worried about the degeneration of the race, many now feared cultural decay. For the philosopher Charles Taylor, once "we're concerned with identity", nothing "is more legitimate than one's aspiration that it is never lost." Hence, a culture needs to be protected not just in the present but through "indefinite future generations".[10]

All this fed into the third key feature of the postwar concept of culture: a vision of a world comprising myriad distinct cultures, not inextricably intertwined, but stiffly separate; a view, too, of human interactions as better understood in terms of cultural differences rather than of social similarities. The French anthropologist Claude Lévi-Strauss, perhaps the most important figure in the discipline after Boas, explained this perspective with a striking simile:

> Cultures are like trains moving each on its own track, at its own speed, and in its own direction. The trains rolling alongside ours are permanently present for us; through the windows of our compartments, we can observe at our leisure the various kinds of car, the faces and gestures of the passengers. But, if on an oblique or parallel track, a train passes in the other direction, we perceive only a vague, fleeting, barely identifiable image, usually just a

momentary blur in our visual field, supplying no information about the event itself and merely irritating us because it interrupts our placid contemplation of the landscape.[11]

For Lévi-Strauss, "Every member of a culture is as tightly bound up with it as this ideal traveller is with his own train": "From birth and... probably even before, the things and beings in our environment establish in each of us an array of complex references forming a system... We literally move along with our reference system, and the cultural systems established outside it are perceptible to us only through the distortions imprinted upon them by our system." Indeed, we may even be "incapable of seeing those other systems". Or, as an activist might demand today, "Stay in your lane!"[12]

These three elements of the Boasian vision created an understanding of cultures as fixed self-contained units, each separated from every other by a sharp discontinuity; of individuals as belonging to one distinct culture, within which all shared a common and unique set of references about the world; of humanity as divided into discrete groups and shaped by differences, not commonalities.

There was, particularly in the last decades of the twentieth century, a tension between a Boasian understanding of discrete cultures and the notion of cultural hybridity and intermingling, which became an indispensable feature of postmodern thinking. For the philosopher Homi Bhabha, the vital metaphor was not of trains passing on different tracks but of "the stairwell as liminal space in-between the designations of identity", the "hither and thither" of which "prevents the identities at either end... from settling into primordial polarities". Yet this postmodern concern with ephemerality, impurity and fragmentation never fully displaced the Boasian view, and writers and thinkers would often talk of hybridity while insisting also on the discreteness of cultures.[13]

The Boasian vision was one of which Herder would have approved. It is also one which, despite Boas' egalitarianism and loathing of racial thinking, Knox and Hunt, Moreton and Ripley, would have understood, for it is their model of a racial world transposed to the terrain of culture. Boas, Lévi-Strauss and their followers helped construct the bridge over which the ghost of racial thinking was smuggled into the body of cultural pluralism. It was the bridge that allowed Julius Lester to speak of "those things uniquely ours which separate us from the white man", that made it possible for Amiri Baraka to insist on the necessity of "the Black Man... [seeing] himself as culturally separate from the white man". It was the bridge over which the politics of identity eventually thronged to plant its flag in a new field.[14]

IV

"Black people are the magical faces at the bottom of society's well. Even the poorest whites, those who must live their lives only a few levels above, gain their self-esteem by gazing down on us. Surely, they must know that their deliverance depends on letting down their ropes. Only by working together is escape possible. Over time, many reach out, but most simply watch, mesmerized into maintaining their unspoken commitment to keeping us where we are, at whatever cost to them, as to us."[15]

That is the arresting image that opens Derrick Bell's 1992 book *Faces at the Bottom of the Well*. It is a work of existential despair, but, for Bell, the only realistic way of thinking about the place in which African Americans find themselves. Racism, he wrote, "is an integral, permanent and indestructible component of this society". Black people "will never gain full equality". Even "those herculean efforts we hail as successful will produce no more than temporary 'peaks of progress', short-lived victories that slide into irrelevance as racial patterns adapt in ways that maintain white dominance. This is a hard-to-accept fact that all history verifies." Not to accept that fact was to do great mental and emotional harm. Since "racial equality is... not a realistic goal", to be "constantly aiming for a status that is unobtainable in a perilously racist America" would lead only to "frustration and despair".[16]

Few people will have heard of Derrick Bell. Yet, few people have been more important in shaping contemporary thinking about race, particularly in America. From Barack Obama to Ta-Nehisi Coates, leading black thinkers have paid tribute to Bell's inspiration. There are not many legal scholars in recent memory, wrote Michelle Alexander, the influential author of *The New Jim Crow*, who "have [had] a greater impact on racial justice thought and advocacy".[17]

Bell is the godfather of what has come to be called Critical Race Theory (CRT). Beginning as a movement within American legal

studies that brought a postmodern sensibility to thinking about the
law, CRT developed into a critique of the liberal "civil rights"
approach to tackling racism, a critique nurtured by a hostility to
universalism, humanism and the Enlightenment. "Enlightenment-
style Western democracy is... the source of black people's subordination", wrote Richard Delgado, one of the movement's founders, because "racism and enlightenment [sic] are the same thing".
Many of the themes that CRT champions—the centrality of race,
rather than of class, to discussions about social issues; the view of
racism as a problem of whiteness; the significance of "white privilege"; the disparagement of the Enlightenment legacy; the politiciza-
tion of identity—became much more widely suffused in twenty-
first-century debates about race and racism, moulding thinkers from
Ibram X. Kendi to Robin DiAngelo.[18]

Born in Pittsburgh in 1930, Bell attended the University of
Pittsburgh's law school, the only black graduate in his class, before
becoming an attorney in the NAACP Legal Defense Fund. As part
of the civil rights assault on Jim Crow, Bell supervised the desegregation of more than 300 schools. Desegregation often led to white
flight, as white families moved elsewhere rather than send their
children to integrated institutions. The result was that many deseg-
regated schools remained segregated, not by formal procedure but
through informal practice. This conundrum led Bell to question
whether it was truly possible to rid society of racism. He had taken
his first step on the road to racial pessimism.

In 1969, Bell joined Harvard Law School. At the end of the
decade, he published perhaps his most celebrated paper, challenging
the conventional view of Brown v Board of Education, the famous
1954 Supreme Court case that invalidated state-sanctioned segregated schools. Desegregation was not the consequence of a moral
desire for racial equality, Bell insisted, but a pragmatic response to
political needs, a recognition that segregation hindered "America's
struggle with communist countries to win the hearts and minds of
emerging third world people" and was "a barrier to further industrialization in the South". Racial progress only occurred when it
aligned with white interests, and when those interests changed, any
attachment to equality was ditched. Whites, he wrote, "simply cannot envision the personal responsibility and the potential sacrifice...
that true equality for blacks will require".[19]

In reality, desegregation was the product of many developments. The American authorities were certainly worried about the image created by Jim Crow and wanted to minimize its propaganda value to the Soviet Union. Desegregation was also a response to the long struggle, not just by black Americans, against racism. The recognition of the immorality of American apartheid played its role, too. And the overthrow of Jim Crow, while it did not bring about the kind of equality African Americans hoped for, nevertheless helped reset the moral dial. The attitude of most Americans to issues from equality to inter-racial marriage was very different by the end of the century than it had been in the era of Jim Crow.

Because racism was ineradicable, so not only would antiracist action "not lead to transcendent change", in Bell's view, but "may indeed, despite our best efforts, be of more help to the system we despise than to the victims of that system whom we are trying to help". And, yet, Bell insisted, antiracists must continue struggling against racism even as they acknowledged that there could be no prospect of success. They had to combine "recognition of the futility of action" with "the unalterable conviction that something must be done, that action must be taken".[20]

Few who were inspired by Bell's work tumbled as far as he did into the well of despair, but pessimism has nevertheless shaped much contemporary thinking about race. "Isn't it time we ask ourselves: What if Bell was right?", Michelle Alexander reflected in a foreword to a new edition of *Faces at the Bottom of the Well* in 2018. "What if justice for the dark faces at 'the bottom of the well' can't actually be won in the United States?... What if racism is permanent? What if?" It is a pessimism rooted in many trends we have already explored: the left's disenchantment with the Enlightenment and with the working class, the degradation of the universalist tradition, the institutionalization of neoliberalism, the enervation of the labour movement. Like Bell himself, Alexander insists that "accepting the permanence of racism in this country does not mean accepting racism".[21]

Yet, challenging racism while believing it to be ineradicable has inevitably shaped the character of antiracism. It has prompted a shift from campaigns for material change to demands for symbolic gestures and representational fairness. After all, if racism is permanent, and attempts to eliminate it futile, then antiracism becomes reduced to little more than a kind of public performance or finger-wagging at white people to make them feel guilty or, at best, an attempt to make the unfairness a little less unfair. "These days", as Paul Gilroy has observed, identity too often "ceases to be an ongoing process of self-making and social interaction", but "becomes instead a thing to be possessed and displayed".[22]

It also becomes a thing to be guarded and policed. For, if racism is permanent and ineradicable, then combating it cannot be about winning equality but can only be about carving out a space within which one can assert a degree of power and autonomy. Hence the demand to "Stay in your lane". Perhaps no issue expresses this better than the controversy over "cultural appropriation".

V

On the evening of 24 August 1955, 14-year-old African American Emmett Till went with some friends to Bryant's Grocery in Money, Mississippi. Living in Chicago, he had come to Mississippi to visit relatives. He walked into the shop and bought two cents' worth of bubble gum. Witnesses claimed that Till flirted with the white shop owner, Carolyn Bryant. Four days after the alleged incident, in the dead of night, her husband Roy Bryant and his half-brother JW Milam, who had been out of town on a trucking job, drove to the house where Till was staying, and kidnapped the boy. They beat him up and mutilated him before shooting him in the head and dumping the body in the Tallahatchie River. Till's body was discovered three days later. Weighted down by a fan blade wrapped around his neck with barbed wire, the body was swollen beyond recognition. The teeth were missing. An ear was severed. An eye was hanging out. The only thing that identified Till was a ring. The following month, an all-white jury found Bryant and Milam not guilty of murder. Protected against double jeopardy, the two men admitted in a 1956 interview with *Look* magazine that they had tortured and murdered the boy. They received $4,000 for their story.[23]

Till's mother Mamie Elizabeth Till-Mobley insisted on an open casket at her son's funeral to expose to the world the savagery of lynchings. She invited photographers to capture the mutilated body.

"I wanted the world to see what they did to my baby", she said. Fifty thousand people saw Emmett Till's disfigured body as it lay in its open casket in church. Millions more saw the photographs in *Jet* magazine, causing shock and outrage. Emmett Till, and the haunting photographs of his broken body, became an indelible, almost ineffable, symbol for the burgeoning civil rights movement.

Sixty years later, the artist Dana Schutz painted "Open Casket", an image of Till in his coffin, drawn from the photographs. The painting was included in the 2017 Whitney Biennial Exhibition in New York. Many objected to a white painter depicting such a traumatic moment in black history. The British artist Hannah Black organized a petition to have the work destroyed. "Although Schutz's intention may be to present white shame", her open letter read, "this shame is not correctly represented as a painting of a dead Black boy by a white artist". According to Black, "the subject matter is not Schutz's; white free speech and white creative freedom have been founded on the constraint of others, and are not natural rights."[24]

A few months later, the novelist Zadie Smith stood in front of the painting with her children. Schutz's work did not impress her—"I didn't feel very much"—but she pondered whether she, a biracial British woman, was deemed black enough for the subject matter to be hers? And what of her children? Their father is white: "by the old racial classifications of America, they are 'quadroons'". "Are my children too white to engage with black suffering?", Smith wondered. "How black is black enough?" And what about Hannah Black herself? She, like Smith, is a British biracial woman. Is she "black enough to write this letter", demanding the painting be destroyed, Smith mused. "Who owns black pain?" Smith was attempting both to untangle the absurdities of racial categories and to push back the inclination to evaluate moral rights by virtue of the group to which individuals are deemed to belong—a practice inextricably bound with racial thinking, and its horrors.[25]

Cultural appropriation has variously been defined as the "unauthorized use of another culture's dance, dress, music, language, folklore, cuisine, traditional medicine, religious symbols, etc" and as "an expression of privilege" which exposes that while "people of color are forced to adopt elements of mainstream white culture, white people can sample at the buffet of other cultures at their leisure, picking and choosing what they wish to consume". Culture in such discussions is unreflexively viewed through a Herderian or Boasian lens, every culture deemed to be a fixed, self-contained unit, every culture separated from every other by a sharp discontinuity, every culture possessing a specific set of traits and forms. But what is it for music or a cuisine—or "pain"—to "belong" to a culture? And who gives permission for someone from another culture to use such cultural forms?[26]

There are few answers to such questions because the debate about cultural appropriation is less about ownership than about gatekeeping—about the tacit rules that define social boundaries, and the legitimacy of carrying cultural baggage across those boundaries. Every society has its gatekeepers, whose role it is to protect certain institutions, maintain the privileges of particular groups and cordon off some beliefs from challenge. Black elites have often tried to silence dissident voices, the NAACP's attitude towards the Scottsboro parents being a good example. Gatekeepers shield not the marginalized but the powerful. Racism itself is a form of gatekeeping, a means of denying racialized groups equal rights, access and opportunities. The policing of cultural appropriation is no different, though the polarities have been reversed, and it is executed in the name of antiracism.

Many critics of cultural appropriation insist that they are opposed not to cultural engagement, but to racism. They want to protect marginalized cultures and to ensure that such cultures speak for themselves and are not simply seen through the eyes of more privileged groups. They want also to ensure that it is not white people but minorities that profit from the promotion of their culture. It is true that cultural engagement does not take place on a level playing field but is shaped by racism and inequality. Racism ensured, for instance, that the great black pioneers of rock 'n' roll rarely received their due, whereas many white artists, from Elvis Presley onwards, were feted as cultural icons. Yet, as Amiri Baraka has observed, the issue here is not that of cultural appropriation at all. "If the Beatles tell me that they learned everything they know from Blind Willie [Johnson]", he told the cultural critic Leonard Schwartz in a radio discussion, "I want to know why Blind Willie is still running an elevator in Jackson, Mississippi. It's that kind of inequality that is abusive, not the actual appropriation of culture because that's normal."[27]

Baraka is highlighting the distinction between campaigns that seek to transform the material conditions of African Americans and campaigns for "recognition" or for the policing of racial boundaries. The campaigns against cultural appropriation expose how the first has been abandoned for the second. Preventing the Beatles from drawing on the work of Blind Willie Johnson would have done little to improve black people's lives. It would not have overthrown Jim Crow laws in the 1950s. It would not rid America of discrimination in the labour market today. Nor will preventing Dana Schutz "profiting" from painting Emmett Till protect the Emmett Tills of today.

Equally troubling is that a campaign such as that against Schutz's work contains, as the American critic Adam Shatz has observed, an "implicit disavowal that acts of radical sympathy, and imaginative identification, are possible across racial lines". Black history, Shatz insists, following in the path of Frederick Douglass and WEB Du Bois and James Baldwin, "is American history" and "confronting it [is] a common burden". That is precisely the perspective that has been lost through the retreat from the universalist standpoint. The danger, as the novelist Kamila Shamsie tweeted (in response to a different controversy over cultural appropriation), is that "'You—other—are unimaginable' is a far more problematic attitude than 'You are imaginable'".[28]

VI

In 1935, while writing his masterpiece *Black Reconstruction in America*, WEB Du Bois pondered the question of why, in the wake of the Civil War, there had not developed working-class solidarity across racial lines. "The South, after the war", he observed, "presented the greatest opportunity for a real national labor movement which the nation ever saw or is likely to see for many decades". Yet, he lamented, "the labor movement, with but few exceptions, never realized the situation. It never had the intelligence or knowledge, as a whole, to see in black slavery or Reconstruction, the kernel and meaning of the labor movement in the United States." The principal reason was "the race philosophy" which "came as a new and terrible thing to make labor unity or labor class-consciousness impossible. So long as the Southern white laborers could be induced to prefer poverty to equality with the Negro, just so long was a labor movement in the South made impossible".[29]

Thirty years later, Theodore Allen was reading Du Bois' work and contemplating the same question: why had there never been a proper working-class movement or labour party in America as there had been in European nations? Allen was a veteran union activist, Marxist and independent scholar whose two-volume *The Invention of the White Race*, first published in the mid-1990s, was a groundbreaking exploration of the emergence of racial ideas in America and foundational for the development of "whiteness studies". He came to the same conclusion as Du Bois—that white workers had been bought off by being invested with a sense of racial superiority over black workers. For cross-racial solidarity to be established, Allen observed in a 1967 pamphlet, white workers had to believe that "An injury to one is an injury to all". Many of Allen's fellow-radicals, he acknowledged, despaired of them ever believing that because "the injury dealt out to the black worker has its counterpart in the privilege of the white worker. To expect the white worker to help wipe out the injury to the Negro is to ask him to oppose his own interests." That interest lay in defending "white-skin privilege". Allen did not necessarily agree. "The race-privilege policy is", he wrote, "contrary to the interests, short-range as well as long-range interests, of not only the Black workers but of the white workers as well". Nevertheless, he remained ambivalent about the possibilities of cross-racial solidarity because he was unsure whether white workers could ever be weaned off racism, ever disabused of the illusion of "white-skin privilege".[30]

Thirty years on again after Allen's 1967 pamphlet, the concept of "white privilege" had become standard currency among Critical Race Theory academics and antiracist activists. This was partly through the work of Allen, and of fellow activist historians such as Noel Ignatiev, who had established the discipline of "whiteness studies" through their retelling the story of how European immigrants to America became "white". By the 1990s, though, the debate was no longer about how to establish cross-racial working-class solidarity. Rather, "white privilege" was now seen simply as something that all white people possessed by virtue of being white. The legal scholar Cheryl Harris, in an influential paper in the *Harvard Law Review*, defined whiteness as "property" that all white people owned. The feminist and antiracist activist Peggy McIntosh explained it "as an invisible package of unearned assets that I can count on cashing in each day, but about which I was 'meant' to remain oblivious". In a celebrated metaphor, she wrote of "an invisible weightless knapsack of special provisions, assurances, tools, maps, guides, codebooks, passports, visas, clothes, compass, emergency gear, and blank checks" that all white people carry with them, but others do not.[31]

Thirty years on again, and today it is a concept that moved from academia to mainstream discussion. From *Good Housekeeping* to *GQ*, popular magazines have published guides to white privilege. Organizations from the National Health Service in Britain to many local councils put out explainers about white privilege. Children's books ask *What is White Privilege?* Trainers such as Robin DiAngelo have become international celebrities, charging thousands of dollars for seminars in which she would castigate white people refusing to accept their racism as exposing "white fragility".[32]

With little public debate or pushback, debates about racism have become framed largely through discussions of whiteness and of white privilege. To make sense of this, and to see why this framing should concern us, it is important to understand the history of the evolution of the concept. What began as an attempt to wrestle with a particular problem about labour organization in America became transformed into a general thesis about white people at the very moment that despair gripped much of the left about the possibilities of building a vibrant labour movement. As the "sympathetic critic" of whiteness studies Peter Kolchin wrote in 2002, "underlying the new interest in white power, privilege, and identity there is evident an intense discouragement over the persistence of racism, the unexpected renewal of nationalism, and the collapse of progressive movements for social change that characterize the current era".[33]

It is not just the shift in the meaning of "white privilege", and its timing, that should give us pause, but also the ways in which the way the concept is deployed. The term "white" is used in different ways in much of the discussion, and those different ways are often conflated. It can be a description of those deemed racially white. It can be an analysis of the power relationships that underly discrimination and bigotry. And it can be a value judgment—whiteness is regarded in some sense as "bad". In an essay for the *Washington Post* in 2015, rabbi Gil Steinlauf wrote that "in a flawed and racist society, we Jewish Americans... must cease to consider ourselves to be part of the social construct of whiteness" and "teach our children that we are, in fact, not white, but simply Jewish". Often it is used in all three senses simultaneously.[34]

Underlying the white privilege thesis are two basic claims. First, that "white" is a useful category in which to place everyone from Elon Musk to a cleaner in a Tesla factory. And, second, that being in such a category imbues people with privileges denied to those not in that category.

The idea that all those deemed white have a common identity and set of interests which may conflict with those of non-whites is, of course, an argument long deployed by racists (the contemporary resurrection of this claim is the theme of the next chapter). It is a claim that most antiracists would reject, recognizing that the interests of white factory workers or shelf-stackers are not the same as those of white bankers or business owners but are far closer to those of black factory workers or Asian shelf-stackers—the very issue with which Du Bois and Allen were wrestling. Why, then, do many ignore this when it comes to the question of "white privilege"? Because, proponents argue, white people do not have to endure the discrimination suffered by non-whites by virtue of their skin colour. At one level, this is true. "Racism" refers to the practice of discrimination against, and bigotry towards, certain social groups; there may be many reasons for such discrimination and bigotry, but one is clearly that those who are non-white are often treated unequally. Projecting this in terms of "white privilege" is, however, flawed. First, it is not a "privilege" not to have to face discrimination or bigotry; it should be the norm. The author Reni Eddo-Lodge acknowledges that it is difficult to define "white privilege" because "it's so difficult to describe an absence". That absence is equal treatment, a right that all should possess. To describe as a "privilege" the fact that one is not being denied equal treatment is to turn the struggle for justice on its head.[35]

Second, the concept of white privilege fails to distinguish between "not being discriminated against or not facing bigotry because of one's skin colour" and "having immunity from discrimination or bigotry because one is white". The distinction is important. Many whites, because of privileges afforded by wealth and class, do have immunity against discrimination. But many others, who are poor or working class, do not. Their experiences of state authority is often similar to that of non-whites. We have already seen this in the discussion about police killings; we will see it again later in this chapter in discussing mass incarceration. In America, someone who is poor and white is more likely to be killed by the police or face imprisonment than wealthy African Americans. It is true that, because of racism, the proportion of black Americans who are wealthy or middle class is far smaller than the proportion of white Americans in those categories. But that is not an argument to erase the fact that having white skin does not necessarily provide materially significant "privilege" whereas being wealthy may do so even if black.

In *Natives*, his reflection on the relationship between race, class and the ghosts of Empire in contemporary Britain, the rapper Akala suggests that "the idea that millions of white people still being relatively poor somehow proves that white privilege does not exist is such a juvenile and historically illiterate argument". After all, he points out, "there were poor whites in the Jim Crow south, apartheid south [sic] Africa and slave colonies of the Caribbean and no one would be silly enough... to claim that white privilege did not exist back then". Yet, the analogies themselves show why the argument is not so "juvenile and historically illiterate". Apartheid societies whether in South Africa or the American South, or slave colonies in the Caribbean, are fundamentally different from modern liberal democracies. However deep-seated may be racism in contemporary Britain or America, the relationship of race, class and privilege is significantly dissimilar to that in apartheid or slave societies.[36]

Eddo-Lodge insists on the importance of "complicating the idea that race and class are distinctly separate rather than intertwined"; in other words, of seeing the intricate interconnections between the two rather than viewing it in Manichean terms. Many contemporary writers make a similar plea even as they push the idea of white privilege. The trouble is, the concept of "white privilege" poses the issue in black and white terms, both literally and metaphorically. By holding whiteness to be an always-significant factor in the life of every white person, the "white privilege" thesis erases the complications, imposing a one-size-fits-all notion of privilege. It fails to tease out the different relations of power that the interactions of race and class imply, and it racializes social divisions unlinked to race.

VII

America locks up more of its citizens than any other nation. In 2019, 639 Americans out of every 100,000 were behind bars, almost double the incarceration rate of Russia and more than five times that of China. It has not always been this way. In 1970, fewer than 200,000 Americans were in jail. By 1980 the figure stood at 316,000. In 2009, the prison population peaked at an astonishing 1,614,000, since when it has slightly fallen, though remaining well over a million in 2019. These are just inmates of federal and state prisons; once those held in local jails, tribal jails, juvenile facilities and immigration detention centres are included, the figure reaches almost two million. The reason for this staggering rise was the law-and-order drive that obsessed America in the last decades of the twentieth century and, in particular, the war on drugs. As with police killings, African Americans have disproportionately borne the brunt of the brutality. The figures are truly shocking. Black Americans are five times as likely to be imprisoned as white Americans. One study suggested that one in three black men born in 2001 were likely to find themselves in jail sometime during their life.[37]

Many activists have viewed mass incarceration as "the new Jim Crow", most notably the lawyer and author Michelle Alexander who adopted that phrase for the title of an influential book. "In the era of colorblindness", she writes, "it is no longer socially permissible, to use race, explicitly, as a justification for discrimination, exclusion and social contempt". So, "we use our criminal justice system to label people of color 'criminals' and then engage in all the practices we supposedly left behind" because "it is perfectly legal to discriminate against criminals in nearly all the ways that it was once legal to discriminate against African Americans". Mass incarceration is "a stunningly comprehensive and well-disguised system of racialized social control that functions in a manner strikingly similar to Jim Crow".[38]

Mass incarceration would seem to be the classic illustration of many of the themes at the heart of CRT: the significance of race; the failures of liberal antiracist policies; the reappearance of racism in new forms rather than its eradication; white privilege as a shield against discriminatory excesses; racism as "an integral, permanent, and indestructible component" of American society. Yet, as James Forman has observed, the story is considerably more complicated; and those complications illustrate many of the flaws of the "white privilege" thesis I have just explored. A former public defender, and now a law professor at Yale, Forman points out that the law-and-order drive and the war on drugs were not simply the products of white racism. They were also supported by black communities. When, in 2014, the Sentencing Project surveyed attitudes to criminal justice policy, it discovered that almost two-thirds of African Americans thought that courts did not treat criminals "harshly enough"—and that, as Forman observes, "even after forty years of tough-on-crime tactics, with their attendant toll on black America".[39]

Black communities in the Seventies and Eighties, Forman notes, were "devastated by historically unprecedented levels of crime and violence", especially during the crack epidemic of the 1980s. In response, black officials, who now controlled many inner cities thanks to shifts brought about partly by the civil rights movement, "advocated tough-on-crime measures in race-conscious terms". Racism certainly "shaped the political, economic, and legal context in which the black community and their elected representatives made their choices" and "narrowed the options available". Forman has long opposed America's "overly punitive criminal justice system" and "the toll that mass incarceration has taken on the African American community". He "agree[s] with much of what the New Jim Crow writers have to say". Nevertheless, it remains the case that the drive towards hardline policing came from within black communities as well as from without; and "we who seek to counter mass incarceration will be hobbled in our efforts if we misunderstand its causes and consequences".[40]

Forman observes also the significance of class as well as race in understanding mass incarceration. "One of the central motivations of Jim Crow", he writes, "was to render class distinctions within the black community irrelevant, at least as far as whites were concerned". It ensured that "blacks of all classes" were subject to "subordination and humiliation". "One of mass incarceration's defining features", however, "is that, unlike Jim Crow, its reach is largely confined to the poorest, least-educated segments of the African American community." A black man "born in the late 1960s who dropped out of high school has a 59% chance of going to prison in his lifetime whereas a black man who attended college has only a 5% chance".[41]

Class distinctions have always existed within African American communities—witness the attitudes of the NAACP elite towards the Scottsboro parents—but since the 1960s a true black middle class has developed, which makes it far more important to take such distinctions into account. The comparison to Jim Crow laws is, Forman insists, headline-grabbing but misguided. The destruction of Jim Crow and the expansion of the black middle class—"changes of this magnitude require us to modify how we discuss race". Unfortunately, "racial justice advocates have been reluctant to acknowledge how class privilege mitigates racial disadvantage". Or, indeed, transforms the meaning of white privilege.[42]

Not only does much of the discussion about mass incarceration ignore class distinctions within black communities, it also often ignores the extent to which whites, too, are the targets. An analysis by Nathaniel Lewis for the People's Project think tank concludes that "race is not a statistically significant factor for many incarceration outcomes, once class is adequately controlled for". His study "provides weight to the assertion that mass incarceration is primarily about the systematic management of the lower classes, regardless of race". Another study by John Clegg and Adaner Usmani shows that the ratio of the incarceration rate of African Americans to that of whites has remained largely steady over the past century. The shifts that have occurred run contrary to the "New Jim Crow" thesis. While there has always proportionately been more black prisoners than white, the ratio of black prisoners to whites rose between 1900 and 1970 but has fallen since 1990—the reverse of what should have been the case if mass incarceration marked the resurrection of

Jim Crow. What has risen dramatically since the 1970s is the incarceration rate among high school dropouts, while the rate among college graduates (black and white) has declined. In 2017, Clegg and Usmani suggest, "a white high school dropout was about fifteen times more likely to be in prison than a black college graduate". Again, this is a story about class, and the policing of the poor, as much as it is about race.[43]

The savagery of mass incarceration in America reveals the complex relationship between race and class. To suggest that is not to "deny racism" or to fall into the trap of "class reductionism" as some have claimed. It is simply not to wish away the complexities of the world. Without facing up to those complexities, it becomes impossible to fashion a strategy whether to oppose racism or to defend working-class interests.

VIII

"Transcending racial consciousness", wrote Georgetown law professor Gary Peller in a seminal CRT paper, "forms a large part of the deep appeal that the integrationism vision has for many". But not for Peller, or for most supporters of Critical Race Theory. Accompanying the preoccupation with whiteness and white privilege is the demand from many to preserve race consciousness, not for whites but for blacks. The integrationist desire to erase race consciousness is itself, according to the critics, a form of white supremacy. "Within black communities", Peller writes, quoting the African-American economist and activist Robert S. Browne, "there is the general skepticism that the negro, even after having transformed himself into a white black-man, will enjoy full acceptance in American society". And there is "doubt that even should complete integration somehow be achieved, it would prove to be really desirable, for its price may be the total absorption and disappearance of the race—a sort of painless genocide".[44]

Unlike white racial consciousness, black racial consciousness is not a form of racism, Peller argues, because "in opposition to the essentializing of race in which white supremacists engaged, [black] nationalists located the meaning of race in history, in the social structures that people—rather than God or some objectified nature—have created". In other words, it is an understanding of race rooted not in biology, but in history and culture. Yet, as we have seen, history and culture provided the new language of race in the postwar world. And, as we shall see in the next chapter, today's white supremacists also root their racial views in history and culture.[45]

A racialized community, Peller argues, is necessary to sustain the "social bonds of identity, recognition, and solidarity". Richard Delgado and Jean Stefancic observe that many now believe "that people of color can best promote their interests through separation from the American mainstream. Some believe that preserving diversity and separateness will benefit all, not just groups of color."[46]

Communities are vital, and racial identity played an important role in allowing African Americans to survive slavery and Jim Crow. But even in the nineteenth century, black communities were not homogenous, nor black and white cultures sharply distinct. That is even more so today.

"Why is it", asked the novelist and essayist Ralph Ellison in 1963, "that so many of those who would tell us the meaning of Negro life never bother to learn how varied it really is?" Ellison was responding to an essay by Irving Howe, socialist, literary critic and editor of *Dissent* magazine, in which he defended the novelist Richard Wright as the authentic voice of African Americans while castigating younger figures, including Ellison and James Baldwin, for their criticisms of Wright and for what he regarded as their betrayal of the black tradition. There is a particular kind of white liberal, Ellison wrote, for whom "unrelieved suffering is the only 'real' Negro experience", and who "when he looks at a Negro... sees not a human being but an abstract embodiment of living hell". "The most distressing aspect of Howe's thinking", he added, was "his Northern white liberal version of the white Southern myth of absolute separation of the races".[47]

Even under Jim Crow, Ellison observed, black cultures and white cultures were deeply entangled. At the same time, what sustained black cultures was not merely "race consciousness" but the capacity to move beyond that consciousness. James Baldwin was "not the product of a Negro store-front church but of the library"; as were Richard Wright and Ellison himself. It was through reading "Marx, Freud, TS Eliot, Pound, Gertrude Stein and Hemingway", through reading "books which seldom, if ever, mentioned Negroes" that Ellison was able to "release" himself "from whatever 'segregated' idea I might have had of my human possibilities". "It is not skin color which makes a Negro American", he insisted, "but cultural heritage as shaped by the American experience". The "Negro American writer", Ellison observed in another essay, is heir not just to the black experience but also "the human experience which is literature" and which may "well be more important to him than his living folk tradition".[48]

In *Omni-Americans*, published in 1970, at the height of Black Power sensibility, the writer, critic and novelist (and friend of Ellison's) Albert Murray challenged the black nationalist account of African American culture. "*American culture*", he wrote, "*even its most rigidly segregated precincts, is patently and irrevocably composite*". The blues, the most black but also the most American of forms, was "*the product of the most complicated culture, and therefore the most complicated sensibility in the modern world*". A generation later, Henry Louis Gates Jr. reminded us that "African American culture... has been the model of multiculturalism and plurality". Black writers and musicians were forever blending myriad forms and traditions. "Even a vernacular form like the spirituals", he observed, "took as its texts the King James version of the Old and New Testaments".[49]

The image of a singular black community bound together by a "race consciousness" was far more plausible at the time Ellison and Murray were writing than it is now. The irony is that the less plausible it became, the more that many antiracists clung to it. A key reason lay in the economic and political shifts in the last decades of the twentieth century that narrowed political possibilities, transformed the understanding of difference and commonalities and had a profound influence on the character of antiracism. The pessimism that had inflected Derrick Bell's thinking now found wider purchase. After the defeat of the black power movement, wrote the feminist and black activist bell hooks, "after so many rebels were slaughtered and lost", after so "many of these voices were silenced by a repressive state", and "others became inarticulate", it "has become necessary to find... new ways to talk about racism and other politics of domination". That new way was through "radical

259

postmodernist practice, most powerfully conceptualized as 'a politics of difference'". The irony is that hooks was a cogent defender of class politics, noting that "Nowadays it is fashionable to talk about race or gender; the uncool subject is class". Nevertheless, she, too, seemed blindsided by the pessimism of our age.[50]

It was against this background that the "politics of identity" emerged as a radical cause. The transformation of the New Social Movements into what we now call identity politics had already begun in the 1970s. "Society as a whole seemed unbudgeable", sociologist and Sixties radical Todd Gitlin wrote; so, many came to believe that "perhaps it was time for specialized subsocieties to rise and flourish". "The principle of separate organization on behalf of distinct interests raged through 'the movement' with amazing speed... One grouping after another insisted on the recognition of difference and the protection of their separate and distinct spheres." Or, as the political philosopher Wendy Brown has put it, "What we have come to call identity politics is partly dependent upon the demise of a critique of capitalism".[51]

The term "identity politics" was coined in 1977 by the American Combahee River Collective, a group of black lesbian militants, in their "Black Feminist Statement". The most radical politics, they argued, came from placing their own experiences at the centre of their struggles. "Focusing upon our own oppression", they wrote, "is embodied in the concept of identity politics". Black radicalism provided a template for many other groups, from women to Native Americans, from Muslims to gays, to look upon social change through the lens of their own cultures, goals and ideals. For the Combahee River Collective, as for many such identity movements in the 1960s and 70s, their specific struggle was inextricably attached to broader campaigns for change. As labour movement organizations and radical struggles disintegrated through the 1980s and beyond, so the recognition of identity became not a means to an end, but an end in itself.

In a 1991 paper on "intersectionality" and identity politics, Kimberlé Crenshaw, who coined the term "intersectionality", distinguished between the claims "I am Black" and "I am a person who happens to be Black". "I am Black" is both "a statement of resistance" and "a positive discourse of self-identity", that "takes the socially imposed identity and empowers it as an anchor of subjectivity". To say "I am a person who happens to be Black", on the other hand, is "straining for a certain universality (in effect 'I am first a person')". While that may be useful in certain contexts, "at this point in history... the most critical resistance strategy for disempowered groups is to occupy and defend a politics of social location rather than to vacate and destroy". In other words, we live in times in which any universalist perspective, or any desire to transcend imposed categories of race, is chimerical, and so we must appropriate for ourselves the identity cages in which we have been placed.[52]

Aims that had previously been seen as reactionary were now embraced as radical. Many became suspicious of the very notion of equality. "Much civil rights reform", bell hooks wrote, "reinforced the idea that black liberation should be defined by the degree to which black people gained equal access to material opportunities and privileges available to whites—jobs, housing, schooling, etc." But these were "ideas about 'freedom'... informed by efforts to imitate the behaviour, lifestyles, and most importantly the values and consciousness of white colonizers". What had been the touchstone of any progressive movement for the previous two centuries—the right to equal access to jobs and housing and schooling—was now regarded by many as imitating the "values and consciousness of white colonizers".[53]

Many today defend identity politics on the grounds that it is simply another name for struggles against racism or women's oppression or homophobia; they claim that those who question identity politics are turning their backs on such struggles. The British writer Nesrine Malik distinguishes between "defensive" and "aggressive" identity politics. The former is "the effort to secure the rights denied to some on the basis of their identity". The latter "is that which seeks domination on the basis of identity". Aggressive identity politics is the politics of race and of whiteness. Defensive identity politics is the struggle for equality for those groups denied it. It is an argument that ignores the social and political context in which the "defensive" politics of identity emerged.[54]

There have been, throughout modernity, struggles against racism, women's oppression and the denial of rights to many "on the basis of their identity". But, for most of that time, such struggles were linked to a radical universalism that insisted on a common humanity and universal rights. There have also always been identitarian movements insisting on embracing racial categories as a means of escaping the burden of racism. But these were mostly seen as conservative. What changed at the end of the twentieth century was that the radical universalist tradition was all but extinguished, allowing identitarians to embrace race consciousness without challenge and to present themselves as the real radicals. The narrative visible in the 1960s, when Malcolm X and black nationalists were mythologized as the radicals and Martin Luther King and the integrationists as conservative, became entrenched by the end of the century.

The politics of identity has transformed the meaning of belongingness and solidarity. An important distinction historically has been that between the inward-looking "binding" politics of identity, and the outward-looking "bridging" politics of solidarity. The former mobilizes by emphasizing shared membership of a particular identity, be that gender, sexuality, race or nation. The politics of solidarity also stresses collective endeavour, but views commonality as emerging not from particular identities but out of a shared set of values and beliefs, and the struggles to win acceptance for those values and beliefs. The distinction is not always clear-cut—elements of both co-exist in many forms of collective politics. It is, however, the politics of solidarity that has crumbled over the past three decades as radical movements have declined and the power of organized labour drained away. For many today, the only form of collective politics that seems possible is that rooted in identity.

The question people ask themselves today is not so much "In what kind of society do I want to live?" as "Who are we?". The two questions are, of course, intimately related, and any sense of social identity must embed an answer to both. But as the political sphere has narrowed, and as mechanisms for political change have eroded, so the answer to the question "In what kind of society do I want to live?" has become shaped less by the kinds of values or institutions people want to establish, than by the kind of people that they imagine they are; and the answer to "Who are we?" has become defined less by the kind of society they want to create than by the history and heritage to which supposedly they belong. The frameworks through which we make sense of the world are not so much political as identitarian; not so much "liberal" or "conservative" or "socialist" as "Muslim" or "white" or "European".

IX

"This is white people doing it to white people, so y'all gonna fight amongst yourselves." Whoopi Goldberg's comments on ABC's *The View* in 2022 about the Holocaust being not "about race" but a form of "white on white" violence were shocking and drew a slew of condemnation. She quickly put out an apology and, after discussing the issue with Jonathan Greenblatt of the Anti-Defamation League, wrote: "I stand corrected."[55]

Goldberg was not denying the Holocaust or the gravity of the catastrophe that befell Jewish people. The discussion on *The View* had been about a Tennessee school board that had removed from the curriculum *Maus*, a graphic novel about the Shoah. Goldberg mocked the censors for being more concerned about nudity and bad language than about the reality of genocide. Nevertheless, the idea of Jews as white and privileged, of racial differences as solely a black and white issue, and of the Holocaust as a quarrel among white folk is so deeply ingrained that even those hostile to racism and to anti-semitism can seem blind to the reality of the Holocaust and of contemporary bigotry against Jews.

The "whiteness" of Jews is a recent phenomenon. It was only in the post-Holocaust world that, in the words of anthropologist Karen Brodkin, "white America embraced Jews and even Jewishness as part of itself". Now, Jewishness was not just "chic in mainstream circles, it also became mainstream", and Jewish intellectuals, such as Hannah Arendt, Susan Sontag, Daniel Bell and Nathan Glazer, became the "interpreters of white America in the 1950s". Yet, however triumphant may have seemed the Jewish entry into whiteness, the story has a different texture to those of other groups—the Irish, the Italians, the Slavs—that followed a similar path, and has a much darker side, too. Throughout modernity, Jews had frequently been the means through which to "think through" wider social concerns. In the late eighteenth century, they were the embodiment of the contest over equality. In the late nineteenth century, they were the personification of modernity and cosmopolitanism for those who despised both. And, in the twentieth century, in the postwar decades, Jews became symbolic of the pernicious quality of whiteness in a way no other group did.[56]

In 1967, James Baldwin published an essay in the *New York Times Magazine* entitled "Negroes are Anti-Semitic Because They are Anti-White". It caused a storm, many accusing him of being antisemitic. That he assuredly was not. Six weeks before he published his *New York Times* essay, Baldwin had resigned from the advisory board of the black magazine *Liberator* in protest at a series of antisemitic articles, "Semitism in the Black Ghetto", that castigated Jews for economic "colonialism". "I think it immoral", Baldwin wrote in a letter to *Freedomways* magazine explaining his resignation, "to blame Harlem on the Jew". "I would like us to do something unprecedented", he added: "to create ourselves without finding it necessary to create an enemy".[57]

In his *New York Times* essay, too, Baldwin argued that the real enemy was not the Jew but the "exploiter". Yet, he racialized the argument in such a way as to make that claim ambiguous. The Jew, Baldwin wrote, "is singled out by Negroes not because he acts differently from other white men, but because he doesn't". "It is bitter", he added, "to watch the Jewish storekeeper locking up his store for the night, and going home. Going, with *your* money in his pocket, to a clean neighbourhood, miles from you, which you will not be allowed to enter".[58]

Baldwin was a subtle and insightful writer, perhaps the most important chronicler of racial confrontation in the 1960s. Yet, the argument about Jewish exploitation of black communities could have been made about any other "white ethnic group"—about Italian shopkeepers or Irish rent collectors or German landlords. But it was not. Jews were singled out, and the exploiters marked as Jews. Where Baldwin was careful not to cross the line into antisemitism, other black intellectuals were happy to leap over it. "The great brainwashing of Negro radical intellectuals", Harold Cruse wrote of his disenchantment with the Communist Party, "was not achieved by capitalism, or the capitalistic bourgeoisie, but by Jewish intellectuals". "When we get ethnocentric and begin to build our black unity, we conflict with Jewish interests", he added. "We confront

Jewish economic interests in our black communities". Cruse's argument exposed both the divisive consequences of communal politics and the way that such politics could encourage bigotry. The black nationalist Julius Lester (who would later convert to Judaism) was even more damning of Jews. In response to criticism that he had read an antisemitic poem in a radio broadcast, Lester claimed that "In America, it is we who are the Jews... it is the Jews who are in the position of being Germans."[59]

Jews, unlike Poles or Italians or the Irish, have long been seen by antisemites as "privileged". Among the more resonant themes of antisemitism are claims that Jews are wealthy and greedy, that they possess inordinate power, that they invisibly control government and the media, that they comprise a sinister, treacherous cabal. Many recent writers have portrayed Jews as "Schrodinger's whites", as a people simultaneously white and not white. But, paradoxically, Jews are also seen as "hyperwhite" in the words of law professor David Schraub, as "the iciest of the ice people", a phrase used by Henry Louis Gates to describe a popular "Afrocentric" thesis that white people are brutal because they are descended from Neanderthals, and Jews especially vicious for being the "'purest' and oldest Neanderthal-Caucasoids". By projecting the problems faced by black people not on to a discriminatory social system or an exploitative economic model, or even on to loathsome landlords and contemptible bosses, but as horrors spawned by "whiteness", it becomes much easier to make the jump from viewing white people as the enemy to seeing Jews as the devils, as the whitest of whites, the iciest of the icemen.[60]

As whiteness has become the currency of antiracism, so the tendency to ignore antisemitism, or even indulge in it, has become more prominent, both within black communities and on the left. There has long been a strand of leftwing antisemitism, rooted in the conflation of Jews with capital and finance and in a Romantic hostility to modernity, represented, as it was for the reactionary right, in the figure of the cosmopolitan Jew. "The whole Jewish world", the nineteenth-century revolutionary anarchist Mikhail Bakunin spat out, "constitutes a single exploiting sect, a sort of bloodsucker people, a collective parasite". Marx and the Rothschilds, were for him, two aspects of the same Jewish conspiracy: "Jewish solidarity, that powerful solidarity that has maintained itself through all history, united them".[61]

Such conspiratorial antisemitism was always a minor strand on the left. It has, nevertheless, been refreshed in recent decades by two developments. The first is hostility to the state of Israel and its brutality towards Palestinians. The identitarian turn on the left has made it easier to target Jews for being Jews, and to hold all Jews responsible for the actions of the state of Israel. It has facilitated the slippage from anti-Zionism into antisemitism, and the blurring of the line between criticizing the policies of Israel and sowing hatred against Jewish people.

The second development is the view of Jews as white and privileged, and therefore the perpetrators of racism but not its victims. In Britain, this became a source of conflict within the Labour Party in the twenty-first century. In his book *Confronting Antisemitism on the Left*, the British leftwing activist Daniel Randall quotes his opponent in a debate about antisemitism as arguing that "Jews are a prosperous, privileged section of the white community... Racism is experience by Black and Asian people, not Jewish people". Randall quotes, too, many Labour Party supporters talking of the Rothschilds as "controlling the world". Nor is it just political activists who cannot see antisemitism. In November 2021, London's Royal Court theatre apologized for naming a money-grabbing billionaire, modelled allegedly on Elon Musk, in Al Smith's play *Rare Earth Mettle*, "Hershel Fink". The character was hastily renamed (to Henry Finn) and the theatre blamed the gaffe on "unconscious bias". It is difficult to know how anyone could fail to see that "Hershel Fink" was an archly Jewish name or that giving such a name to an unscrupulous capitalist would be to play on deep-rooted racist stereotypes. Yet, as writer Jo Glanville pointed out, it is plausible in the sense that "the association of Jews with power and money is so deeply entrenched in our culture that it isn't even questioned".[62]

Th main source of antisemitism remains today the reactionary right. Most of the physical attacks on Jews in the West are from far-right groups or Islamists. The issue of antisemitism on the left, and among antiracists, nevertheless, is a worrying trend. The more we view racism as the problem of whiteness, the more such trends will be strengthened.

10

IDENTITARIANS ALL

THE GHOSTLY AFTERLIVES OF RACE

I

In 1965, Britain passed its first Race Relations Act, outlawing discrimination on the "grounds of colour, race, or ethnic or national origins" in public places. Three years later, a second Race Relations Act made it a crime to promote racial hatred. In between these two Acts, homosexuality was legalized in 1967, as was abortion. In 1970, the Equal Pay Act prohibited discrimination between men and women in terms of pay and conditions. In the midst of these landmark laws marking the beginning of a new, more socially liberal age, the Labour government published in 1969 a white paper called *In Place of Strife*. Its aim was to reduce the power of trade unions. The white paper did not lead to legislation, but influenced future laws making it more difficult to take strike action and outlawing many acts of solidarity.

The contrast between a swathe of laws that removed, or at least reduced, social and political discrimination and legislation that constrained working-class rights was not only marked but also framed the course of policy and law-making over the next half century. Britain became increasingly socially liberal. Between 1989 and 2019, the proportion of the population that thought that gay relationships were wrong fell from 40 per cent to 13 per cent; the numbers opposed to abortions halved, as did those who thought it wrong to have a child outside of marriage. When the first British

Social Attitudes Survey was published in 1983, more than 50 per cent of whites would not countenance a spouse of a different race. By 2020, nine out of ten Britons declared themselves happy for their child to marry someone of another ethnic group. Just three per cent thought you had to be white to be "truly British".[1]

While legislation and attitudes about social issues became increasingly liberal, trade union laws became increasingly restrictive. Labour Party leaders were as keen as Conservatives to curb union power. In the run-up to the 1997 general election, Labour leader Tony Blair, responding to criticisms that the party was too close to the unions, insisted that he had no intention of re-empowering them. "The essential elements of the trade union legislation of the 1980s will remain", he wrote. "There will be no return to secondary action, flying pickets, strikes without ballots, the closed shop and all the rest." "The changes that we do propose", he added, would still "leave British law the most restrictive on trade unions in the Western world".[2]

The result has been the sapping of influence and numbers. Union membership fell from 13.2m in 1979 to a record low of 6.2m in 2016. Fewer than one in four employees is unionized. Many studies have shown the importance of unionization in reducing inequality. Between 1937 and 1979, union membership in Britain doubled while the share of income going to the top one per cent fell by two-thirds. Between 1979 and 2014, membership of unions fell by a half and the share of income for the richest one per cent more than doubled. In America, too, there is "consistent evidence that unions reduce inequality".[3]

The liberalization of social mores and the restrictions on trade union activity are rarely considered in tandem because they are seen as belonging to different narratives. Yet, taken together, they tell an important story about our understanding of equality. They tell us, for instance, why most nations have tolerated economic inequality even as they have sought to reduce racial inequalities. Just as in America, though in a very different way, the economic and the political became detached in Britain, too, as they did in most Western nations. In any struggle for equality, both sides of the equation are important; both the expansion of political rights for minority groups and women, on the one hand, and the demands for all to enjoy decent pay, good housing, adequate welfare benefits and sound social infrastructure, on the other. This is so not least because disproportionate numbers of black and minority populations are working class and poor. In separating the two strands, not only has it been more difficult to advance either kind of equality, but the two have seemingly been set one against each other.

The free-market policies that came to dominate the latter decades of the twentieth century were more able to accommodate equality at a political than at an economic level. This made it easier for many, especially sections of white workers, to be persuaded that the rise of economic inequality, and the lack of social resources, were the products of too great an emphasis on minority rights. It made it easier to blame migrants and minorities for their social problems. The kinds of social fissures that racism had previously fostered now became nurtured by policies aiming to reduce inequalities.

This chapter looks at how the separation of the economic and the political has led to issues of class being viewed in identitarian terms and to the resurrection of notions of "white identity". It shows how the far right has been able to exploit the language of pluralism and diversity to rebrand racist ideas; and how mainstream conservatives have helped rehabilitate far-right claims about immigration, Muslims and whiteness. Finally, I explore what it needs for us to be able to transcend racial categories and escape the identitarian trap.

II

In his influential 2017 book *The Road to Somewhere*, writer and researcher David Goodhart describes a Britain divided "between the people who see the world from Anywhere and the people who see it from Somewhere". "Anywheres", who "dominate our culture and society", have "portable" identities, and their worldview is rooted in a form of "progressive individualism". They place a "high value on autonomy, mobility and novelty and a much lower value on group identity, tradition and national social contracts". They are "comfortable with immigration, European integration and... human rights" and with "most forms of equality (though not necessarily economic)". "Somewheres", in contrast, are more "rooted and usually have 'ascribed' identities—Scottish farmer, working class Geordie,

Cornish housewife—based on group belonging and particular places". They are "more socially conservative" and "feel uncomfortable about many aspects of cultural and economic change—such as mass immigration, an achievement society in which they struggle to achieve, the reduced status of non-graduate employment and more fluid gender roles".[4]

We have heard throughout this book echoes of the contrast between those deemed to espouse an "abstract" universalism and those who derive their ideals and values from particular histories, traditions and places. We can hear it in Maurice Barrès' late nineteenth-century condemnation of the "Kantianism" that turns "our young Lorrainers, Provençaux, Bretons and Parisians... into an abstract ideal man, everywhere identical with himself, while our need is for men firmly rooted in our soil, in our history, in our national conscience". Goodhart's argument is not, however, simply a replay of previous *cris de coeur*. He is speaking also to a new set of political and social divides that have upended political alignments, eroded the old distinction of left and right, led social democratic parties, as well as mainstream centre-right ones, in many Western countries to implode, and nurtured a new populism. He is writing in an age in which the major political fault line in Europe and America is not between left and right, between social democracy and conservatism, but between those who feel at home in—or at least are willing to accommodate themselves to—a globalized world and those who feel left out, dispossessed and voiceless. These are broadly the groups that Goodhart labels "Anywheres" and "Somewheres".[5]

The Anywheres/Somewheres divide explains also, for Goodhart, one particular aspect of the realignment—the re-emergence of white identity as a political phenomenon and of the "white working class" as a significant social category. Goodhart champions the interests and identity of the white working class, whom he views as having been neglected by the "Anywheres" elite. It is an argument that has become common among communitarian and "postliberal" thinkers on both sides of the Atlantic—Michael Sandel, Thomas Frank, Michael Walzer, Michael Lind, Christophe Guilluy, Matthew Goodwin, Maurice Glasman. Postliberals are perhaps best described as former liberals who have become repelled by the excessive individualism of liberalism, and are now shaped as much by the "faith, flag and family" conservatism of Edmund Burke as by the ideas of John Stuart Mill.

In one sense, the Anywheres/Somewheres distinction is a pithy way of talking about the tension between universalist and particularist viewpoints. It is also both more and less than that. From a historical perspective, Goodhart's "Somewheres" are relatively recognizable as carriers of the tradition that originates with Burke and Herder. It is a tradition that views culture as the organic binding for communities, and insists that communities are constituted through history and constrained by values defined as much by place and tradition as by reason and necessity.

The Anywheres, as described by Goodhart, convey, however, a selective form of universalism. Their worldview, rooted as it is in a philosophy of individualism, a contempt for the "lower orders" and the adoption of "portable" identities, is, to a degree, derived from the liberal universalists of the nineteenth century. Yet, as we have seen through this book, this was a standpoint challenged by a more radical tradition, embodied in figures as diverse as Toussaint Louverture, Frederick Douglass, Sylvia Pankhurst, Claude McKay, and CLR James. These were universalists who rejected liberal individualism, embraced the significance of collective action, were hostile to market philosophy, indeed often hostile to capitalism, and strongly anti-imperialist.

Goodhart's remark about Anywheres being "comfortable with… most forms of equality (though not necessarily economic)" reveals the distance between the "Anywheres" and the radical universalists for whom the goal of economic equality was inextricably woven into their mission. In contrast to the elitist philosophies of nineteenth-century liberal imperialists or twenty-first-century globalists, this was a tradition of insurgent universalism that placed working-class struggles at the heart of their project. They were universalists who drew on aspects of both "Somewheres" and "Anywheres". The Anywheres that Goodhart describes, as well as his Anywheres/Somewheres divide, only make sense in the absence of the radical universalist tradition.

There are, in other words, two distinct challenges to liberal individualism: one from the conservative Burke/Herder tradition inimical to universalism, the other from a radical universalism that was as ill-disposed to conservative particularism as it was to liberal elitism. That radical universalism has today largely disappeared as a social force and been seemingly erased from historical memory, too. We have seen the consequences of that disappearance for the antiracist struggle. It has equally shaped perceptions of whiteness and of the Somewheres/Anywheres division.

Postliberal champions of the "Somewheres" are generally hostile to identity politics, insisting on the importance of the "common good". "Fifty years ago", Goodhart writes, "there was no such thing as identity politics; now, it is what mainly motivates the young, London left... The Twitter accounts of Labour activists are more about rape culture or bullying than economic inequality"; a cadre of "middle-class radicals in search of non-economic justifications for their radicalism". In fact, as we have seen, fifty years ago—indeed 150 years ago—there was such a thing as identity politics; it was just not called "identity politics". Both in the concept of race and in certain strands of opposition to racism, the identitarian viewpoint has a long history.[6]

For all their disparagement of identity politics, postliberals are as attached to it as the "Anywheres"; it is just a different form of identity politics, rooted in nation, place or race rather than in race, gender, sex or sexuality. Racial identities are important to both sides, though expressed in different ways. Many postliberals, as we shall see, demand recognition for white identities and are sympathetic to the specific cultural needs of the white working class.

The late philosopher Roger Scruton was no postliberal but an authentic conservative. His Burkean views on culture and nationhood have, however, profoundly influenced postliberal thinkers. The concept of race, Scruton acknowledged, had been discredited; nevertheless, "it is difficult to avoid terms like 'race', not least because they accurately reflect ways of *conceiving social unity*". The idea of race "may still perform a function" denoting as it does "a continuity across generations, based in kinship and intermarriage, but supported also by a consciousness of common descent", though that continuity was not "entirely biological" but "cultural", too. The Boasian bridge that allowed race to be imported into culture was even more important for conservatives than it was for the left. "The real price of community", Scruton concluded, "is sanctity, intolerance, exclusion, and a sense that life's meaning depends upon obedience, and also on vigilance against the enemy". Postliberals, as much as conservatives such as Scruton, think of communities as rooted in the politics of identity and exclusion. In imagining the "common good", they see the "good" as defined through a restricted notion of the "common".[7]

Many aspects of the postliberal critique of contemporary capitalism and liberalism ring true: the rejection of excessive individualism, the excoriation of "technocratic neoliberalism", the anger at soaring inequality, the ire at the abandonment of the working class by social democratic parties. The conclusions they draw from this critique are, however, questionable. The social and political changes that accompanied the slippage of the postwar order into neoliberalism eroded the radical universalist tradition, powered the cultural turn and the emergence of identitarian politics, and infused antiracist movements with a sense of pessimism. Something similar engulfed working-class communities, too.

On both sides of the Atlantic, economic and social changes combined with political shifts to create a world that felt far more precarious and out of control. Old industries declined; labour markets were deregulated; trade union rights were curtailed; the gig economy emerged; inequality soared; and society became more atomized and fragmented. And all at a time when social democratic parties in Europe, and the Democrats in America, increasingly detached themselves from their old working-class constituencies. Many sections of the working class became economically and politically marginalized, and infused with a sense of anger and disaffection. The forms of social organization that once gave working-class lives identity, solidarity and dignity, disappeared.

Cornel West, the American philosopher and socialist activist, has spoken of the "increasing class division and differentiation" within African American communities in the last decades of the twentieth century. It is a process that has helped create, on the one hand "a significant black middle class, highly anxiety-ridden, insecure, willing to be co-opted and incorporated into the powers that be, concerned with racism to the degree that it poses constraints on upward social mobility", and, on the other, "a devastated black industrial working class" cut adrift by deindustrialization and "an underclass that embodies a kind of walking nihilism". What emerged from this, he observed, was "tremendous hopelessness". So it was within many white working-class communities, too. The economists Anne Case and Angus Deaton coined the phrase "deaths of despair" to describe the shocking drop in longevity among sections of working-class whites, caused mainly by a startling rise in fatalities from suicide, alcoholism and drug overdoses.[8]

The marginalization of the working class, and its political voicelessness, was the product largely of economic and political changes. Many, however, came to see it as a cultural loss. In part, the very decline of working-class power, and the weakening of labour organizations and social democratic parties, helped obscure the economic and political roots of social problems. When the working class had a significant presence in politics, it was easy to see how issues of housing or wages related to economic and social policy. The more the working class was marginalized, the less class was employed as a lens through which to understand social problems. As class declined as an explanatory tool, culture increasingly became, as we have seen, the medium through which social issues were refracted.

Many sections of the working class came also to see their problems in cultural terms. They, too, turned to the language of identity to express their discontent. Class became seen not as a political but as a cultural, even racial, attribute. Commentators today frequently talk of the "white working class" but rarely about the black working class or the Muslim working class. Minorities are regarded as belonging to almost classless "communities". Class divisions are viewed primarily as the property of white populations. As the category of the "white working class" gained traction, it was its whiteness as much as its class location that came to define it.

Once class identity came to be seen as a cultural attribute, those regarded as culturally different became viewed as threats; identity became bound together, in Scruton's words, by "intolerance, exclusion, and... vigilance against the enemy." For racial minorities, the growth of inward-looking identity-based solidarity erased important distinctions within communities, and led to the view that white people were the source of racism. Similarly, as white workers saw solidarity as shaped by culture and ethnicity, they became more hostile towards immigrants and minorities.

III

"Will the earth be reduced to something homogeneous because of deculturalizing and depersonalizing trends for which American imperialism is now the most cynical and arrogant vector? Or will people find the means for the necessary resistance in their beliefs, traditions, and ways of seeing the world? This is really the decisive question that has been raised at the beginning of the next millennium."[9]

That might read like an anti-globalist screed from a leftwing radical. It is in fact from the pen of Alain de Benoist, the founder of the *Nouvelle Droite* in France, and a philosophical mentor of the contemporary far right. Just as the left effected a "cultural turn" in the postwar years, so did the far right. Pluralism has, as we have seen, an ambiguous history. It is fundamental to modern ideas of multiculturalism and tolerance. It is also at the heart of reactionary traditions and of the racist challenge to Enlightenment universalism. The left and the right do not deploy pluralism in the same fashion, the former using it to embrace group differences within societies, the latter to assert differences between peoples; it is the distinction between *multiculturalism* and *ethnopluralism*. That distinction, though, as we shall see, is not as clear-cut as might first appear.

As reactionary and racist organizations, which had enjoyed the limelight in the prewar years, were pushed into the shadows in the post-Holocaust world, many on the far right were forced to rethink their views of race, identity and difference. Benoist became a key figure in this rethinking. Born during the Second World War in a small town near Tours, Benoist cut his political teeth within the traditional fascist milieu, most notably through the far-right opposition to Algerian independence. In the 1960s, after the French defeat in Algeria and the fall of the Fourth Republic, he began recognizing the need to move beyond discredited arguments rooted in biological racism, and to engage in a cultural war to reclaim intellectual ground. Benoist helped found, in the months before the eruptions of May 1968, the Groupement de Recherche et d'Études pour la Civilisation Européenne (Research and Study Group for European Civilization or GRECE), a thinktank that became a kind of Frankfurt School for the far right.

The *Nouvelle Droite* drew in part from traditional themes and sources. It proclaimed its hostility to the Enlightenment, moder-

275

nity, equality, democracy, and liberalism, and insisted on the importance of tradition and hierarchy. It found sustenance in the French reactionary tradition from Joseph de Maistre to Charles Maurras, and from German rightwing thinkers, especially the inter-war "conservative revolutionaries", such as Ernst Jünger and Carl Schmitt. It drew, too, upon a very different tradition: that of the New Left that emerged in the late 1950s. From the New Left, the French New Right borrowed arguments about the significance of culture, its hostility to globalization, its anti-Americanism and its embrace of the Italian Marxist philosopher Antonio Gramsci. Benoist took from Gramsci the belief that conquest of power comes only after conquest of culture. Liberalism was so entrenched that its values survived irrespective of who was in power. Anti-liberals, Benoist argued, had to fight battles not on the streets but in people's minds, at the level of ideas, and of "metapolitics". This he called the tactic of "right-wing Gramscianism".[10]

At the heart of Benoist's philosophy was the abandonment of racial superiority in favour of cultural difference, and the reworking of the relationship between community, identity and diversity. "The true wealth of the world", he insisted, "is first and foremost the diversity of its cultures and peoples". It is in being different that a people finds its meaning and identity, both of which are drawn, indeed in certain senses are inseparable, from its culture and heritage. "Different cultures provide different responses to essential questions"; hence "all attempts to unify them end up destroying them". It was a *volkish* vision: "Everyone inherits a 'constituent community' which precedes him and which will constitute the root of his values and norms". The individual "discovers his goals rather than choosing them", and builds his identity through that discovery. So, "to find out who I am, I first have to know where I am".[11]

"Ethnopluralism" seemed not to possess the taint of biological racism; but by fixing cultures to specific geographic locations and by insisting that to belong to a culture one had to be descended from the original inhabitants of that location, the *Nouvelle Droite* found in "culture" the synonym for "race"; a find later borrowed by conservatives and postliberals. Immigrants must always remain outsiders because they were carriers of distinct cultures and histories, and so could never be absorbed into those of the host nation. To return to

276

Lévi-Strauss's simile, host and immigrant sat on different trains on different tracks; a simile as apt for hostile ethnopluralism as it is for celebratory multiculturalism.

Benoist loathed not just assimilation but also "mixed" marriages, because "one cannot be at the same time for race mixing [*métissage*] and for diversity, since the immediate consequence of the first is to reduce the second". As he thought it impractical to deport all immigrants and their descendants from France, Benoist proposed instead the establishment of parallel communities to allow both the "indigenous" and the immigrant "to keep alive the structures of their collective cultural lives". It is a solution in which "the equal remains different". Citizenship, for Benoist, should be reserved for those who are "one of us". To be a citizen is to "belong... to a homeland and a past". Immigrants could—or, at least, should—never be citizens. Democracy works only where "demos and ethnos coincide".[12]

There are moments when Benoist sounds less like a racist reactionary than a leftwing radical. "Undertaken under the aegis of missionaries, armies and merchants", he wrote in his co-authored *Manifesto for a European Renaissance*, "the Westernisation of the planet has represented an imperialist movement fed by the desire to erase all otherness by imposing on the world a supposedly superior model invariably presented as 'progress'." "Homogenising universalism", he added, "is only the projection and the mask of an ethnocentrism extended over the whole planet." That this could have come from the pen of Richard Delgado or Kimberlé Crenshaw reveals not Benoist's radical credentials but the reactionary roots of much of contemporary radical identity politics. It is not that Delgado or Crenshaw belong to the far right; it is rather that the identitarian philosophies of both left and right draw from the same well of difference, are freighted by the same hostility to universalism, and so succumb to the same distorted vision of the world.[13]

IV

"The soul of our people", Marine Le Pen told a Front National May Day rally as she stood in front of a statue of Jeanne d'Arc in Paris, is forged through "the links of a chain that ties us to the past through our history and to the future through our will to achieve our destiny." It might have been Burke. Or Herder. Or Barrès. Or Benoist. It is the celebration of a collective soul forged through history, the idea of which has coursed from nineteenth-century Romantics to twenty-first-century reactionaries.[14]

The Front National was founded in 1972 out of various far-right fragments, in an attempt, like the *Nouvelle Droite*, to find a footing in a new world. As a leading neo-fascist put it in 1979, "this *realpolitik* of the Right, which the generation of Alain de Benoist offers us, is perhaps the only route which remains open to us to leave the ghetto in which the Right finds itself trapped". Jean-Marie Le Pen, regarded as a moderate in far-right circles, was installed as its leader and public face. Many figures moved in the 1970s from GRECE to the FN; many ideas, too, including the concept of ethnopluralism and hostility to immigration as undermining difference. Peoples are not "superior or inferior, they are different", claimed Le Pen, which is why "I love North Africans, but their place is in the Maghreb".[15]

In 1974, Jean-Marie Le Pen took 0.8 per cent of the vote in the Presidential election. In 2002 he shocked France by coming second to Jacques Chirac and winning almost 18 per cent of the vote in the run-off. But Le Pen was never able properly to shake off either his rootedness in fascism or his indelible antisemitism. His daughter Marine Le Pen, taking over the reins of the party in 2011, went much further in detoxifying the FN, even to the point of expelling her father from the party in 2015 after he described the Holocaust as a "minor detail". In 2018 she renamed the Front National the Rassemblement National (RN). At its heart, however, remained the Benoist ethnopluralist programme.

Three intertwined issues dominated the worldview of Le Pen fille: hostility to globalism, to immigration and to Islam. Globalism, for Marine Le Len, was an "ideology that far exceeds mere globalization and which aims to standardize cultures, to encourage nomadism, the permanent movement of uprooted people from one continent to another, to make them interchangeable and, in essence, to render them anonymous". Like Benoist, Le Pen's opposition to immigrants was framed as respecting difference. "The world will only survive through human and cultural diversity, through biodiversity", she insisted. The only difference that really mattered, however, was that between the "French way of life" and the rest.[16]

Le Pen's hostility to globalism is matched only by her antagonism towards Islam. With "the Islamization of our country", she claimed, "the majority [of French people] no longer feel at home in France". Muslims had "taken charge of entire neighbourhoods where they impose their vision, their culture, their proscriptions". In some senses, Muslims took the place in twenty-first-century far-right demonology that had, in previous generations, been occupied by Jews. But the role of Muslims in the reactionary mind was different from that of Jews. Jews were, and still are, viewed as a people that invisibly control government and the media and comprise a sinister, treacherous global cabal. Muslims, on the other hand, are regarded as "invaders" and "colonisers", undermining French culture not by wielding cosmopolitan power but by replacing one culture with another.[17]

Le Pen detoxified the FN to the extent that it became the main opposition party in the 2010s, though that was the consequence as much of the collapse of the traditional left and Gaullists as of the rise of the far right. In the Presidential elections of 2022, fears that Le Pen might defeat the unpopular incumbent Emmanuel Macron never materialized; nevertheless, Le Pen won more than 41 per cent of the vote in the second-round run-off.

The success of Le Pen lay not just in her ability to exploit anger at globalization. It lay also in her ability to marry reactionary hostility to immigrants and Muslims to economic and social policies that once were the staple of the left: defence of jobs, support for the welfare state, opposition to austerity. It proved immensely appealing as traditional leftwing parties moved away from their old working-class constituencies at just the time working-class lives became more precarious. As the economic and the political became unstitched, the far right restitched them to their own template. This has been the case not just in France, but throughout the Western world, where the melding of reactionary xenophobia and appeals to working-class anger has undergird the populist upsurge of the early decades of the twenty-first century.

Where populists gained power—Donald Trump in America, Boris Johnson in Britain, Matteo Salvini in Italy—the consequences have generally been dismal for working-class people, with reduced public spending, stagnating wages, cuts in welfare benefits, little change in inequality, and tax cuts for the rich. Nevertheless, the abandonment by the left of class-based arguments and policies, combined with the influence of identitarian perspectives and an acceptance that immigrants are the cause of working-class decline has made it easier for rightwing populists to seize the moment. The result is a new kind of mass politics and the refashioning of the original reactionary politics of identity for a new age.

V

"We are Generation Identity… We have stopped believing that Khader is our brother, the planet our village and humanity our family. We have discovered that we have roots and ancestors—and thus a future. Our only inheritance is our blood, our soil, and our identity… This is not a mere manifesto, it's a declaration of war."

It was a declaration of war on a YouTube video. But for all its comically dramatic music and overheated rhetoric, the launch in 2012 of Génération Identitaire, or Generation Identity, marked an important point in the development of modern reactionary identitarianism. Ten years earlier, a group of French far-right activists, many linked to the *Nouvelle Droite*, had formed the Bloc Identitaire which became the heart of a network of far-right identitarian groups and of which Génération Identitaire was the youth wing. The movement was banned by the French government in March 2021 for "incitement of discrimination, hatred and violence". By then it had spawned a dozen other groups across Europe, and its influence had crossed the Atlantic, too.[18]

The Bloc Identitaire drew on the *Nouvelle Droite* for both individuals and themes. Its key leitmotifs are familiar: opposition to globalization, defence of ethnopluralism and white identity, hostility to immigration and Islam. The Identitarians feared that demographic change would sweep away white Europeans. "The cradle", Adriano Scianca, a leading figure in the Italian Identitarian movement, believed, is "the most powerful weapon" and when "the baby cots are empty, civilization dies", an echo of Theodore Roosevelt's claim that "competition between the races" reduced itself "to the warfare of the cradle". For late nineteenth-century white supremacists, the declining birth-rate of Anglo-Saxons created the alarming possibility of the only true white race in America being over-run by "the immigrant European horde". A century later, the fear is of Europeans being swamped by hordes from beyond the continent.[19]

Far more than the postwar *Nouvelle Droite*, the figures around the Identitarian movements of the twenty-first century evince a visceral hatred of Islam. Gisèle Littman, an Egyptian-born Jewish woman who wrote under the name of Bat Ye'or (Hebrew for "Daughter of the Nile"), coined the term "Eurabia". It described a grand conspiracy theory in which the EU, led by French elites, implemented a secret plan to sell Europe to Muslims in exchange for oil. Europe, Ye'or told the Israeli newspaper *Haaretz*, "will become a political satellite of the Arab and Muslim world". Europeans would be reduced to the condition of "dhimmitude"—the permanent status of second-class subjects of Islamic rule. The Israeli historian Robert Wistrich dismissed Ye'or's fantasies as "the protocols of the elders of Brussels". In the wake of 9/11, however, the fantasies took flight, and not just on the fringes of politics. The mainstream British writer Melanie Phillips has become an advocate of the "dhimmitude" thesis, as have influential figures such as Niall Ferguson and Bruce Bawer in America.[20]

Generation Identity is no mass movement; membership of its various groups are tiny. Nevertheless, it has helped shape public debate, promoting an aggressive form of reactionary identitarianism that has percolated far beyond the far right. "Europe is committing suicide... by the end of the lifespans of most people currently alive, Europe will not be Europe and the peoples of Europe will have lost the only place in the world we had to call home." That could be Alain de Benoist or Guillaume Faye or Fabrice Robert, or any number of *Nouvelle Droite* or Génération Identitaire polemicists. In fact, it is Douglas Murray, in the opening to his bestseller *The Strange Death of Europe*. Murray is a leading figure in British conservative circles, associate editor of the *Spectator* magazine, former associate director of the neoconservative Henry Jackson Society and author of a string of popular books. He writes of "the replacement of large parts of the European populations by other people" and worries that "London has become a foreign country" because "in 23 of London's thirty-three boroughs 'white Britons' are now in a minority", again echoing Generation Identity.[21]

The main themes in Murray's argument were steeped in traditional racial thinking. The term "race suicide" was coined by the American sociologist Edward Ross, and popularized by Theodore Roosevelt to express their fears that Anglo-Saxons were being outbred by inferior immigrants from southern and eastern Europe. The white supremacist Theodore Lothrop Stoddard warned that the white ancestral "homeland" of the Caucasus had become a "racially brown man's land in which white blood survives only as vestigial traces of vanishing significance". The same was happening in Europe, too. "What assurance", he wondered, could there be "that the present world order may not swiftly and utterly pass away?" These ideas were for much of the postwar era pushed to the racist fringes. Sustained by the *Nouvelle Droite* and Génération Identitaire, these fringe arguments have now become appropriated by many strands of mainstream conservatism.

The 2010s saw a series of books warning of Europe "committing suicide", such as Thilo Sarrazin's *Deutschland schafft sich ab* ("Germany Abolishes Itself"), Éric Zemmour's *Le Suicide français* ("French Suicide") and Michel Houellebecq's novel *Soumission* ("Submission"). Sarrazin, former SPD finance minister for the state of Berlin, and executive board member of Germany's central bank, bemoaned the declining white population and the high level of immigrant fertility, the combination leading to Germany being both less intelligent, less moral and no longer Germany. For Zemmour, a television journalist who became a candidate in the 2022 Presidential elections, Europe was committing "premeditated suicide", the left having "betrayed the people in the name of minorities". The philosopher and public intellectual Alain Finkielkraut echoed that thought when he told journalist Sasha Polakow-Suransky that immigration was leading to the "planned demise of Europe".[22]

The "Great Replacement" conspiracy theory, a staple of the far right, has also gained a foothold in mainstream conservatism. In 2011, the novelist and white nationalist conspiracy theorist Renaud Camus published *Le Grand Remplacement* in which he claimed that globalists had created the "replaceable human, without any national, ethnic or cultural specificity", allowing *les élites remplacistes*—"the replacing elites"—to swap white Europeans for non-Europeans. He described non-Europeans in Europe as "colonists", the *élites rempla-*

cistes as "collaborationists", and the process of replacement as "geno-cide by substitution". Camus dedicated his book to the two "proph-ets" that had shaped his thinking, the British anti-immigration politician Enoch Powell and the French writer Jean Raspail, whose 1973 dystopian novel *The Camp of the Saints* tells of a fleet of immi-grants from India overwhelming France, and its white population, and has become a cult hit for identitarians across the globe.[23]

In Britain, too, similar fears have become part of the conservative conversation. Like Murray, the London-based American novelist Lionel Shriver fears the de-whitening of London and projects her version of replacement theory. "The lineages of white Britons in their homeland commonly go back hundreds of years," she writes, and yet they have to "submissively accept" the "ethnic transforma-tion of the UK... without a peep of protest". Westerners, she adds, are being forced "to passively accept and even abet incursions by foreigners so massive that the native-born are effectively surrender-ing their territory without a shot fired". The distinguished econo-mist Paul Collier is another figure apprehensive about "the indige-nous British" becoming "a minority in their own capital". Political scientist Eric Kaufmann thinks it legitimate to promote white "racial self-interest" and to use such racial self-interest to limit immigra-tion, so that in a majority white country, immigrants should be mainly white to enable "assimilation".[24]

Identitarian arguments have become even more entrenched on the other side of the Atlantic, from the far right to mainstream Republicanism. The white nationalist and neo-Nazi Richard Spencer, who claims to have invented the term "alt-right", replays many of the themes of reactionary identitarianism: whites as vic-tims of cultural "dispossession", immigration as a "proxy war" against whites. He advocates "peaceful ethnic cleansing" and the creation of "an ethno-state that would be a gathering point of all Europeans", one "based on very different ideals than... the Declaration of Independence".[25]

The Presidential victory of Donald Trump in 2016 provided new opportunities, as alt-right identitarians such Stephen Miller and Steve Bannon entered the White House. Bannon, then editor of the alt-right website *Breitbart*, was fond of dropping Generation Identity names and themes into his conversation. "It's really an invasion", he said of the 2015 migration crisis in Europe. "I call it the Camp of the Saints."[26]

Even before the Trump ascendancy, conservatives were humming to many of the European refrains. In the question at the heart of Christopher Caldwell's 2009 book *Reflections on the Revolution in Europe*—"Can Europe be the same with different people in it?"—is embedded the idea that Europe was made by a particular group of people and that immigrants—different people—would undo it. He echoes, too, the claim that migration is a form of "colonization" and that migrants come to "supplant" European culture. Caldwell hails Jean Raspail's *The Camp of the Saints* as capturing "the complexity of the modern world".[27]

After 2016, the Great Replacement theory became a commonplace in Republican circles. "We can't restore our civilization with somebody else's babies", Iowan Congressman Steve King tweeted. Fox News' Tucker Carlson has constantly charged the Democrats with trying "to change the racial mix of the country... a policy [that] is called 'the great replacement', the replacement of legacy Americans with more obedient people from far-away countries". Polls show that a third of Americans and nearly two-thirds of Trump supporters believe in the Great Replacement Theory and that a secret cabal "is trying to replace native-born Americans with immigrants for electoral gains".[28]

One of the ironies is that many of the conservatives who fret most about "white decline" are also among the most strident critics of identity politics. According to Douglas Murray, identity politics "atomizes society into different interest groups", and its "consequences... are deranged as well as dementing". But not, apparently, when worrying that "Only 44.9 per cent of London residents are now white British" or that Europeans are being driven out of their homeland. Taking part in a debate in defence of the proposition that "identity politics is tearing society apart", Lionel Shriver argued that she had been a "fierce advocate" of the US civil rights movement because its goal was "to break down the artificial barriers between us" and "to release us into seeing each other not as black or white... but as individual people". "The colour of my skin," she added, "is an arbitrary accident" and "the boxes into which I have been born are confinements I have struggled to get out of and I would wish that liberation to everyone else." Except, it seems, if you are a non-white immigrant. Then, the "arbitrary accident" of birth becomes an essential feature of one's identity, the "artificial barriers between us" need to be recognized as insurmountable impediments to assimilation, the "confinements" of ethnic boxes maintained and people seen not as "individuals" but as "black or white".[29]

Most conservative critics of identity politics are not opposed to identity politics, just to the identity politics of the left. They despise Black Lives Matter for its "racism" and condemn the divisiveness of a concept such as "white privilege". But they want to keep London (and Paris and Berlin) primarily white and to protect the European homeland from being colonized by marauding immigrants. All of which takes us to the deeper problem with the mainstream right's embrace of white identity. The reactionary right—*Nouvelle Droite*, Generation Identity, the alt-right in America—uses the language of diversity and identity as a means of rebranding racism. Many on the mainstream right rehearse elements of this rebranding, even as they castigate the excesses of white nationalism. Murray "unequivocally" condemns the "racism exhibited by people pursuing white ethno-nationalism" while also giving a nod to the Great Replacement theory and to the importance of whiteness. It is occupying the grey zone in which one can claim attachment to the moral framework of postwar antiracism but also maintain the freedom to replay perniciously racist arguments helping to normalize them.[30]

Beyond the grey zone lies white nationalist terror. Over the past twenty years, we have witnessed a series of mass murders committed in the name of white nationalism, all primed by conspiracy theories about immigration, Muslims, Jews, the Great Replacement and white genocide. In 2011, Anders Breivik killed eight people by detonating a van bomb in Oslo, then shooting dead another 69 at a Workers' Youth League summer camp on the island of Utøya. He published a 1500-page online manifesto entitled *2083: A European Declaration of Independence* which blamed the Frankfurt School and "cultural Marxism" for policies of mass immigration, multiculturalism and political correctness, and drew on the work of Richard Spencer and Bat Ye'or, as well as more mainstream figures such as the British commentator Melanie Phillips. When, in 2018, Robert Bowers shot dead eleven people at the Tree of Life

Synagogue in Pittsburgh, Pennsylvania, he claimed that Jews were committing "genocide" against whites by leading a conspiracy to bring Muslims into the country. In 2019, Australian Brenton Tarrant murdered fifty-one people, and injured forty, in mass shootings in two mosques, Al Noor and Linwood Islamic, in Christchurch, New Zealand. Tarrant had links with Generation Identity. In 2022, Payton Gendron shot dead 10 people in a supermarket in Buffalo, New York state, almost all of whom were black. His 180-page manifesto described African Americans and immigrants as "replacers" who "invade our lands, live on our soil, attack and replace our people".[31]

These are but a few incidents on the trail of white nationalist terror attacks in the twenty-first century. What makes them particularly shocking is the contrast between the savagery of the racist violence and societies that place such great store on moral opposition to racism. The normalization of white identity, and the adoption by mainstream conservatives of notions such "race suicide" and the loss of the "white homeland", provides the bridge between the two.

VI

"The attack was not an attack on diversity, but an attack in the name of diversity. To ensure diverse peoples remain diverse, separate, unique, undiluted [and] unrestrained in cultural or ethnic expression and autonomy. To ensure that the peoples of the world remain true to their traditions and faiths and do not become watered down and corrupted by the influence of outsiders." The lines were written by Brenton Tarrant. The "attack" was his murderous rampage at two mosques in Christchurch. And the words appear in his manifesto "The Great Replacement".[32]

If there are red flags raised about the way that the darker themes of Generation Identity have seeped into mainstream conservative thinking, there are also questions to be asked about the relationship between liberal and leftwing ideas of identity and pluralism and those of the reactionary right. From one perspective, there is no equivalence between the two. One emerged from the decay of genuine movements for social change and betterment, the other from the attempt to restore the fortunes of the far right after the disintegration of fascist organizations in the post-Holocaust world. Yet, liberal views of cultural diversity can seem distressingly like those of reactionaries.

The Canadian Will Kymlicka is perhaps the leading philosopher of multiculturalism today. In a discussion of indigenous cultures, he argues that while "it is right and proper that the character of a culture change as a result of the choices of its members", it is different if the culture is "being threatened... by people outside the culture". It is, for Kymlicka, "one thing to learn from the larger world; it is another to be swamped by it". It is a phrase that should make us sit up and take notice. "Swamped" is a word beloved of the reactionary right. It was deployed by Margaret Thatcher in a TV interview in 1978 to describe fears about the arrival in Britain of people from "the new Commonwealth or Pakistan". In an attempt to win votes from supporters of the neo-Nazi National Front, she warned that "people are really rather afraid that this country might be rather swamped by people with a different culture". It is also the sentiment expressed by today's Generation Identity activists to stop immigration and preserve European culture.[33]

Kymlicka was speaking, of course, of marginalized peoples who lacked the power to prevent themselves from being "swamped". That, though, is also how reactionary identitarians view the "indigenous" populations of Europe—as peoples powerless when facing up to the globalized elites, their promotion of immigration and imposition of the ideology of "sameness". "European peoples", Fabrice Robert, one of the founders of the Bloc Identitaire, claimed, "have the same rights as the tribes of the Amazon". It may be an absurd claim, but the absurdity should not blind us to the ease with which the far right can appropriate and exploit the language of diversity and victimhood. Once it becomes a matter of principle to protect identity from decay and peoples from being swamped, then we embark on a road that leads to Generation Identity. "If one of the major questions of the 20th century was the right of peoples to self-determination", insisted Philippe Vardon, another figure who has travelled to-and-fro between Bloc Identitaire and the Front National, "THE [sic] central question of our century is the right of peoples to self-preservation".[34]

It is not just in the demand that cultures be protected that liberal multiculturalism and reactionary identitarianism find common cause. It is also in the insistence that peoples of different cultures think, believe and act in fundamentally distinct ways. In 2020, the Smithsonian's National Museum of African American History and Culture in Washington DC published a chart demonstrating the distinctive features of "white culture". These included an "emphasis on the scientific method" and on "rational, linear thinking", the "Protestant work ethic" and a belief that "Hard work is the key to success", "future orientation" and a willingness to "plan for the future". After a public outcry, the museum withdrew the chart. Its updated page on "whiteness" still maintains that "white people, their customs, culture, and beliefs operate as the standard by which all other groups of [sic] are compared", presenting "white culture" as a single thing and all white people as alike in their "customs, culture and beliefs".[35]

In the nineteenth century, racists regarded science, rationality and hard work as white traits, and as expressions of white superiority. Those confronting racism dismissed such claims, insisting that these were universal traits and universal goods. Many of today's antiracists, though, view such qualities as the racists once did, as peculiarly white, and so reject, not the claims that these are white traits, but the traits themselves as tainted by whiteness. This is where the obsession with whiteness leads to: a *volkish* view of social differences.

What links identitarians of left and right is a common hostility to universalism, a rejection of Enlightenment ideals as simultaneously ethnocentric, the product of European culture, and insufficiently ethnocentric, steamrollering cultural differences to impose a universalist perspective. That hostility has not emerged from the same place. For the right, antipathy to universalism, and scepticism about Enlightenment ideals, is stitched into the fabric of a philosophy woven from the threads of hierarchy, inequality and tradition. For the left, belief in universalism, which once was foundational to its worldview, has ebbed away, largely because of disbelief that it is possible to overcome the constraints placed upon us, reach across fissures of race and identity, and create a movement to transcend those divisions. Or even that one *should* pursue such a project.

"I will resist every attempt to categorize me", Pauli Murray wrote in 1945, "to place me in some caste, or to assign me to some segregated pigeonhole". Today, the willingness to cling to one's pigeonhole, one's identity, to categorize myself and others, is all that we seem to possess. As hopes for social change have eroded, many have been led to hunker down in their separate laagers; and the more one hunkers down, the more the laager becomes the only way through which to perceive the world, the more that one's race or identity looms ever larger in one's consciousness.[36]

"The earthquake cannot be subpoenaed. The typhoon will not bend under indictment", Ta-Nehisi Coates wrote in his book *Between the World and Me*. Coates is probably the most celebrated African American essayist of the early twenty-first century, a figure who, in the words of the late Toni Morrison, "fill[s] the intellectual void that plagued me after James Baldwin died". Written as a letter to his son Samori, *Between the World and Me* is a beautifully crafted meditation on the place of black people in American society. It is also a deeply pessimistic one. Like Derrick Bell, Coates seems to view racism as "integral, permanent and indestructible". It can no more be challenged by human will than an earthquake or a typhoon. "My portion of the American galaxy", he writes, is one "where [black] bodies were enslaved by a tenacious gravity", while "the other, liberated portion" is always beyond reach. Coates follows a commonplace in much contemporary African American writing: to talk of "black bodies" rather than of black people, as if speaking of beings divested of agency. It is a fatalism that would have been alien to Pauli Murray. "When my brothers try to draw a circle to exclude me", she insisted, "I shall draw a larger circle to include them. Where they speak out for the privileges of a puny group, I shall shout for the rights of all mankind."[37]

Murray recognized both the need to build solidarity outwards, drawing others in, and the possibilities of bending the world towards more universal forms of justice. Coates, too, sees the importance of struggle; indeed, he tells his son, it is all that he can offer him. But it is a different kind of struggle to that envisaged by Murray; a struggle, not in hope of redemption, but to tend the flame of remembrance. "Struggle for the memory of your ancestors", he tells Samori. "Struggle for your grandmother and grandfather, for your name". A struggle not to shape the future but to not forget the past.[38]

In his history of the idea of race, Ivan Hannaford, drawing upon the work of Hannah Arendt, observed that "racial" ideas became a means of marginalizing the "political". The "political idea", Hannaford wrote, involves "a disposition to see people not in terms of where they came from and what they looked like but in terms of membership of a public arena". Politics ensures that rights, duties and obligations flow not from the essence of one's being—from nature or identity—but from one's beliefs and actions as citizens. The racial view takes the opposite stance, insisting that "the rights, duties and obligations which once flowed from a politics that *released* man from Nature" are now deemed to be rooted "in nature and directly derived from it regardless of the postulates of politics".[39]

Rooting identity and difference in history and culture rather than in race and biology does not alter this. Identitarian politics, whether of left and right, also views people "in terms of where they came from and what they looked like" not in "terms of membership of a public arena". Kanye West cannot be black because he has white thoughts. Dana Schutz cannot portray black pain because she is white. Immigrants are colonizers. London is not London if it is not majority white. Like racial thinking, the identitarian perspective fractures civic space and fragments the political sphere. Once we accept that social conversations can be limited by one's identity, we begin fencing off the common pastures of society.

Politics can be deeply divisive—it cleaves society across ideological lines. But it also provides the opportunity to champion not race or identity, but values and ideals, and in so doing to unite across ethnic or cultural divisions. What matters in political struggles is not who you are, but what you believe; the reverse is true in identity struggles. Political conflicts are often useful because they repose social problems in a way that asks: "How can we change society to overcome that problem?" To view racism politically, for instance, we need to ask, "What are its social roots and what structural changes are required to combat it?" We might disagree on the answer, but the debate itself is a useful one. Political conflicts are the kinds of conflicts necessary for social transformation. The turn to identity has encouraged us to repose political problems as issues of culture or ethnicity or faith, and so transformed political conflicts into forms that make them neither useful nor resolvable. Rather than ask about the material changes that might enable justice in the present, it demands recognition for one's particular identity and redress for injustices in the past. The demand to "stay in your lane" is the antithesis of politics; it is to shun forms of political engagement that can be socially transformative.

The unstitching of the economic and the political is both cause and consequence of this. It encourages an identitarian view of social problems by delinking race and class and obscuring the social and political roots of both working-class inequalities and racial injustices. Just as in the nineteenth century racial identity was used to break-up class alliances, and to persuade white workers that their interests lay in their whiteness, not in their class location, so today the language of identity leads to the same place, though without necessarily the conscious intention of doing so. It encourages workers to define themselves in terms of race rather than of class. At the same time, the increasing purchase of identitarian claims makes it easier to cleave the political from the economic and to view both in terms of identity.

VII

"The Negro is not. Any more than the white man."[40]

More than seventy years after Frantz Fanon wrote those lines in *Black Skins, White Masks*, they still feel unsettling. That they should do so exposes the deeply conflicted relationship we still possess with race. We mostly despise racism and yet cannot imagine a world without racial categorization. Indeed, many imagine that protecting racial identities is necessary, essential even, to the antiracist project.

In his 2019 book *Self-Portrait in Black and White*, the American writer Thomas Chatterton Williams reflects on his attempts to move beyond viewing himself and the world in racial categories. "I have to believe", he writes, that "the best aspects of Enlightenment universalism... can and should be salvaged and disentangled from the documented imperfections and biases of the past... I have to *believe* it is possible that all human beings are capable of such transcendence." "It is my hope", he adds, "that as many people as possible, of all skin tones and hair textures, will come to turn away from the racial delusion."[41]

And, yet, it is not so simple. Williams decides that he is an "ex-black" because racial categories "cannot adequately capture" who he is, nor who his daughter is. I, too, don't see myself in terms of racial categories. But race is not something that as individuals we can scrub away from this world. Race is an idea, a false idea; but it has material roots and arises out of social practice. Not to believe in race cannot simply be an individual decision. It also has to be a collective movement, a movement that not only disavows racial categories but aims to dismantle, too, the social practice of racism.[42]

The concept of race emerged in the eighteenth century as the medium through which could be understood many of the contradictions of modernity. Most importantly, it made sense of, and provided a justification for, the persistence of inequalities and enslavement in societies that had proclaimed their fidelity to equality. It provided a mechanism that, consciously or unconsciously, could disrupt assertions of class solidarity. And it was a means through which anxieties about social decay could express themselves.

The most cogent, deep-seated, far-reaching challenge to the concept of race came through the radical universalist tradition. It was a tradition that included such disparate, and politically distinct, figures as Denis Diderot and Toussaint Louverture, Frederick Douglass and WEB Du Bois, Sylvia Pankhurst and CLR James, Pauli Murray and James Baldwin. What links such diverse leaders and activists is an insistence on the universal application of equality and a desire to build solidarity across the fissures of race and identity. It is a tradition that challenged both racism and the racialization of people; that is, both the practice of discrimination and the imposition of racial categories on people, often as a means of justifying such discrimination. The erosion of that tradition created a social space that came to be filled by identity politics. As the broader struggles for social transformation have faded, people have tended to retreat into their particular cultures, and to embrace more parochial forms of identity.

Human beings live neither in the "particular" nor the "universal". All humans define themselves both through their many immediate, rooted identities—a woman, an engineer, a Parisian, a Jew, an FC Barcelona fan, a devourer of Satyajit Ray films—and in terms of more universal aspirations. Those aspirations are framed by the character of politics and of social engagement. Humanity manifests itself in concrete local forms and these are the starting points in understanding the more abstract concept of human universality. Equally, it is the more universal sense of being human that gives our local rooted identities context and meaning. What links the particular and the universal is the conscious activity through which humans make and remake their world, through politics and art and social struggles. These allow us to transcend our immediate, local identities and to reach out and discover more universal forms of our humanness, not as abstract beliefs but in concrete expressions of empathy and solidarity.

From the Haitian Revolution to the Grunwick strike, from the suffragette movement to the anti-apartheid struggle, from hosting Ukrainian refugees to campaigning for the Uyghurs in China, our engagement with the world allows us to move beyond our immediate concerns and to place those concerns in a more expansive, more universal context. The opposite is also true: when politics seems frayed and social movements have disintegrated, the link between the local and the global, between the particular and the universal, becomes strained, even broken. We are left with looking at the world through David Goodhart's eyes, as it were, reducing it to a forced (and false) dichotomy of "Somewheres" vs "Anywheres", constrained expressions of local identity set against rhetorical forms of universalism. A particularism within which people find refuge in opposition to a universalism that expresses a contempt for ordinary people and their struggles. An inward-looking solidarity frequently rooted in intolerance and exclusion versus a cosmopolitanism that often celebrates the erosion of community and democracy.

"Any human being properly motivated and educated is capable of outgrowing the bounds and divisions of identity, of touching the universal", Williams writes. The problem, though, is not merely that of motivation and education. It is also the social context within which we fashion our relationships to others. To transcend race, to break the bounds of identity politics, requires us to resurrect radical universalism not as an idea but as a social movement. It requires us to think of racism, not as a singular problem, but in its connection with other forms of inequalities. It requires us to restitch the economic and the political. To transcend the concept of race requires not just an intellectual revolution, but a social one, too.[43]

NOTES AND REFERENCES

INTRODUCTION: RETELLING THE STORY OF RACE

1. For details of the Grunwick strike, see Dromey and Taylor (1978); Sudhari and Pearson (2018).
2. Rothkopf (2017).

1. THE INVENTION OF EQUALITY

1. Johnson, "Taxation No Tyranny" [http://www.samueljohnson.com/tnt.html; accessed 30 September 2020]. Stuurman (2017), 2.
2. For a discussion of the debate about race as a natural and as a social concept, see Malik (2008), esp. 13–59. For an early iteration of the argument that "race did not give birth to racism. Racism gave birth to race" see Malik (1996). Barbara Fields has developed a similar argument: see Fields (1990) and Fields & Fields (2012).
3. Jaspers (2014), 1.
4. Mo Tzu (1967), §III.
5. Kenny (2004), 281.
6. Paul, Galatians 3:28 (New English Version); Holland (2019), 68.
7. MacCulloch (2009), 115, 114; Paul, 1 Corinthians 7:20.
8. Fogel (1989), 201; Augustine, (1998), 943; Garnsey (1996), 29.
9. Holland (2019), 124; Gerbner (2018); Davis (1988), 291–332; Lay (1738), 44.
10. Blackburn (1988), 44.
11. Kant (1784), 2; Darnton (1982), 2; Adorno & Horkheimer (1997).
12. Foucault, "What is Enlightenment?", in Foucault (2020), 42.
13. Hume, (1748a), Section 8, part 1, E 8.7, SBN 83–4; Diderot (1992), 85.
14. von Humboldt (2020), vol. 1, 341.
15. Israel (2006), 545–6; Stuurman (2017), 258, 259.
16. Luther, "Against the Robbing and Murdering Hordes of Peasants" in Lund (2002), 44.
17. Martyn Mclaughlin, "David Hume's ties to Grenadian plantations

revealed", *The Scotsman*, 17 July 2020; Hume (1748a) Section 8, part 1, E 8.7, SBN 83-4; Hume (1748b), NC 20n6.1, Mil 208.

18. All three of Kant's essays on race are in Kant (2007a).
19. Kant, "Physical Geography" in Kant (2012), 576; Eze, "The Color of Reason" in Eze (1997b), 116.
20. Jefferson (1801), 273–4, 278, 276.
21. Mills (2005), 170–1; Eze, "Introduction" to Eze (1997a), 5.
22. Jones (2001), 2030–1; Israel (2011), 231.
23. Diderot, "Encyclopédie", in Diderot and d'Alembert (2017).
24. Muthu (2003), 81.
25. Diderot (1992), 212; Muthu (2003), 87; Raynal (2006), 77.
26. Israel (2011),18.
27. Darnton (1982), 24; Blom (2010),17.
28. Darnton (1982), 40.
29. Diderot, "Encyclopédie", in Diderot and d'Alembert (2017).
30. Israel (2006), 551–2.
31. "An Agreement of the People" [https://oll.libertyfund.org/pages/1647-the-agreement-of-the-people-as-presented-to-the-council-of-the-army; accessed 31 October 2020]; Steel (2015), 3; Hill (2002),128. Two more versions of "An Agreement of the People" were published in 1648 and 1649, the third, the most radical of the three, signed jointly by the leading Levellers John Lilburne, Richard Overton, William Walwyn and Thomas Prince.
32. Hill (2002), 129, 130.
33. Hume (1742), note M; Hobsbawm (1977), 36.
34. Smith (1776), vol. 1, bk. IV, ch. 2; bk. I, ch. 8; vol. 2, bk. V, ch. 1, pt. 2; Smith (1759), part 1, sect. 3, ch. 3.
35. Ferguson (1757), 24.
36. Rousseau (1984), 109.
37. Stedman Jones (2008), 53.
38. Hoare (1820), 52–61; Drescher (1986), 39–40; Fryer (1984), 119–20; Olusoga (2016), 125–7; Lyall (2017), 46–7.
39. Gibbon (1846), 312.
40. Davis (1988), 398.
41. Hague (2008), loc. 8091.
42. Davis (1999), 50; Blackburn (1988), 50.

2. THE INVENTION OF RACE

1. Sollas (1924), 121.
2. Haddon (1924), 1, 2; Stocking (1982), 59; Barkar (1992), 100–1.
3. Bernier, "A New Division of the Earth" in Bernasconi and Lott (2000), 1–4.

4. Moore (2007), 4; Davis (1984), 32–51.

5. Frederickson (2015), 47.

6. Lovejoy (1936).

7. Linnaei (1758), 20–2.

8. Marks (1995), 51–2.

9. Blumenbach (1865), 269.

10. Ibid., 98–9.

11. Gossett (1963), 52.

12. Muthu (2003), 268.

13. Kleingeld (2007); Kant (1795), 12.

14. Sikka (2011), 22.

15. Herder (2016), 140, 141 (italics in the original).

16. Herder (2004), 30 (italics in the original).

17. Herder (2016), 203; Herder (2002), 50; Berlin (1976), 165, 180.

18. Herder (2016), 296.

19. Rushdie, "In Good Faith" in Rushdie (1991), 394; Herder (2016), 212–3.

20. Sikka (2011), 130.

21. Herder (2016), 128–9.

22. Sikka (2011), 138.

23. For a discussion of early forms of the Counter-Enlightenment, see McMahon (2001).

24. Burke (1790), 22; Burke (1968), 138.

25. Bagehot, "Letters on the French Coup", in Bagehot (1915).

26. Pick (1989), 56; Arendt (2017), 223.

27. Berger, "Francisco de Goya" in Berger (2021), 175.

28. Marx and Engels (2004), 4.

29. Niebuhr (1847), vol. 1, xxxi.

30. Blanckaert (1988), 25.

31. Gobineau (1915), 36, xiv.

32. Gobineau (1915), 207, 206, 205; Mosse (1978), 53.

33. Zeitlin (1968), 75.

34. Hall (2012), 208.

35. McLennan (1896), 16, 10; Mill (1820), vol. 2, 190.

36. Huxley, "Emancipation: Black and White" in Huxley (1870).

37. Stepan (1982), 24.

38. Prichard (1836–47), vol. 3, iv.

39. Desmond (1989), 388; Richards (1989).

40. Knox (1850), 7, 29.

41. Knox (1850), 314, 179.

42. Darwin (1981), vol. 1, 201, 240.

43. Burrow (1966), 130.

44. Stanton (1960), 144; Morton (1839), 1–2.
45. Nott and Gliddon (1854), 465; (1857), 399–400.
46. Stepan (1982), 4.
47. Beddoe (1912), 182.

3. THE INVENTION OF WHITE IDENTITY

1. Allen (1998); the quote first appeared on the back cover of vol. 1 of Allen (1997).
2. Sluiter (1997); Thornton (1998).
3. Sluiter (1997), 396 n4; "Presidential Proclamation—Establishment of the Fort Monroe National Monument" [https://obamawhitehouse. archives.gov/the-press-office/2011/11/01/presidential-proclamation-establishment-fort-monroe-national-monument; accessed 26 January 2022]; Jake Silverstein, "Why We Published the 1619 Project", *New York Times*, 20 December 2019; President's Advisory 1776 Commission (2021).
4. Davis (1984), 52.
5. Ligon (1657), 44.
6. Morgan (1975), 127, 80.
7. Ibid., 129.
8. Fields and Fields (2012), 125.
9. Morgan (1975), 313.
10. Ibid., 155, 327.
11. Ibid, 333, 335.
12. Crèvecoeur (1904), 54.
13. Franklin (1918), 10 (italics in the original).
14. Nott and Gliddon (1854), 89 (italics in original); Nott, Appendix to Gobineau (1856), 498.
15. Dillingham (1911), 2, 30, 18.
16. Heffer (2012), 1.
17. Heffer (2012), 167; Carlyle (1853), 8, 42; Emerson, "Carlyle" in Emerson (2000), 837–41.
18. Field (2001); Emerson, "English Traits" in Emerson (2000), 485, 612.
19. Ignatiev (1995), 49.
20. Martin (2014), 52; Morton (1839), 16.
21. Beddoe (1885), 5, 9, 10.
22. Ignatiev (1995); Roediger "Whiteness and Ethnicity in History of 'White Ethnics' in the United States", in Roediger (1994), 181–98; Man (1950), 97–8.
23. Ripley (1908).
24. Ross (1914), 285–6.

25. For Roosevelt's racial ideas see Dyer (1990); Roosevelt (1889–96), vol. 3,128–9.
26. Roosevelt (1889–96) vol. 1, 13; Dyer (1990), 54, 145, 152, 155.
27. Pearson (1914–30), vol. 3 A, 348.
28. Galton (1904), 1; Grant (1916), 47.
29. Himmelfarb (1984), 358; Ellis (1916), 401.
30. Kevles (1995), 48.
31. Pichot (2009), 259.
32. Isenberg (2017), xxviii.
33. Painter (2010), 258.
34. Chase (1980), 144–53; Painter (2010), 271–3.
35. Chase (1980),150, 149.
36. Laughlin (1922), 446–51; Laughlin (1930), 17; Buck v. Bell, 274 US 200. [https://www.courtlistener.com/opinion/101076/buck-v-bell/; accessed 13 March 2021]; Chase (1980), 135.
37. Davenport (1913), 212, 214, 216, 217, 219, 222.
38. Goddard (1917), 243, 252.
39. Painter (2010), 283.
40. Brigham (1923), xxi, 159, 174, 145.
41. Koven and Götzke (2010),133; Denvir (2020), 143; Jacobson (1998), 83.
42. Semmel (1962); Hutton (1996), 31.
43. Lorimer (1978),195.
44. Ibid.
45. "Slaves and Labourers", *Saturday Review*, 16 January 1864.
46. Cannadine (2001), 8.
47. Ibid., 59, 125.
48. Lorimer (1978), 34; Ward (1855), 284–5; Douglass (1855), 366–7, 390–1; *Times*, 6 April 1847; *Times*, 8 April 1847.
49. Lorimer (1978), 68.
50. Booth (1890), 11–12.
51. Himmelfarb (1984), 366.
52. Pick (1989), 63.
53. Ibid., 60.
54. Gumplowicz (1893), 234, 235, 210.
55. Ward (1914), 203–12.
56. Webb (1979), 173, 174.
57. Freud (1918), 52, 15; Rieff (1961), 63.
58. Huxley (1929), 163.
59. Du Bois (2007c), 3.
60. "Mr. Chamberlain on the Australian Colonies", *Times*, 12 November 1895.

61. Olusoga and Erichsen (2010), 110, 87, 88; Smith (1980).
62. O'Sullivan (1845), 2; Gossett (1963), 318; Kramer (2002),1341.
63. Giddings (1901), 243; Strong (1900),183.
64. Jacobson (1998), 208, 209.
65. Ross (1911), 47; Roosevelt (1894), 366.
66. Jacobson (1998), 92; Stoddard (1921), 259.
67. Pearson (1893), 85.
68. Lake and Reynolds (2008), 93.
69. Stoddard (1921), 21,13, 9, 259–60, 298.

4. THE REINVENTION OF JEW-HATRED

1. David Baddiel, "David Baddiel on antisemitism: the oldest racism is no longer lurking in the shadows", *Sunday Times*, 30 May 2021.
2. Baron cited in Feldman (1993), 124; Blumenkranz cited in Rodinson (1983), 94–5; Moore (2007), 4.
3. Kates (1989), 214.
4. Ibid., 213–5.
5. Sorkin (2019), 2; Vital (1999), 29.
6. Lévi-Strauss (1963), 89; Schechter (2003), 36.
7. Kates (1989), 232.
8. Hunt (1996), 75, 76.
9. Cesarani (2002); Dubin (2017); Schama (2018), 369–71; Sorkin (2019), 17–20, 25–7, 75–9.
10. Hyman (1998), 5; Sorkin (2019), 96; Mendes-Flohr and Reinharz (1995), 117.
11. Mendes-Flohr and Reinharz (1995), 118.
12. Mendes-Flohr and Reinharz (1995), 150–1; Sorkin (2019), 5.
13. Mendes-Flohr and Reinharz (1995), 115; Low (1979), 412.
14. Arendt (2007), 62, 64.
15. Arendt (2017), 73.
16. Herder (2016), 283, 284, 285; Apsler (1943), 4, 6.
17. Chamberlain (1911), vol. 1, 330.
18. Bein (1990), 594.
19. Pulzer (1988), 55.
20. Birnbaum (2001), 114; Schama (2018), 641; Mosse (1978), 168.
21. Fine and Spencer (2017), 35; Wheen (1999), 56; Marx (1975), 226 (italics in the original).
22. Arendt (2017), 44.
23. Stern (1961), 121, 31.
24. Pulzer (1988), 236, 36.
25. Stern (1961), 141, 63.

26. Pulzer (1988), 28, 291, 292.
27. Jones (1824), vol. 1, 28.
28. Benes (2006), 169.
29. Benes (2006),169–70, 176, Halbfass (1988), 139.
30. Zimmerman (1999).
31. Mosse (1978), 92; Zimmerman (1999), 428.
32. Burrow (2000), 3.
33. Mosse (1978), 105.
34. Chamberlain (1911), vol. 1, 267, 271.
35. Ibid., 269, 263.
36. Ibid., 202, 200, lxv.
37. Ibid., 331, 330, 339, 480.
38. Ibid., 577, 578.

5. BARBARISM COMES HOME

1. Du Bois (2007d), 15; Arendt (2017), 270.
 2. Roosevelt (1889–96), vol. 3, 129; Dilke (1888), 188.
 3. Hull (2005), 56.
 4. Hull (2005), 33.
 5. Olusoga and Erichsen (2010), 140–8; Hull (2005), 47–69.
 6. Olusoga and Erichsen (2010), 155, 148.
 7. Olusoga and Erichsen (2010), 152, 157; Hull (2005), 64, 68.
 8. Forth (2012), iv; "Weyler in Cuba", *New York Times*, 12 February 1896, 4; Pitzer (2017).
 9. Silvester and Gewald (2003), xx–xxi.
10. Hull (2005), 78; Olusoga and Erichsen (2010), 210.
11. Olusoga and Erichsen (2010), 229–30, 189; Hull (2005), 88.
12. Farrar (1867), 148, 151–2.
13. Traverso (2003), 57–8.
14. Kidd (1894), 46.
15. Traverso (2003), 58–9.
16. Packenham (1992), 239–53; Hochschild (2019), 75–87.
17. Hochschild (2019), 16.
18. Ibid., 226, 233, 4.
19. Ibid., 259.
20. Northrup (1988), 99–100; Higginson (1989), 10, 5.
21. "50% think Belgian colonists did more good than harm in Congo", *The Brussels Times*, 12 July 2020 [https://www.brusselstimes.com/news/belgium-all-news/121215/50-think-belgian-colonists-did-more-good-than-harm-in-congo/; accessed 2 September 2021].
22. Gilley (2017), 1. For a recent account of the British Empire's rootedness in violence, see Elkins (2020).

23. Gott (2011), 44.
24. Reynolds (2001), 53.
25. Ibid., 78.
26. Hughes (2003), 120; Ryan (2012), xix; Reynolds (2001), 76–7, 85.
27. Reynolds (2001), 94, 115.
28. Ibid., 127.
29. Mazower (2008), 586; Brendon (2000), 262–82; Campbell (2017); Labanca (2004); Traverso (2003), 67.
30. Mayer (2012), 91.
31. Hitler (1992), 60, 347, 295, 604, 605, (italics in the original).
32. Churchill, "Zionism versus Bolshevism", *Illustrated Sunday Herald*, 8 February 1920, 5.
33. Crim (2011), 628–9.
34. Childers (1983); Childers (1984); Hamilton (1982); King et al. (2008).
35. Burleigh and Wippermann (1991), 44–50, 77–96; Friedländer (1997), 26–40, 111–171. There were, in fact, three laws that Hitler announced. The third made the swastika the official flag of Germany.
36. White (2009), Bessel (1984) and (2004); Fischer (1983).
37. Bessel (2004).
38. Whitman (2018), 5, 93–113.
39. Ibid., 121, 122, 123.
40. Ibid., 119, 109 (italics in the original).
41. Guettel (2012), 133–4, 141–2, 149, 150.
42. Whitman (2018), 127–8, 5; Friedländer (1997), 147–55.
43. Kühl (1994), 25; Burleigh and Wippermann (1991), 48–9, 173.
44. Friedlander (1995); Burleigh and Wippermann (1991),142–67.
45. Burleigh and Wippermann (1991), 51–2.
46. Black (2003), 284–314; Schafft (2004), 45–58.
47. Kühl (1994), 75; Kevles (1995), 164–92.
48. Ellinger (1942), 141–3; Stoddard (1940), 205, 193–6.
49. Hitler (1953), 33, 24.
50. Hitler (1992), 128–9; Padover (1935),167, 165–6; Engels (1849); Mazower (2008), 16.
51. Mazower (2008), 558, 4, 150, 584.
52. "Nazi Persecution of Soviet Prisoners", Holocaust Encyclopedia, United States Holocaust Memorial Museum [https://encyclopedia.ushmm.org/content/en/article/nazi-persecution-of-soviet-prisoners-of-war; accessed 10 July 2020]; Foerster (1986); Weingartner (1996).
53. Mazower (2008), 173–4, 368–415; Kershaw (2008), 60–88.
54. Heydrich (2017), 210.
55. Müller (1979), 12.
56. Olusoga and Erichsen (2010), 224.

57. Friedländer, (1990), 100 (italics in the original). The Arendt observation is in Arendt (2006), 279. Many of the original essays in the *Historikerstreit* are collected in Piper (1993). For the broader debate, see Baldwin (1990); Maier (1988); Kershaw (1995), ch. 9.
58. Césaire (2000), 36.

6. WHOSE UNIVERSAL?

1. Jackson and Bacon (2010), 133.
2. Césaire (1981), 24; for details of American responses to the Haitian Revolution see Jackson and Bacon (2010) and Byrd (2020).
3. Fanon (1990), 253.
4. Ibid., 251, 252.
5. Hazareesingh (2020), 11.
6. For the history of the Haitian Revolution see Dubois (2004), Fick (1991), Hazareesingh (2020).
7. Dubois (2004), 18, 39–40; Blackburn (1997), 431–49; Curtin (1969), 78–9.
8. Dubois (2004), 21, 85; Blackburn (1988), 166, 167, 179.
9. Dubois (2004), 62; Blackburn (1988), 188–90.
10. Dubois (2004), 87–9.
11. James (1980b), ix.
12. Dubois (2012), 137–54, 97–104.
13. Genovese (1979), 3, xix.
14. Trouillot (1995), 103; Sala-Molins (2006), 124.
15. Blackburn (1991), 89.
16. Fick (1991), 44–5; Nesbitt (2008), 73; Scott (2020), 107, 113.
17. Hazareesingh (2020), 47; Dubois (2004), 105; Nesbitt (2008), 76; Piquionne (1998).
18. Hazareesingh (2020), 11.
19. "The Trial of Mr. Eyre", letter from ES Beesly, *Bee-Hive*, 18 August 1866.
20. Plain Dealer, "The Working Men of Jamaica", *Bee-Hive*, 16 December 1865; Plain Dealer, "The Next House on Fire", *Bee-Hive*, 1 September 1866.
21. "The Indian Struggle", *The People's Paper*, 5 September 1857; "Progress of the Indian Insurrection", *The People's Paper*, 19 September 1857.
22. Mill (2003), 81.
23. Mill (1858).
24. Turley (2004), 170 (italics in the original).
25. Charles Forsdick and Christian Høgsbjerg, "Introduction" in Forsdick and Høgsbjerg (2017), 16, 33, 31, 25.

26. Høgsbjerg (2014), 63.
27. James (1980b), 283.
28. Gilroy (1993); Equiano (2001).
29. Blyden (1997), 10; Mudimbe (2016), 70; Walker (2001), 26; see also Lynch (1967), 58–65.
30. Clarke (1974), 20; see also Grant (2010).
31. Grant (2010), 265.
32. Moses (1972), 46, 45.
33. Du Bois (2007a), 77.
34. Du Bois (2007a), 59; Du Bois (1915), 241; Du Bois (2015), 407–8.
35. Gilmore (2008), 31–66.
36. Gilmore (2008), 153–4; Robinson (1988), 361; Joshua Yaffa, "A Black Communist's Disappearance in Stalin's Russia", *New Yorker*, 18 October 2021.
37. Degras (1955), vol. 1, 163–4, 401.
38. Makalani (2011), 117, 95.
39. Mockler (2003); Brendon (2000), 262–82.
40. Brendon (2000), 275; Høgsbjerg (2014), 91.
41. Hill (1986), 69; Høgsbjerg (2014), 94.
42. Du Bois (2007a), 59; Du Bois (2015), 386; Padmore (1931).
43. Nardal (1928), 5.
44. Fanon (2008), 176; Singh (1998), 76; Macey (2000), 28.
45. Macey (2000), 93, 100, 103–4 (italics in the original).
46. Fanon (2008), 82.
47. Du Bois (2007c), 8; Fanon (2008), 170.
48. Diagne (2018); Césaire (1987), 82; Senghor (1964), 74; Sartre (1964), 18.
49. Fanon (1988), 34, 42–3.
50. Fanon (2008), 175, 176, 179.
51. Fanon (1988), 18; Fanon (1990), 173–4; Fanon (2008), 180.
52. Fanon (2008), 176.
53. Fanon (1990), 251, 252, 254.
54. Ibid., 253, 254.
55. Fanon (2008), 121.

7. SOLIDARITY FRACTURED

1. Rosenberg (1988); Shugg (1938), 547–56; Foner (2017), 66–9.
2. Foner & Lewis (1989), 244–5.
3. "The Meaning of July Fourth For the Negro", in Douglass (1999), 188–206.
4. "Oration in Memory of Abraham Lincoln", in Douglass (1999), 616–24.

5. Jonathan W. White and Scott Sandage, "What Frederick Douglass Had to Say About Monuments", *Smithsonian Magazine*, 30 June 2020.

6. "Protesters denounce Abraham Lincoln statue in D.C., urge removal of Emancipation Memorial", *Washington Post*, 26 June 2020.

7. "A Letter from the President", *New York Tribune*, 23 August 1862; Greeley's editorial, "The Prayer of Twenty Millions", was published on 19 August 1862.

8. "Nemesis", in Douglass (1999), 451.

9. Litwack (1961), 74–93; Foner (2010), 14–16; de Tocqueville (2003), 402.

10. "The Claims of the Negro Ethnologically Considered", in Douglass (1999), 296.

11. "They Glory in their Shame", *Colored American*, 10 June 1837; Sinha (2016), 365.

12. Olmsted (1861), vol. 1, 13; Morris (1954), 220.

13. Morris (1954), 220.

14. "Southern South Carolina—Its Social and Political Character", *New York Times*, 23 November 1861; Morris (1954), 223.

15. Forret (2006), 141, 15.

16. Graham (2018).

17. "The Anniversaries", *New York Times*, 10 May 1865.

18. "The Anniversaries", *New York Times*, 10 May 1865; Blight (2018), 469.

19. Foner (2005), 90; Foner (1994), 458.

20. Johnson (1967–2000), vol. 3, 144; vol. 13, 287, 288; Foner (2014), 180.

21. Foner (2014), 199–205.

22. Avins (1966), 809.

23. Stanton, Anthony and Gage (1882), vol. 2, 382, 383.

24. Ibid., 353.

25. Ginzberg (2009), 122.

26. Stanton, Anthony and Gage (1882), vol. 2, 383.

27. Woodward (1991); Benedict (1980), 489–524.

28. Bernstein (1956); Stowell 2008); Stowell (1999).

29. Bernstein (1971); *New York Times*, 28 December 1873; *New York Times*, 20 January 1874.

30. Pike (1874), 66, 67, 12, 63.

31. Slaughter-House Cases, 83 U.S. (16 Wall.) 36 (1873) [https://tile.loc.gov/storage-services/service/ll/usrep/usrep083/usrep083036/usrep083036.pdf; accessed 12 December 2020]; Foner (2014), 529–30, 437; Keith (2007); Lane (2008); Pope (2015); United States v. Cruikshank, 92 U.S. 542 (1875) [https://supreme.justia.com/cases/federal/us/92/542/; accessed 12 December 2020].

32. Civil Rights Cases, 109 U.S. 3 (1883) [https://tile.loc.gov/storage-services/service/ll/usrep/usrep109/usrep109003/usrep109003.pdf; accessed 12 December 2020]; Howard (1999), 124–33; Goldstone (2012).

33. Howard (1999),132 (italics in the original).

34. Du Bois (2007b), 24.

35. Foner (2017), 53–6.

36. Foner and Lewis (1978–84), vol. 3, 112, 111.

37. Ibid., vol. 3, 109, 116, 122, 106–7.

38. Ibid., vol. 3, 133.

39. Foner (2017), 5; Foner and Lewis (1989), 152.

40. Foner (2017), 60–2; Foner and Lewis (1978–84), vol. 3, 143–239; DeSantis (2016).

41. Foner (2017), 61–3.

42. Ibid., 71–7.

43. Ibid., 76.

44. For a history of the IWW, see Renshaw (1999) and Cole, Struthers and Zimmer (2017).

45. Zucchino, (2020); Tyson, (2006); Umfleet (2006); Wooley (1977); Kirk (2002).

46. Woodward (1938),18; Bloom (2019), 51.

47. Tyson, (2006), 7, 8; Zucchino (2020), 79–89.

48. Tyson (2006), 7, 9, 6, 8.

49. Ibid., 8, 9, 10.

50. Williamson (1975); Woodward (1974), 12; Rabinowitz (1976), 325–50.

51. Woodward (1974), 68.

52. Kousser (1974), 45–82; Bloom (2019), 54.

53. Equal Justice Initiative (2017); Litwack (1998), 286–7. See also Waldrep (2005), Giddings (2008), Wells (1991).

54. Du Bois (2007b), 573.

55. Kousser (1974), 144.

56. Kousser (1974), 49, 208; Bloom (2019), 62, 63.

57. Kyle (1901), vol. 7, 554.

58. Whites (1988), 450, 453.

59. Du Bois (2007b), 573.

60. Hughes (1994), 41.

61. Woodward (1974), 74; Plessy v. Ferguson, 163 U.S. 537 (1896) [https://supreme.justia.com/cases/federal/us/163/537/; accessed 20 December 2021].

62. "Reconstruction and Disfranchisement", *Atlantic Monthly* (October 1901), cited in Woodward (1974), 72.

63. Woodward (1938), 29, 32.
64. A transcript of the speech can be found at http://historymatters.gmu. edu/d/39/; accessed 20 December 2021].
65. Du Bois (2007c), 39–40.

8. FROM CLASS SOLIDARITY TO BLACK LIVES MATTER

1. Carter (1969); see also Solomon (1998),191–206; Kelley (2015), 78–91; Gilmore (2008), 118–28.
2. Carter (1969), 18, 20.
3. For the story of communist work in the American South, see Gilmore (2008), Solomon (1998) and Kelley (2015).
4. Kelley (2015), 92, 93, 109.
5. Ibid., 109.
6. Miller *et* al. (2001), 401–5, 427–8.
7. Murray (1967).
8. Du Bois, "Postscript", *Crisis*, September 1931, 315.
9. Solomon (1998), 198, 199; Carter (1969), 90–1.
10. Lewis (2000), 546–53; Marable (1991), 27–8.
11. Caute (1978), 27, 70, 71.
12. Lauren (1996), 201.
13. "Adolph Hitler, KKK", *Afro-American*, 9 Sept. 1933, 16; Gilmore (2008), 171; for accounts of the "red summer", see Voogd (2008) and McWhirter (2011).
14. Ruchames (1953), 28, 29.
15. Korstad (2003); Korstad and Lichtenstein (1988). The UCAPAWA was later renamed the Food, Tobacco, Agricultural, and Allied Workers (FTA).
16. Korstad (2003), 251.
17. Korstad and Lichtenstein (1988), 791.
18. Korstad (2003), 258.
19. Korstad and Lichtenstein (1988), 789.
20. Murray (2018), 163; Gilmore (2008), 285.
21. For the seminal paper on the "long civil rights movement" see Hall (2005).
22. Malcolm X (1968), 118.
23. Lee (1996); Malcom X (1968), 292.
24. Malcolm X (1968), 378, 484; Perry (1992), 237.
25. Malcom X (1968), 411, 403–6.
26. Ibid, 452, 447, 454 (italics in original).
27. Payne and Payne (2020), 454; Lewis (1998), 287–8.
28. Malcolm X (1968), 454 (italics in original).

29. Garrow (1988), 545, 554, 555; Joseph (2020), 270.
30. Honey (2018), 154, 120; "Formula For Discord", *New York Times*, 17 August 1967, 36.
31. Honey (2007).
32. Marable (1991), 93–4, 92–3; Baldwin "A Report from Occupied Territory", in Baldwin (1998), 734, 730.
33. Marable (1991), 92, 96.
34. Bloom and Martin (2016), 2; Crouch (1997), 253.
35. Bloom and Martin (2016), 19–62; Jones and Jeffries (1998), 29–31.
36. Bloom and Martin (2016), 370.
37. Cruse (2009), 201, 82, 86, 91 (italics in the original).
38. Malcom X (1968), 425; Carmichael and Hamilton (1967), 44 (italics in the original).
39. Lester (1968), 91, 87, 84–5.
40. Neal (1968), 30; Baraka "The Legacy of Malcolm X, and the Coming of the Black Nation", in Baraka (2009), 165, 166, 167.
41. Baraka, "A Radical View of Newark", *New York Times*, 17 October 1976; Baraka (1997), 458.
42. Marable (1991), 97; Johnson (2007), loc 1071.
43. Marable (1991), 98.
44. "The Jogger and the Wolf Pack", *New York Times*, 26 April 189; Robert D. McFadden and Susan Saulny, "A Crime Revisited: The Decision; 13 Years Later, Official Reversal in Jogger Attack", *New York Times*, 6 December 2002; Byfield (2014).
45. Kelley (2015), xxi.
46. "1,050 people have been shot and killed by police in the past year", *Washington Post*, 6 May 2022 [https://www.washingtonpost.com/graphics/investigations/police-shootings-database/; accessed 7 May 2022]; Mapping Police Violence [https://mappingpoliceviolence.org/; accessed 6 September 2022].
47. Fryer (2017); Fryer (2019); Reilly (2020), 7; Sentencing Project (2018); Gelman, Fagan and Kiss (2007).
48. Sahara et al. (2019); Edwards, Hedwig & Esposito (2019); Mike Males, "Who are the police killing?", Center for Juvenile and Criminal Justice, 26 August 2014 [http://www.cjcj.org/news/8113; accessed 6 May 2022]; John Creamer, "Inequalities Persist despite decline in poverty for all major race and Hispanic origin groups", United States Census Bureau, 15 September 2020 [https://www.census.gov/library/stories/2020/09/poverty-rates-for-blacks-and-hispanics-reached-historic-lows-in-2019.html; accessed 6 May 2022].
49. Feldman *et* al. (2019); Feldman (2020).
50. Alysia Santo and R.G. Dunlop, "Where Police Killings Often Meet With

Silence: Rural America", *New York Times*, 25 September 2021; Adam Rothman and Barbara J. Fields, "The Death of Hannah Fizer", *Dissent*, 24 July 2020.

51. Banfield (1974), 63, 57, 59, 60, 61, 72.
52. Lewis (1966), xlii, xlv, xliv; Banfield (1974), ix.
53. Banfield (1974), 96.
54. Moynihan (1965), chs. III & IV.
55. Kelling and Wilson (1982).
56. Alexander (2010), 41; Haldeman (1994), 53.
57. Weitzer (1999), 819, 841–2.
58. Vitale (2017), 3; Fuentes (2013), 155; Baldwin (1998), 728–38; see also Balko (2013).
59. Daytrian Wilken, "The Black Sanitation Workers Who Are Saying, 'I Am a Man'", *New York Times*, 20 July 2020.
60. Black Lives Matter, "What we believe" [https://uca.edu/training/files/2020/09/black-Lives-Matter-Handout.pdf; accessed 6 May 2022]; Grant (2010), 265; Fanon (1990), 126; Lewis (1998), 287–8; Baraka (1997), 342.
61. Amir Khafagy, "Black Lives Matter on the Picket Line", *Discourse Blog* [https://www.discourseblog.com/p/black-lives-matter-on-the-picket?s=r; accessed 6 May 2022]; Matt Sledge, "New Orleans sanitation worker protest enters second week; dispute centers on pay, conditions", *Nola*, 11 May 2020. [https://www.nola.com/news/coronavirus/article_336a7742–93d3–11ea-a344–1bdefd47e647.html; accessed 6 May 2022]; See also: Anthony McCauley, "Labor agency investigating New Orleans garbage contractor Metro Services as workers move to unionize", *Nola*, 24 June 2020 [https://www.nola.com/news/business/article_b37bb7ee-b64b-11ea-ac72-eb8ecb99b035.html; accessed 6 May 2022].

9. STAY IN YOUR LANE!

1. "Kanye West Stirs Up TMZ Newsroom Over Trump, Slavery, Free Thought" [https://www.youtube.com/watch?v=s_M4LkYra5k&t=2s; accessed 25 May 2022].
2. Coates (2018); Appiah (1994), 162.
3. Ijeoma Oluo, "How should white people talk about Kanye West?", *Guardian*, 3 May 2018.
4. Jeffries (2017), 211–19.
5. Marcuse (1966), 4.
6. Todorov (1993), 68.
7. Jeffries (2017), 303; Mills (1960); Hughes, "The Sea Change" in Hughes (1987), 135–6.

8. For an account of the work of Boas and his circle see King (2019).

9. Boas (1922), 240; White (1949), 181; Stocking (1982), 227.

10. Kymlicka (1995), 86; Taylor (1994), 40, 41 n16.

11. Lévi-Strauss (1985), 10.

12. Ibid., 11.

13. Bhabha (1994), 4; Harvey (1990), 44.

14. Lester (1968), 91; Baraka (2009), 166.

15. Bell (1992a), dedication page.

16. Bell (1992a), xxi, 15; Bell (1992b), 302.

17. Alexander (2018), ix.

18. Delgado (2012).

19. Bell (1980), 524, 525, 522–3.

20. Bell (1992a), 247, 248.

21. Alexander (2018), xiv, xviii.

22. Gilroy (2000), 103.

23. Tyson (2017); Anderson (2015).

24. Hannah Black, "Open letter to the curators and staff of the Whitney Museum" [https://blackcontemporaryart.tumblr.com/post/158661 755087/please-read-share-hannah-blacks-open-letter-to; accessed 19 May 2022].

25. Smith (2017).

26. Nadra Kareem Nittle, "A Guide to Understanding and Avoiding Cultural Appropriation", ThoughtCo, 4 February 2021 [https://www. thoughtco.com/cultural-appropriation-and-why-iits-wrong-2834561; accessed 29 May 2022]; Nicki Lisa Cole, "Definition of Cultural Appropriation: What It Is, Why It Matters and How to Avoid It" [https://writingtheother.com/wp-content/uploads/2018/08/ Definition-of-Cultural-Appropriation.pdf; accessed 29 May 2022].

27. Amiri Baraka interviewed by Leonard Schwartz on KAOS-FM's "Cross Cultural Poetics", #141, 19 May 2007 [https://writing.upenn.edu/ pennsound/x/XCP.php#141; accessed 29 May 2022].

28. Shatz (2019); Kamila Shamsie [https://twitter.com/kamilashamsie/sta tus/774721046209503233?lang=en-gb; accessed 25 May 2022].

29. Du Bois (2007b), 290, 557.

30. Allen (1967), 172: Allen (1972).

31. Harris (1993): McIntosh (1988).

32. Lizz Schumer, "What White Privilege Really Means—and How to Work on It", *Good Housekeeping*, 29 June 2020 [https://www.goodhousekeep-ing.com/life/a32948548/what-is-white-privilege/; accessed 24 May 2022]; Olive Pometsey, "White Privilege: A Primer", *GQ*, 22 January 2020 [https://www.gq-magazine.co.uk/politics/article/what-is-white-privilege; accessed 24 May 2022]; NHS Providers, "Changing Mindsets:

Confronting White Privilege in the NHS" [https://nhsproviders.org/inclusive-leadership/changing-mindsets-confronting-white-privilege-in-the-nhs; accessed 24 May 2022]; Gloucestershire County Council, "Dispelling the Myths: White Privilege" [https://www.gloucestershire.gov.uk/your-community/black-history-month/black-history-month-2020/dispelling-the-myths/white-privilege/; accessed 24 May 2022]; Blocker Anderson (2022); DiAngelo (2019).

33. Kolchin (2002), 167.
34. Gil Steinlauf, "Jews struggled for decades to become white. Now we must give up white privilege to fight racism", *Washington Post*, 22 September 2015.
35. Eddo-Lodge (2018), 86.
36. Akala (2018), 63.
37. "Criminal Justice Facts", The Sentencing Project, 2020. [https://www.sentencingproject.org/criminal-justice-facts/; accessed 12 May 2022]; James Cullen, "History of Mass Incarceration, Brennan Centre for Justice, 20 July 2018 [https://www.brennancenter.org/our-work/analysis-opinion/history-mass-incarceration; accessed 12 May 2022]; Leah Sakala, "Breaking Down Mass Incarceration in the 2010 Census: State-by-State Incarceration Rates by Race/Ethnicity", Prison Policy Initiative, 28 May 2014 [https://www.prisonpolicy.org/reports/rates.html; accessed 12 May 2022].
38. Alexander (2010), 2, 4.
39. Forman (2017), 9.
40. Ibid., 10, 11–12; Forman (2012), 103–4.
41. Forman (2012), 131, 132.
42. Ibid., 134.
43. Lewis (2017); Clegg and Usmani (2019).
44. Peller (1990), 131, 135.
45. Ibid., 138.
46. Peller (1990), 138; 1663; Delgado and Stefancic (1994), 162.
47. Ellison, "The World and the Jug", in Ellison (2003), 156, 159, 163.
48. Ibid., 163, 164, 177; Ellison "Change the Joke and Slip the Yoke" in Ellison (2003), 112.
49. Murray (2020), 23, 152–3 (italics in the original); Gates (1992), xvii.
50. hooks (1991), 25; hooks (2000), vii.
51. Gitlin (1995), 100; Brown (1995), 59.
52. Crenshaw (1991), 1297.
53. hooks (1991), 15–16.
54. Malik (2019), 139–40.
55. This episode of *The View* is on YouTube [https://www.youtube.com/watch?v=AhITfM4bqO8; accessed 24 May 2022]; Goldberg published

her apology on Twitter [https://twitter.com/WhoopiGoldberg/status/1488320164517101574; accessed 24 May 2022].

56. Brodkin (1998), 140, 142, 143.
57. Baldwin, "Anti-Semitism and Black Power", in Baldwin (2010), 253, 251.
58. "Baldwin, "Negroes are Anti-Semitic Because They are Anti-White", in Baldwin (1998), 746, 741 (italics in the original).
59. Cruse (1969), 158; Cruse, "My Jewish Problem and Theirs", in Hentoff (1969), 184–5; Julius Lester, "A Response", in Hentoff (1969), 232.
60. Schraub (2019), 393; Henry Louis Gates Jr., "Black Demagogues and Pseudo-Scholars", *New York Times*, 20 July 1992. Gates was referring to Michael Bradley's thesis in his book *The Iceman Inheritance*.
61. Wheen (1999), 340.
62. Randall (2021), 197; Jo Glanville, "Formerly known as", *London Review of Books*, 10 November 2021 [https://www.lrb.co.uk/blog/2021/november/formerly-known-as; accessed 24 May 2022].

10. IDENTITARIANS ALL: THE GHOSTLY AFTERLIVES OF RACE

1. "How British moral attitudes have changed in the last 30 years", The Policy Institute at King's College London, October 2019 [https://www.ipsos.com/sites/default/files/ct/news/documents/2019–10/moral_attitudes_2019.pdf; accessed 8 June 2022]; Airey and Jowell (1983); Rob Ford, "A close inspection of the British Social Attitudes Survey shows that racial prejudice is in long-term decline", *Democratic Audit*, 27 August 2014 [https://www.democraticaudit.com/2014/08/27/a-close-inspection-of-the-british-social-attitudes-survey-shows-that-racial-prejudice-is-in-long-term-decline/; accessed 8 June 2022] "Race and Ethnicity in Britain", Ipsos Mori, June 2020 [https://www.ipsos.com/sites/default/files/ct/news/documents/2020–06/race-inequality-june-2020-charts.pdf; accessed 8 June 2022].
2. Tony Blair, "We won't look back to the 1970s", *Times*, 31 March 1997.
3. "Trade Union Membership, UK 1995–2020: Statistical Bulletin", Department of Business, Energy and Industrial Strategy [https://assets.publishing.service.gov.uk/government/uploads/system/uploads/attachment_data/file/989116/Trade-union-membership-2020-statistical-bulletin.pdf; accessed 11 June 2022]; McNicholas *et* al. (2020); Dromey (2018).
4. Goodhart (2017), 3, 5.
5. Pulzer (1988), 55.
6. Goodhart (2017), 79.
7. Scruton (1990), 59, 66 (italics in the original).
8. Stephanson & West (1989), 276; Case and Deaton (2020).

9. Benoist, "The Idea of Empire" in Benoist (2018), loc. 749.

10. Rueda (2021), 217.

11. Benoist & Champetier (2012), 28, 26; Benoist, "On Identity" in Benoist (2018), loc. 4132, 4164, 4361.

12. Rose (2021), 107; Benoist and Champetier (2012), 35; Benoist, "On Identity" in Benoist (2018), loc 4215; Benoist (2011), 24, 23.

13. Benoist & Champetier (2012), 28–9.

14. Eltchaninoff (2018), 158.

15. Marcus (1995), 23; Bar-on (2007), 127.

16. Eltchaninoff (2018), 66, 77.

17. Ibid., 126, 125.

18. The Génération Identitaire website has been shut down. An English translation of the text of the video can be found in Generation Identity (2013), 9–11; the most comprehensive study of the Identitarian movements is Zúquete (2018).

19. Zúquete (2018), 129; Dyer (1990), 145.

20. Ye'or (2005); Zia-Ebrahimi (2018); Adi Schwartz, "Protocols of the Elders of Brussels", *Haaretz*, 20 June 2006.

21. Murray (2018), 1, 3; Douglas Murray, "Census That Reveals a Troubling Future", *Standpoint*, 25 February 2013.

22. Stoddard (1921), 5; Zemmour (2015), 523; Polakow-Suransky (2017), 130.

23. Camus (2015), loc. 248; Raspail (1975), 180; Polakow-Suransky (2017), 212.

24. "Lionel Shriver, "Would you like London to be overrun with Americans like me?", *Spectator*, 28 August 2021; Collier (2013), 101; Kaufmann (2017); Kaufmann (2018), 522–5.

25. Bar-on (2019), 226.

26. Polakow-Suransky (2017), 291.

27. Caldwell (2009), 7.

28. Philip Bump, "Rep. Steve King warns that 'our civilization' can't be restored with 'somebody else's babies'", *Washington Post*, 12 March 2017; Judd Legum, "Republicans have invoked the 'great replacement' theory over and over", *Guardian*, 17 May 2022 [https://www.theguardian.com/commentisfree/2022/may/17/republicans-have-invoked-the-great-replacement-theory-over-and-over-and-over; accessed 10 June 2022]; Nicholas Confessore and Karen Yourish, "A Fringe Conspiracy Theory, Fostered Online, Is Refashioned by the G.O.P.", *New York Times*, 15 May 2022; Tucker Carlson, "Joe Biden revealed why he supports illegal immigration in 2015, he wants to change the country", Fox News, 23 September 2021 [https://www.foxnews.com/opinion/tucker-carlson-joe-biden-revealed-why-supports-illegal-immigration-

2015-change-the-country; accessed 10 June 2022]; "Immigration Attitudes and Conspiratorial Thinkers: A Study Issued on the 10th Anniversary of The Associated Press-NORC Center for Public Affairs Research" [https://apnorc.org/projects/immigration-attitudes-and-conspiratorial-thinkers/; accessed 10 June 2020]; Andrew Romano, "Poll: 61% of Trump voters agree with idea behind 'great replacement' conspiracy theory" [https://news.yahoo.com/hed-poll-61-of-trump-voters-agree-with-idea-behind-great-replacement-conspiracy-the-ory-090004062.html; accessed 10 June 2020].

29. Murray (2019), 3, 4; Lionel Shriver speaking at an Intelligence Squared debate on "Identity Politics is Tearing Society Apart", 22 May 2019 [https://www.youtube.com/watch?v=hVMYfuzhbxk; accessed 31 May 2022].

30. Murray (2019), 122.

31. Michael Feola, "How 'great replacement' theory led to the Buffalo mass shooting", *Washington Post*, 25 May 2022; Lara Keay, "Buffalo shooting: What is the 'great replacement theory' mentioned in Payton Gendron's manifesto?", Sky News, 18 May 2022 [https://news.sky.com/story/buffalo-shooting-what-is-the-great-replacement-theory-mentioned-in-payton-gendrons-manifesto-12615069; accessed 10 June 2022].

32. Brenton Tarrant, "The Great Replacement" [https://img-prod.ilfoglio.it/userUpload/The_Great_Replacementconvertito.pdf; accessed 30 May 2022].

33. Kymlicka (1995), 104–5; Margaret Thatcher Foundation, "TV Interview for Granada World In Action ('rather swamped')", 27 January 1978 [https://www.margaretthatcher.org/document/103485; accessed 30 May 2022].

34. Zúquete (2018), 133, 31.

35. Marina Watts, "In Smithsonian Race Guidelines, Rational Thinking and Hard Work Are White Values", *Newsweek*, 17 July 2020 [https://www.newsweek.com/smithsonian-race-guidelines-rational-thinking-hard-work-are-white-values-1518333; accessed 31 May 2022]; National Museum of African History and Culture, "Whiteness" [https://nmaahc.si.edu/learn/talking-about-race/topics/whiteness; accessed 31 May 2022].

36. Murray (1945), 22.

37. Coates (2015), 83, 20–1; Murray (1945), 24.

38. Coates (2015), 151.

39. Hannaford (1996), 12 (italics in the original).

40. Fanon (2008), 180.

41. Williams (2019), 137–8, 153–4 (italics in original).

42. Ibid., 159, 160.

43. Ibid., 137.

BIBLIOGRAPHY

Adi, Hakim (2018) *Pan-Africanism: A History*, Bloomsbury Academic.

Adorno, Theodor W. & Horkheimer, Max (1997; first pub. 1944) *Dialectic of Enlightenment*, Verso.

Airey, CR & Jowell, R. (1983) British Social Attitudes Survey, National Centre for Social Research.

Akala (2018), *Natives: Race and Class in the Ruins of Empire*, Two Roads.

Alexander, Michelle (2010) *The New Jim Crow: Mass Incarceration in the Age of Colorblindness*, New Press.

———— (2018) "Foreword" to Bell (1992).

Allen, Theodore W. (1994 & 1997) *The Invention of the White Race*, 2 vols., Verso.

———— (1998) "Summary of the Argument of *The Invention of the White Race*", *Cultural Logic*, 2.

———— (1972) "The Most Vulnerable Point", Paper presented to the Conference of Easter and Mideastern Shop and Community Organizers, 20 October 1972 [https://credo.library.umass.edu/view/pageturn/mums1021-s02-i013/#page/1/mode/1up; accessed 14 May 2022].

———— (1967) "Can White Workers Radicals be Radicalised?" in Ignatin, Noel, and Allen, Ted (2011) "White Blindspot", 167–181.

Anderson, Devery S. (2015) *Emmett Till: The Murder That Shocked the World and Propelled the Civil Rights Movement*, University Press of Mississippi.

Appiah, Kwame Anthony (1994) "Identity, Authenticity, Survival: Multicultural Societies and Social Reproduction", in Guttman (1994), 149–63.

Apsler, Alfred (1943) "Herder and the Jews", *Monatshefte fur Deutschen Unterricht*, 35 (1), 1–15.

Arendt, Hannah, (2017; first pub. 1951) *The Origins of Totalitarianism*, Penguin.

———— (2007) *The Jewish Writings*, Shocken.

———— (2006; first pub. 1963) *Eichmann in Jerusalem: A Report on the Banality of Evil*, Penguin.

315

Armitage, David (2004) "John Locke, Carolina and the Two Treatises of Government", *Political Theory*, 35 (5), 602–27.

Augustine (1998) *The City of God Against the Pagans*, Cambridge University Press.

Avins, Alfred (1966) "The Fifteenth Amendment and Literary Tests: The Original Intent", *Stanford Law Review*, 18 (5), 808–22.

Baddiel, David (2021) *Jews Don't Count: How Identity Politics Failed One Particular Identity*, TLS Books.

Bagehot, Walter (1915) *The Works and Life of Walter Bagehot: The Works in Nine Volumes. The Life in One Volume*, Longmans, Green, and Co., Vol. 1 [https://oll.libertyfund.org/titles/2258; accessed 18 November 2020].

Baldwin, James (2010) *The Cross of Redemption: Uncollected Writings*, Vintage.

———— (1998) *Collected Essays*, Library of America.

Baldwin, Peter (ed.) (1990) *Reworking the Past: Hitler, the Holocaust and the Historians' Debate*, Beacon Press.

Balko, Radley (2013) *Rise of the Warrior Cop: The Militarization of America's Police Forces*, Public Affairs.

Banfield, Edward C. (1974) *The Heavenly City Revisited*, Little, Brown.

Baraka, Amiri (2009) *The LeRoi Jones/Amiri Baraka Reader*, Basic Books.

———— (1997; first pub. 1984) *The Autobiography of LeRoi Jones*, Lawrence Hill.

Barkar, Elazar (1992) *The Retreat of Scientific Racism: Changing Concepts of Race in Britain and the United States between the World Wars*, Cambridge University Press.

Bar-on, Tamir (2007) *Where Have All The Fascists Gone?*, Ashgate.

———— (2019) "Richard B. Spencer and the Alt-Right" in Sedgwick (2019), 224–41.

Beddoe, John (1912), *The Anthropological History of Europe: Being the Rhind Lectures for 1891*, Alexander Gardner.

———— (1885) *The Races of Britain: A Contribution to the Anthropology of Western Europe*, Trubner & Co.

Bein, Alex (1990) *The Jewish Question: Biography of a World Problem*, Herzel Press.

Bell, Derrick (1992a) *Faces at the Bottom of the Well: The Permanence of Racism*, Basic Books.

———— (1992b) "Racial Realism" in Crenshaw et al. (1995), 302–12.

———— (1980) "Brown v. Board of Education and the Interest-Convergence Dilemma", *Harvard Law Review*, 93 (3), 518–33.

Benedict, Michael Les (1980) "Southern Democrats in the Crisis of 1876–1877: A Reconsideration of Reunion and Reaction", *Journal of Southern History* 46 (4), 489–524.

Benedict, Ruth, (1961; first pub. 1935) *Patterns of Culture*, Routledge.

Benes, Tuska (2006) "From Indo-Germans to Aryans: Philology and the Racialization of Salvationist National Rhetoric, 1806–30", in Eigen and Larrimore (2006) 167–81.

Benoist, Alain de (2018) *Democracy and Populism: The Telos Essays*, Telos Press ebook.

———— (2011) *The Problem of Democracy*, Arktos.

Benoist, Alain de & Champetier, Charles (2012) *Manifesto for a European Renaissance*, Arktos.

Berger, John (2021) *Portraits*, Verso.

Berlin, Isaiah (1976) *Vico and Herder: Two Studies in the History of Ideas*, Hogarth Press.

Bernasconi, Robert (ed.) (2001a) *Race*, Blackwell.

———— (2001b) "Who invented the concept of race?", in Bernasconi (2001a) 11–36.

Bernasconi, Robert & Lott, Tommy L., (eds.) (2000) *The Idea of Race*, Hackett.

Bernasconi, Robert & Mann, Anika Maaza, (2005) "The Contradictions of Racism: Locke, Slavery and the Two Treatises", in Vals (2005), 89–107.

Bernier, François, "A New Division of the Earth" in Bernasconi & Lott (2000), 1–4.

Bernstein, Samuel (1971) "The Impact of the Paris Commune in the United States", *Massachusetts Review*, 12 (3), 435–46.

———— (1956) "American Labor in the Long Depression, 1873–1878", *Science & Society*, 20 (1), 59–83.

Bessel, Richard (1984) *Political Violence and the Rise of Nazism: The Storm Troopers in Eastern Germany 1925–1934*, Yale University Press.

———— (2004) "The Nazi Capture of Power", *Journal of Contemporary History*, 39 (2), 169–88.

Bhabha, Homi K. (1994) *The Location of Culture*, Routledge.

Biddiss, Michael D. (ed.) (1979) *Images of Race*, Leicester University Press.

Birnbaum, Pierre (2001) *The Idea of France*, Hill & Wang.

Black, Edwin (2003) *War Against the Weak: Eugenics and America's Campaign to Create a Master Race*, Four Walls Eight Windows.

Black, Robert (1975) *Fascism in Germany: How Hitler Destroyed the World's Most Powerful Labour Movement*, Steyn [Online at https://www.marxists.org/subject/fascism/blick/germany.pdf; accessed 19 July 2021].

Blackburn, Robin (2011) *An Unfinished Revolution: Karl Marx and Abraham Lincoln*, Verso.

——— (1997) *The Making of New World Slavery: From the Baroque to the Modern 1492–1800*, Verso.

——— (1988) *The Overthrow of Colonial Slavery: 1776–1848*, Verso.

——— (1991) "The French Revolution and New World Slavery", in Osborne (ed.) (1991), 73–89.

Blanckaert, Claude, (1988) "On the Origins on French Ethnology", in Stocking (1988) 18–55.

Blanning, Tim (2010) *The Romantic Revolution*, Weidenfeld & Nicolson.

Blight, David W. (2018) *Frederick Douglass: Prophet of Freedom*, Simon & Schuster.

Blocker Anderson, Brandee (2022) *What is White Privilege?*, Antiracism Academy LLC.

Blom, Philipp (2010) *A Wicked Company: The Forgotten Radicalism of the European Enlightenment*, Basic Books.

Bloom, Jack M. (2019; 2nd edn.; first pub. 1987) *Class, Race and the Civil Rights Movement*, Indiana University Press.

Bloom, Joshua, and Waldo, Jr,. E. Martin, (2016) *Black Against Empire: The History and Politics of the Black Panther Party*, University of California Press.

Blumenbach, Johann Friedrich (1865) *The Anthropological Treatises of Johann Friedrich Blumenbach*, Longman, Green, Longman, Roberts & Green.

Blyden, Edward Wilmot, (1997; first pub. 1908) *African Life and Customs*, Black Classic Press.

Boas, Franz (1922) *The Mind of Primitive Man*, Macmillan.

Bolton, Charles C. (1994) *Poor Whites of the Antebellum South*, Duke University Press.

Bonsal, Stephen (1994) *Unfinished Business*, Michael Joseph.

Booth, William (1890) *In Darkest England: And the Way Out*, Funk & Wagnalls.

BIBLIOGRAPHY

Brendon, Piers (2000) *The Dark Valley: A Panorama of the 1930s*, Jonathan Cape.

Brewer, Holly (2017) "Slavery, Sovereignty, and 'Inheritable Blood': Reconsidering John Locke and the Origins of American Slavery", *American Historical Review*, 122 (4), 1038–78.

Brigham, Carl C. (1923) *A Study of American Intelligence*, Princeton University Press.

Broadie, Alexander (ed.) (2003) *The Cambridge Companion to the Scottish Enlightenment*, Cambridge University Press.

Brodkin, Karen (1998) *How Jews Became White Folks: And What that Says About Race in America*, Rutgers University Press.

Brown, Wendy (1995) *States of Injury: Power and Freedom in Late Modernity*, Princeton University Press.

Buffon, Georges Louis Leclerc, comte de (1780–5) *Natural History: General and Particular*, William Creech [http://name.umdl.umich.edu/004880992.0001.003; accessed 13 September 2020].

Buhle, Paul (ed.) (1986) *CLR James: His Life and Work*, Allison & Busby.

Burke, Edmund (1968; first pub. 1790) *Reflections on the Revolution in France: And on the Proceedings in Certain Societies in London Relative to That Event*, Penguin.

———— (1790) "Substance of the speech of the Right Honourable Edmund Burke, in thr [sic] debate on the army estimates, in the House of Commons, on Tuesday, the 9th day of February, 1790", Early English Books Online Text Creation Partnership, 2011 [https://quod.lib.umich.edu/e/ecco/004902170.0001.000/1:2?rgn=div1;view=toc; accessed 17 November 2020].

Burleigh, Michael & Wippermann, Wolfgang (1991) *The Racial State: Germany 1933–1945*, Cambridge University Press.

Burrow, John (2000) *The Crisis of Reason: European Thought, 1848–1914*, Yale University Press.

———— (1966) *Evolution and Society: A Study in Victorian Social Theory*, Cambridge University Press.

Byfield, Natalie (2014) *Savage Portrayals: Race, Media and the Central Park Jogger Story*, Temple University Press.

Byrd, Brandon R. (2020) *The Black Republic: African Americans and the Fate of Haiti*, University of Pennsylvania Press.

Caldwell, Christopher (2009) *Reflections on the Revolution in Europe: Immigration, Islam and the West*, Penguin.

Camp, Jordan T. & Kelley, Robin DG (2013) "Black Radicalism, Marxism, and Collective Memory: An Interview with Robin D. G. Kelley", *American Quarterly*, 65 (1), 215–30.

Campbell, Ian (2017) *The Addis Ababa Massacre: Italy's National Shame*, Hurst.

Camus, Renaud (2015; first pub. 2011) *Le Grand Remplacement: Introduction au Remplacisme Global*, Chateau de Plieux.

Cannadine, David, (2001) *Ornamentalism: How the British Saw Their Empire*, Allen Lane.

Carlyle, Thomas (1853) *Occasional Discourse on the Nigger Question*, Thomas Bosworth.

Carmichael, Stokely & Hamilton, Charles V. (1967) *Black Power: The Politics of Liberation in America*, Vintage.

Carter, Dan T. (1969) *Scottsboro: A Tragedy of the American South*, Louisiana State University Press.

Case, Anne and Deaton, Angus (2020) *Deaths of Despair and the Future of Capitalism*, Princeton University Press.

Caute, David (1978) *The Great Fear: The Anti-Communist Purge Under Truman and Eisenhower*, Secker and Warburg.

Césaire, Aimé (2004) *Discours sur le Colonialisme, Suivi de Discours sur la Négritude*, Présence Africaine.

———— (2000) *Discourse on Colonialism*, Monthly Review Press.

———— (1981) *Toussaint Louverture: La Révolution Fançaise et le Problème Colonial*, Présence Africaine.

———— (1987) "Discours sur la Négritude"in Césaire (2004); also available online [http://blog.ac-versailles.fr/lelu/public/ALTERITE/DISCOURS_NEGRITUDE.pdf; accessed 1 July 2022].

Cesarani, David (2002) *Port Jews: Jewish Communities in Cosmopolitan Maritime Trading Centres 1550–1950*, Frank Cass.

Chamberlain, Houston Stewart, (1911; first pub. 1899) *The Foundations of the Nineteenth Century* (2 Vols.), John Lane.

Chase, Allan (1980; first pub. 1975) *The Legacy of Malthus: The Social Costs of the New Scientific Racism*, University of Illinois Press.

Childers, Thomas (1983) *The Nazi Voter: The Social Foundations of Fascism in Germany, 1919–1933*, University of North Carolina Press.

———— (1984) "Who, Indeed, Did Vote for Hitler?", *Central European History*, 17 (1), 45–53.

Clark, JCD (ed.) (1990) *Ideas and Politics in Modern Britain*, Macmillan.

Clarke, John Henrik (1974) "Marcus Garvey: The Harlem Years", *Black Scholar*, 5 (4), 17–23.

Clegg, John and Usmani, Adaner (2019) "The Economic Origins of Mass Incarceration", *Catalyst*, 3 (3).

Coates, Ta-Nehisi, (2015) *Between the World and Me*, Text Publishing Company.

———— (2018) "I'm not black, I'm Kanye", *The Atlantic*, 7 May 2018.

Cole, Peter, Struthers, David & Zimmer, Kenyon (eds.) (2017), *Wobblies of the World: A Global History of the IWW*, Pluto.

Collier, Paul (2013) *Exodus: Immigration and Multiculturalism in the 21st Century*, Allen Lane.

Crenshaw, Kimberlé (1991) "Mapping the Margins: Intersectionality, Identity Politics, and Violence against Women of Color", *Stanford Law Review*, 43 (6), 1241–99.

Crenshaw, Kimberlé, Gotanda, Neil, Peller, Gary & Thomas, Kendall (eds.) (1995) *Critical Race Theory: The Key Writings that Formed a Movement*, New Press.

Crèvecoeur, John Hector St. John (1904; first pub. 1782) *Letters from an American Farmer*, Fox, Duffield & Company.

Crim, Brian E. (2011) "'Our Most Serious Enemy': The Specter of Judeo-Bolshevism in the German Military Community, 1914–1923", *Central European History*, 44 (4), 624–41.

Crouch, Stanley (1997) *The All-American Skin Game, Or the Decoy of Race*, Vintage.

Cruse, Harold (2009; first pub. 1968) *Rebellion or Revolution?*, University of Minnesota Press.

———— (1969; first pub. 1967) *The Crisis of the Negro Intellectual*, WH Allen.

Curtin, Philip D. (1969) *The Atlantic Slave Trade: A Census*, University of Wisconsin Press.

Dailey, Jane, (2012) "The Sexual Politics of Race in World War II America", in Kruse & Tuck (2012), 145–70.

Darnton, Robert (1996) *The Forbidden Best-Sellers of Pre-Revolutionary France*, W.W. Norton.

———— (1982) *The Literary Underground of the Old Regime*, Harvard University Press.

Darwin, Charles, (1998; first pub. 1872) *The Expressions of the Emotions in Man and Other Animals*, Harper Collins.

———— (1981; first pub. 1871) *The Descent of Man and Selection in Relation to Sex*, Princeton University Press.

———— (1968; first pub. 1859) *The Origin of Species By Means of Natural Selection Or the Preservation of Favoured Races in the Struggle for Life*, Penguin.

Davenport, Charles Benedict (1913) *Heredity in Relation to Eugenics*, Henry Holt.

Davis, David Brion (1999; first pub. 1975) *The Problem of Slavery in the Age of Revolution 1770–1823*, Oxford University Press.

———— (1988; first pub. 1966) *The Problem of Slavery in Western Culture*, Oxford University Press.

———— (1984) *Slavery and Human Progress*, Oxford University Press.

Degras, Jane, (ed.) (1955) *The Communist International, 1919–1943: Documents*, 3 vols., Royal Institute of International Affairs.

Delgado, Richard (2012) "Rodrigo's Seventh Chronicle: Race, Democracy, and the State", Alabama Law Scholarly Commons Working Paper [https://scholarship.law.ua.edu/fac_working_papers/235; accessed 17 May 2022].

Delgado, Richard, and Stefancic, Jean (2017) *Critical Race Theory: An Introduction*, New York University Press.

———— (1994) "Critical Race Theory, An Annotated Bibliography 1993: A Year of Transition", *University of Colorado Law Review*, 66, 159–93.

Denvir, Daniel (2020) *All-American Nativism: How the Bipartisan War on Immigrants Explains Politics As We Know It*, Verso.

DeSantis, John (2016) *The Thibodaux Massacre: Racial Violence and the 1887 Sugar Cane Labor Strike*, History Press.

Desmond, Adrian (1989) *The Politics of Evolution: Morphology, Medicine and Reform in Radical London*, University of Chicago Press.

Diagne, Souleymane Bachir (2018) "Négritude", *Stanford Encyclopedia of Philosophy* [https://plato.stanford.edu/archives/sum2018/entries/negritude/; accessed 16 November 2020].

DiAngelo, Robin (2019) *White Fragility: Why It's So Hard for White People to Talk About Racism*, Penguin.

Diderot, Denis (1992) *Political Writings*, Cambridge University Press.

Diderot, Denis, & d'Alembert, Jean le Rond (eds.) (2017) *Encyclopédie, ou dictionnaire raisonné des sciences, des arts et des métiers, etc.*, University of Chicago: ARTFL Encyclopédie Project (Autumn 2017 Edition),

Robert Morrissey and Glenn Roe (eds.), [http://encyclopedie.uchicago.edu/ accessed 6 October 2020]).

Dilke, Charles Wentworth (1888; first pub. 1869) *Greater Britain: A Record of Travel in English-Speaking Countries During 1866–67*, Macmillan & Co..

Dillingham, William P. (1911) *A Dictionary of Races and Peoples: Reports of the Immigration Commission, Vol. 5*, US Government Printing Office, 1911.

Douglass, Frederick (2017) *Narrative of the Life of Frederick Douglass, An American Slave, Written By Himself*, WW Norton.

———— (1999) *Selected Speeches and Writings*, ed. Philip Foner, Lawrence Hill Books.

———— (1855) *My Bondage and My Freedom*, Miller, Orton & Mulligan.

Drescher, Seymour (1986) *Capitalism and Antislavery: British Mobilization in Comparative Perspective*, Oxford University Press.

Dromey, Jack (2018) *Power to the People: How Stronger Unions Can Deliver Economic Justice*, IPPR.

Dromey, Jack & Taylor, Graham (1978) *Grunwick: The Workers' Story*, Lawrence & Wishart.

Dubin, Lois (2017) "Port Jews Revisited: Commerce and Culture in the Age of European Expansion", in Karp & Sutcliffe (2017) 550–75.

DuBois, Ellen Carol (1999) *Feminism and Suffrage: The Emergence of an Independent Women's Movement in America, 1848–1869*, Cornell University Press.

Dubois, Laurent (2012) *Haiti: The Aftershocks of History*, Picador.

———— (2004) *Avengers of the New World: The Story of the Haitian Revolution*, Harvard University Press.

Du Bois, WEB (2007a; first pub. 1940) *Dusk of Dawn: An Essay Toward An Autobiography of a Race Concept*, Oxford University Press.

———— (2007b; first pub. 1935) *Black Reconstruction in America: An Essay Toward a History of the Part Which Black Folk Played in the Attempt to Reconstruct Democracy in America, 1860–1880*, Oxford University Press.

———— (2007c; first pub. 1903) *The Souls of Black Folk*, Oxford University Press.

———— (2007d) *The World and Africa and Color and Democracy*, Oxford University Press.

———— (1915) *The Negro*, Henry Holt.

———— (2015) "The Negro Mind Reaches Out" in Locke (2015), 385–414.

Dyer, Thomas G. (1990) *Theodore Roosevelt and the Idea of Race*, Louisiana State Press.

Eddo-Lodge, Reni (2018) *Why I Am No Longer Talking to White People About Race*, Bloomsbury.

Edwards, Frank, Hedwig, Lee & Esposito, Michael (2019) "Risk of being killed by police use of force in the United States by age, race–ethnicity, and sex", PNAS 116 (34), 16793–98 [https://www.pnas.org/doi/10.1073/pnas.1821204116; accessed 6 May 2020].

Eigen, Sara & Larrimore, Mark, (eds.) (2006) *The German Invention of Race*, State University of New York Press.

Elkins, Caroline (2022) *Legacy of Violence: A History of the British Empire*, Bodley Head.

Ellinger, TUH (1942) "On the Breeding of Aryans and Other Genetic Problems of Wartime Germany", *Journal of Heredity*, 33, 141–3.

Ellis, Havelock (1916) *The Task of Social Hygiene*, Houghton Mifflin.

Ellison, Ralph (2003) *The Collected Essays of Ralph Ellison*, Modern Library.

Eltchaninoff, Michel (2018) *Inside the Mind of Marine Le Pen*, Hurst.

Emerson, Ralph Waldo (2000) *The Essential Writings of Ralph Waldo Emerson*, The Modern Library.

Engels, Friedrich (1849) "The Magyar Struggle", *Neue Rheinische Zeitung*, 13 January 1849 [online at: https://marxists.architexturez.net/archive/marx/works/1849/01/13.htm; accessed 22 August 2021].

Equal Justice Initiative (2017) *Lynching in America: Confronting the Legacy of Racial Terror* (3rd ed.), Equal Justice Initiative.

Equiano, Olaudah (2001; first pub. 1789) *The interesting narrative of the life of Olaudah Equiano, or Gustavus Vassa, the African*, WW Norton.

Eze, Emmanuel Chukwudi (ed.) (1997a) *Race and the Enlightenment: A Reader*, Blackwell.

———— (ed.) (1997b) *Post-Colonial African Philosophy: A Critical Reader*, Blackwell.

Fanon, Frantz (2008; first pub. 1952) *Black Skin, White Masks*, Pluto Press.

———— (1990; first pub. 1961) *The Wretched of the Earth*, Penguin.

———— (1988; first pub. 1964) *Toward the African Revolution: Political Essays*, Grove Press.

Farrar, Frederic William (1867) "Aptitudes of Race", in Biddiss (1979), 141–55.

Feldman, Justin (2020) *Police Killings in the US: Inequalities by Race/Ethnicity and Socioeconomic Position*, People's Policy Project [https://

www.peoplespolicyproject.org/wp-content/uploads/2020/06/
PoliceKillings.pdf; accessed 6 May 2022].

Feldman, Justin M., Gruskin, Sofia, Coul, Brent A. & Krieger, Nancy (2019) "Police-Related Deaths and Neighborhood Economic and Racial/Ethnic Polarization, United States, 2015–2016", *American Journal of Public Health* 109, 458–64,.

Feldman, Louis H. (1993) *Jew and Gentile in the Ancient World:*
Attitudes and Interactions from Alexander to Justinian, Princeton University Press.

Ferguson, Adam (1809; first pub. 1767) *Essay on the History of Civil Society*, 7th edition, Hastings, Etheridge & Bliss.

———— (1757) *The Morality of Stage Plays Seriously Considered* [https://archive.org/details/moralityofstage00ferguoft/page/n5/mode/2up; accessed 28 November 2020].

Ferguson, Niall (2004) *Empire: How Britain Made the Modern World*, Penguin.

Fick, Carolyn (1991) *The Making of Haiti: The Saint Domingue Revolution from Below*, University of Tennessee Press.

Field, Peter (2001) "The Strange Case of Emerson and Race", *American Nineteenth Century History*, 2, 1–32.

Fields, Barbara Jeanne (1990) "Slavery, Race and Ideology in the United States of America", *New Left Review*, 181, 95–118.

Fields, Karen E. & Fields Barbara J. (2012) *Racecraft: The Soul of Inequality in American Life*, Verso.

Fine, Robert & Spencer, Philip (2017) *Antisemitism and the Left: On the Return of the Jewish Question*, Manchester University Press.

Fischer, Conan (1983) *Stormtroopers: A Social, Economic and Ideological Analysis, 1929–1935*, Allen & Unwin.

Foerster, Juergen (1986) "The German Army and the Ideological War Against the Soviet Union", in Hirschfeld (1986), 15–29.

Fogel, Robert William (1989) *Without Consent Or Contract: The Rise and Fall of American Slavery*, WW Norton.

Foner, Eric (2014; first pub.1988) *Reconstruction: America's Unfinished Revolution 1863–1877*, Harper Perennial.

———— (2010) *The Fiery Trial: Abraham Lincoln and American Slavery*, WW Norton.

———— (2005) *Forever Free: The Story of Emancipation and Reconstruction*, Vintage.

BIBLIOGRAPHY

———— (1998) *The Story of American Freedom*, WW Norton.

———— (1994) "The Meaning of Freedom in the Age of Emancipation", *Journal of American History*, 81 (2), 435–60.

Foner, Philip S. (2017; first pub. 1974) *Organized Labor and the Black Worker 1619–1981*, Haymarket.

———— (1947–1994) *History of the Labor Movement in the United States, 10 vols.*, International Publishers.

Foner, Phillip S. & Lewis, Ronald L. (eds.) (1989) *Black Workers: A Documentary History From Colonial Times to the Present*, Temple University Press.

———— (eds.) (1978–84) *The Black Worker* (8 vols), Temple University Press.

Forman, James Jr. (2017) *Locking Up Our Own: Crime and Punishment in Black America*, Abacus.

———— (2012) "Racial Critiques of Mass Incarceration: Beyond the New Jim Crow", *NYU Law Review*, 87 (1), Yale Law School, Public Law Working Paper No. 243 [https://ssrn.com/abstract=1966018; accessed 12 May 2022].

Forret, Jeff (2006) *Race Relations at the Margins: Slaves and Poor Whites in the Antebellum Southern Countryside*, Louisiana State University Press.

Forsdick, Charles & Høgsbjerg, Christian (2017) *The Black Jacobins Reader*, Duke University Press.

Forth, Aidan Alexander Henry (2012) *Empire of Camps: British Imperialism and the Concentration of Civilians, 1876–1903*, PhD Dissertation, Stanford University [online at https://stacks.stanford.edu/file/druid:pp244vv2180/Dissertation%20FINAL-augmented.pdf; accessed 22 June 2020].

Foucault, Michel (2020; first pub.1984) *The Foucault Reader*, Penguin.

Franklin, Benjamin (1918; first pub. 1755) *Observations Concerning the Increase of Mankind, Peopling of Countries, Etc*, William Abbatt.

Frederickson, George M. (2015) *Racism: A Short History*, Princeton University Press.

Freud, Sigmund (2018; first pub. 1921) *Group Psychology and the Analysis of the Ego*, Logos.

Friedlander, Henry (1995) *The Origins of Nazi Genocide: From Euthanasia to the Final Solution*, University of North Carolina Press.

Friedländer, Saul (1997) *Nazi Germany and the Jews: The Years of Persecution 1933–39*, Weidenfeld & Nicolson.

———— (1990) "Some Reflections on the Historicization of National Socialism", in Baldwin (1990), 88–101.

Fryer, Peter (1984) *Staying Power: The History of Black People in Britain*, Pluto Press.

Fryer, Roland G. Jr. (2019) "An Empirical Analysis of Racial Differences in Police Use of Force", *Journal of Political Economy*, 127 (3).

———— (2018) "Reconciling Results on Racial Differences in Police Shootings", *NBER Working Paper Series* [https://www.nber.org/system/files/working_papers/w24238/w24238.pdf; accessed 6 May 2020].

Fuentes, Annette (2013) *Lockdown High: When the Schoolhouse Becomes a Jailhouse*, Verso.

Galton, Francis (1869) *Hereditary Genius: An Inquiry Into Its Laws and Consequences*, Macmillan.

———— (1904) "Eugenics: Its Definition, Scope and Aims", *American Journal of Sociology*, 10 (1), 1–6.

———— (1865) "Hereditary Character and Talent", *Macmillan's Magazine*, 12, 157–66.

Garnsey, Peter (1996), *Ideas of Slavery from Aristotle to Augustine*, Cambridge University Press.

Garrow, David J. (1988; first pub. 1986) *Bearing the Cross: Martin Luther King Jr. and the Southern Christian Leadership Conference*, Vintage.

Garvey, Marcus (2006; first pub. 1923/5) *The Philosophy & Opinions of Marcus Garvey: Or African for the Africans* (ed. Amy Jacques-Garvey), Routledge.

Gates, Henry Louis, Jr. (1992) *Loose Canons: Notes on the Culture Wars*, Oxford University Press.

Gelman, Andrew, Fagan, Jeffrey & Kiss, Alex, (2007) "An Analysis of the New York City Police Department's 'Stop-and-Frisk' Policy in the Context of Claims of Racial Bias", *Journal of the American Statistical Association*, 102 (479), 813–23.

Generation Identity (2013) *We Are Generation Identity*, Arktos Media.

Genovese, Eugene D. (1979) *From Rebellion to Revolution: Afro-American Slave Revolts in the Making of the Modern World*, Louisiana State University Press.

Gerbner, Katharine (2018) *Christian Slavery: Conversion and Race in the Protestant Atlantic World*, University of Pennsylvania Press

BIBLIOGRAPHY

Gibbon, Edward (1846) *The Auto-Biography of Edward Gibbon Esq. Illustrated from His Letters, with Occasional Notes and Narratives*, Turner & Hayden.

Giddings, Franklin Henry (1901) *Democracy and Empire: With Studies of Their Psychological, Economic and Moral Foundations*, Macmillan.

Giddings, Paula J. (2008) *Ida: A Sword Among Lions: Ida B. Wells and the Campaign Against Lynching*, Amistad.

———— (1993) *The Black Atlantic: Modernity and Double Consciousness*, Verso.

Gilley, Bruce (2017) The case for colonialism, *Third World Quarterly* [http://www.web.pdx.edu/~gilleyb/2_The%20case%20for%20colonialism_at2Oct2017.pdf; accessed 20 December 2020].

Gilmore, Glenda Elizabeth (2008) *Defying Dixie: The Radical Roots of Civil Rights, 1919–1950*, WW Norton.

Gilroy, Paul (2000) *Against Race: Imagining Political Culture Beyond the Color Line*, Belknap Press.

———— (1993) *The Black Atlantic: Modernity and Double Consciousness*, Verso.

Ginzberg, Lori D. (2009) *Elizabeth Cady Stanton: An American Life*, Hill & Wang.

Gitlin, Todd (1995) *The Twilight of Common Dreams: Why America is Wracked by Culture Wars*, Metropolitan Books.

Gobineau, Arthur de (1915; first pub. 1853) *The Inequality of Human Races*, William Heinemann.

———— (1856) *Moral and Intellectual Diversity of Races, With Particular Reference to Their Respective Influence In the Civil and Political History of Mankind*, JB Lippincott.

Goddard, Henry H. (1917) "Mental Tests and the Immigrant", *The Journal of Delinquency* 2 (5), 243–77.

Goldstone, Lawrence (2012) *Inherently Unequal: The Betrayal of Equal Rights by the Supreme Court, 1865–1903*, Bloomsbury.

Golob, Sacha & Timmermann, Jens, (eds.) (2017) *The Cambridge History of Moral Philosophy*, Cambridge University Press.

Goodhart, David (2017) *The Road to Somewhere: The Populist Revolt and the Future of Politics*, Hurst.

Gordon, Ann D. (ed.) (1997–2012) *The Selected Papers of Elizabeth Cady Stanton & Susan B. Anthony*, 6 vols., Rutgers University Press.

Gossett, Thomas F. (1963) *Race: The History of an Idea in America*, Oxford University Press.

BIBLIOGRAPHY

Gott, Richard (2011) *Britain's Empire: Resistance, Repression and Revolt*, Verso.

Graham, Barbara L. (2018) *Social Identity and the Law: Race, Sexuality and Intersectionality*, Routledge.

Grant, Colin (2010) *Negro with a Hat: The Rise and Fall of Marcus Garvey*, Oxford University Press.

Grant, Madison (1916) *The Passing of the Great Race: Or the Racial Basis of European History*, Charles Scribner's Sons.

Guettel, Jens-Uwe (2012) *German Expansionism, Imperial Liberalism and the United States, 1776–1945*, Cambridge University Press.

Gumplowicz, Louis (1893) *La Lutte des Races: Recherches Sociologiques*, Guillaumin.

Gutmann, Amy (ed.) (1994) *Multiculturalism: Examining the Politics of Recognition*, Princeton University Press.

Haddon, AC (1924) *The Races of Man and Their Distribution*, Cambridge University Press.

Hague, William (2008) *William Wilberforce: The Life of the Great Anti-Slave Trade Campaigner*, Harper.

Halbfass, Wilhelm (1988) *India and Europe: An Essay in Understanding*, State University of New York Press.

Haldeman, HR (1994) *The Haldeman Diaries: Inside the Nixon White House*, GP Putnam's Sons.

Hall, Catherine (2012) *Macauley and Son: Architects of Imperial Britain*, Yale University Press.

Hall, Jacqueline Dowd (2005) "The Long Civil Rights Movement and the Political Uses of the Past", *Journal of American History*, 91 (4), 1233–63.

Hamilton, Richard (1982) *Who Voted For Hitler?*, Princeton University Press.

Hammerschlag, Sarah (2010) *The Figural Jew: Politics and Identity in Postwar French Thought*, University of Chicago Press.

Hannaford, Ivan (1996) *Race: The History of an Idea in the West*, John Hopkins University Press.

Harris, Cheryl I. (1993) "Whiteness as Property", in Crenshaw et al. (1995), 276–91.

Harris, James A. (2017) "Shaftesbury, Hutcheson and the Moral Sense" in Golob and Timmermann (2017), 325–37.

Harris, Joel Chandler (1890) *Life of Henry W. Grady: Including His Writings and Speeches*, Cassell.

Harvey, David (1990) *The Condition of Postmodernity: An Enquiry Into the Origins of Cultural Change*, Blackwell.

Hazareesingh, Sudhir (2020) *Black Spartacus: The Epic Life of Toussaint Louverture*, Allen Lane.

Heffer, Simon (2012; first pub. 1995) *Moral Desperado: A Life of Thomas Carlyle*, Faber & Faber.

Hentoff, Nat (ed.) (1969) *Black Anti-Semitism and Jewish Racism*, Richard W. Bacon.

Herder, Johann Gottfried (2016; first pub. in 4 vols. 1784–91) *Outlines of a Philosophy of a History of Man*, Random Shack.

——— (2004) *Another Philosophy of History and Selected Political Writings*, Hackett.

——— (2002) *Philosophical Writings*, Cambridge University Press.

Heydrich, Reinhard (2017) "The Final Solution", in MacArthur (2017), 209–11.

Higginson, John (1989) *A Working Class in the Making: Belgian Colonial Labor Policy, Private Enterprise, and the African Mineworker, 1907–1951*, University of Wisconsin Press.

Hill, Christopher (2002; first pub. 1961) *The Century of Revolution: 1603–1714*, Routledge.

Hill, Robert (1986) "In England", in Buhle (1986), 61–80.

Himmelfarb, Gertrude (1984) *The Idea of Poverty: England in the Early Industrial Age*, Faber & Faber.

Hirschfeld, Gerhard, (ed.) (1986) *The Policies of Genocide: Jews and Soviet Prisoners of War in Nazi Germany*, Routledge.

Hitler, Adolf (1992; first pub. 1925) *Mein Kampf*, Pimlico.

——— (1953) *Hitler's Table Talk, 1941–1944*, Weidenfeld & Nicolson.

Hoare, Prince (1820) *Memoirs of Granville Sharpe, Esq.: Composed From His Own Manuscripts and the Authentic Documents in Possession of His Family and of the African Institution*, Henry Colburn.

Hobsbawm, Eric (1977; first pub. 1962) *The Age of Revolution: Europe 1789–1848*, Abacus.

Hobson, John Arthur (1902) *Imperialism: A Study*, James Nisbet.

Hochschild, Adam (2019; first pub. 1998) *King Leopold's Ghost: A Story of Greed, Terror and Heroism in Colonial Africa*, Picador.

Høgsbjerg, Christian (2014) *CLR James in Imperial Britain*, Duke University Press.

BIBLIOGRAPHY

Holland, Tom (2019) *Dominion: The Making of the Western Mind*, Little, Brown.

Honey, Michael K. (2018) *To the Promised Land: Martin Luther King and the Fight for Economic Justice*, WW Norton.

———— (2007) *Going Down Jericho Road: The Memphis Strike, Martin Luther King's Last Campaign*, WW Norton.

hooks, bell (2000), *Where We Stand: Class Matters*, Routledge.

———— (1991) *Yearning: Race, Gender and Cultural Politics*, Turnaround.

Howard, John R. (1999) *The Shifting Wind: The Supreme Court and Civil Rights from Reconstruction to Brown*, State University of New York Press.

Hughes, Langston (1994) *The Return of Simple*, Hill & Wang.

Hughes, Robert (2003; first pub. 1986) *The Fatal Shore: A History of the Transportation of Convicts to Australia, 1787–1868*, Vintage.

Hughes, H. Stuart (1987) *Between Commitment and Disillusion*, Weslyan University Press.

Hull, Isabel V. (2005) *Absolute Destruction: Military Culture and the Practices of War in Imperial Germany*, Cornell University Press.

Humboldt, Alexander von (2020) *Cosmos*, 5 vols., Outlook Verlag.

Hume, David (1748a) *An Enquiry Concerning Human Understanding*, Hume Texts Online [https://davidhume.org/texts/e/full; accessed 20 September 2020].

———— (1748b), "Of National Characters", Hume Texts Online [https://davidhume.org/texts/empl1/nc; accessed 23 September 2020].

———— (1742) "Of the Middle Station of Life", Hume Texts Online [https://davidhume.org/texts/empw/ms; accessed 28 October 2020].

Hunt, Lynn (1996) *The French Revolution and Human Rights: A Brief History with Documents*, Bedford.

Hutton, C. (1996) "The Defeat of the Morant Bay Rebellion", *Jamaican Historical Review*, 19, 30–8.

Huxley, Aldous (1929; first pub. 1927) *Proper Studies*, Chatto & Windus.

Huxley, Thomas Henry (1870) *Lay Sermons, Addresses and Reviews*, Macmillan & Co.

Hyman, Paula E. (1998) *The Jews of Modern France*, University of California Press.

Ignatiev, Noel (1995) *How the Irish Became White*, Routledge.

BIBLIOGRAPHY

Ignatin, Noel, and Allen, Ted (2011) "White Blindspot" in Davidson, Carl (ed.). *Revolutionary Youth & the New Working Class: The Praxis Papers, the Port Authority Statement, the RYM Documents and Other Lost Writings of SDS*, Changemaker Publications. 148–81 [http://www.sds-1960s.org/WhiteBlindspot.pdf; accessed 14 May 2022].

Isenberg, Nancy (2017) *White Trash: The 400-year Untold Story of Class in America*, Atlantic.

Israel, Jonathan (2011) *Democratic Enlightenment: Philosophy, Revolution and Human Rights 1750–1790*, Oxford University Press.

———— (2006) *Enlightenment Contested: Philosophy, Modernity and the Emancipation of Man 1670–1752*, Oxford University Press.

Jacobson, Matthew Frye (1998) *Whiteness of a Different Color: European Immigrants and the Alchemy of Race*, Harvard University Press.

Jackson, Maurice & Bacon, Jacqueline (eds.) (2010) *African Americans and the Haitian Revolution: Selected Essays and Historical Documents*, Routledge.

Jamaica Royal Commission (1866) *Report of the Jamaican Royal Commission, 1866*, HM Stationery Office.

James, CLR (2019; first pub. 1963) *Beyond a Boundary*, Vintage.

———— (1980a) *Spheres of Existence: Selected Writings*, Allison & Busby.

———— (1980b; first pub. 1938) *The Black Jacobins, Toussaint L'Ouverture and the San Domingo Revolution*, Allison & Busby.

———— (1938) *A History of Negro Revolt*, Fact.

Jaspers, Karl (2014; first pub. 1949) *The Origin and Goal of History*, Routledge Revivals.

Jefferson, Thomas (1801; first pub. 1787) *Notes on the State of Virginia*, RT Rawle.

Jeffries, Stuart (2017) *Grand Hotel Abyss: The Lives of the Frankfurt School*, Verso.

Johnson, Andrew (1967–2000) *The Papers of Andrew Johnson*, 16 vols., University of Tennessee Press.

Johnson, Cedric (2007) *Revolutionaries to Race Leaders: Black Power and the Making of African American Politics*, University of Minnesota Press.

Jones, Charles E. (ed.) (1998) *The Black Panther Party (Reconsidered)*, Black Classic Press.

Jones, Charles E. & Jeffries, Judson L. (1998) "'Don't Believe the Hype': Debunking the Panther Mythology", in Jones (1998), 25–56.

Jones, Derek (2001) *Censorship: A World Encyclopaedia*, Routledge.

Jones, William (1824) *Discourses Delivered Before the Asiatic Society and Miscellaneous Papers on the Religion, Poetry, Literature, Etc, of the Nations of India*, Charles S. Arnold.

Joseph, Peniel E. (2020) *The Sword and the Shield: The Revolutionary Lives of Malcolm X and Martin Luther King Jr.*, Basic Books.

Kant, Immanuel (2012) *Natural Science*, Cambridge University Press.

———— (2007a) *Anthropology, History and Education*, Cambridge University Press.

———— (1795) *Towards Perpetual Peace: A Philosophical Sketch* [https://www.earlymoderntexts.com/assets/pdfs/kant1795.pdf; accessed 17 January 2021].

———— (2007b) "On the Different Races of Human Beings", in Kant (2007a), 82–97.

———— (1784) "What is Enlightenment?" [https://archive.org/details/AnswerTheQuestionWhatIsEnlightenment/mode/2up; accessed 22 September 2020].

Karp, Jonathan & Sutcliffe, Adam (eds.) (2017) *The Cambridge History of Judaism vol. 7: The Early Modern World*, Cambridge University Press.

Kates, Gary (1989) "Jews into Frenchman: Nationality and Representation in Revolutionary France", *Social Research*, 56 (1) 213–32.

Kaufmann, Eric (2018) *Whiteshift: Populism, Immigration and the Future of White Majorities*, Allen Lane.

———— (2017) *"Racial Self-interest" Is Not Racism: Ethno-demographic Interests and the Immigration Debate*, Policy Exchange.

Keith, Leeanna (2007) *The Colfax Massacre: The Untold Story of Black Power, White Terror and the Death of Reconstruction*, Oxford University Press.

Kelley, Robin DG (2015; first pub. 1990) *Hammer and Hoe: Alabama Communists During the Great Depression*, University of North Carolina Press.

Kelling, George L. & Wilson, James Q. (1982) "Broken Windows", *The Atlantic*, March 1982.

Kenny, Anthony (2004) *Ancient Philosophy (A New History of Philosophy, Vol. 1)*, Clarendon Press.

Kershaw, Ian (2008) *Hitler, the Germans and the Final Solution*, International Institute for Holocaust Research/Yale University Press.

———— (1995) *The Nazi Dictatorship: Problems and Perspectives of Interpretation*, Edward Arnold.

Kevles, Daniel J. (1995; first pub. 1985) *In the Name of Eugenics: Genetics and the Uses of Heredity*, Harvard University Press.

Kidd, Benjamin (1894) *Social Evolution*, Macmillan.

King, Charles (2019) *Gods of the Upper Air: How a Circle of Renegade Anthropologists Reinvented Race, Sex and Gender in the Twentieth Century*, Anchor.

King, Gary, Rosen, Ori, Tanner, Martin & Wagner, Alexander F. (2008) "Ordinary Economic Voting Behavior in the Extraordinary Election of Adolf Hitler", *Journal of Economic History*, 68 (4), 951–96.

King, Martin Luther Jr. (2010; first pub. 1968) *Where Do We Go From Here: Chaos or Community?*, Beacon Press.

———— (1986) *A Testament of Hope: Essential Writings and Speeches* (ed. James N. Washington), Harper One.

Kirk, J. Allen (2002) "A Statement of Facts Concerning the Bloody Riot in Wilmington N.C.", Academic Affairs Library, University of North Carolina [https://docsouth.unc.edu/nc/kirk/kirk.html; accessed 20 November 2020].

Kleingeld, Pauline (2007) "Kant's Second Thoughts on Race", *The Philosophical Quarterly*, 57 (229), 573–92.

Knox, Robert (1850) *The Races of Men: A Fragment*, Lea & Blanchard.

Kolchin, Peter (2002) "Whiteness Studies: The New History of Race in America", *Journal of American History*, 89 (1), 154–73.

Korstad, Robert Rogers (2003) *Civil Rights Unionism: Tobacco Workers and the Struggle for Democracy in the Mid-Twentieth-Century South*, University of North Carolina Press.

Korstad, Robert & Lichtenstein, Norman (1988) "Opportunities Found and Lost: Labor, Radicals, and the Early Civil Rights Movement", *Journal of American History*, 75 (3), 786–811.

Kousser, J. Morgan (1974) *The Shaping of Southern Politics: Suffrage Restriction and the Establishment of the One-Party South, 1880–1910*, Yale University Press.

Koven, Steven G. & Götzke, Frank (2010) *American Immigration Policy: Confronting the Nation's Challenges*, Springer.

Kramer, Paul A. (2002) "Empires, Exceptions, and Anglo-Saxons: Race and Rule between the British and United States Empires, 1880–1910", *Journal of American History*, 88 (4), 1315–53.

Kruse, Kevin M. & Tuck, Stephen (2012) *Fog of War: The Second World War and the Civil Rights Movement*, Oxford University Press.

Kühl, Stefan (1994) *The Nazi Connection: Eugenics, American Racism and German National Socialism*, Oxford University Press.

Kyle, James H. (1901), *Report of the Industrial Commission on the Relations and Conditions of Capital and Labor Employed in Manufactures and General Business*, vol. 7, US Government Printing Office.

Kymlicka, Will (1995) *Multicultural Citizenship: A Liberal Theory of Minority Right*, Clarendon Press.

Labanca, Nicola (2004) "Colonial Rule, Colonial Repression and War Crimes in the Italian Colonies", *Journal of Modern Italian Studies*, 9 (3), 300–13.

Lake, Marilyn & Reynolds, Henry (2008) *Drawing the Global Colour Line: White Men's Countries and the International Challenge of Racial Equality*, Cambridge University Press.

Lane, Charles (2008) *The Day Freedom Died: The Colfax Massacre, the Supreme Court, and the Betrayal of Reconstruction*, Henry Holt.

Laughlin, Harry H. (1930) *The Legal Status of Eugenical Sterilization: History and Analysis of Litigation Under the Virginia Sterilization Statute, Which Led to a Decision of the Supreme Court of the United States Upholding the Statute*, Psychopathic Laboratory of the Municipal Court of Chicago [*Buck v Bell Documents*, 79: https://readingroom.law.gsu.edu/buckvbell/79; accessed 13 March 2021].

———— (1922) *Eugenical Sterilization in the United States: A Report of the Psychopathic Laboratory of the Municipal Court of Chicago*, Psychopathic Laboratory of the Municipal Court of Chicago.

Lauren, Paul Gordon (1996; first pub. 1988) *Power and Prejudice: The Politics and Diplomacy of Racial Discrimination*, Westview Press.

Lay, Benjamin (1738) *All Slave-Keepers that Keep the Innocent in Bondage, Apostates Pretending to Lay Claim to the Pure & Holy Christian Religion*, Evans Early American Imprint collection [http://name.umdl.umich.edu/N03401.0001.001; accessed 26 October 2020].

Le Bon, Gustave (1898) *The Psychology of Peoples*, Macmillan.

Lee, Martha F. (1996) *The Nation of Islam: An American Millenarian Movement*, Syracuse University Press.

Lepore, Jill (2018) *These Truths: A History of the United States*, WW Norton.

Lester, Julius (1968) *Look Out Whitey! Black Power's Gon' Get Your Mama!*, Grove Press.

Levi, Primo (1988) *The Drowned and the Saved*, Abacus.

BIBLIOGRAPHY

Lévi-Strauss, Claude (1985; first pub. 1983) *The View from Afar*, Penguin.
———— (1963) *Totemism*, Beacon Press.

Lewis, David Levering (2000) *W.E.B. Du Bois: The Fight for Equality and the American Century, 1919–1963*, Henry Holt.

Lewis, John, (with Michael D'Orso) (1998) *Walking with the Wind: A Memoir of the Movement*, Simon & Schuster.

Lewis, Nathaniel (2017) *Mass Incarceration: New Jim Crow, Class War, Or Both?*, People's Policy Project [https://www.peoplespolicyproject. org/wp-content/uploads/2018/01/MassIncarcerationPaper.pdf; accessed 6 May 2022].

Lewis, Oscar (1966), *La Vida: A Puerto Rican Family in a Culture of Poverty— San Juan and New York*, Random House.

Ligon, Richard (1657) *A True and Exact History of the Island of Barbados*, Humphrey Mosley.

Lind, Michael (2020) *The New Class War: Saving Democracy from the Metropolitan Elite*, Atlantic.

Linnaei, Caroli, Carl (1758) *Systema naturae per regna tria naturae, secundum classes, ordines, genera, species, cum characteribus, differentiis, synonymis, locis*, Holmiae.

Litwack, Leon F. (1998) *Trouble in Mind: Black Southerners in the Age of Jim Crow*, Vintage.
———— (1961) *North of Slavery: The Negro in the Free States, 1790–1860*, University of Chicago Press.

Locke, Alain (ed.) (2015; first pub. 1925) *The New Negro: An Interpretation*, Martino.

Locke, John (2010) *A Letter Concerning Toleration*, Liberty Fund [https:// oll.libertyfund.org/titles/locke-a-letter-concerning-toleration-and-other-writings; accessed 26 October 2020].
———— (1988) *Two Treatises of Government*, Cambridge University Press.

Lorimer, Douglas A. (1978) *Colour, Class and the Victorians: English Attitudes to the Negro in the Mid-Nineteenth Century*, Leicester University Press.

Lovejoy, Arthur O. (1936) *The Great Chain of Being: A Study of the History of an Idea*, Harvard University Press.

Low, Alfred (1979) *Jews in the Eyes of Germans from the Enlightenment to Imperial Germany*, Institute for the Study of Human Issues.

Lund, Eric (2002) *Documents from the History of Lutheranism, 1517–1750*, Fortress Press.

Lyall, Andrew (2017) *Granville Sharp's Cases on Slavery*, Bloomsbury.

Lynch, Hollis R. (1967) *Edward Wilmot Blyden: Pan-Negro Patriot, 1832–1912*, Oxford University Press.

———— (1965) "Edward W, Blyden: Pioneer West African Nationalist", *Journal of African History*, 6 (3), 373–88.

MacArthur, Brian, (ed.) (2017) *The Penguin Book of Modern Speeches*, Penguin.

MacCulloch, Diarmaid (2009) *A History of Christianity: The First Three Thousand Years*, Allen Lane.

Macey, David (2000) *Frantz Fanon: A Life*, Granta.

Maier, Charles S. (1988) *The Unmasterable Past: History, Holocaust and German National Identity*, Harvard University Press.

Makalani, Minkah (2011) *In the Cause of Freedom: Radical Black Internationalism from Harlem to London, 1917–1939*, University of North Carolina Press.

Malcolm X & Haley, Alex (1968; first pub. 1965) *The Autobiography of Malcolm X*, Penguin.

Malik, Kenan (2014) *The Quest for a Moral Compass: A Global History of Ethics*, Atlantic.

———— (2009) *From Fatwa to Jihad: The Rushdie Affair and its Legacy*, Atlantic.

———— (2008) *Strange Fruit: Why Both Sides Are Wrong in the Race Debate*, Oneworld.

———— (1996) *The Meaning of Race: Race, History and Culture in Western Society*, Macmillan.

Malik, Nesrine (2019) *We Need New Stories: Challenging the Toxic Myths Behind Our Age of Discontent*, Weidenfeld & Nicolson.

Man, Albon P. Jr. (1950) "The Irish in New York in the Early Eighteen-Sixties", *Irish Historical Studies*, 7 (26), 87–108.

Marable, Manning (1991) *Race, Reform and Rebellion: The Second Reconstruction in Black America, 1945–1990*, Macmillan.

Marcus, Jonathan (1995) *The National Front and French Politics: The Resistible Rise of Jean-Marie Le Pen*, New York University Press.

Marcuse, Herbert (1966; first pub. 1955) *Eros and Civilisation: A Philosophical Inquiry Into Freud*, Beacon Press.

Marks, Jonathan (1995) *Human Biodiversity: Genes, Race and History*, Aldine de Gruyter.

Martin, Amy E. (2014) "Victorian Ireland: Race and the Category of the Human", *Victorian Review*, 40 (1), 52–7.

BIBLIOGRAPHY

Marx, Karl (1975) *Early Writings*, Penguin.

Marx, Karl & Engels, Friedrich (2004; first pub. 1848) *The Communist Manifesto*, Penguin.

May, Henry F. (1976) *The Enlightenment in America*, Oxford University Press.

Mayer, Arno J. (2012; first pub. 1988) *Why Did the Heavens Not Darken?: The "Final Solution" in History*, Verso.

Mazower, Mark (2008) *Hitler's Empire: Nazi Rule in Occupied Europe*, Penguin.

McIntosh, Peggy (1988) "White Privilege and Male Privilege: A Personal Account of Coming to See Correspondences Through Work in Women's Studies" [https://nationalseedproject.org/Key-SEED-Texts/white-privilege-and-male-privilege; accessed 17 May 2022].

McKivigan, John R., Husband, Julie & Kaufman, Heather L., (eds.) (2018) *The Speeches of Frederick Douglass: A Critical Edition*, Yale University Press.

McLennan, John Ferguson (1896) *Studies in Ancient History, Second Series: Comprising an Inquiry into the Origins of Exogamy*, McMillan.

McMahon, Darrin M. (2001) *Enemies of the Enlightenment: The French Counter Enlightenment and the Making of Modernity*, Oxford University Press.

McNicholas, Celine, Rhinehart, Lynn, Poydock, Margaret, Shierholz, Heidi & Perez, Daniel (2020) "Why unions are good for workers—especially in a crisis like COVID-19", Economic Policy Institute, 25 August 2020 [https://www.epi.org/publication/why-unions-are-good-for-workers-especially-in-a-crisis-like-covid-19-12-policies-that-would-boost-worker-rights-safety-and-wages/; accessed 11 June 2021].

McWhirter, Cameron (2011) *Red Summer: The Summer of 1919 and the Awakening of Black America*, Henry Holt.

Megargee, Geoffrey P. (ed.) (2009) *Early Camps, Youth Camps, and Concentration Camps and Subcamps under the SS-Business Administration Main Office (WVHA): Encyclopedia of Camps and Ghettos, 1933–1945 vol 1*, Indiana University Press.

Mendes-Flohr, Paul & Reinharz, Jehuda (eds.) (1995) *The Jew in the Modern World: A Documentary History*, Oxford University Press.

Meritt, Keri Leigh (2017) *Masterless Men: Poor Whites and Slavery in the Antebellum South*, Cambridge University Press.

Mill, James (1820) *The History of British India*, 6 vols., 2nd edn., Baldwin, Cradock & Joy.

Mill, John Stuart (2003; first pub. 1859) *On Liberty*, Yale University Press.

———— (1858), *Memorandum of the Improvements in the Administration of India During the Last Thirty Years, And the Petition of the East India Company to Parliament*, Wm. H. Allen & Co..

Miller, James A., Pennybacker Susan D. & Rosenhaft, Eve (2001) "Mother Ada Wright and the International Campaign to Free the Scottsboro Boys, 1931–1934", *American Historical Review*, 106 (2), 387–430.

Mills, Charles W. (1997) *The Racial Contract*, Cornell University Press.

———— 2005, "Kant's Untenmenschen" in Vals (2005),169–93.

Mills, C. Wright (1960) "Letter to the New Left", *New Left Review*, 5 (September/October 1960), 18.

Mockler, Anthony (2003; first pub. 1984) *Haile Selassie's War*, Signal Books.

Moore, RI (2007) *The Formation of a Persecuting Society: Authority and Deviance in Western Europe 950–1250*, 2nd edn., Blackwell.

Morgan, Edmund (1975) *American Slavery, American Freedom: The Ordeal of Colonial Virginia*, WW Norton.

Morris, Richard B. (1954) "The Measure of Bondage in Slave States", *Mississippi Valley Historical Review*, 41(2), 219–40.

Morton, Samuel George (1839) *Crania Americana: A Comparative View of the Skulls of Various Aboriginal Nations of North and South America In Which is Prefixed an Essay on the Varieties of the Human Species*, J. Dobson.

Moses, Wilson J. (1972) "Marcus Garvey: A Reappraisal", *Black Scholar*, 4 (3), 38–49.

Mosse, George L. (1978) *Toward the Final Solution: A History of European Racism*, JM Dent.

Mo Tzu (1967) *Basic Writings of Mo Tzu, Hsün Tzu and Han Fei Tzu*, Columbia University Press.

Moynihan, Daniel (1965) *The Negro Family: The Case for National Action*, Office of Policy Planning and Research United States Department of Labor.

Mudimbe, VY (2016) *The Mudimbe Reader*, University of Virginia Press.

Müller, Filip (1979) *Eyewitness Auschwitz: Three Years in the Gas Chambers*, Ivan R. Dee/US Holocaust Memorial Museum.

Murray, Albert (2020; first pub. 1970) *The Omni-Americans: Some Alternatives to the Folklore of White Supremacy*, Library of America.

Murray, Douglas (2019) *The Madness of Crowds: Gender, Race and Identity*, Bloomsbury.

——— (2018) *The Strange Death of Europe: Immigration, Identity and Islam*, Bloomsbury.

Murray, Jr., Hugh T. (1967) "The NAACP versus the Communist Party: The Scottsboro Rape Cases, 1931–1932", *Phylon*, 28 (3), 276–87.

Murray, Pauli (2018; first pub. 1987) *Song in a Weary Throat: Memoir of an American Pilgrimage*, Liveright.

——— (1945) "An American Credo", *Common Ground* 5 (2), 22–4.

Muthu, Sankar (2003) *Enlightenment Against Empire*, Princeton University Press.

Nardal, Jane (1928) "L'Internationalisme Noir", *La Dépêche Africaine*, 1.

Neal, Larry (1968) "The Black Arts Movement", *Drama Review*, 12 (4), 28–39.

Nesbitt, Nick (2008) *Universal Emancipation: The Haitian Revolution and the Radical Enlightenment*, University of Virginia Press.

Niebuhr, BG (1847; first pub. 1828) *The History of Rome*, 5 vols., Taylor and Walton.

Northrup, David (1988) *Beyond the Bend in the River: African Labor in Eastern Zaire, 1865–1940*, Ohio University Center for International Studies.

Nott, Josiah C. (1849) *Two Lectures on the Connection Between the Biblical and Physical History of Man*, Bartlett and Welford.

Nott, JC & Gliddon, GR (1857) *Indigenous Races of the Earth: Or New Chapters of Ethnology*, JB Lippincott.

——— (1854) *Types of Mankind: Or Ethnological Researches Based on Ancient Monuments, Paintings, Sculptures and Crania of Races, and Upon the Natural, Geographical, Philological and Biblical History*, Lippincott, Grambo & Co..

Olmsted, Frederick Law (1861) *The Cotton Kingdom: A Traveller's Observation on Cotton and Slavery*, 2 vols., Mason Brothers.

Olusoga, David (2016) *Black and British: A Forgotten History*, Macmillan.

Olusoga, David & Erichsen, Casper W. (2010) *The Kaiser's Holocaust: Germany's Forgotten Genocide*, Faber & Faber.

Osborne, Peter, (ed.) (1991) *Socialism and the Limits of Liberalism*, Verso.

O'Sullivan, John (July–August 1845) "Annexation", *United States Magazine and Democratic Review*, 17 (1), 5–10.

Packenham, Thomas (1992) *The Scramble for Africa 1876–1912*, Abacus.

Padmore, George (1931) *The Life and Struggles of Negro Toilers*, RILU [https://www.marxists.org/archive/padmore/1931/negro-toilers/index.htm; accessed 8 March 2021).

Padover, SK (1935) "Treitschke: Forerunner of Hitlerism", *Pacific Historical Review*, 4 (2), 161–70.

Painter, Nell Irvin (2010) *The History of White People*, WW Norton.

Payne, Les & Payne, Tamara (2020) *The Dead Are Arising: The Life of Malcolm X*, Penguin.

Pearson, Charles H. (1893) *National Life and Character: A Forecast*, Macmillan.

Pearson, Karl (1914–30) *The Life, Letters and Labours of Francis Galton*, 3 vols., Cambridge University Press [online at https://galton.org/pearson/; accessed 3 March 2021].

Peller, Gary (1990) "Race Consciousness" in Crenshaw *et al.* (1995), 127–58.

Perry, Bruce (1992) *Malcolm: The Life of a Man Who Changed Black America*, Station Hill.

Pichot, André (2009; first pub. 2001) *The Pure Society: From Darwin to Hitler*, Verso.

Pick, Daniel (1989) *Faces of Degeneration: A European Disorder, c.1848–1918*, Cambridge University Press.

Pike, James S. (1874) *The Prostate State: South Carolina Under Negro Government*, D Appleton.

Piper, Ernst, (ed.) (1993) *Forever in the Shadow of Hitler?: Original Documents of the Historikerstriet, the Controversy Concerning the Singularity of the Holocaust*, Humanities Press.

Piquionne, Nathalie (1998) "Lettre de Jean-François, Biassou et Belair, juillet 1792", *Annales Historiques de la Révolution Française*, 311, 132–9.

Pitzer, Andrea (2017) *One Long Night: A Global History of Concentration Camps*, Little, Brown.

Polakow-Suransky, Sasha (2017) *Go Back to Where You Came From: The Backlash Against Immigration and the Fate of Western Democracy*, Hurst.

Pope, James Gray (2015) "Snubbed Landmark: Why United States v. Cruikshank (1876) Belongs at the Heart of the American Constitutional Canon", *Harvard Civil Rights-Civil Liberties Law Review*, 50 (1), 385–447.

Powers, HH (Sept. 1898) "The War as a Suggestion of Manifest Destiny", *Annals of the American Academy of Political and Social Science*, 12, 1–20.

President's Advisory 1776 Commission (2021) *The 1776 Report* [https://trumpwhitehouse.archives.gov/wp-content/uploads/2021/01/The-Presidents-Advisory-1776-Commission-Final-Report.pdf; accessed 16 March 2021].

Prichard, James Cowles (1836–47) *Researches into the Physical History of Mankind*, 5 vols. (3rd edn.), Sherwood, Gilbert & Piper.

Pulzer, Paul (1988; first pub. 1964) *The Rise of Political Anti-Semitism in Germany and Austria*, Harvard University Press.

Rabinowitz, Howard N. (1976) "From Exclusion to Segregation: Southern Race Relations, 1865–1890", *Journal of American History*, 63 (2), 325–50.

Randall, Daniel (2021) *Confronting Antisemitism on the Left: Arguments for Socialists*, No Pasaran Media.

Raspail, Jean (1975; first pub. 1973) *The Camp of the Saints*, Charles Scribner's Sons.

Raynal, Guillaume Thomas (2006) *A History of the Two Indies: A Translated Selection of Writings from Raynal's Histoire philosophique et politique des établissements des Européens dans les Deux Indes*, Routledge.

Reilly, Wilfred (2020) *Taboo: 10 Facts (You Can't Talk About)*, Regnery.

Renshaw, Patrick (1999; first pub. 1967) *The Wobblies: The Story of the IWW and Syndicalism in the United States*, Ivan R. Dee.

Reports of the Immigration Commission (1911) *Statements and Recommendations Submitted by Societies and Organizations Interested in the Subject of Immigration*, Government Printing Office.

Reynolds, Henry (2001) *An Indelible Stain? The Question of Genocide in Australia's History*, Viking.

Richards, Evelleen (1989) "The 'Moral Anatomy' of Robert Knox: The interplay between biological and social thought in Victorian scientific naturalism", *Journal of the History of Biology*, 22 (3), 373–436.

Rieff, Philip (1961; first pub. 1959) *Freud: The Mind of a Moralist*, Doubleday.

Ripley, William Z. (1899) *The Races of Europe: A Sociological Study*, D. Appleton.

――― (1908) "Races in the United States", *Atlantic Monthly*, 102 (6), 745–75.

BIBLIOGRAPHY

Robinson, Robert (with Jonathan Slevin) (1988) *Black on Red: My 44 Years Inside the Soviet Union*, Acropolis.

Rodinson, Maxime (1983) *Cult, Ghetto and State: The Persistence of the Jewish Question*, Al Saqi Books.

Roediger, David (1994) *Towards the Abolition of Whiteness: Essays on Race, Politics and Working Class History*, Verso.

Roosevelt, Theodore (1889–96) *The Winning of the West*, 4 vols., GP Putnam's.

———— (1894) "National Life and Character", *Sewanee Review*, 2 (3), 353–76.

Rose, Matthew (2021) *A World after Liberalism: Philosophers of the Radical Right*, Yale University Press.

Rosenberg, Daniel (1988) *New Orleans Dockworkers: Race, Labor and Unionism 1892–1923*, State University of New York Press.

Ross, Edward Alsworth (1914) *The Old World in the New: The Significance of the Past and Present Immigration to the American People*, Century.

———— (1911) *The Changing Chinese: The Conflict of Oriental and Western Cultures in China*, Century.

Rothkopf, David (2017) "The Shallow State", *Foreign Policy*, 22 February 2017.

Rousseau, Jean-Jacques (1984) *A Discourse on Inequality*, Penguin.

Ruchames, Louis (1953) *Race, Jobs and Politics: The Story of the FEPC*, Columbia University Press.

Rudwick, Elliott M. (1959) "DuBois versus Garvey: Race Propagandists at War", *Journal of Negro Education*, 28 (4), 421–9.

Rueda, Daniel (2021) "Alain de Benoist, ethnopluralism and the cultural turn in racism", *Patterns of Prejudice*, 55 (3), 213–35.

Rushdie, Salman (1991) *Imaginary Homelands: Essays and Criticism 1981–1991*, Granta.

Ryan, Lyndall (2012) *Tasmanian Aborigines: A History Since 1803*, Allen & Unwin.

Sahara, Fabina, *et al.* (2019) "Fatal police violence by race and state in the USA, 1980–2019: a network meta-regression", *Lancet*, 398, 1239–55.

Said, Edward W. (1993) *Culture and Imperialism*, Chatto & Windus.

———— (1991; first pub. 1978) *Orientalism: Western Conceptions of the Orient*, Penguin.

Sala-Molins, Louis (2006; first pub. 1992) *Dark Side of the Light: Slavery and the French Enlightenment*, University of Minnesota Press.

Sandel, Michael & Cowley, Jason (2016) "Michael Sandel: The energy of the Brexiteers and Trump is born of the failure of elites", *New Statesman*, 13 June 2016.

Sartre, Jean-Paul (1964) "Black Orpheus", *Massachusetts Review*, 6 (1), 13–52.

Schafft, Gretchen E. (2004) *From Racism to Genocide: Anthropology in the Third Reich*, University of Illinois Press.

Schama, Simon (2018) *Belonging: The Story of the Jews 1492–1900*, Vintage.

Schechter, Ronald (2003) *Obstinate Hebrews: Representations of Jews in France 1715–1815*, University of California Press.

Schraub, David (2019) "White Jews: An Intersectional Approach", *AJS Review* 43 (2), 379–407.

Scott, Julius S. (2020; first pub. 2018) *The Common Wind: Afro-American Currents in the Age of the Haitian Revolution*, Verso.

Scruton, Roger (1990) "In Defence of the Nation", in Clark (1990), 53–86.

Sedgwick, Mark (ed.) (2019) *Key Thinkers of the Radical Right: Behind the New Threat to Liberal Democracy*, Oxford University Press.

Semmel, Bernard (1962) *The Governor Eyre Controversy*, Macgibbon & Kee.

Senghor, Léopold Sédar, (1964) *On African Socialism*, Pall Mall Press.

Sentencing Project (2018) *Report to the United Nations on Racial Disparities in the U.S. Criminal Justice System* [https://www.sentencingproject.org/publications/un-report-on-racial-disparities/; accessed 6 May 2020].

Shatz, Adam (2017) "Raw Material", *London Review of Books*, 24 March 2017 [https://www.lrb.co.uk/blog/2017/march/raw-material; accessed 25 May 2022].

Shugg, Roger W. (1938) "The New Orleans General Strike of 1892", *Louisiana Historical Quarterly*, 21, 547–60.

Sikka, Sonia (2011) *Herder on Humanity and Cultural Difference: Enlightened Relativism*, Cambridge University Press.

Silvester, Jeremy & Gewald, Jan-Bart (2003) *Words Cannot be Found: German Colonial Rule in Namibia: An Annotated Reprint of the 1918 Blue Book*, Brill.

Singh, Nikhil Pal (1998) "The Black Panthers and the 'Undeveloped Country' of the Left", in Jones (1998), 57–105.

Sinha, Manisha (2016) *The Slave's Cause: A History of Abolition*, Yale University Press.

Sloane, Hans (1707) *A Voyage to the Islands Madera, Barbados, Nieves, S. Christophers and Jamaica*, vol. 1, B.M..

Sluiter, Engel (1997) "New Light on the '20. and Odd Negroes' Arriving in Virginia, August 1619", *William and Mary Quarterly*, 54 (2), 395–8.

Smith, Adam (1896; first pub. 1763) *Lectures on Justice, Police, Revenue and Arms*, Clarendon Press.

———— (1759) *The Theory of Moral Sentiments; or, An Essay Towards an Analysis of the Principles by Which Men Naturally Judge Concerning the Conduct and Character, First of Their Neighbours, and Afterwards of Themselves*, Henry G. Bohn [https://oll.libertyfund.org/titles/2620; accessed 18 November 2020].

———— (1776) *An Inquiry Into the Nature and Causes of the Wealth of Nations*, 2 vols., Metheun (https://oll.libertyfund.org/title/smith-an-inquiry-into-the-nature-and-causes-of-the-wealth-of-nations-cannan-ed-in-2-vols; accessed 18 November 2020).

Smith, Woodruff D. (1980) "Friedrich Ratzel and the Origins of Lebensraum", *German Studies Review*, 3 (1), 51–68.

Smith, Zadie (2017) "Getting In and Out", *Harper's Magazine*, July 2017 [https://harpers.org/archive/2017/07/getting-in-and-out/; accessed 20 May 2022].

Sollas, W.J. (1924; first pub. 1911) *Ancient Hunters and Their Modern Representatives*, Macmillan.

Solomon, Mark (1998) *The Cry Was Unity: Communists and African Americans, 1917–1936*, University Press of Mississippi.

Sorkin, David (2019) *Jewish Emancipation: A History Across Five Centuries*, Princeton University Press.

Stanton, Elizabeth Cady, Anthony, Susan B. & Gage, Matilda Joslyn (eds.) (1882) *History of Woman Suffrage*, 3 vols., Fowler & Wells.

Stanton, William (1960) *The Leopard's Spots: Scientific Attitudes to Race in America 1815–1859*, University of Chicago Press.

Stedman Jones, Gareth (2008; first pub. 2004) *An End to Poverty? A Historical Debate*, Columbia University Press.

Steel, Pet (2015) *The Levellers Movement: An Account of Perhaps the First Political Movement to Represent the Ordinary People*, SERTUC [https://levellersday.files.wordpress.com/2013/03/the-levellers-movement.pdf; accessed 4 November 2020].

Stepan, Nancy (1982) *The Idea of Race in Science: Great Britain 1800–1960*, Macmillan Press.

Stephanson, Anders & West, Cornell (1989) "Interview with Cornell West", *Social Text*, 21, 269–86.

Stern, Fritz (1961) *The Politics of Cultural Despair: A Study in the Rise of the Germanic Ideology*, University of California Press.

Stocking, George Jr., (ed.) (1988) *Bones, Bodies, Behaviour: Essays on Biological Anthropology* (*History of Anthropology*, vol. 5), University of Wisconsin Press.

———— (1982; first pub. 1968) *Race, Evolution and Culture: Essays in the History of Anthropology*, University of Chicago Press.

Stoddard, Lothrop (1940) *Into the Darkness: Nazi Germany Today*, Duell, Sloan & Pearce.

———— (1922) *The Revolt Against Civilization: The Menace of the Under Man*, Charles Scribner's Sons.

———— (1921) *The Rising Tide of Color Against White World-Supremacy*, Charles Scribner's Sons.

Stowell, David O. (ed.) (2008) *The Great Strikes of 1877*, University of Illinois Press.

———— (1999) *Streets, Railroads and the Great Strike of 1877*, University of Chicago Press.

Strong, Josiah (1900) *Expansion Under New World-Conditions*, Baker & Taylor.

Stuurman, Siep (2017) *The Invention of Humanity: Equality and Cultural Difference in World History*, Harvard University Press.

Sundari, Anitha, and Pearson, Ruth (2018) *Striking Women: Struggles & Strategies of South Asian Women Workers from Grunwick to Gate Gourmet*, Lawrence & Wishart.

Táíwò, Olúfémi O. (2022) *Elite Capture: How the Powerful Took Over Identity Politics (and Everything Else)*, Pluto.

Taylor, Charles (1994) "The Politics of Recognition" in Gutmann (1994), 25–73.

"The Fundamental Constitutions of Carolina" (1669) Yale Law School Avalon Project [https://avalon.law.yale.edu/17th_century/nc05.asp; accessed 22 September 2020].

Thornton, John (1998) "The African Experience of the '20. and Odd Negroes' Arriving in Virginia in 1619", *The William and Mary Quarterly*, 55 (3), 421–34.

Tocqueville, Alexis de (2003; first pub. 1835 & 1840) *Democracy in America and Two Essays on America*, Penguin.

Todorov, Tzvetan (1993) *On Human Diversity: Nationalism, Racism and Exoticism in French Thought*, Harvard University Press.

Tone, John Lawrence (2008) *War and Genocide in Cuba, 1895–1898*, University of North Carolina Press.

Traverso, Enzo (2003) *The Origins of Nazi Violence*, New Press.

Trouillot, Michel-Rolph (1995) *Silencing the Past: Power and the Production of History*, Beacon Press.

Turley, David (2004) *The Culture of English Antislavery, 1780–1860*, Routledge.

Tyson, Timothy B. (2017) *The Blood of Emmett Till*, Simon & Schuster.

———— (2006) "The Ghosts of 1898: Wilmington's Race Riot and the Rise of White Supremacy", *News & Observer* (17 November 2006).

Umfleet, Le Ra (2006) *1898 Wilmington Race Riot Report*, 1898 Wilmington Race Riot Commission & North Carolina Office of Cultural Resources.

Vals, Andrew, (ed.) (2005) *Race and Racism in Modern Philosophy*, Cornell University Press.

Vital, David (1999) *A People Apart: The Jews in Europe 1789–1939*, Oxford University Press.

Vitale, Alex S. (2017) *The End of Policing*, Verso.

Voogd, Jan (2008) *Race Riots and Resistance: The Red Summer of 1919*, Peter Lang.

Waldrep, Christopher (2005) *Lynching in America: A History in Documents*, NYU Press.

Walker, Clarence Earl (2001) *We Can't Go Home Again: An Argument About Afrocentrism*, Oxford University Press.

Wallace, Alfred Russell (1864) "The Origin of Human Races and the Antiquity of Man Deduced from the Theory of 'Natural Selection'", *Journal of the Anthropological Society of London*, 2, clviii–clxxxvii.

Ward, Lester F. (1914; first pub. 1903) *Pure Sociology: A Treatise on the Origin and Spontaneous Development of Society*, Macmillan.

Ward, Samuel Ringgold (1855) *Autobiography of a Fugitive Negro: His Anti-Slavery Labours in the United States, Canada and England*, John Snow.

Webb, Beatrice (1979; first pub. 1926) *My Apprenticeship*, Cambridge University Press.

———— (1889–1898) *Typescript Diary*, 1 January 1889–March 1898, LSE Digital Library [https://digital.library.lse.ac.uk/objects/lse:wip502kaf; accessed on 24 April 2021].

Weingartner, James (1996) "War against Subhumans: Comparisons between the German War Against the Soviet Union and the American War against Japan, 1941–1945", *The Historian*, 58 (3), 557–73.

Weitzer, Ronald (1999) "Citizens' perceptions of police misconduct: Race and neighborhood context", *Justice Quarterly*, 16 (4), 819–46.

Wells, Ida B. (1991) *Crusade for Justice: The Autobiography of Ida B. Wells*, Chicago University Press.

Wheen, Francis (1999) *Karl Marx*, Fourth Estate.

White, Joseph Robert (2009) "Introduction to the Early Camps", in Megargee (2009), 3–180.

White, Leslie, A. (1949) *The Science of Culture: A Study of Man and Civilization*, Grove Press.

Whites, Lee-Ann (1988) "The De Graffenried Controversy: Class, Race, and Gender in the New South", *Journal of Southern History*, 54 (3), 449–78.

Whitman, James Q. (2018) *Hitler's American Model: The United States and the Making of Nazi Race Law*, Princeton University Press.

Whitman, Walt (1995; first pub. 1882) *Specimen Days and Collect*, Dover.

Williams, Thomas Chatterton (2019) *Self-Portrait in Black and White: Unlearning Race*, John Murray.

Williamson, Joel (1975) *After Slavery: The Negro in South Carolina During Reconstruction, 1861–1877*, WW Norton.

Wood, Amy Louise (2009) *Lynching and Spectacle: Witnessing Racial Violence in America, 1890–1940*, University of North Carolina Press.

Wood, Graeme (2017) "His Kampf", *The Atlantic*, June 2017.

Woodward, C. Vann (1991; first pub. 1951) *Reunion and Reaction: The Compromise of 1877 and the End of Reconstruction*, Oxford University Press.

———— (1974; 3rd revised edn., first pub. 1955) *The Strange Career of Jim Crow*, Oxford University Press.

———— (1971; first pub. 1951) *Origins of the New South, 1877–1913*, Louisiana State University Press.

———— (1938) "Tom Watson and the Negro in Agrarian Politics", *Journal of Southern History*, 4 (1), 14–33.

Wooley, Robert, H. (1977) *Race and Politics: The Evolution of the White Supremacy Campaign of 1898 in North Carolina*, PhD dissertation, University of North Carolina.

Wynes, Charles E. (1975) "James Wormley of the Wormley Hotel Agreement", *Centennial Review*, 19 (1), 397–401.

Ye'or, Bat (2005) *Eurabia: The Euro-Arab Axis*, Fairleigh Dickinson University Press.

Zeitlin, Irving (1968) *Ideology and the Development of Sociological Theory*, Prentice Hall.

Zemmour, Éric (2015) *Le Suicide Français*, Albin Michel.

Zia-Ebrahimi, Reza (2018) "When the Elders of Zion Relocated to Eurabia: Conspiratorial Racialization in Antisemitism and Islamophobia", *Patterns of Prejudice*, 52 (4), 314–37.

Zimmerman, Andrew (1999) "Anti-Semitism as Skill: Rudolf Virchow's 'Schulstatistik' and the Racial Composition of Germany", *Central European History*, 32 (4), 409–29.

Zucchino, David (2020) *Wilmington's Lie: The Murderous Coup of 1898 and the Rise of White Supremacy*, Atlantic Monthly Press.

Zúquete, José Pedro (2018) *The Identitarians: The Movement Against Glabalism and Islam in Europe*, University of Notre Dame Press.

INDEX

INDEX

INDEX